ATTACK ON TITAN

32

HAJIME ISAYAMA

THE CHARACTERS OF ATTACK ON TITAN

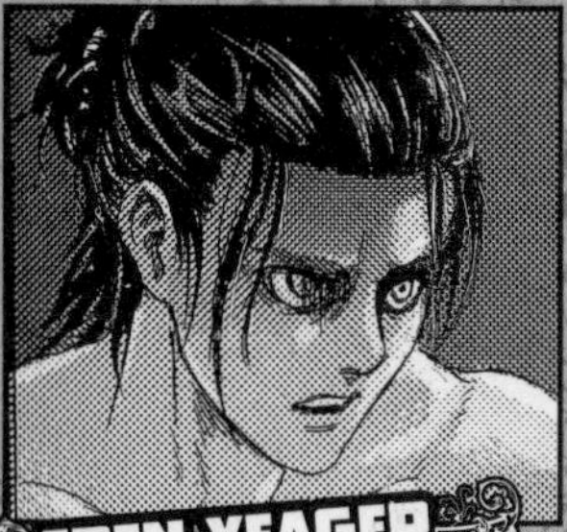

EREN YEAGER

FROM THE 104TH TRAINING CORPS; NOW IN THE SURVEY CORPS. HOLDS THE POWER OF THE ATTACK TITAN AND THE FOUNDING TITAN. BOLDLY INFILTRATED MARLEY ON HIS OWN.

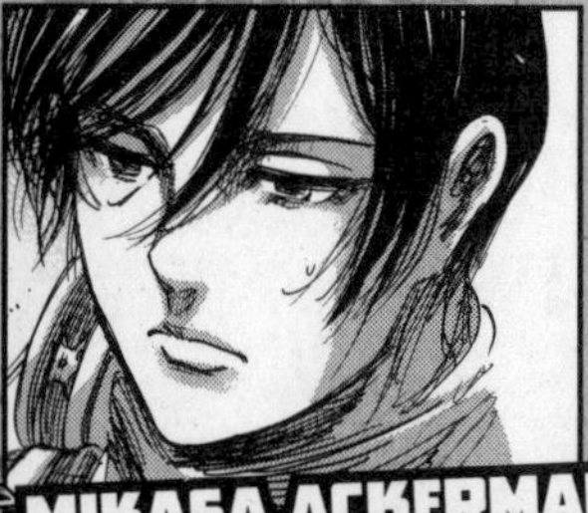

MIKASA ACKERMAN

FROM THE 104TH TRAINING CORPS; NOW IN THE SURVEY CORPS. SHE HAS SHOWN INCREDIBLE COMBAT ABILITIES EVER SINCE SHE WAS A RECRUIT. SHE SEES PROTECTING EREN AS HER MISSION.

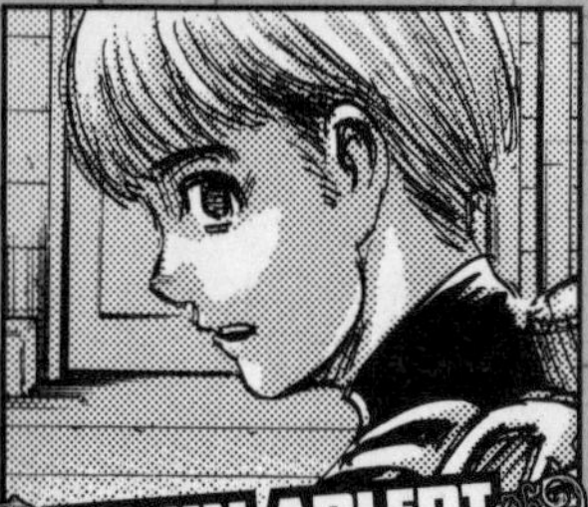

ARMIN ARLERT

FROM THE 104TH TRAINING CORPS; NOW IN THE SURVEY CORPS. HOLDS THE POWER OF THE COLOSSUS TITAN. HE HAS SAVED HIS COMRADES COUNTLESS TIMES WITH HIS SHARP INTELLECT AND BRAVERY.

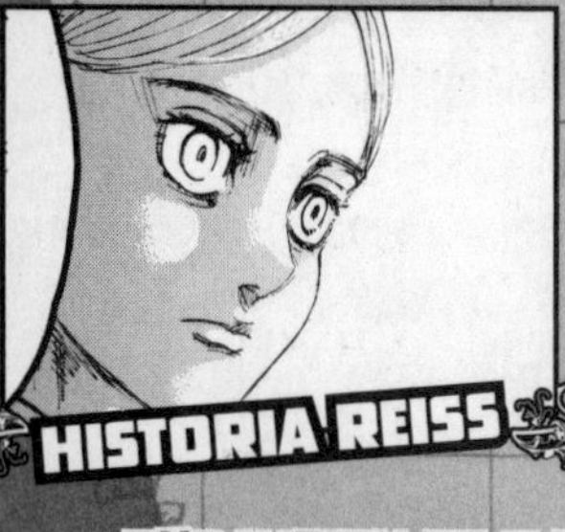

HISTORIA REISS

A DESCENDANT OF THE REISS FAMILY, THE TRUE ROYAL BLOODLINE, HISTO-RIA HAS ASCENDED TO THE THRONE AS QUEEN. SHE ONCE BELONGED TO THE SURVEY CORPS UNDER THE NAME KRISTA LENZ.

THE NATION OF ELDIA [THE ISLAND OF PARADIS]

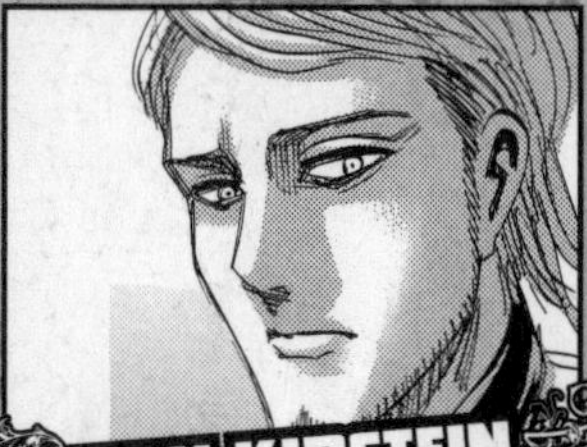

JEAN KIRSTEIN

FROM THE 104TH TRAINING CORPS; NOW IN THE SURVEY CORPS. ONCE KNOWN FOR HIS SARCASTIC PERSONALITY, HE HAS NOW GROWN INTO A LEADER.

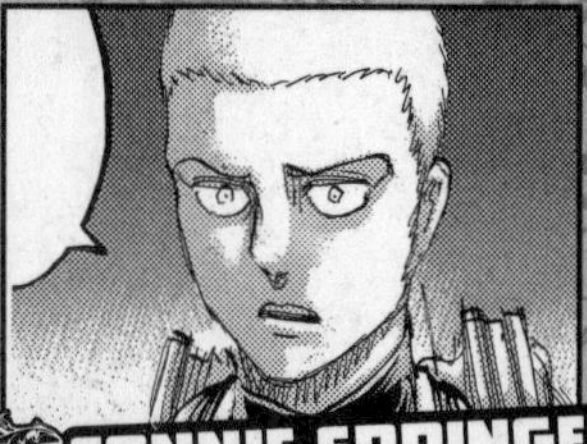

CONNIE SPRINGER

FROM THE 104TH TRAINING CORPS; NOW IN THE SURVEY CORPS. HE IS CHEERFUL IN PERSONALITY, BUT FINDS HIMSELF LOSING EVERYONE IMPORTANT TO HIM... ORIGINALLY FROM RAGAKO VILLAGE.

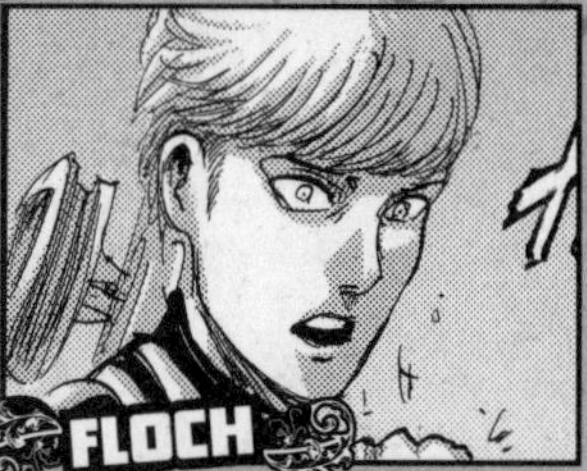

FLOCH

A MEMBER OF THE SURVEY CORPS. A SURVIVOR OF THE DECISIVE BATTLE FOR SHIGANSHINA DISTRICT, WHICH CLAIMED MANY LIVES, INCLUDING ERWIN'S.

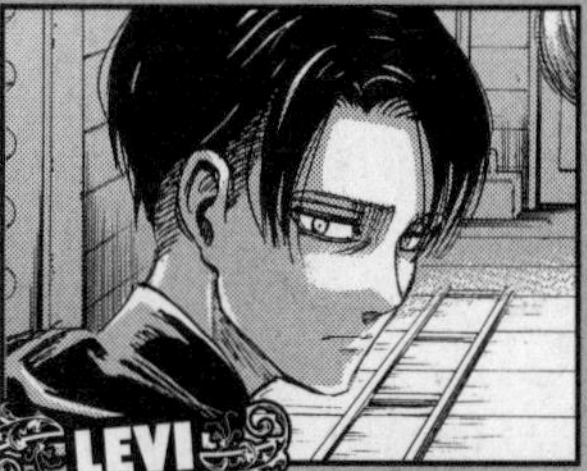

LEVI

CAPTAIN OF THE SURVEY CORPS. KNOWN AS "HUMANITY'S STRONGEST SOLDIER." HE FIGHTS THROUGH HIS STRUGGLES IN ORDER TO CARRY ON HIS GOOD FRIEND ERWIN'S DYING WISHES.

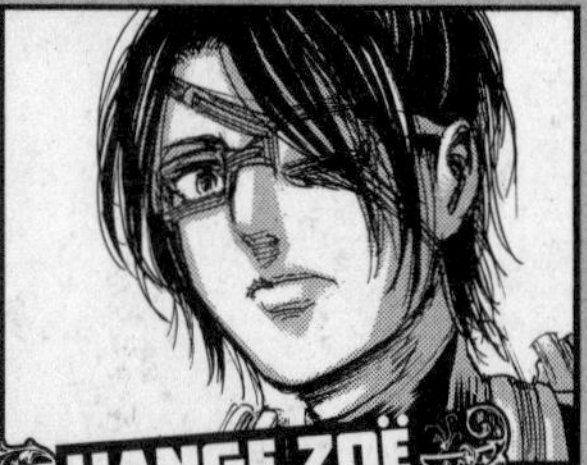

HANGE ZOË

COMMANDER OF THE SURVEY CORPS. KEEN POWERS OF OBSERVATION LED ERWIN TO NAME HANGE HIS SUCCESSOR DESPITE OBVIOUS ECCENTRICITIES.

THE ELDIAN WARRIORS OF THE MARLEYAN ARMY

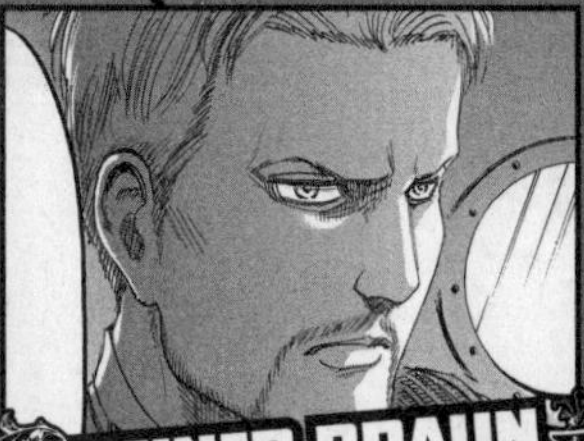

REINER BRAUN

HOLDS THE ARMORED TITAN WITHIN HIM. SINCE HE WAS THE ONLY ONE TO MAKE IT BACK FROM THE MISSION ON PARADIS, HE SUFFERS FROM A GUILTY CONSCIENCE.

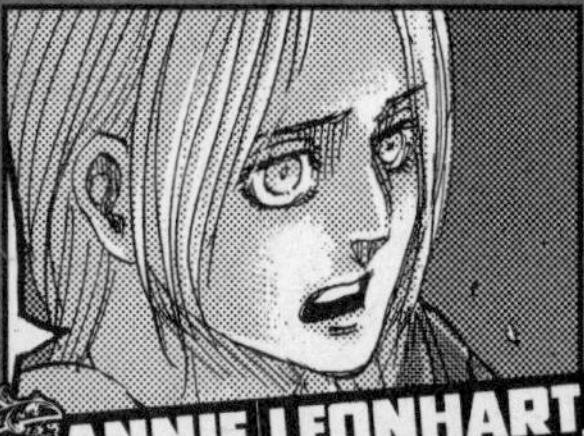

ANNIE LEONHART

ANNIE HOLDS THE FEMALE TITAN WITHIN HER. HER HARDENED STATE WAS UNDONE BY THE POWER OF THE FOUNDING TITAN, WAKING HER FROM HER FOUR YEARS OF SLEEP.

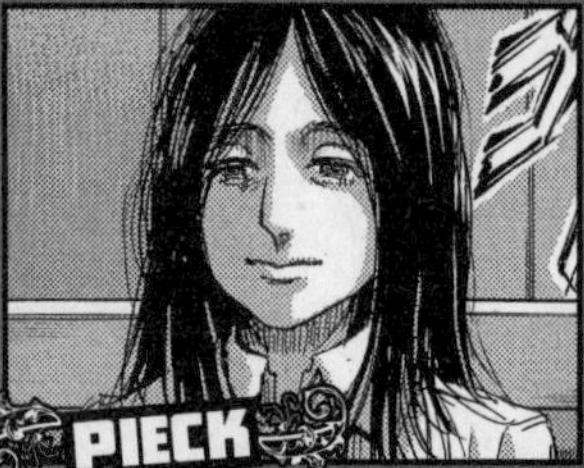

PIECK

HOLDS THE CART TITAN WITHIN HER, CARRYING THE PANZER UNIT ON THE BACK OF THE "CARTMAN" TO FIGHT. HIGHLY PERCEPTIVE.

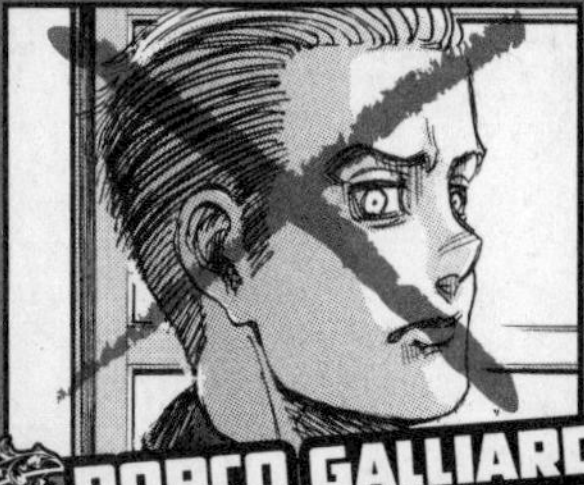

PORCO GALLIARD

HOLDS THE JAW TITAN WITHIN HIM. THERE IS STRIFE BETWEEN HIM AND REINER OVER BOTH THE INHERITANCE OF THE ARMORED TITAN AND THE DEATH OF HIS OLDER BROTHER, MARCEL.

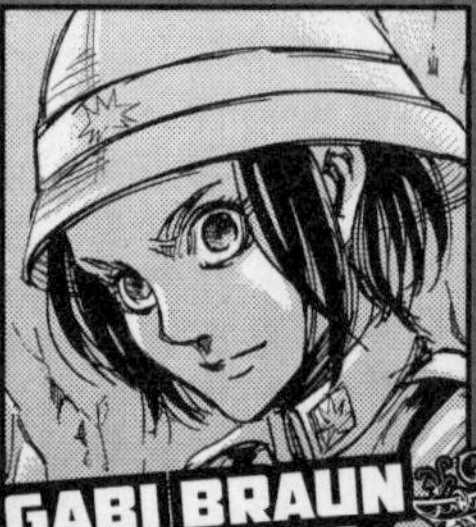

GABI BRAUN

BOLD DESPITE HER SMALL SIZE, GABI IS A DYNAMIC WARRIOR CANDIDATE. HER GOAL IS TO EVENTUALLY INHERIT THE ARMORED TITAN. REINER'S COUSIN.

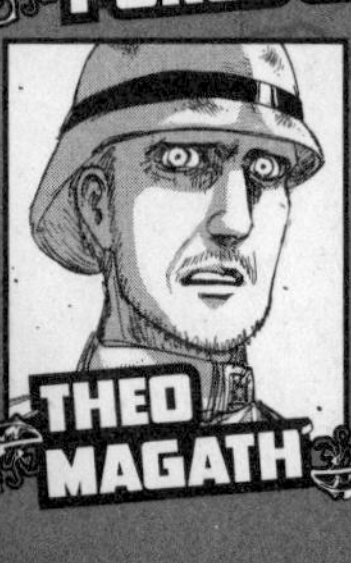

THEO MAGATH

A MARLEYAN WHO LEADS A UNIT OF ELDIANS. PROMOTED TO GENERAL.

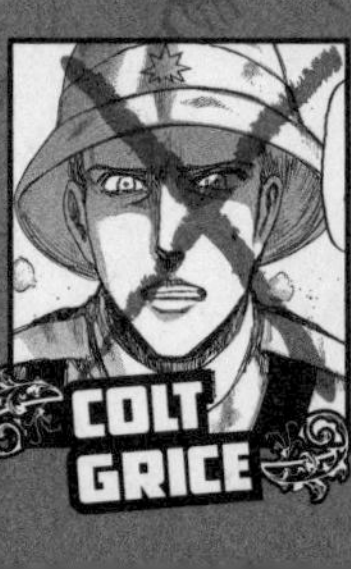

COLT GRICE

FALCO'S OLDER BROTHER. THE OLDEST OF THE WARRIOR CANDIDATES, AND, IN EFFECT, THEIR LEADER.

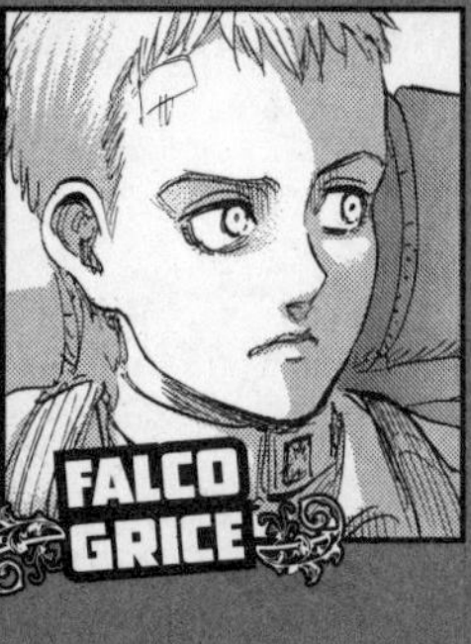

FALCO GRICE

A WARRIOR CANDIDATE HE HAS AFFECTION FOR GABI AND WANTS TO PROTECT HER. DURING EREN'S TIME INFILTRATING MARLEY, FALCO CAME IN CONTA WITH EREN WITHOUT REALIZING HIS TRUE IDENTITY.

THE ANTI-MARLEYAN VOLUNTEERS

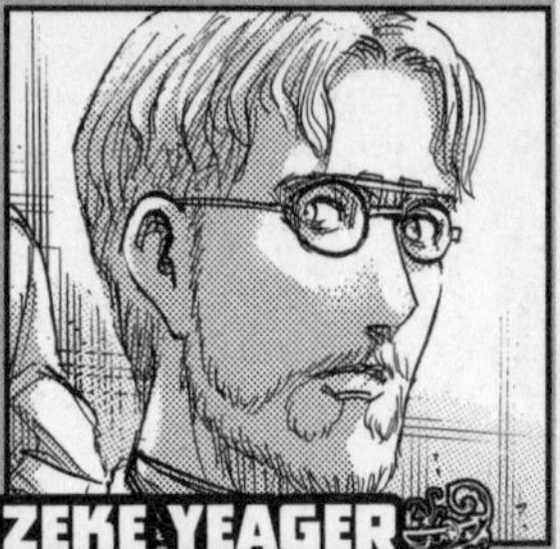

ZEKE YEAGER

HOLDS THE POWER OF THE BEAST TITAN. A LEADER OF THE WARRIORS, HE WAS ONCE KNOWN AS "THE WONDER CHILD." HIS MOTHER IS A DESCENDANT OF THE ROYAL BLOODLINE. HE IS ALSO EREN'S HALF-BROTHER.

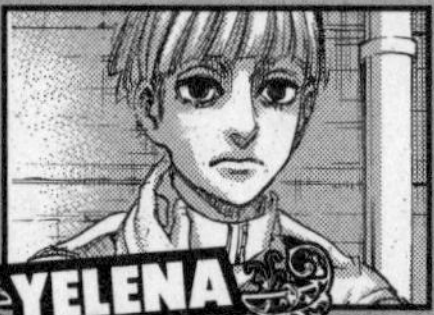

YELENA

YELENA COMMANDS THE VOLUNTEERS AND FOLLOWS ZEKE. SHE DRESSED AS A MAN DURING THE EXPEDITION TO MARLEY IN ORDER TO WORK IN SECRET.

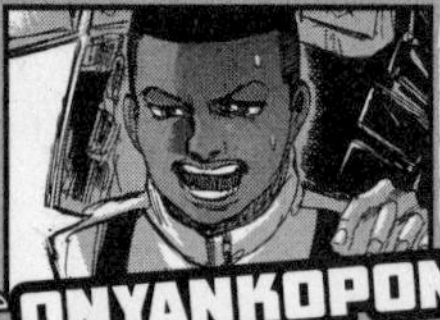

ONYANKOPON

AFTER TRAVELING TO PARADIS WITH YELENA, HE TELLS ITS INHABITANTS OF MARLEY'S ADVANCED CULTURE.

ATTACK on TITAN

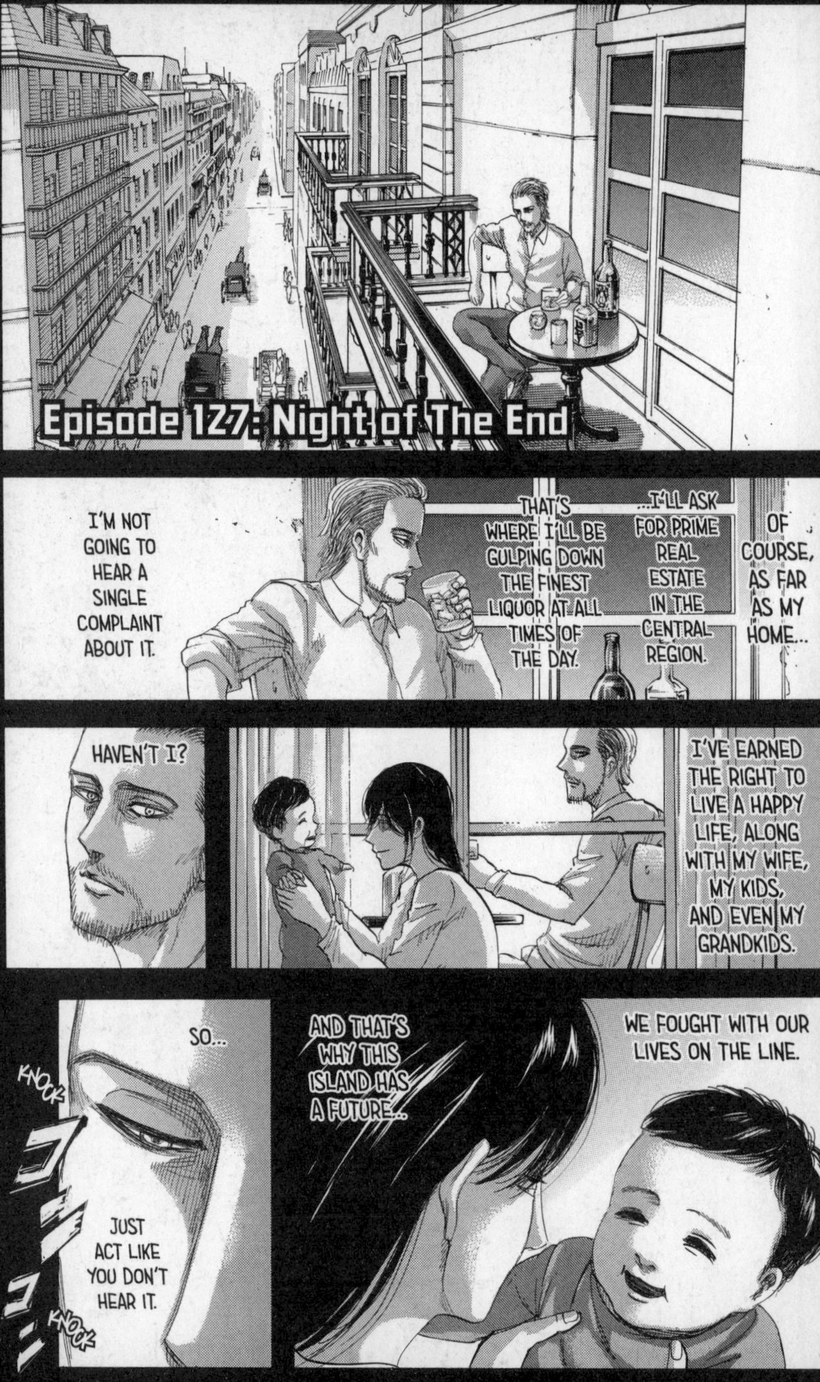
Episode 127: Night of The End
OF COURSE, AS FAR AS MY HOME...
...I'LL ASK FOR PRIME REAL ESTATE IN THE CENTRAL REGION.
THAT'S WHERE I'LL BE GULPING DOWN THE FINEST LIQUOR AT ALL TIMES OF THE DAY.
I'M NOT GOING TO HEAR A SINGLE COMPLAINT ABOUT IT.
I'VE EARNED THE RIGHT TO LIVE A HAPPY LIFE, ALONG WITH MY WIFE, MY KIDS, AND EVEN MY GRANDKIDS.
HAVEN'T I?
WE FOUGHT WITH OUR LIVES ON THE LINE.
AND THAT'S WHY THIS ISLAND HAS A FUTURE...
SO...
KNOCK
JUST ACT LIKE YOU DON'T HEAR IT.
KNOCK

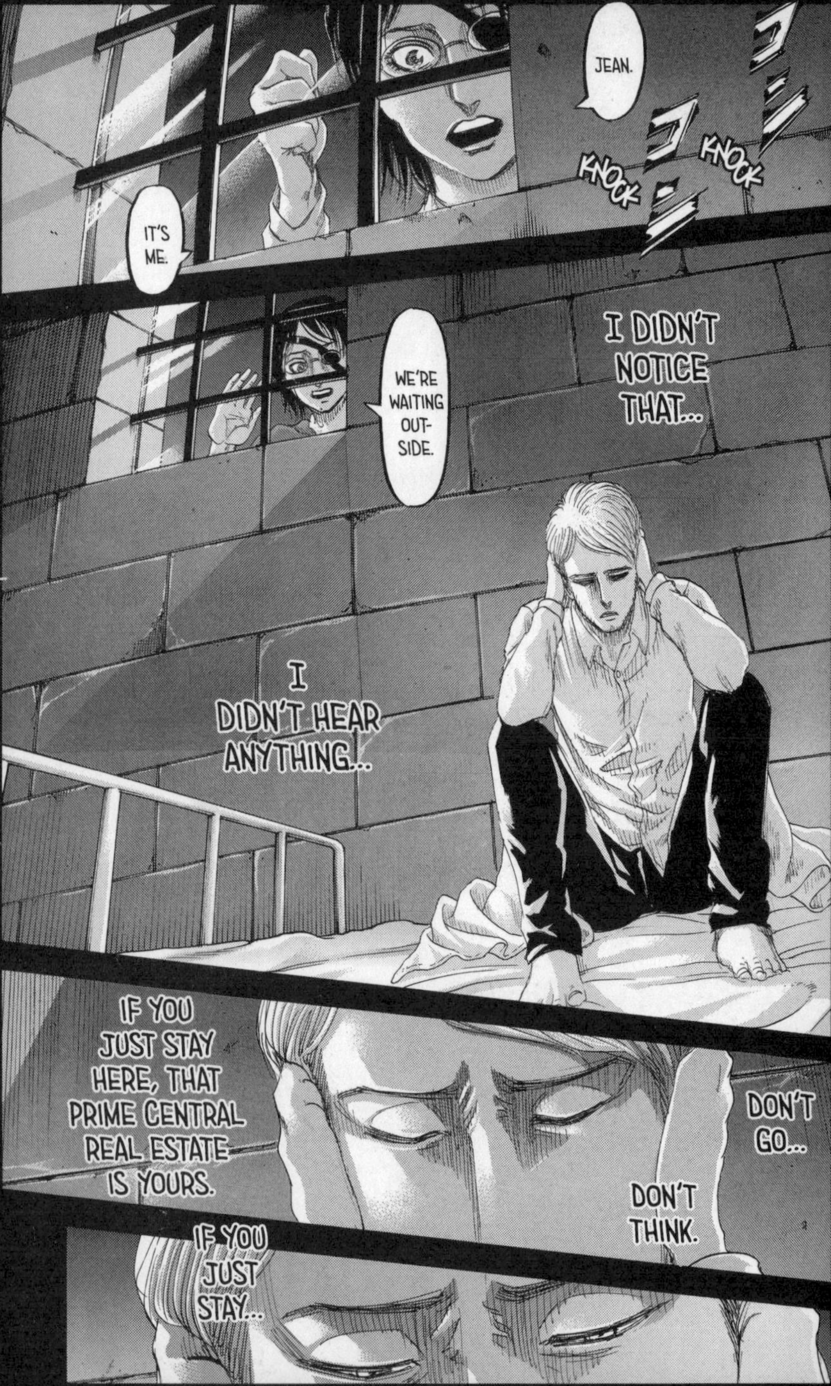
JEAN.
KNOCK
KNOCK
IT'S ME.
WE'RE WAITING OUTSIDE.
I DIDN'T NOTICE THAT...
I DIDN'T HEAR ANYTHING...
DON'T GO...
DON'T THINK.
IF YOU JUST STAY HERE, THAT PRIME CENTRAL REAL ESTATE IS YOURS.
IF YOU JUST STAY...

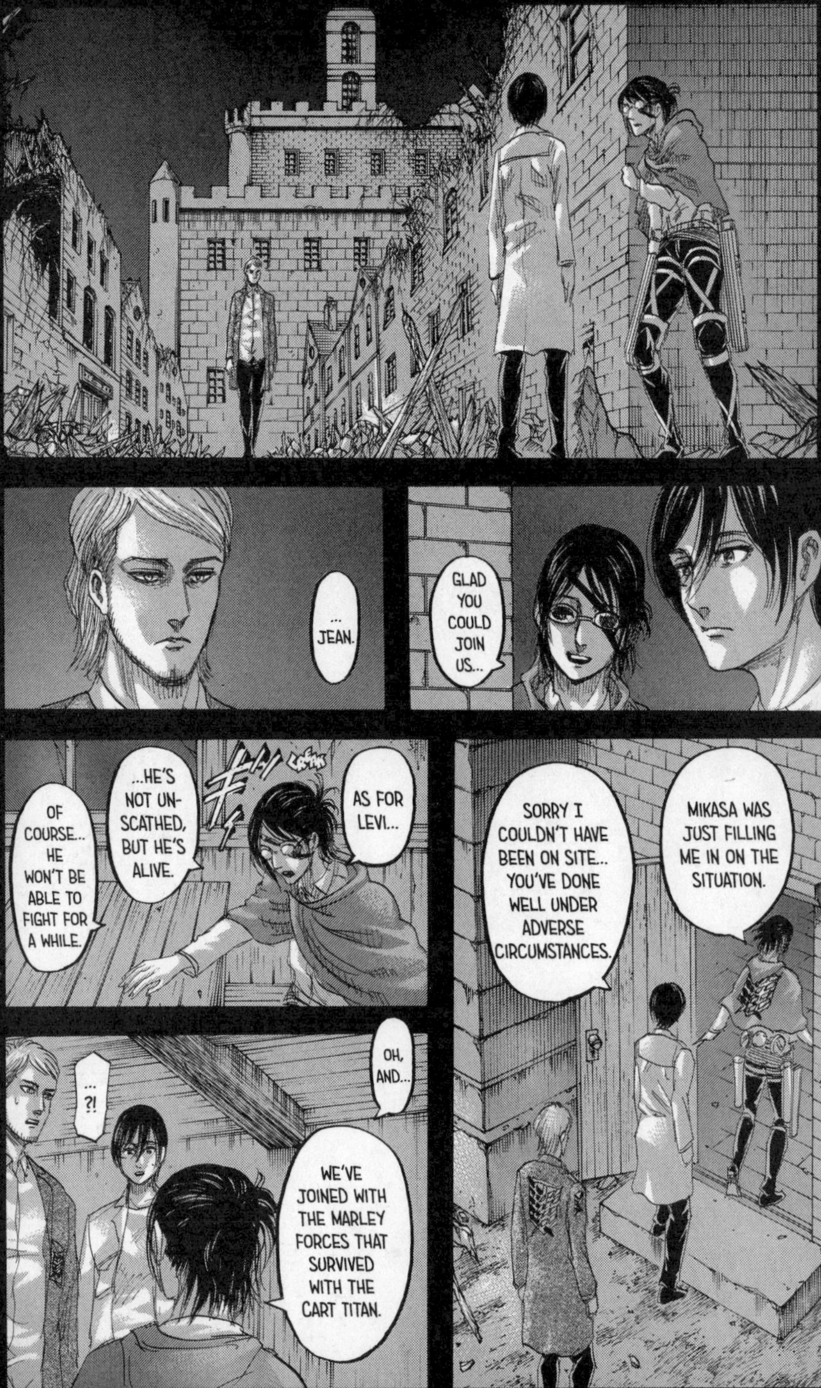
GLAD YOU COULD JOIN US...
... JEAN.
MIKASA WAS JUST FILLING ME IN ON THE SITUATION.
SORRY I COULDN'T HAVE BEEN ON SITE... YOU'VE DONE WELL UNDER ADVERSE CIRCUMSTANCES.
AS FOR LEVI...
...HE'S NOT UN-SCATHED, BUT HE'S ALIVE.
OF COURSE... HE WON'T BE ABLE TO FIGHT FOR A WHILE.
OH, AND...
WE'VE JOINED WITH THE MARLEY FORCES THAT SURVIVED WITH THE CART TITAN.
... ?!

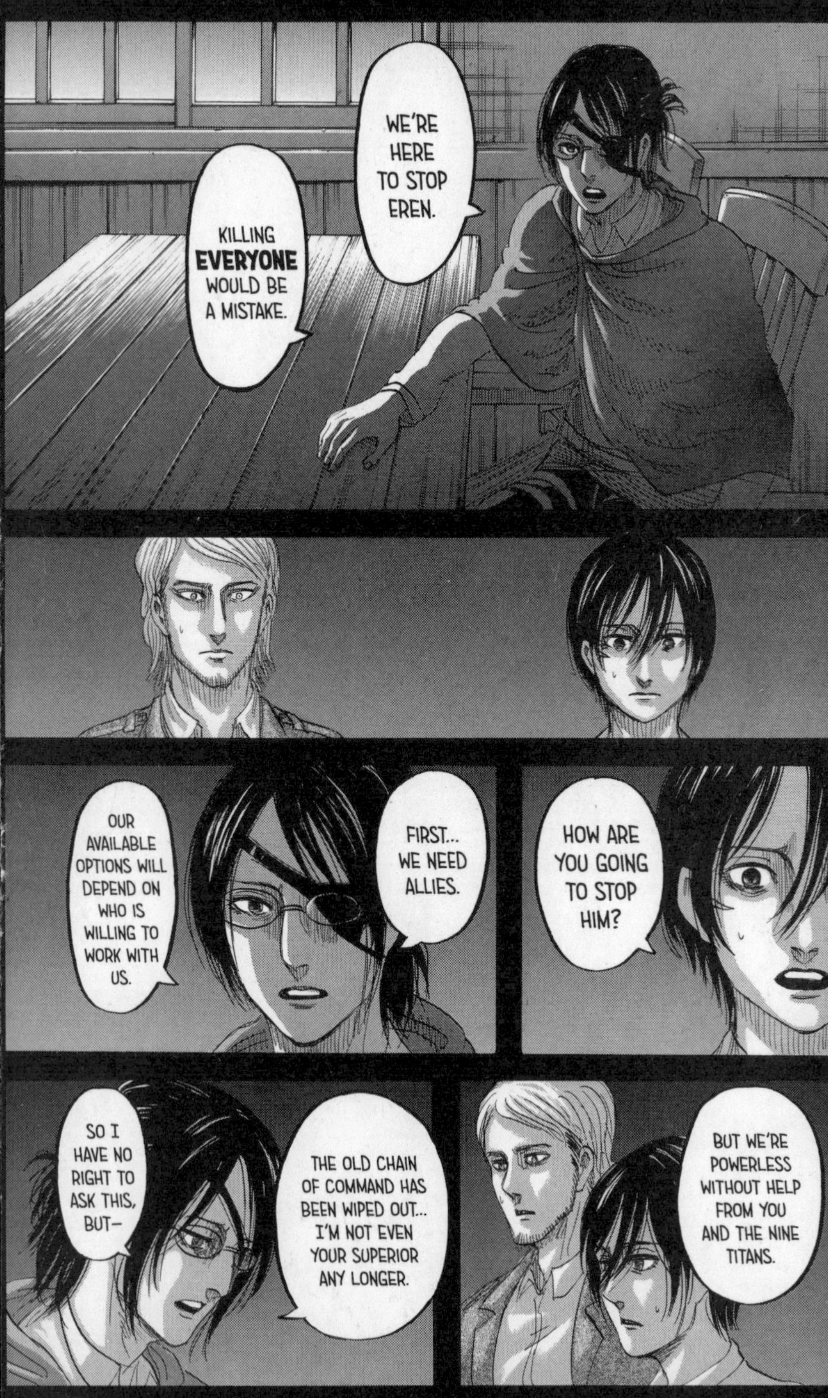
WE'RE HERE TO STOP EREN.
KILLING **EVERYONE** WOULD BE A MISTAKE.
HOW ARE YOU GOING TO STOP HIM?
FIRST... WE NEED ALLIES.
OUR AVAILABLE OPTIONS WILL DEPEND ON WHO IS WILLING TO WORK WITH US.
BUT WE'RE POWERLESS WITHOUT HELP FROM YOU AND THE NINE TITANS.
THE OLD CHAIN OF COMMAND HAS BEEN WIPED OUT... I'M NOT EVEN YOUR SUPERIOR ANY LONGER.
SO I HAVE NO RIGHT TO ASK THIS, BUT—

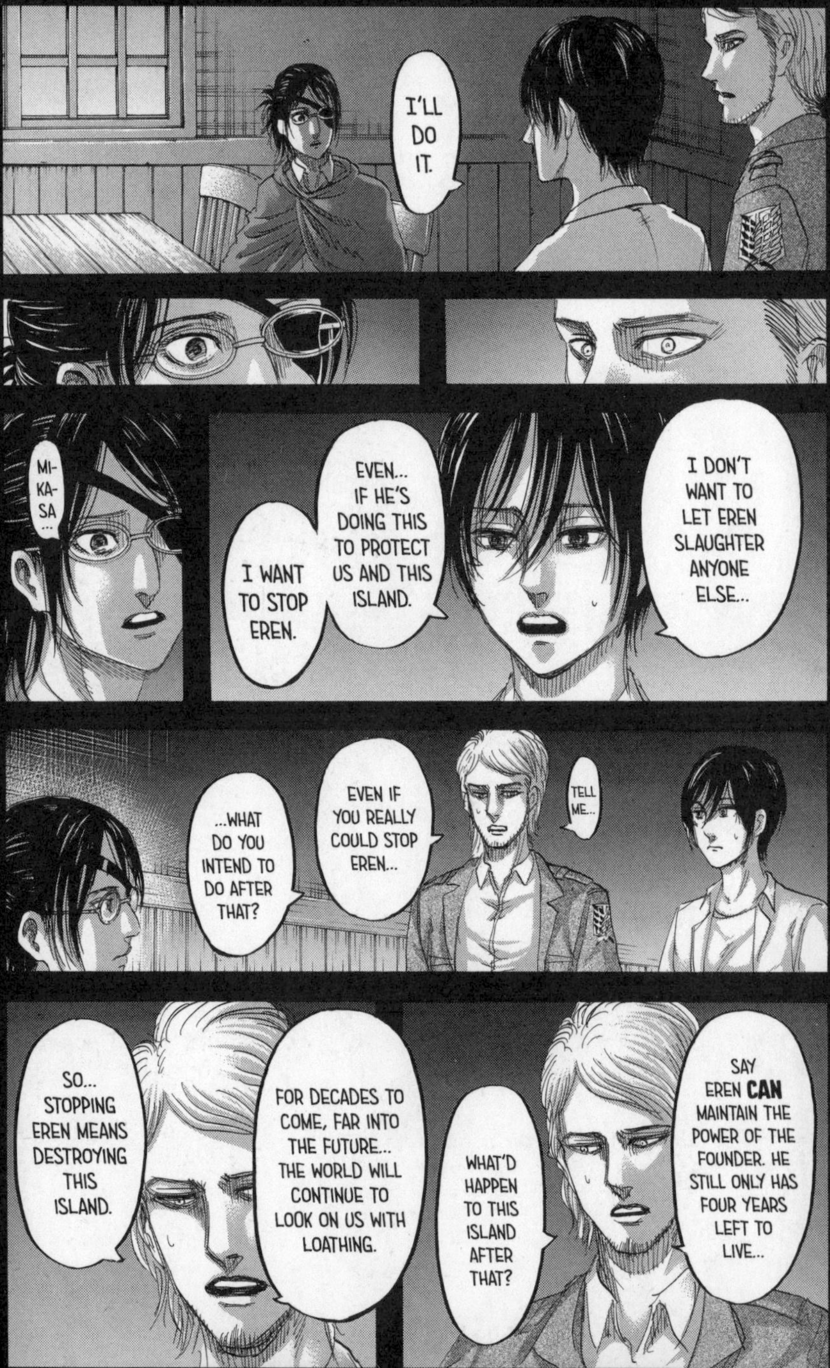
I'LL DO IT.
I DON'T WANT TO LET EREN SLAUGHTER ANYONE ELSE...
EVEN... IF HE'S DOING THIS TO PROTECT US AND THIS ISLAND.
I WANT TO STOP EREN.
MI-KA-SA...
TELL ME...
EVEN IF YOU REALLY COULD STOP EREN...
...WHAT DO YOU INTEND TO DO AFTER THAT?
SAY EREN **CAN** MAINTAIN THE POWER OF THE FOUNDER. HE STILL ONLY HAS FOUR YEARS LEFT TO LIVE...
WHAT'D HAPPEN TO THIS ISLAND AFTER THAT?
FOR DECADES TO COME, FAR INTO THE FUTURE... THE WORLD WILL CONTINUE TO LOOK ON US WITH LOATHING.
SO... STOPPING EREN MEANS DESTROYING THIS ISLAND.

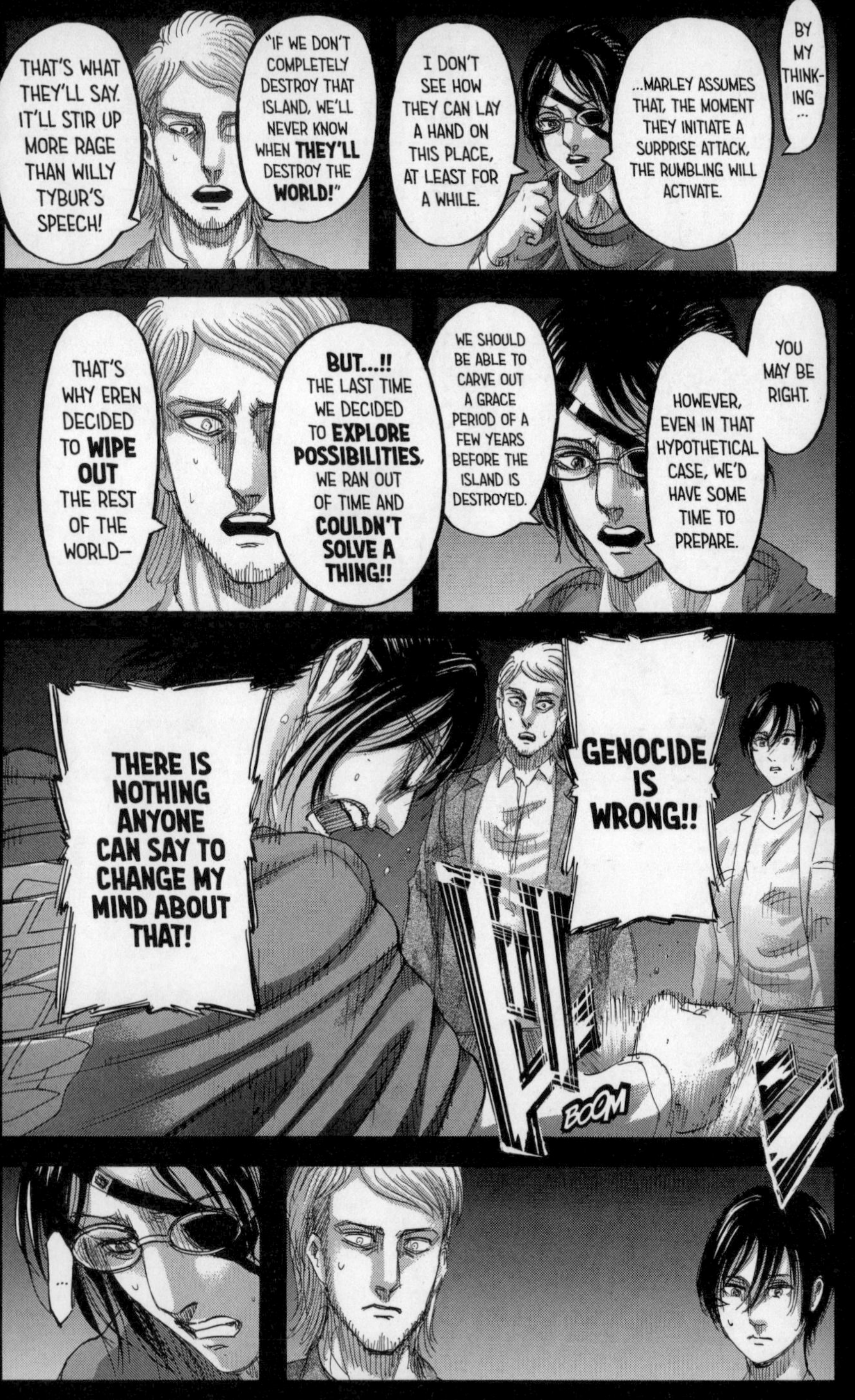

BY MY THINKING...
...MARLEY ASSUMES THAT, THE MOMENT THEY INITIATE A SURPRISE ATTACK, THE RUMBLING WILL ACTIVATE.
I DON'T SEE HOW THEY CAN LAY A HAND ON THIS PLACE, AT LEAST FOR A WHILE.
"IF WE DON'T COMPLETELY DESTROY THAT ISLAND, WE'LL NEVER KNOW WHEN **THEY'LL** DESTROY THE **WORLD!**"
THAT'S WHAT THEY'LL SAY. IT'LL STIR UP MORE RAGE THAN WILLY TYBUR'S SPEECH!
YOU MAY BE RIGHT.
HOWEVER, EVEN IN THAT HYPOTHETICAL CASE, WE'D HAVE SOME TIME TO PREPARE.
WE SHOULD BE ABLE TO CARVE OUT A GRACE PERIOD OF A FEW YEARS BEFORE THE ISLAND IS DESTROYED.
BUT...!! THE LAST TIME WE DECIDED TO **EXPLORE POSSIBILITIES,** WE RAN OUT OF TIME AND **COULDN'T SOLVE A THING!!**
THAT'S WHY EREN DECIDED TO **WIPE OUT** THE REST OF THE WORLD—
GENOCIDE IS WRONG!!
THERE IS NOTHING ANYONE CAN SAY TO CHANGE MY MIND ABOUT THAT!
BOOM
...

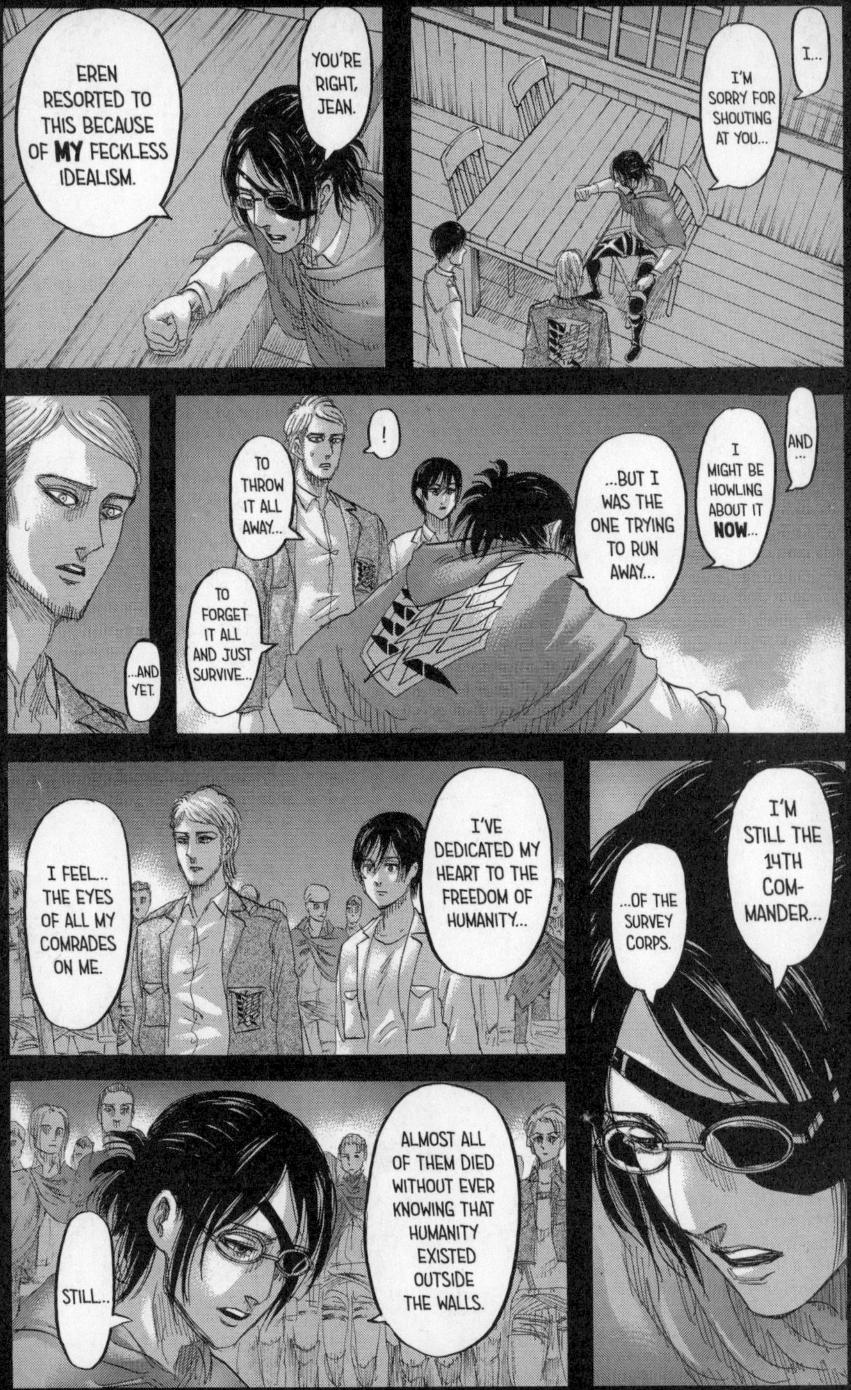
I...
I'M SORRY FOR SHOUTING AT YOU...
YOU'RE RIGHT, JEAN.
EREN RESORTED TO THIS BECAUSE OF **MY** FECKLESS IDEALISM.
AND...
I MIGHT BE HOWLING ABOUT IT **NOW**...
...BUT I WAS THE ONE TRYING TO RUN AWAY...
!
TO THROW IT ALL AWAY...
TO FORGET IT ALL AND JUST SURVIVE...
...AND YET.
I'M STILL THE 14TH COMMANDER...
...OF THE SURVEY CORPS.
I'VE DEDICATED MY HEART TO THE FREEDOM OF HUMANITY...
I FEEL... THE EYES OF ALL MY COMRADES ON ME.
ALMOST ALL OF THEM DIED WITHOUT EVER KNOWING THAT HUMANITY EXISTED OUTSIDE THE WALLS.
STILL...

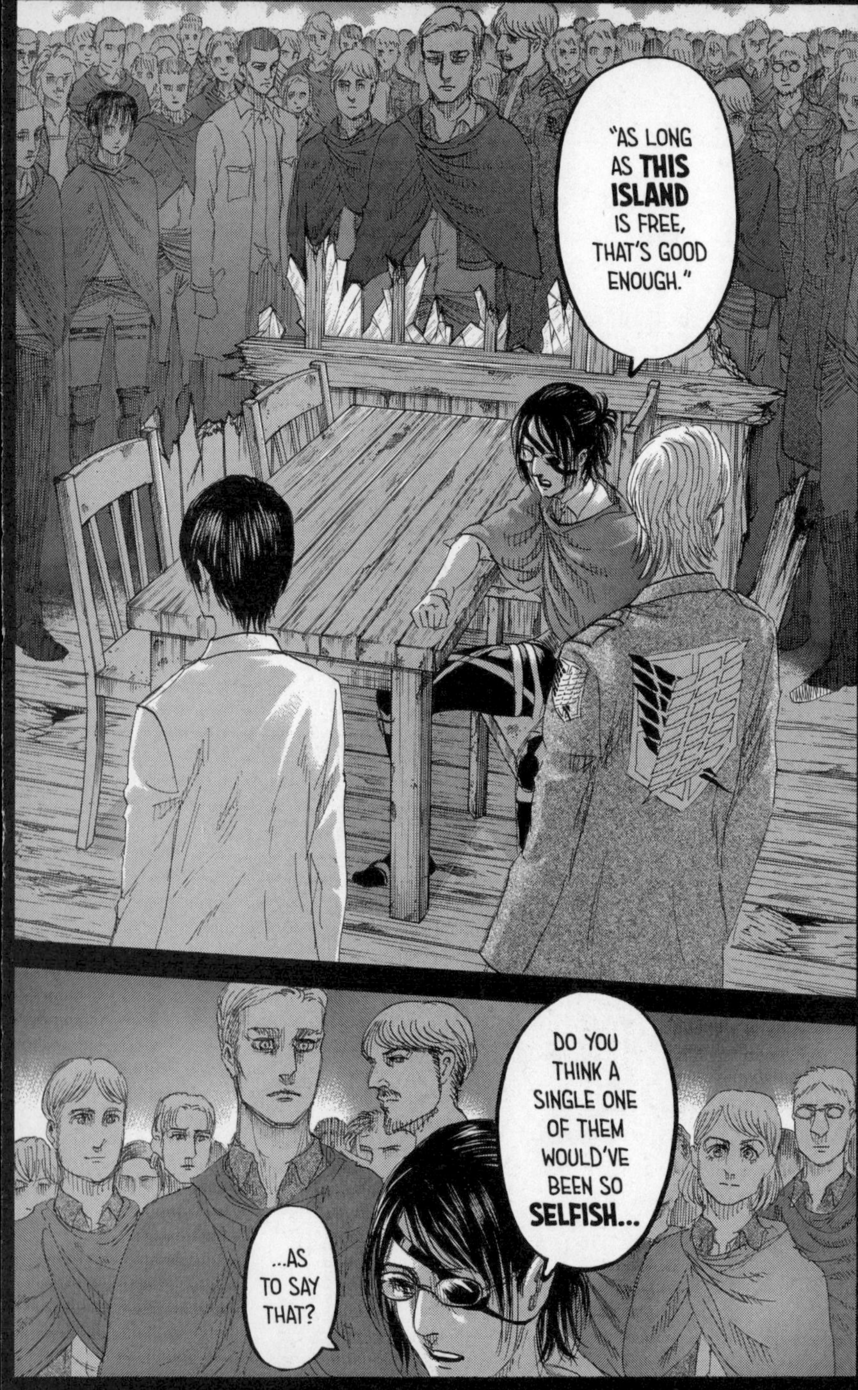
"AS LONG AS **THIS ISLAND** IS FREE, THAT'S GOOD ENOUGH."
DO YOU THINK A SINGLE ONE OF THEM WOULD'VE BEEN SO **SELFISH...**
...AS TO SAY THAT?

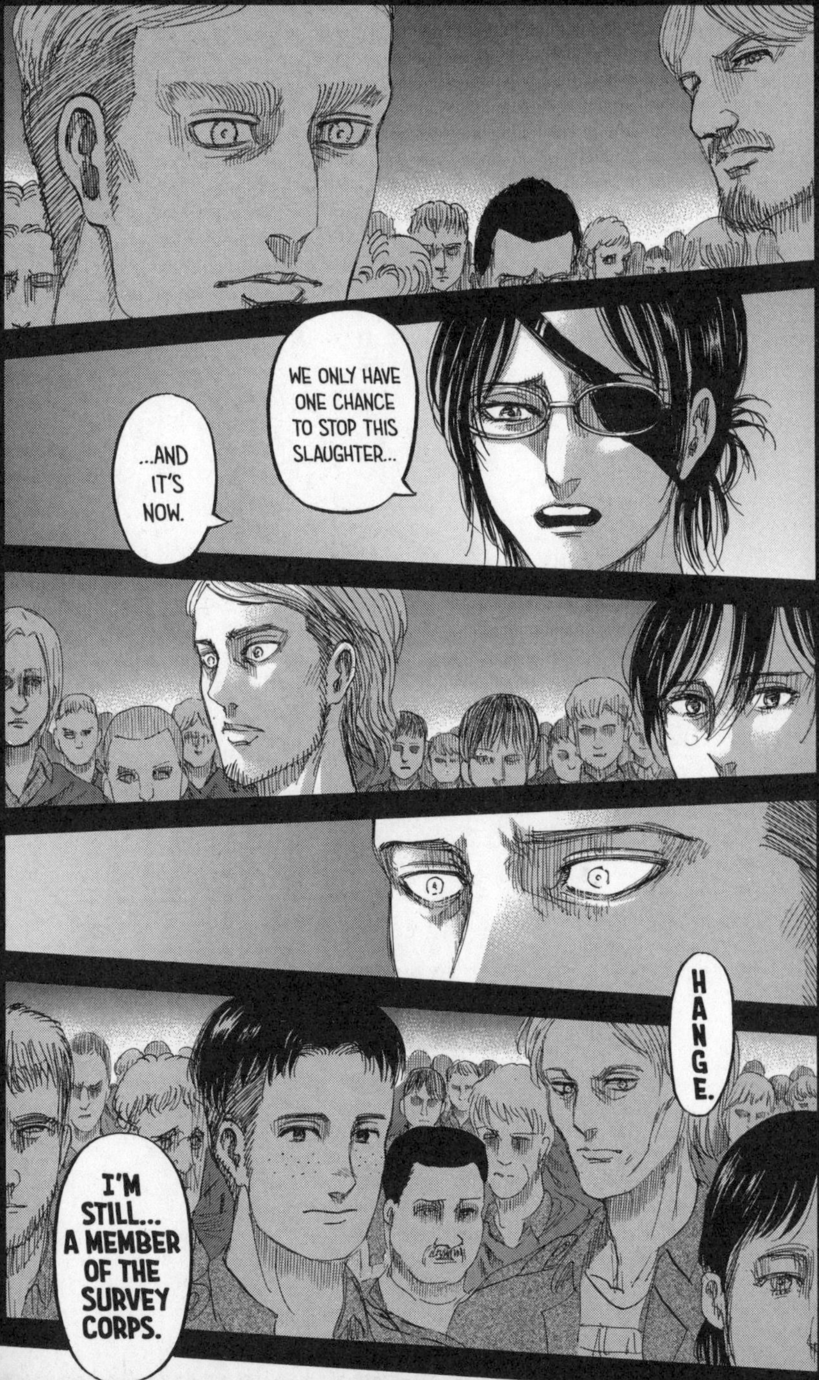
WE ONLY HAVE ONE CHANCE TO STOP THIS SLAUGHTER...
...AND IT'S NOW.
HANGE.
I'M STILL... A MEMBER OF THE SURVEY CORPS.

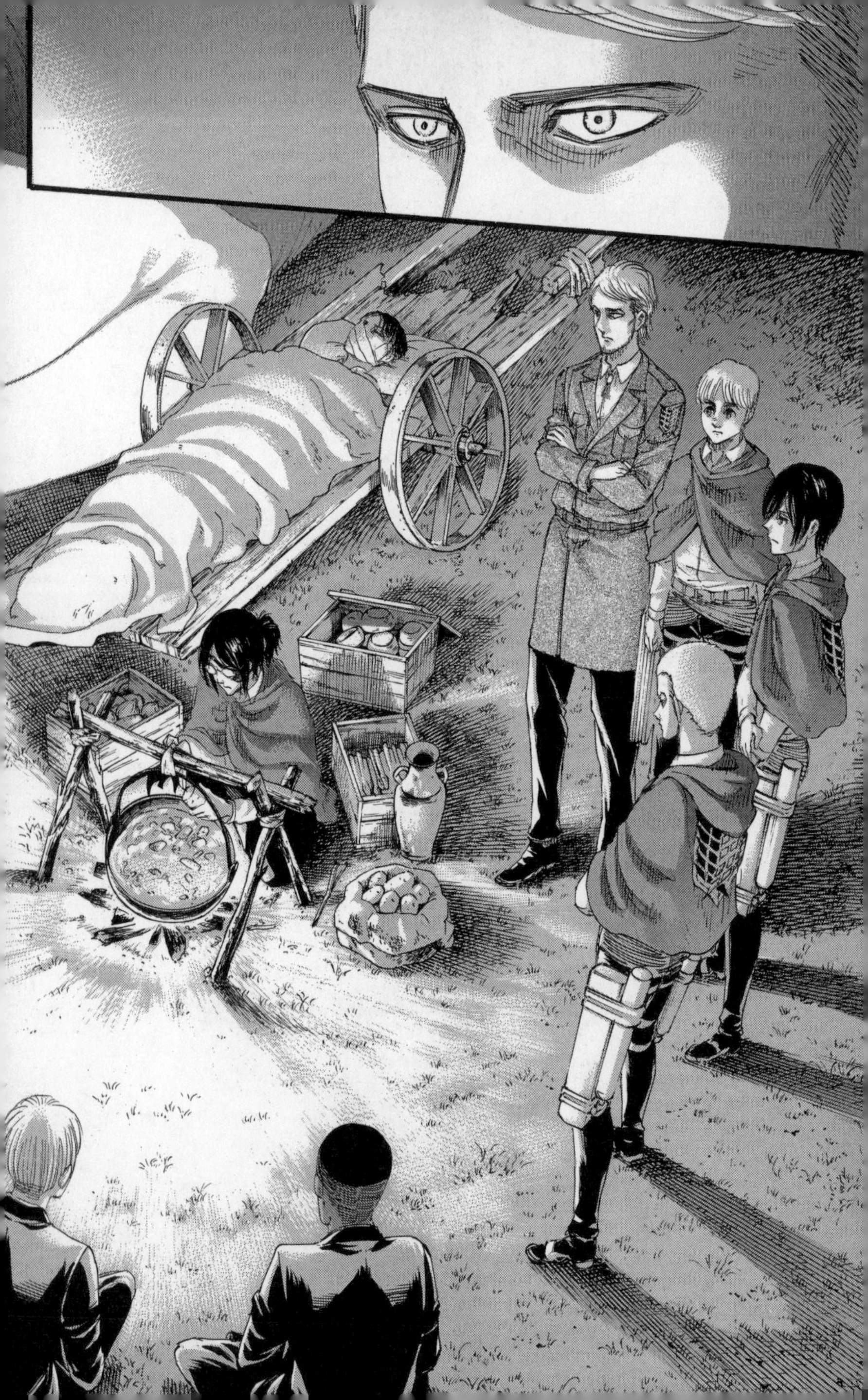

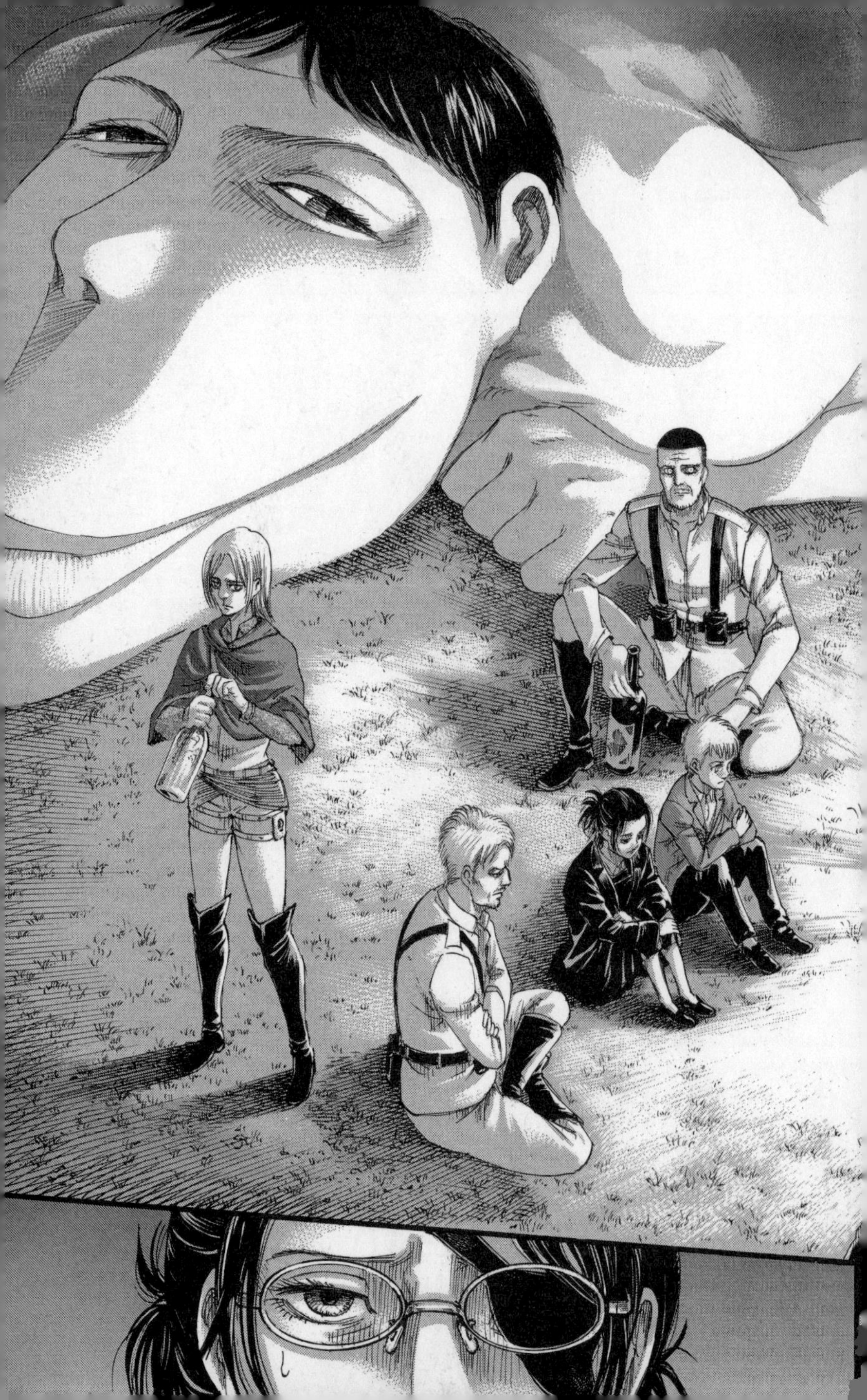

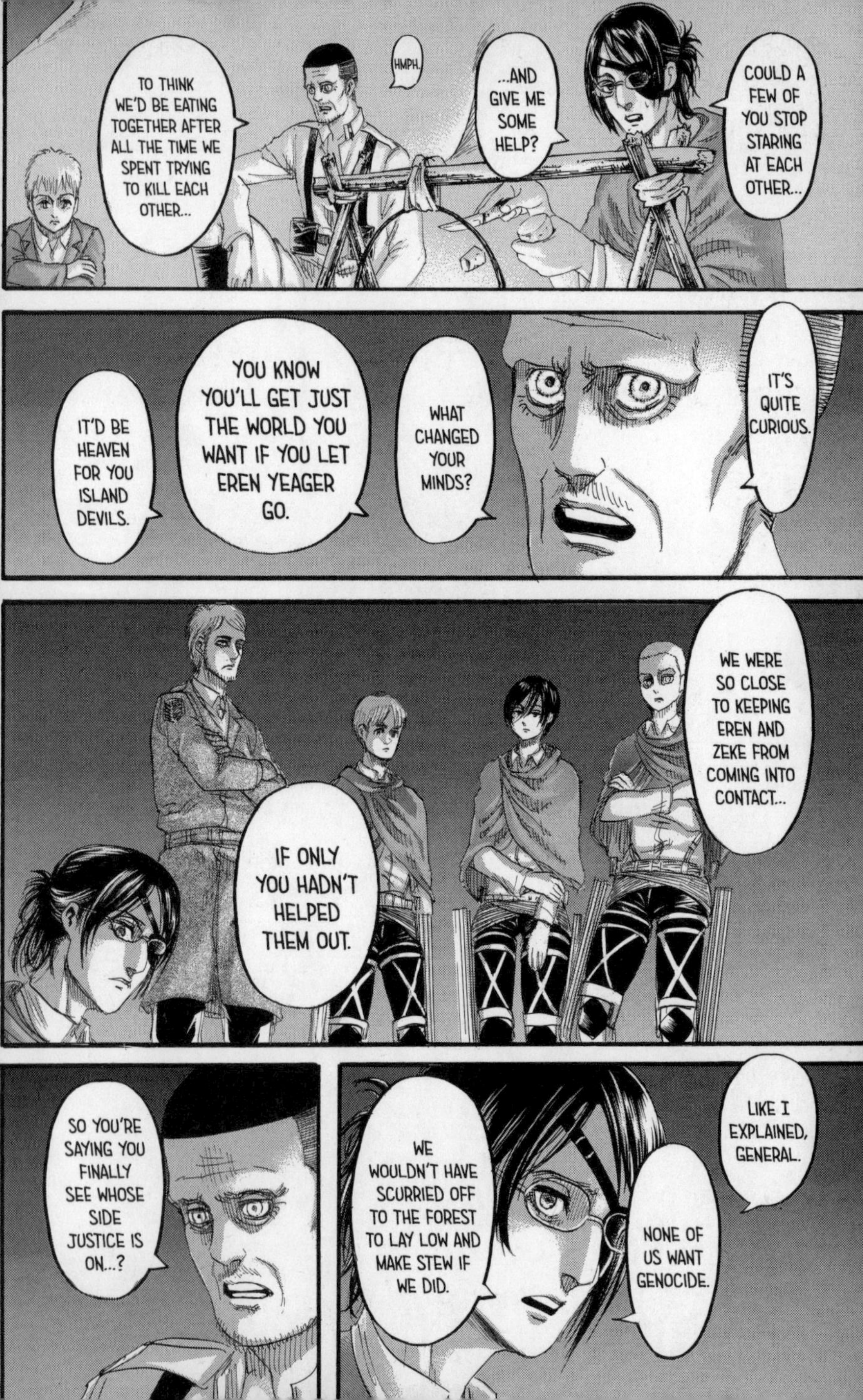
COULD A FEW OF YOU STOP STARING AT EACH OTHER...
...AND GIVE ME SOME HELP?
HMPH.
TO THINK WE'D BE EATING TOGETHER AFTER ALL THE TIME WE SPENT TRYING TO KILL EACH OTHER...
IT'S QUITE CURIOUS.
WHAT CHANGED YOUR MINDS?
YOU KNOW YOU'LL GET JUST THE WORLD YOU WANT IF YOU LET EREN YEAGER GO.
IT'D BE HEAVEN FOR YOU ISLAND DEVILS.
WE WERE SO CLOSE TO KEEPING EREN AND ZEKE FROM COMING INTO CONTACT...
IF ONLY YOU HADN'T HELPED THEM OUT.
LIKE I EXPLAINED, GENERAL.
NONE OF US WANT GENOCIDE.
WE WOULDN'T HAVE SCURRIED OFF TO THE FOREST TO LAY LOW AND MAKE STEW IF WE DID.
SO YOU'RE SAYING YOU FINALLY SEE WHOSE SIDE JUSTICE IS ON...?

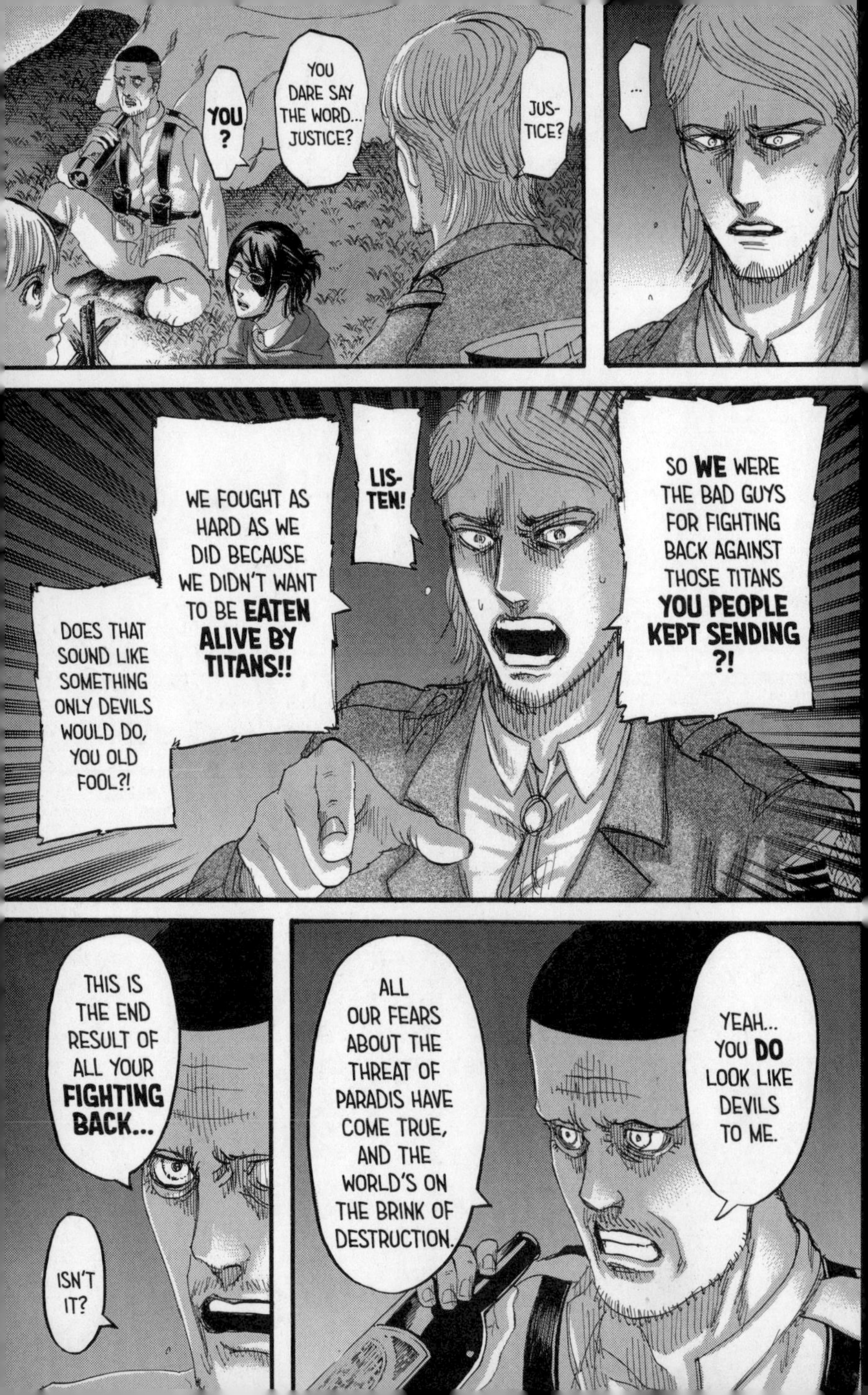
...
JUSTICE?
YOU DARE SAY THE WORD... JUSTICE?
YOU ?
SO **WE** WERE THE BAD GUYS FOR FIGHTING BACK AGAINST THOSE TITANS **YOU PEOPLE KEPT SENDING ?!**
LISTEN!
WE FOUGHT AS HARD AS WE DID BECAUSE WE DIDN'T WANT TO BE **EATEN ALIVE BY TITANS!!**
DOES THAT SOUND LIKE SOMETHING ONLY DEVILS WOULD DO, YOU OLD FOOL?!
YEAH... YOU **DO** LOOK LIKE DEVILS TO ME.
ALL OUR FEARS ABOUT THE THREAT OF PARADIS HAVE COME TRUE, AND THE WORLD'S ON THE BRINK OF DESTRUCTION.
THIS IS THE END RESULT OF ALL YOUR **FIGHTING BACK...**
ISN'T IT?

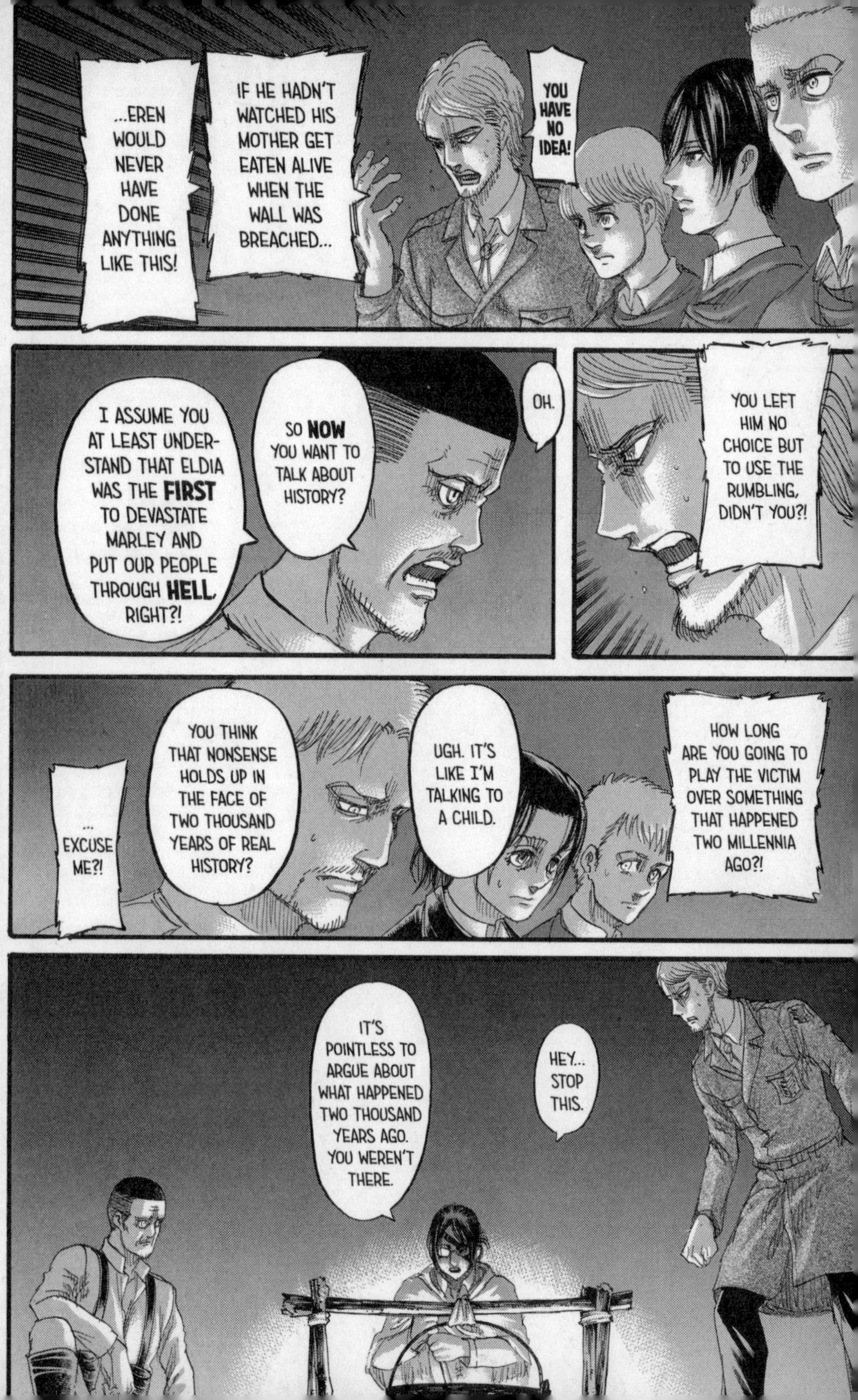
YOU HAVE NO IDEA!
IF HE HADN'T WATCHED HIS MOTHER GET EATEN ALIVE WHEN THE WALL WAS BREACHED...
...EREN WOULD NEVER HAVE DONE ANYTHING LIKE THIS!
YOU LEFT HIM NO CHOICE BUT TO USE THE RUMBLING, DIDN'T YOU?!
OH.
SO **NOW** YOU WANT TO TALK ABOUT HISTORY?
I ASSUME YOU AT LEAST UNDERSTAND THAT ELDIA WAS THE **FIRST** TO DEVASTATE MARLEY AND PUT OUR PEOPLE THROUGH **HELL**, RIGHT?!
HOW LONG ARE YOU GOING TO PLAY THE VICTIM OVER SOMETHING THAT HAPPENED TWO MILLENNIA AGO?!
UGH. IT'S LIKE I'M TALKING TO A CHILD.
YOU THINK THAT NONSENSE HOLDS UP IN THE FACE OF TWO THOUSAND YEARS OF REAL HISTORY?
...EXCUSE ME?!
HEY... STOP THIS.
IT'S POINTLESS TO ARGUE ABOUT WHAT HAPPENED TWO THOUSAND YEARS AGO. YOU WEREN'T THERE.

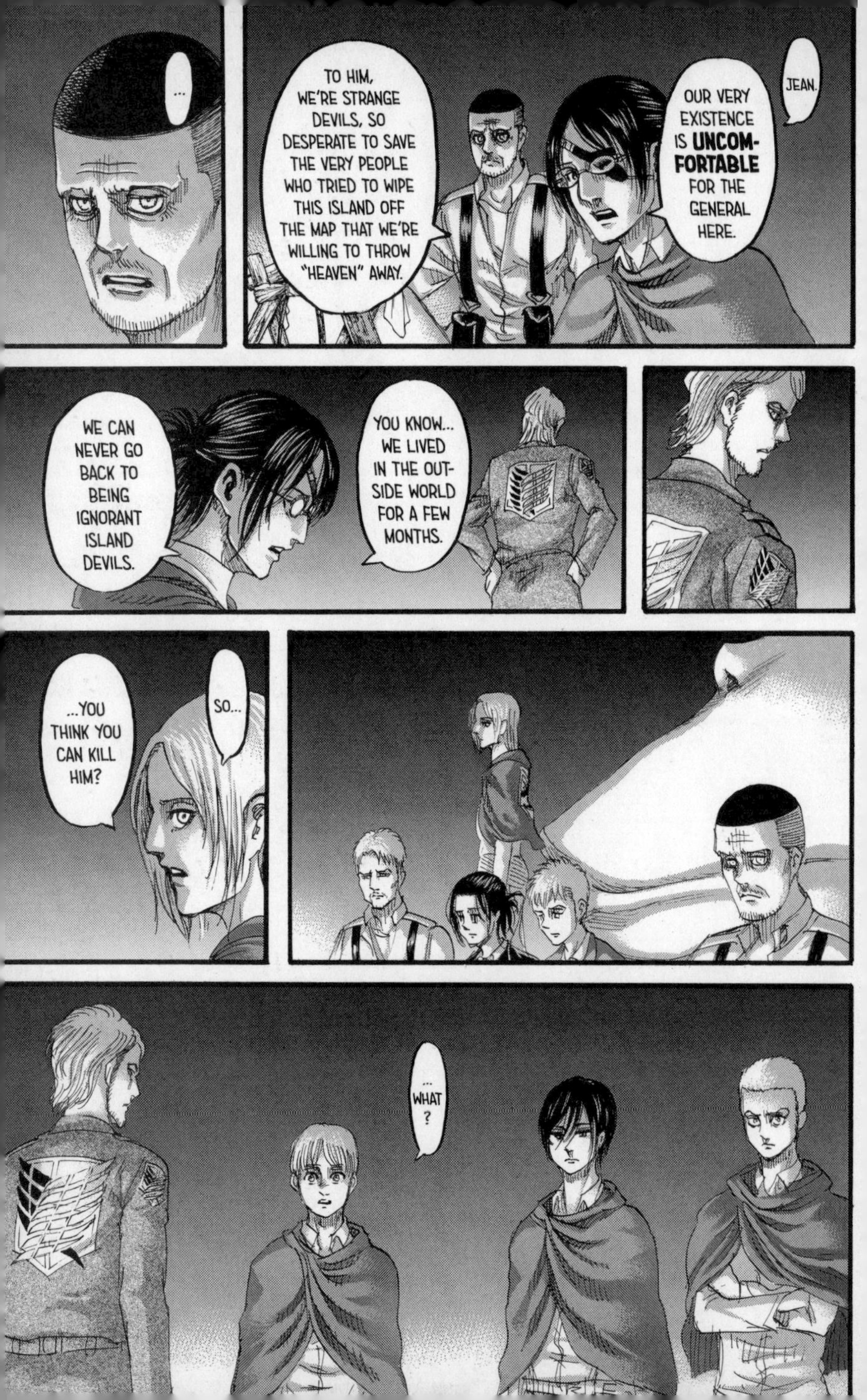
JEAN.
OUR VERY EXISTENCE IS **UNCOMFORTABLE** FOR THE GENERAL HERE.
TO HIM, WE'RE STRANGE DEVILS, SO DESPERATE TO SAVE THE VERY PEOPLE WHO TRIED TO WIPE THIS ISLAND OFF THE MAP THAT WE'RE WILLING TO THROW "HEAVEN" AWAY.
...
YOU KNOW... WE LIVED IN THE OUTSIDE WORLD FOR A FEW MONTHS.
WE CAN NEVER GO BACK TO BEING IGNORANT ISLAND DEVILS.
SO...
...YOU THINK YOU CAN KILL HIM?
...WHAT?

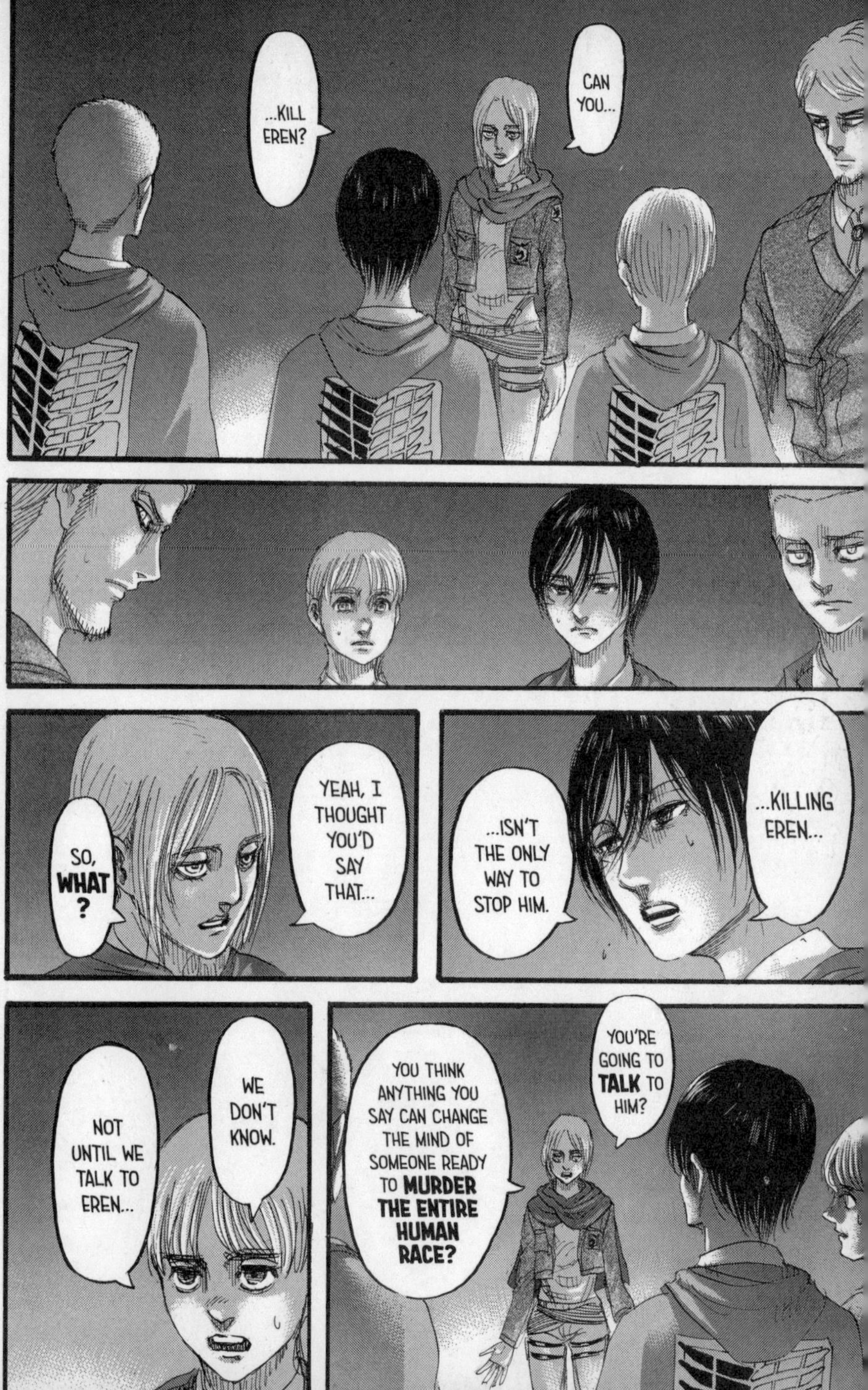
CAN YOU...
...KILL EREN?
...KILLING EREN...
...ISN'T THE ONLY WAY TO STOP HIM.
YEAH, I THOUGHT YOU'D SAY THAT...
SO, **WHAT**?
YOU'RE GOING TO **TALK** TO HIM?
YOU THINK ANYTHING YOU SAY CAN CHANGE THE MIND OF SOMEONE READY TO **MURDER THE ENTIRE HUMAN RACE?**
WE DON'T KNOW.
NOT UNTIL WE TALK TO EREN...

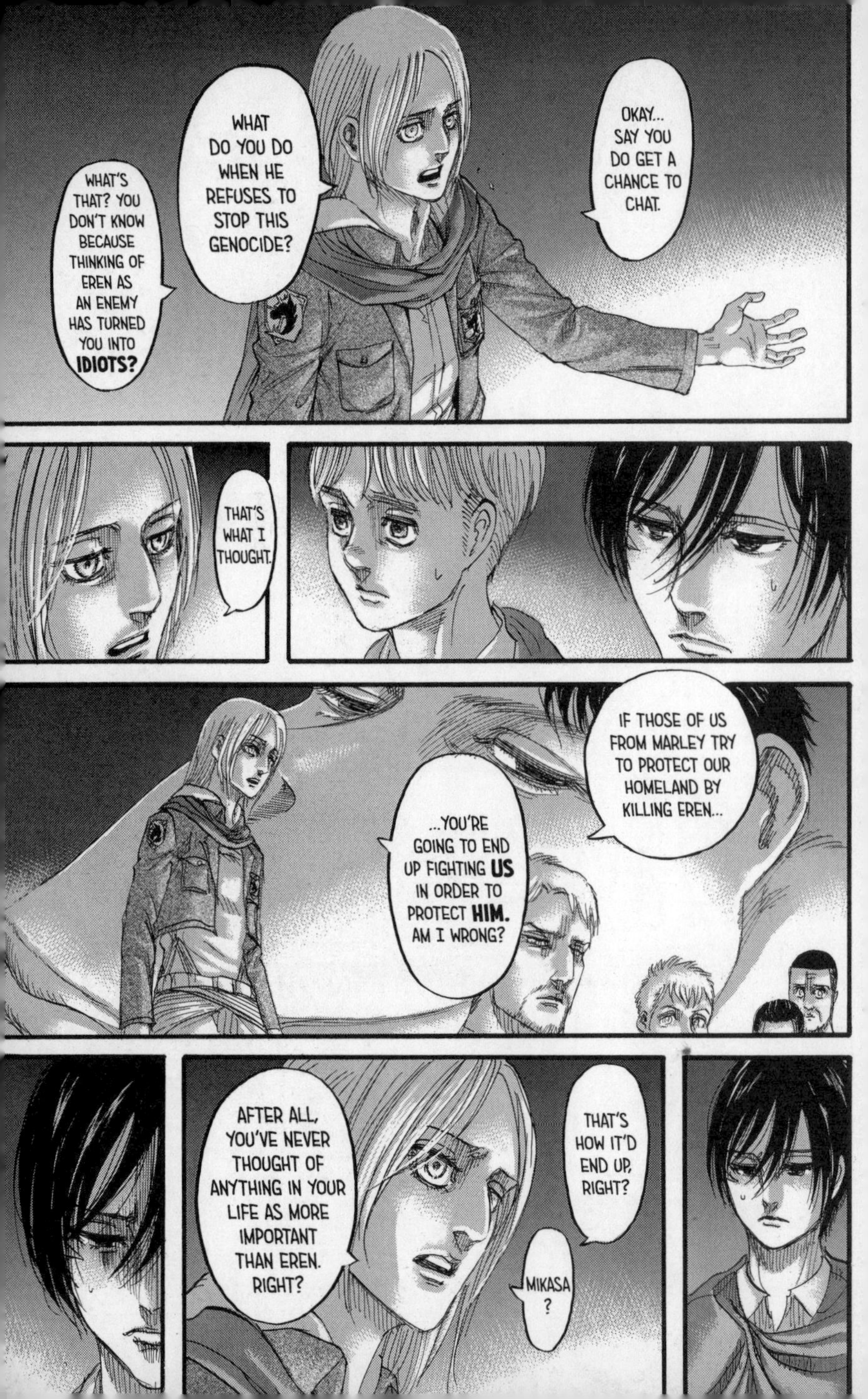
OKAY... SAY YOU DO GET A CHANCE TO CHAT.
WHAT DO YOU DO WHEN HE REFUSES TO STOP THIS GENOCIDE?
WHAT'S THAT? YOU DON'T KNOW BECAUSE THINKING OF EREN AS AN ENEMY HAS TURNED YOU INTO **IDIOTS?**
THAT'S WHAT I THOUGHT.
IF THOSE OF US FROM MARLEY TRY TO PROTECT OUR HOMELAND BY KILLING EREN...
...YOU'RE GOING TO END UP FIGHTING **US** IN ORDER TO PROTECT **HIM.** AM I WRONG?
THAT'S HOW IT'D END UP, RIGHT?
AFTER ALL, YOU'VE NEVER THOUGHT OF ANYTHING IN YOUR LIFE AS MORE IMPORTANT THAN EREN. RIGHT?
MIKASA ?

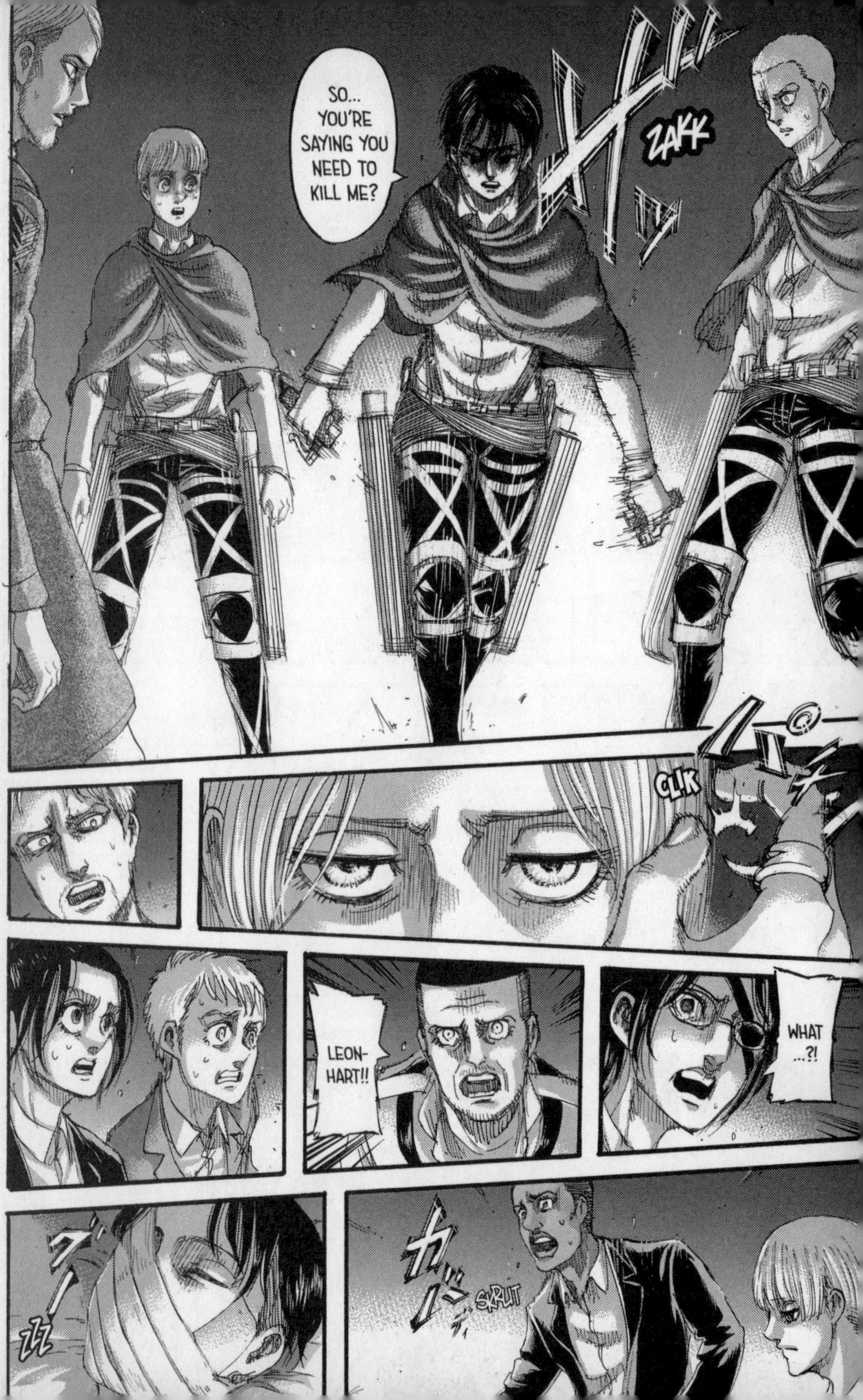
SO... YOU'RE SAYING YOU NEED TO KILL ME?
ZAKK
CLIK
WHAT ...?!
LEON-HART!!
SKRUT
ZZZ

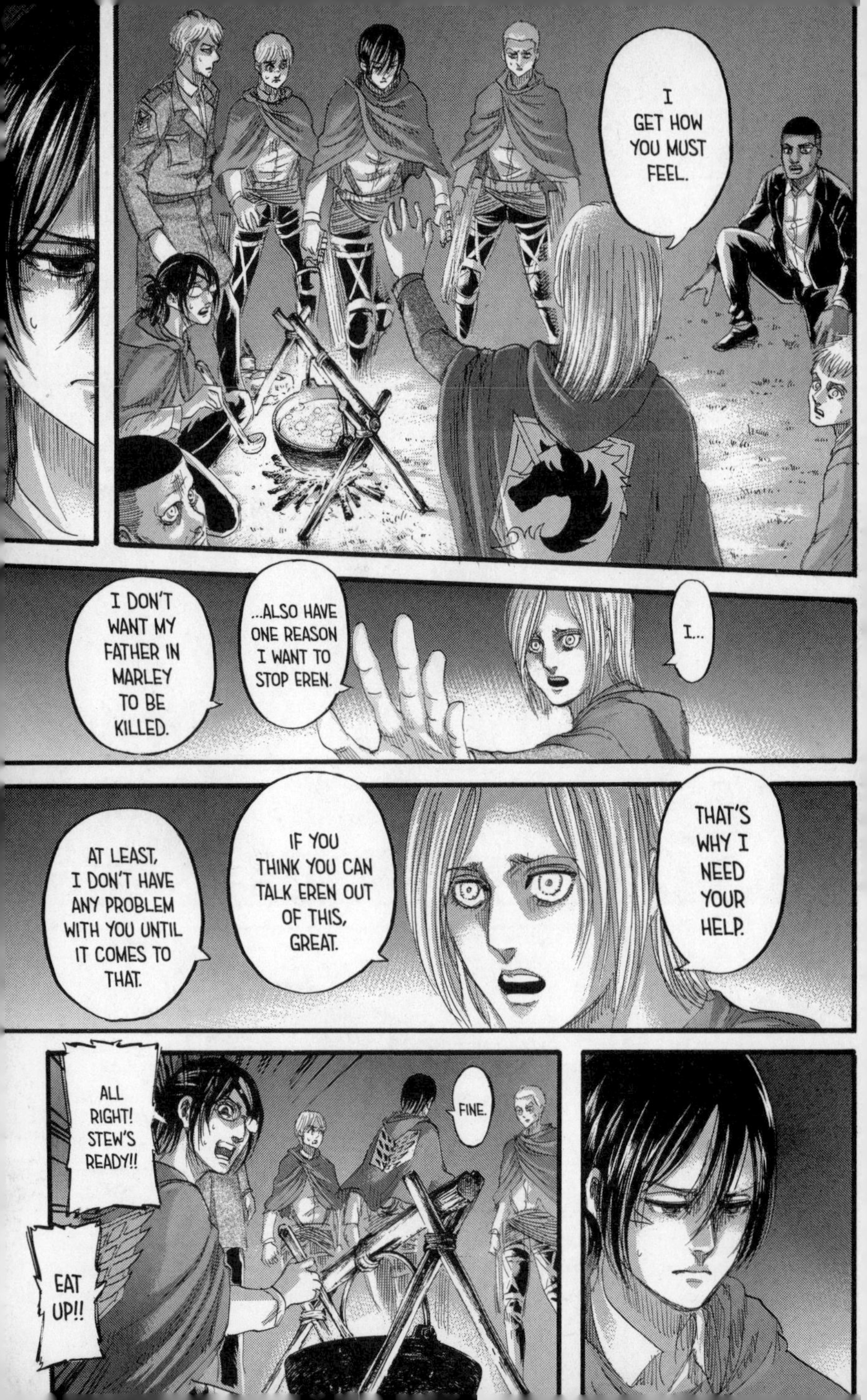
I GET HOW YOU MUST FEEL.
I...
...ALSO HAVE ONE REASON I WANT TO STOP EREN.
I DON'T WANT MY FATHER IN MARLEY TO BE KILLED.
THAT'S WHY I NEED YOUR HELP.
IF YOU THINK YOU CAN TALK EREN OUT OF THIS, GREAT.
AT LEAST, I DON'T HAVE ANY PROBLEM WITH YOU UNTIL IT COMES TO THAT.
FINE.
ALL RIGHT! STEW'S READY!!
EAT UP!!

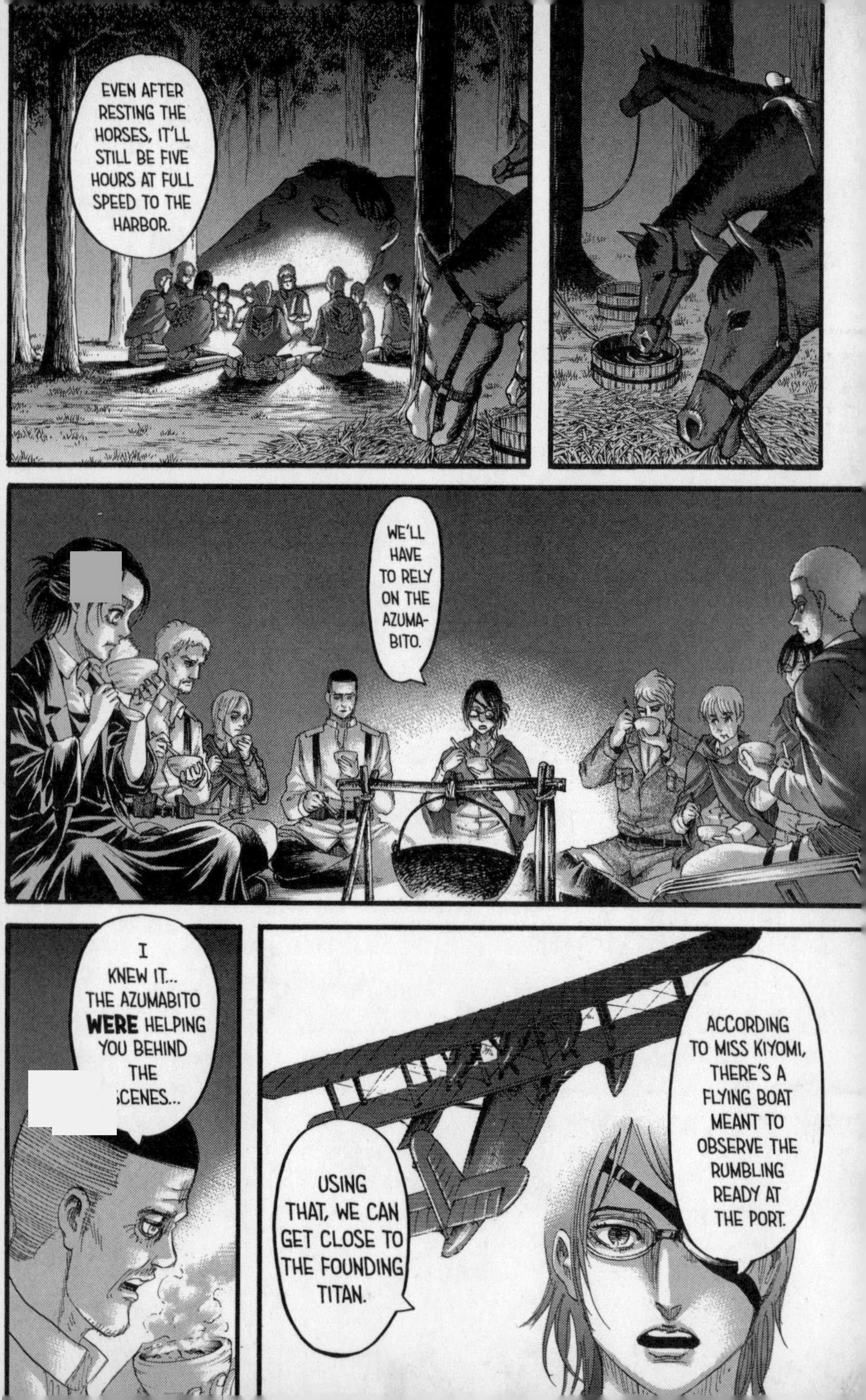
EVEN AFTER RESTING THE HORSES, IT'LL STILL BE FIVE HOURS AT FULL SPEED TO THE HARBOR.
WE'LL HAVE TO RELY ON THE AZUMABITO.
ACCORDING TO MISS KIYOMI, THERE'S A FLYING BOAT MEANT TO OBSERVE THE RUMBLING READY AT THE PORT.
USING THAT, WE CAN GET CLOSE TO THE FOUNDING TITAN.
I KNEW IT... THE AZUMABITO **WERE** HELPING YOU BEHIND THE SCENES...

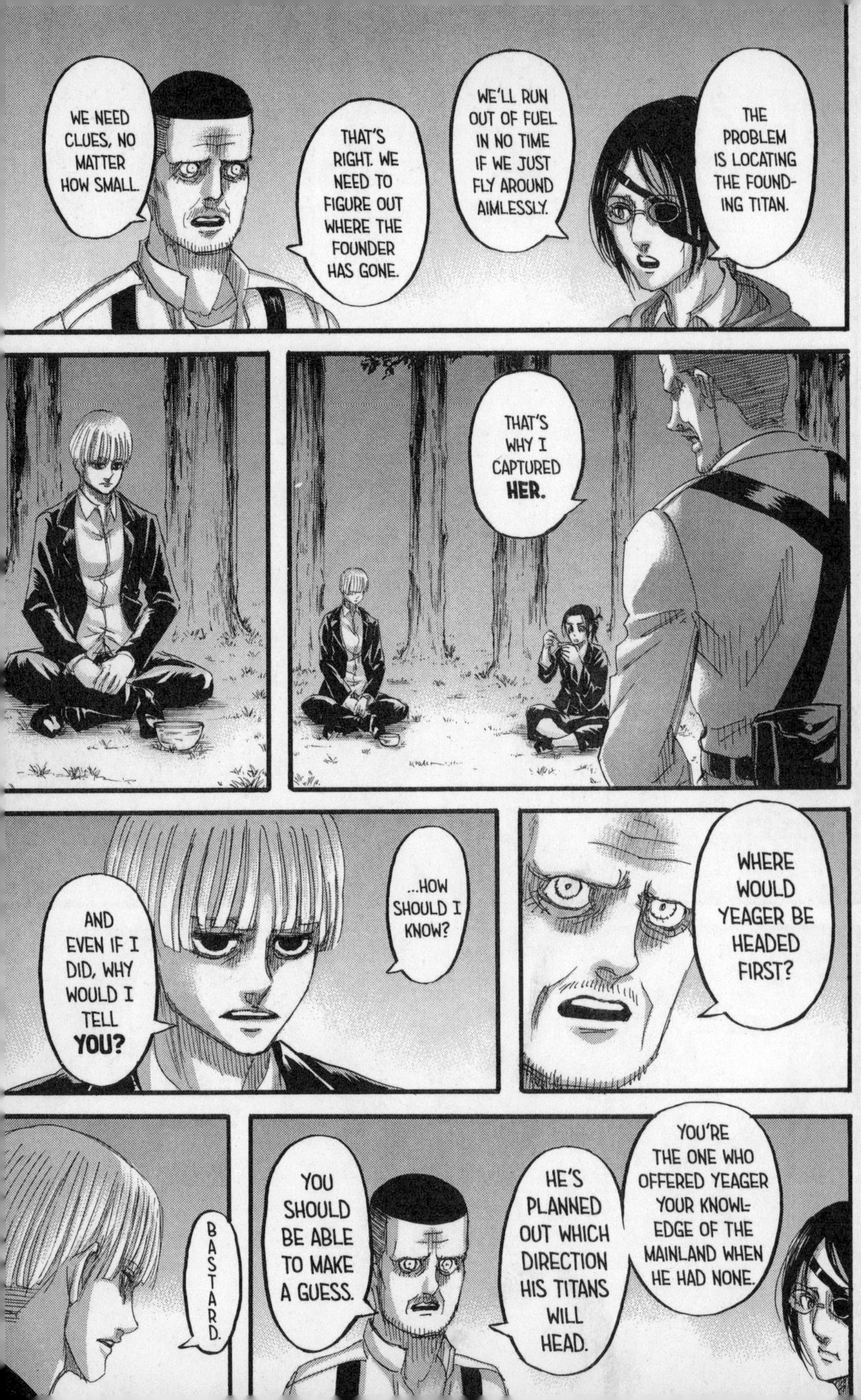
THE PROBLEM IS LOCATING THE FOUNDING TITAN.
WE'LL RUN OUT OF FUEL IN NO TIME IF WE JUST FLY AROUND AIMLESSLY.
THAT'S RIGHT. WE NEED TO FIGURE OUT WHERE THE FOUNDER HAS GONE.
WE NEED CLUES, NO MATTER HOW SMALL.
THAT'S WHY I CAPTURED **HER.**
WHERE WOULD YEAGER BE HEADED FIRST?
...HOW SHOULD I KNOW?
AND EVEN IF I DID, WHY WOULD I TELL **YOU?**
YOU'RE THE ONE WHO OFFERED YEAGER YOUR KNOWLEDGE OF THE MAINLAND WHEN HE HAD NONE.
HE'S PLANNED OUT WHICH DIRECTION HIS TITANS WILL HEAD.
YOU SHOULD BE ABLE TO MAKE A GUESS.
BASTARD.

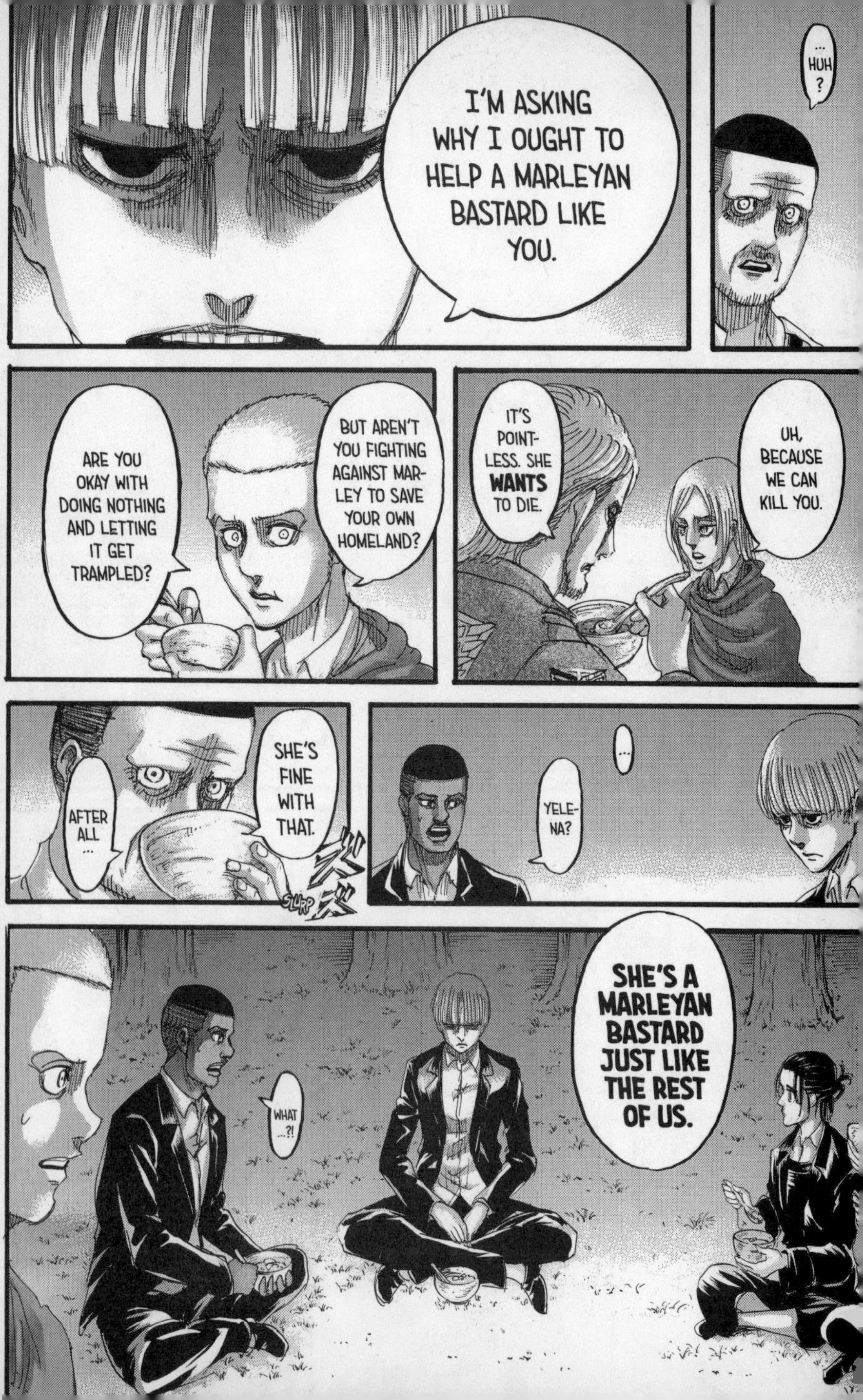
...HUH?
I'M ASKING WHY I OUGHT TO HELP A MARLEYAN BASTARD LIKE YOU.
UH, BECAUSE WE CAN KILL YOU.
IT'S POINTLESS. SHE **WANTS** TO DIE.
BUT AREN'T YOU FIGHTING AGAINST MARLEY TO SAVE YOUR OWN HOMELAND?
ARE YOU OKAY WITH DOING NOTHING AND LETTING IT GET TRAMPLED?
...
YELENA?
SHE'S FINE WITH THAT.
AFTER ALL...
SLURP
SHE'S A MARLEYAN BASTARD JUST LIKE THE REST OF US.
WHAT...?!

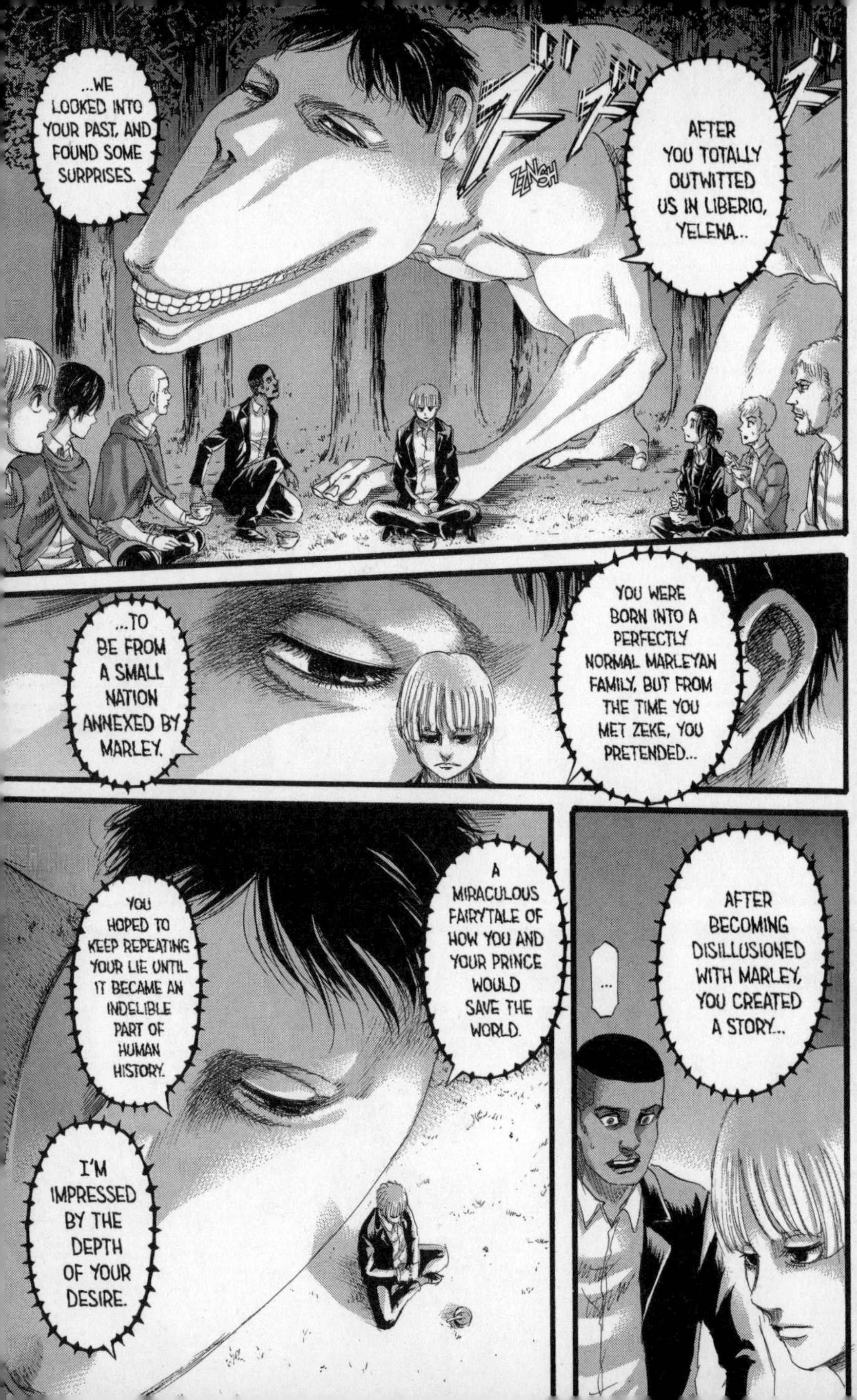
AFTER YOU TOTALLY OUTWITTED US IN LIBERIO, YELENA...
ZZNSH
...WE LOOKED INTO YOUR PAST, AND FOUND SOME SURPRISES.
YOU WERE BORN INTO A PERFECTLY NORMAL MARLEYAN FAMILY, BUT FROM THE TIME YOU MET ZEKE, YOU PRETENDED...
...TO BE FROM A SMALL NATION ANNEXED BY MARLEY.
AFTER BECOMING DISILLUSIONED WITH MARLEY, YOU CREATED A STORY...
...
A MIRACULOUS FAIRYTALE OF HOW YOU AND YOUR PRINCE WOULD SAVE THE WORLD.
YOU HOPED TO KEEP REPEATING YOUR LIE UNTIL IT BECAME AN INDELIBLE PART OF HUMAN HISTORY.
I'M IMPRESSED BY THE DEPTH OF YOUR DESIRE.

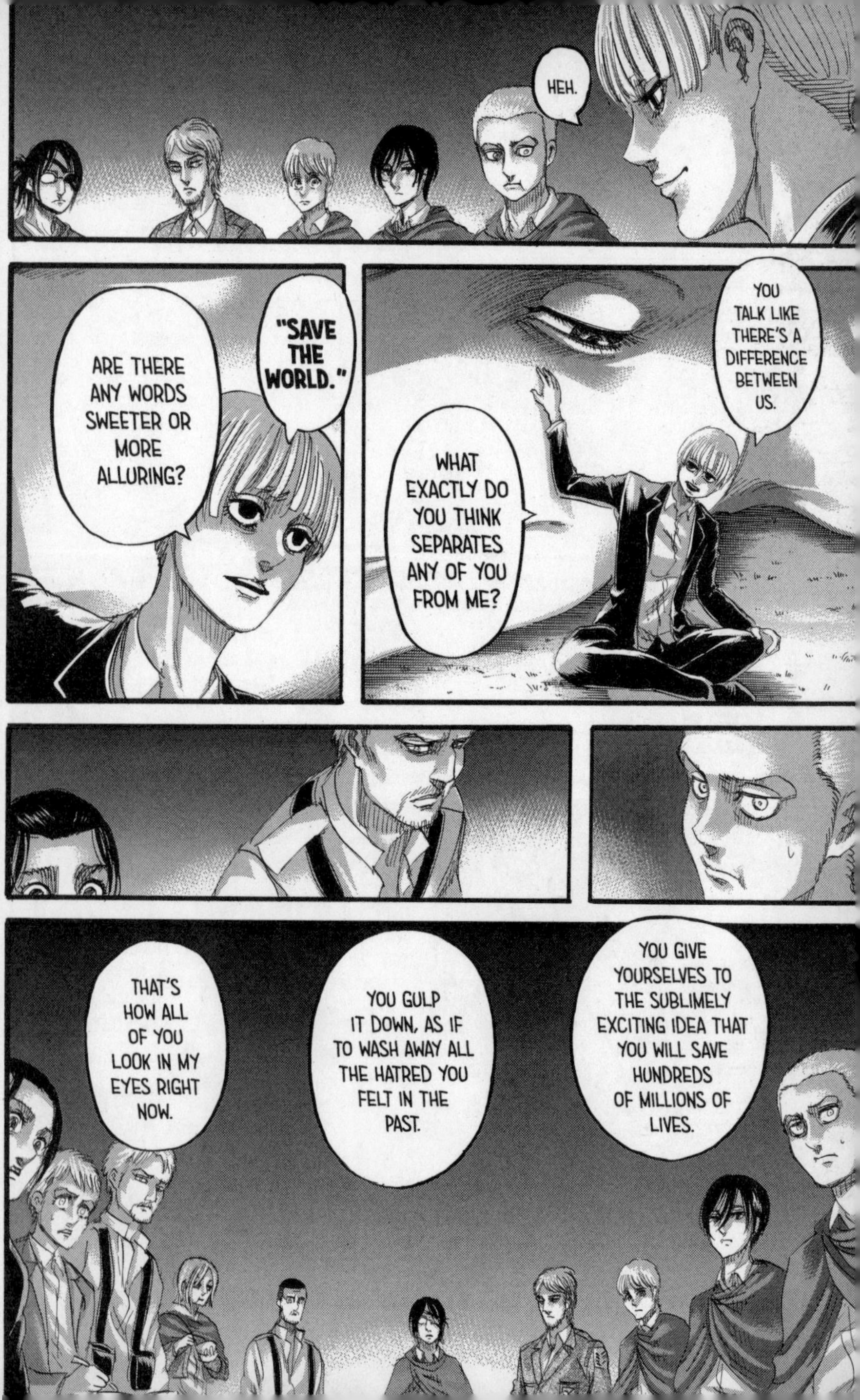
HEH.
YOU TALK LIKE THERE'S A DIFFERENCE BETWEEN US.
WHAT EXACTLY DO YOU THINK SEPARATES ANY OF YOU FROM ME?
"SAVE THE WORLD."
ARE THERE ANY WORDS SWEETER OR MORE ALLURING?
YOU GIVE YOURSELVES TO THE SUBLIMELY EXCITING IDEA THAT YOU WILL SAVE HUNDREDS OF MILLIONS OF LIVES.
YOU GULP IT DOWN, AS IF TO WASH AWAY ALL THE HATRED YOU FELT IN THE PAST.
THAT'S HOW ALL OF YOU LOOK IN MY EYES RIGHT NOW.

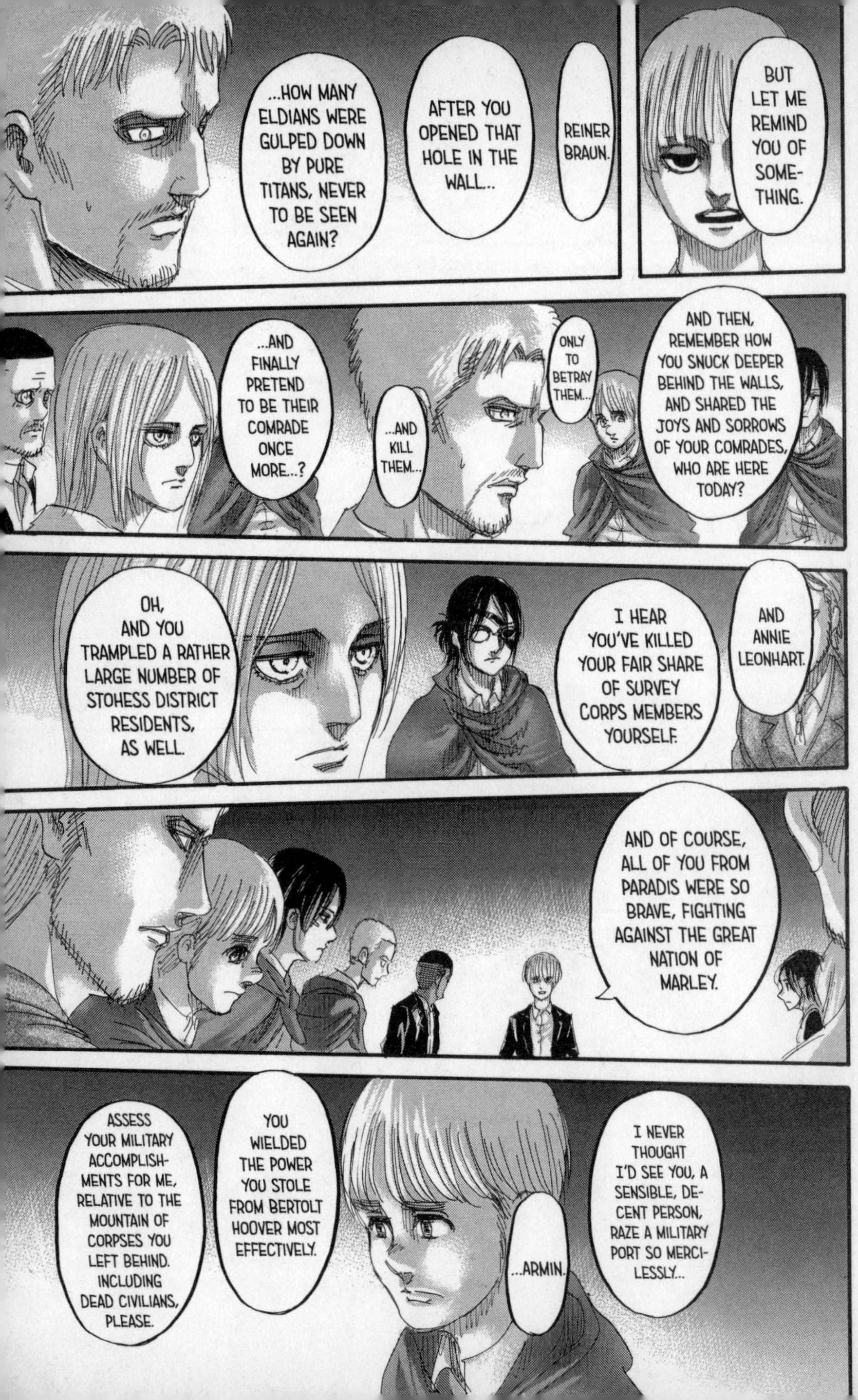
BUT LET ME REMIND YOU OF SOME-THING.
REINER BRAUN.
AFTER YOU OPENED THAT HOLE IN THE WALL...
...HOW MANY ELDIANS WERE GULPED DOWN BY PURE TITANS, NEVER TO BE SEEN AGAIN?
AND THEN, REMEMBER HOW YOU SNUCK DEEPER BEHIND THE WALLS, AND SHARED THE JOYS AND SORROWS OF YOUR COMRADES, WHO ARE HERE TODAY?
ONLY TO BETRAY THEM...
...AND KILL THEM...
...AND FINALLY PRETEND TO BE THEIR COMRADE ONCE MORE...?
AND ANNIE LEONHART.
I HEAR YOU'VE KILLED YOUR FAIR SHARE OF SURVEY CORPS MEMBERS YOURSELF.
OH, AND YOU TRAMPLED A RATHER LARGE NUMBER OF STOHESS DISTRICT RESIDENTS, AS WELL.
AND OF COURSE, ALL OF YOU FROM PARADIS WERE SO BRAVE, FIGHTING AGAINST THE GREAT NATION OF MARLEY.
I NEVER THOUGHT I'D SEE YOU, A SENSIBLE, DE-CENT PERSON, RAZE A MILITARY PORT SO MERCI-LESSLY...
...ARMIN.
YOU WIELDED THE POWER YOU STOLE FROM BERTOLT HOOVER MOST EFFECTIVELY.
ASSESS YOUR MILITARY ACCOMPLISH-MENTS FOR ME, RELATIVE TO THE MOUNTAIN OF CORPSES YOU LEFT BEHIND. INCLUDING DEAD CIVILIANS, PLEASE.

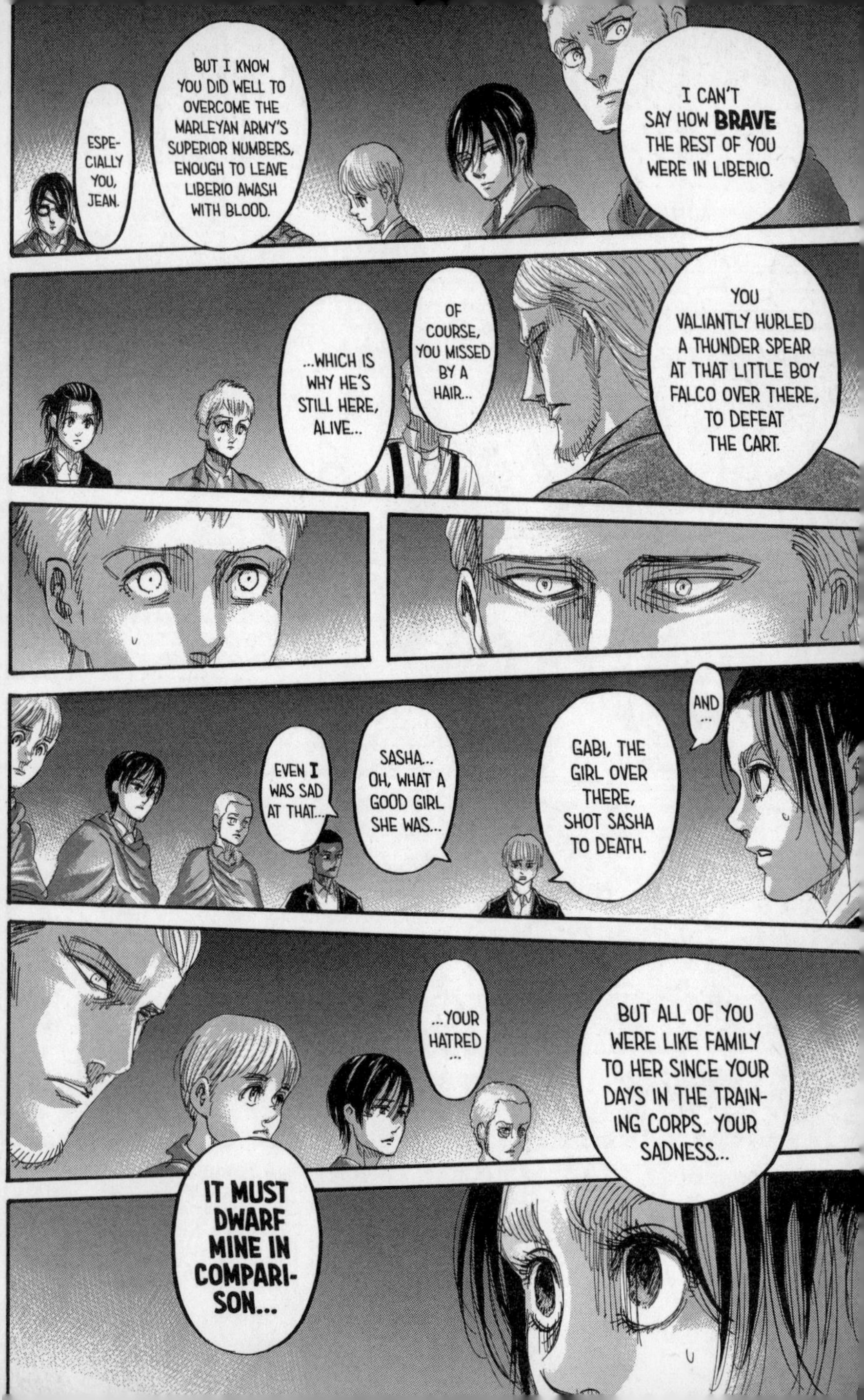

I CAN'T SAY HOW **BRAVE** THE REST OF YOU WERE IN LIBERIO.
BUT I KNOW YOU DID WELL TO OVERCOME THE MARLEYAN ARMY'S SUPERIOR NUMBERS, ENOUGH TO LEAVE LIBERIO AWASH WITH BLOOD.
ESPE-CIALLY YOU, JEAN.
YOU VALIANTLY HURLED A THUNDER SPEAR AT THAT LITTLE BOY FALCO OVER THERE, TO DEFEAT THE CART.
OF COURSE, YOU MISSED BY A HAIR...
...WHICH IS WHY HE'S STILL HERE, ALIVE...
AND...
GABI, THE GIRL OVER THERE, SHOT SASHA TO DEATH.
SASHA... OH, WHAT A GOOD GIRL SHE WAS...
EVEN **I** WAS SAD AT THAT...
BUT ALL OF YOU WERE LIKE FAMILY TO HER SINCE YOUR DAYS IN THE TRAIN-ING CORPS. YOUR SADNESS...
...YOUR HATRED...
IT MUST DWARF MINE IN COMPARI-SON...

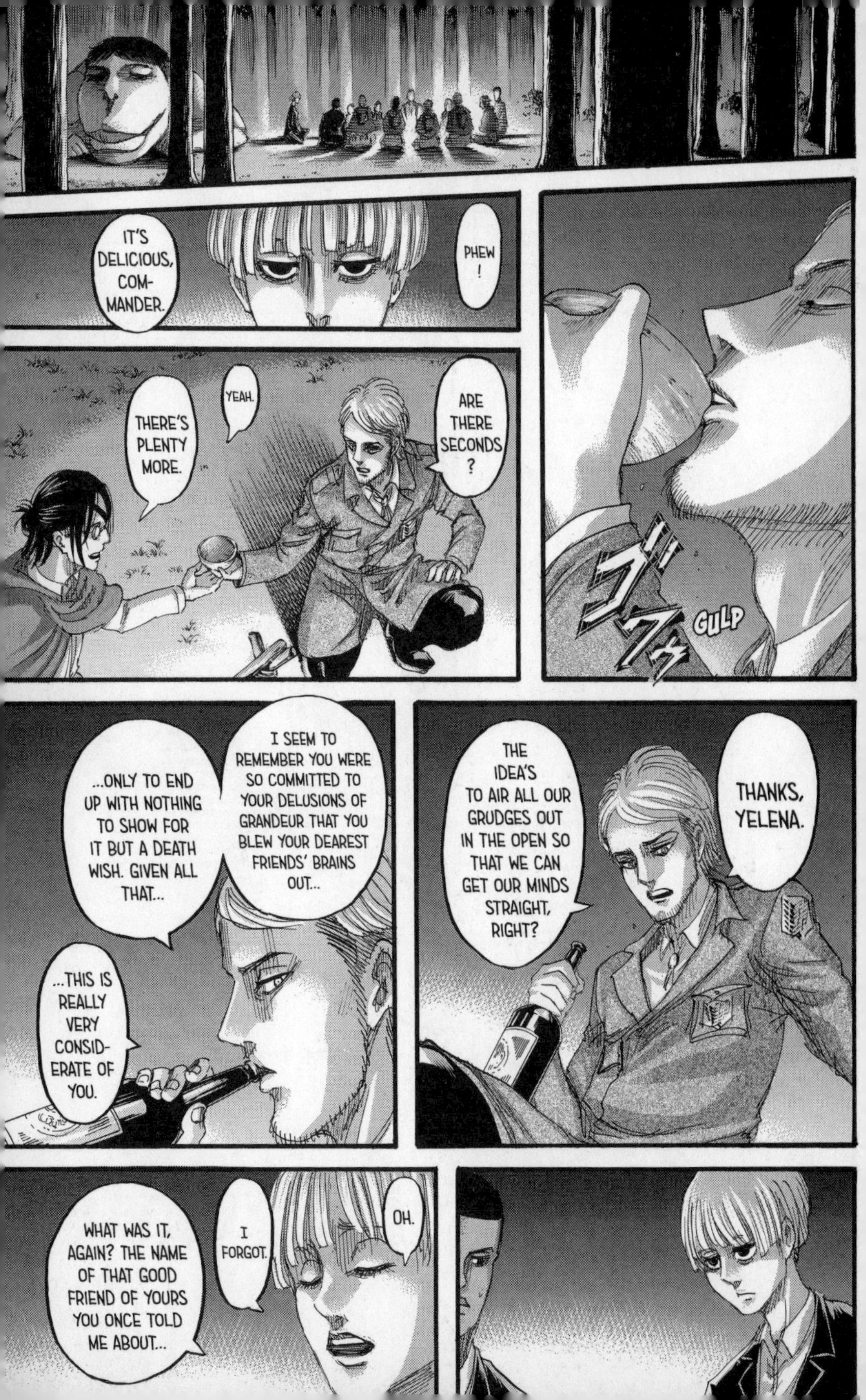
GULP
PHEW!
IT'S DELICIOUS, COM-MANDER.
ARE THERE SECONDS?
YEAH.
THERE'S PLENTY MORE.
THANKS, YELENA.
THE IDEA'S TO AIR ALL OUR GRUDGES OUT IN THE OPEN SO THAT WE CAN GET OUR MINDS STRAIGHT, RIGHT?
I SEEM TO REMEMBER YOU WERE SO COMMITTED TO YOUR DELUSIONS OF GRANDEUR THAT YOU BLEW YOUR DEAREST FRIENDS' BRAINS OUT...
...ONLY TO END UP WITH NOTHING TO SHOW FOR IT BUT A DEATH WISH. GIVEN ALL THAT...
...THIS IS REALLY VERY CONSID-ERATE OF YOU.
OH.
I FORGOT.
WHAT WAS IT, AGAIN? THE NAME OF THAT GOOD FRIEND OF YOURS YOU ONCE TOLD ME ABOUT...

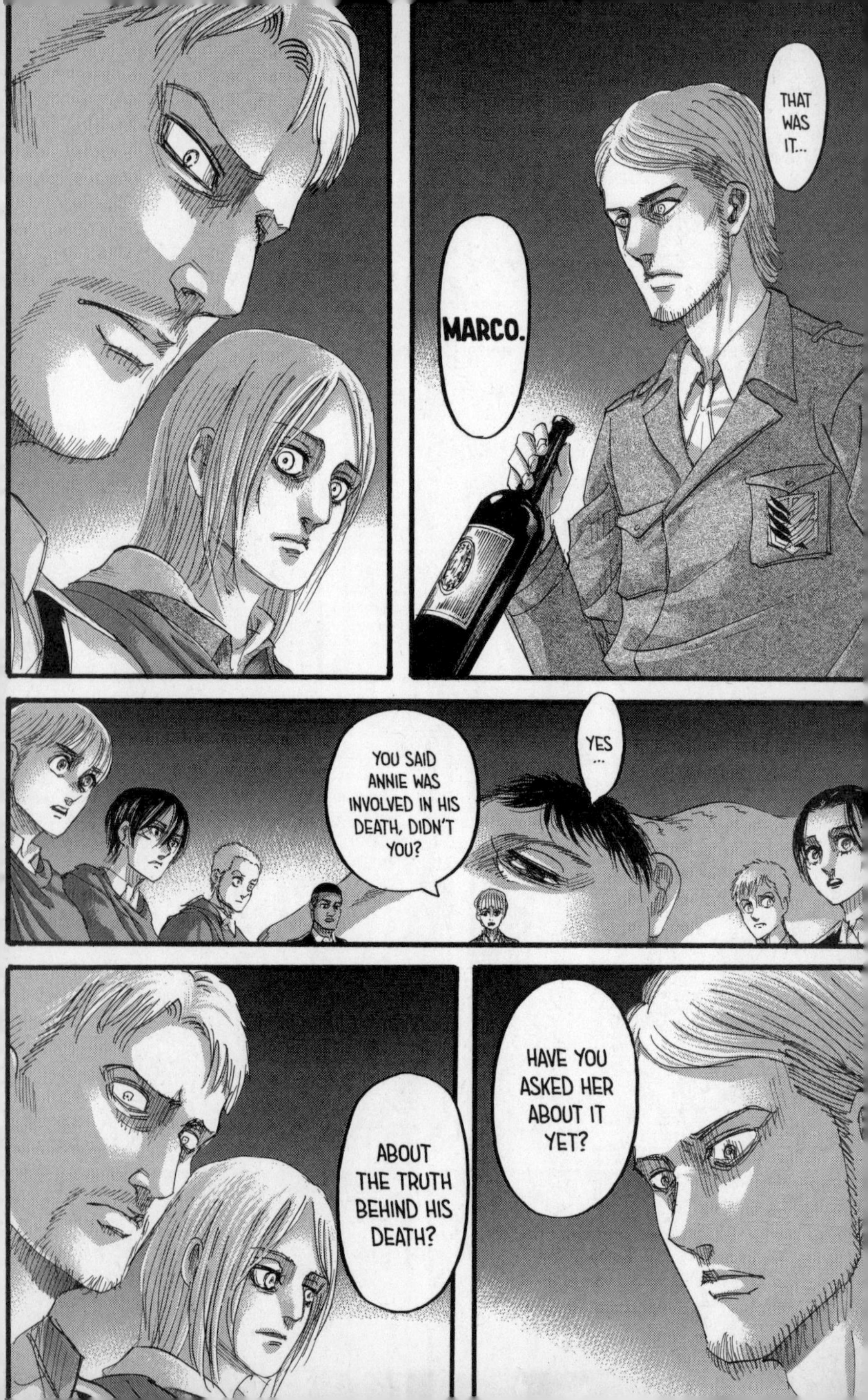
THAT WAS IT...
MARCO.
YES...
YOU SAID ANNIE WAS INVOLVED IN HIS DEATH, DIDN'T YOU?
HAVE YOU ASKED HER ABOUT IT YET?
ABOUT THE TRUTH BEHIND HIS DEATH?

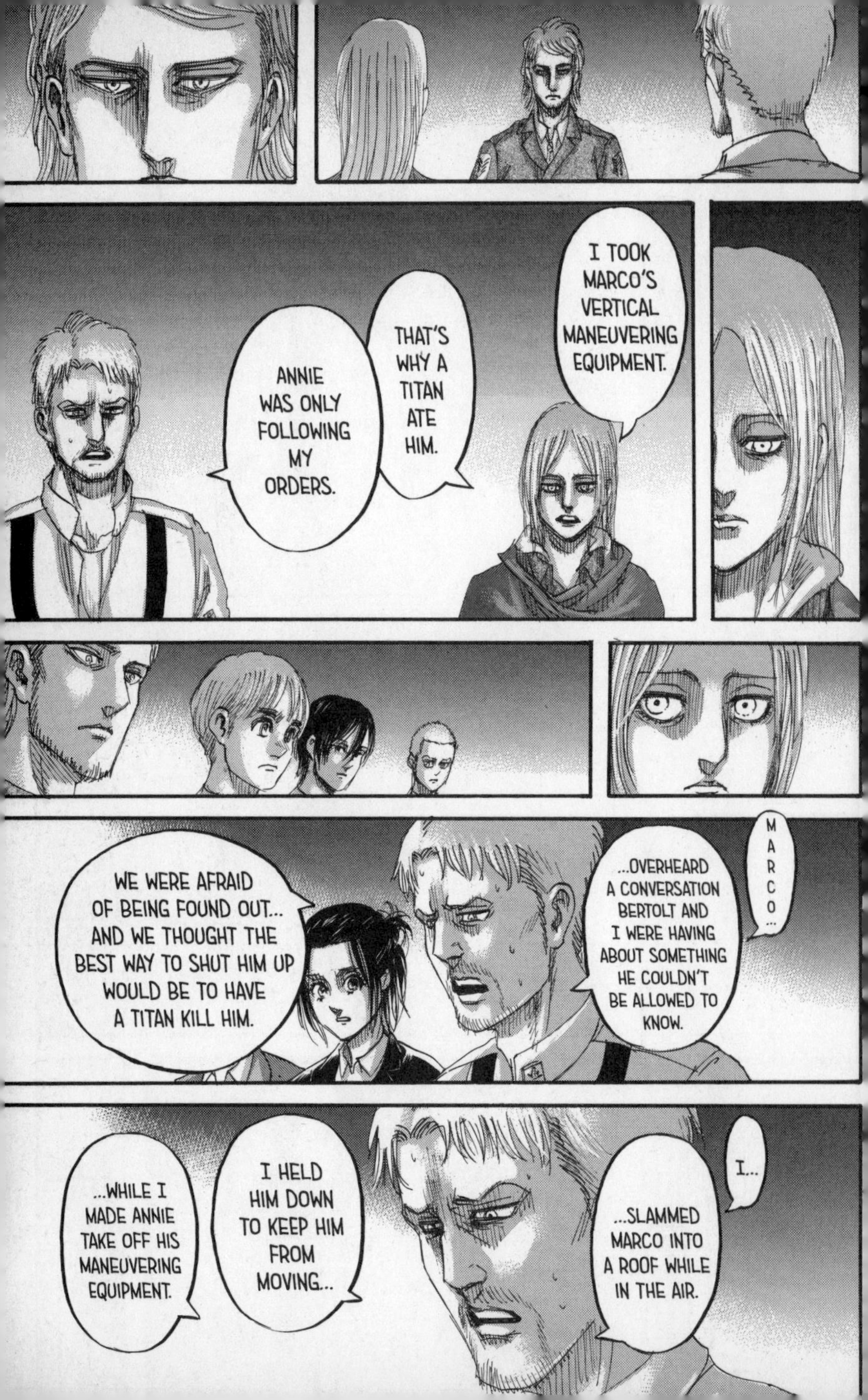
I TOOK MARCO'S VERTICAL MANEUVERING EQUIPMENT.
THAT'S WHY A TITAN ATE HIM.
ANNIE WAS ONLY FOLLOWING MY ORDERS.
MARCO...
...OVERHEARD A CONVERSATION BERTOLT AND I WERE HAVING ABOUT SOMETHING HE COULDN'T BE ALLOWED TO KNOW.
WE WERE AFRAID OF BEING FOUND OUT... AND WE THOUGHT THE BEST WAY TO SHUT HIM UP WOULD BE TO HAVE A TITAN KILL HIM.
I...
...SLAMMED MARCO INTO A ROOF WHILE IN THE AIR.
I HELD HIM DOWN TO KEEP HIM FROM MOVING...
...WHILE I MADE ANNIE TAKE OFF HIS MANEUVERING EQUIPMENT.

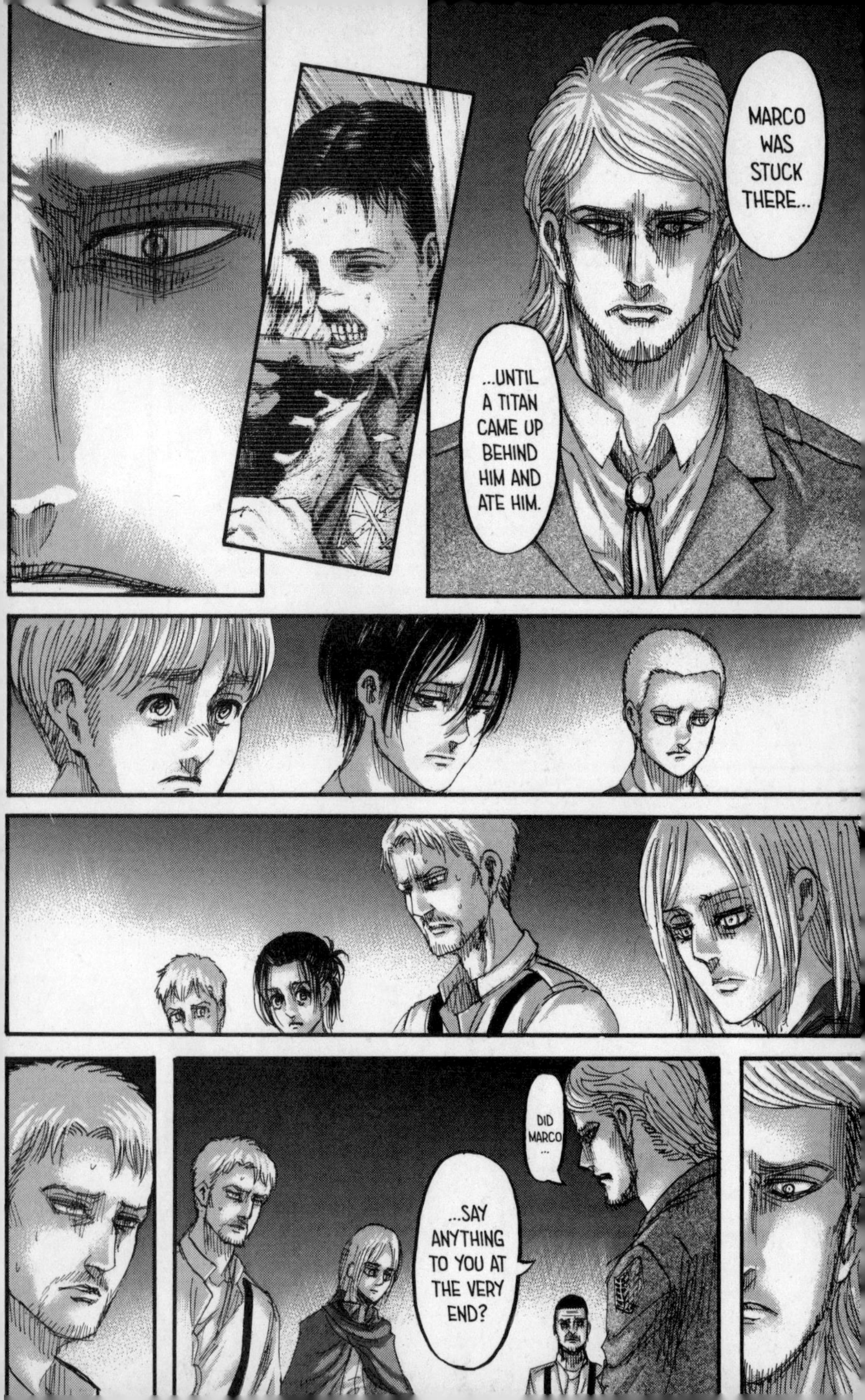
MARCO WAS STUCK THERE...
...UNTIL A TITAN CAME UP BEHIND HIM AND ATE HIM.
DID MARCO ...
...SAY ANYTHING TO YOU AT THE VERY END?

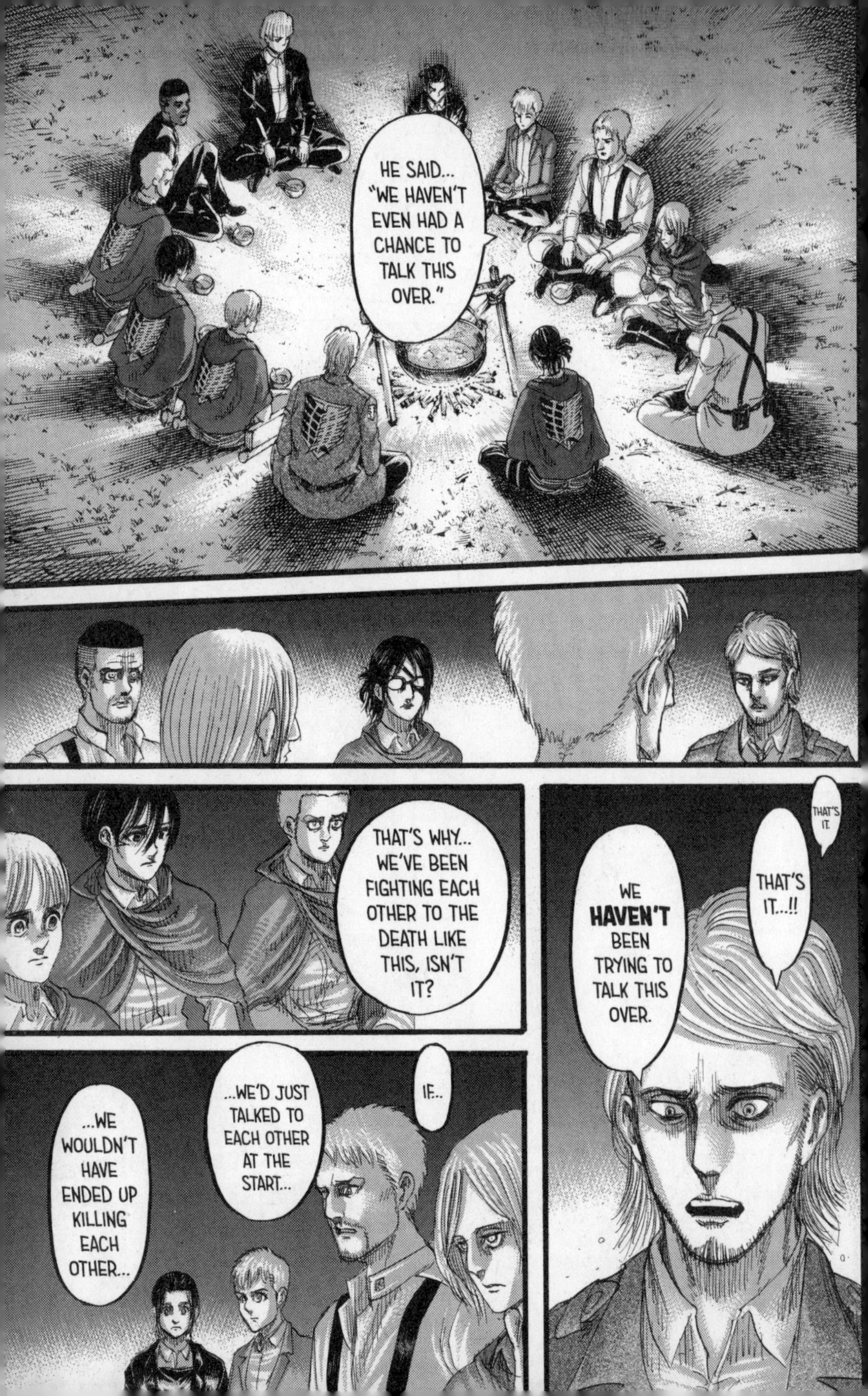
HE SAID... "WE HAVEN'T EVEN HAD A CHANCE TO TALK THIS OVER."
THAT'S IT.
THAT'S IT...!!
WE **HAVEN'T** BEEN TRYING TO TALK THIS OVER.
THAT'S WHY... WE'VE BEEN FIGHTING EACH OTHER TO THE DEATH LIKE THIS, ISN'T IT?
IF...
...WE'D JUST TALKED TO EACH OTHER AT THE START...
...WE WOULDN'T HAVE ENDED UP KILLING EACH OTHER...

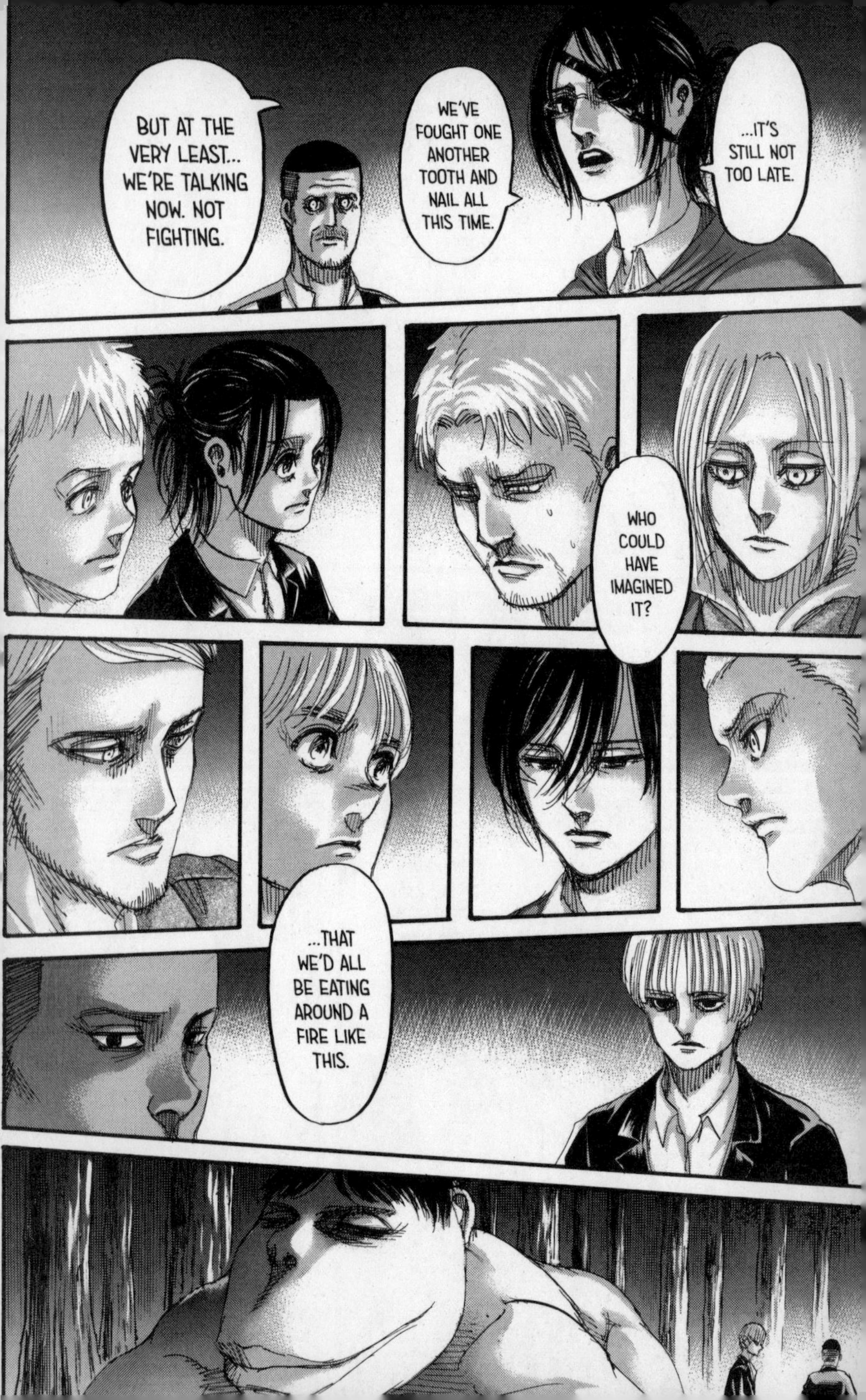
...IT'S STILL NOT TOO LATE.
WE'VE FOUGHT ONE ANOTHER TOOTH AND NAIL ALL THIS TIME.
BUT AT THE VERY LEAST... WE'RE TALKING NOW. NOT FIGHTING.
WHO COULD HAVE IMAGINED IT?
...THAT WE'D ALL BE EATING AROUND A FIRE LIKE THIS.

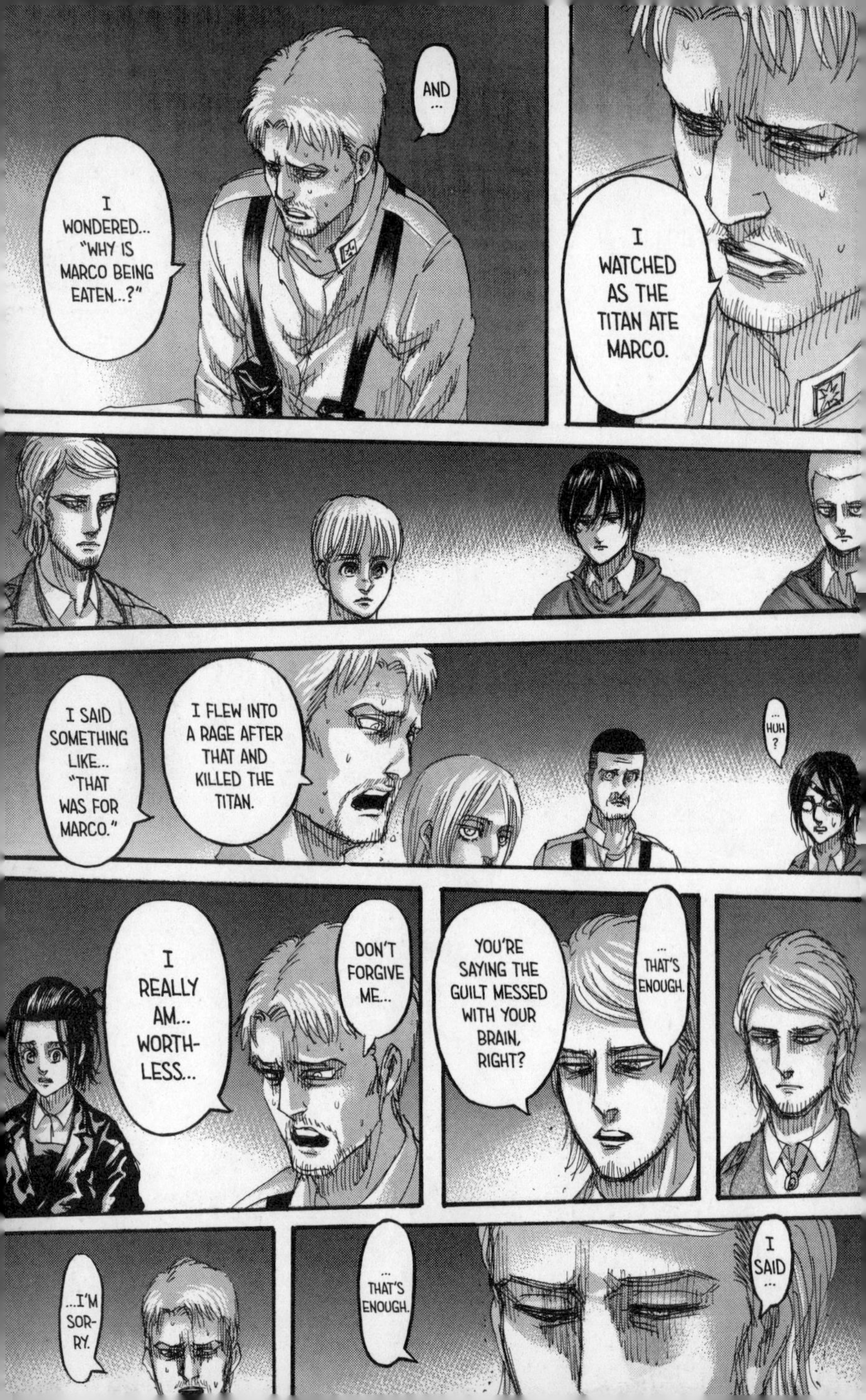
I WATCHED AS THE TITAN ATE MARCO.
AND ...
I WONDERED... "WHY IS MARCO BEING EATEN...?"
... HUH ?
I FLEW INTO A RAGE AFTER THAT AND KILLED THE TITAN.
I SAID SOMETHING LIKE... "THAT WAS FOR MARCO."
... THAT'S ENOUGH.
YOU'RE SAYING THE GUILT MESSED WITH YOUR BRAIN, RIGHT?
DON'T FORGIVE ME...
I REALLY AM... WORTH-LESS...
I SAID ...
... THAT'S ENOUGH.
...I'M SOR-RY.

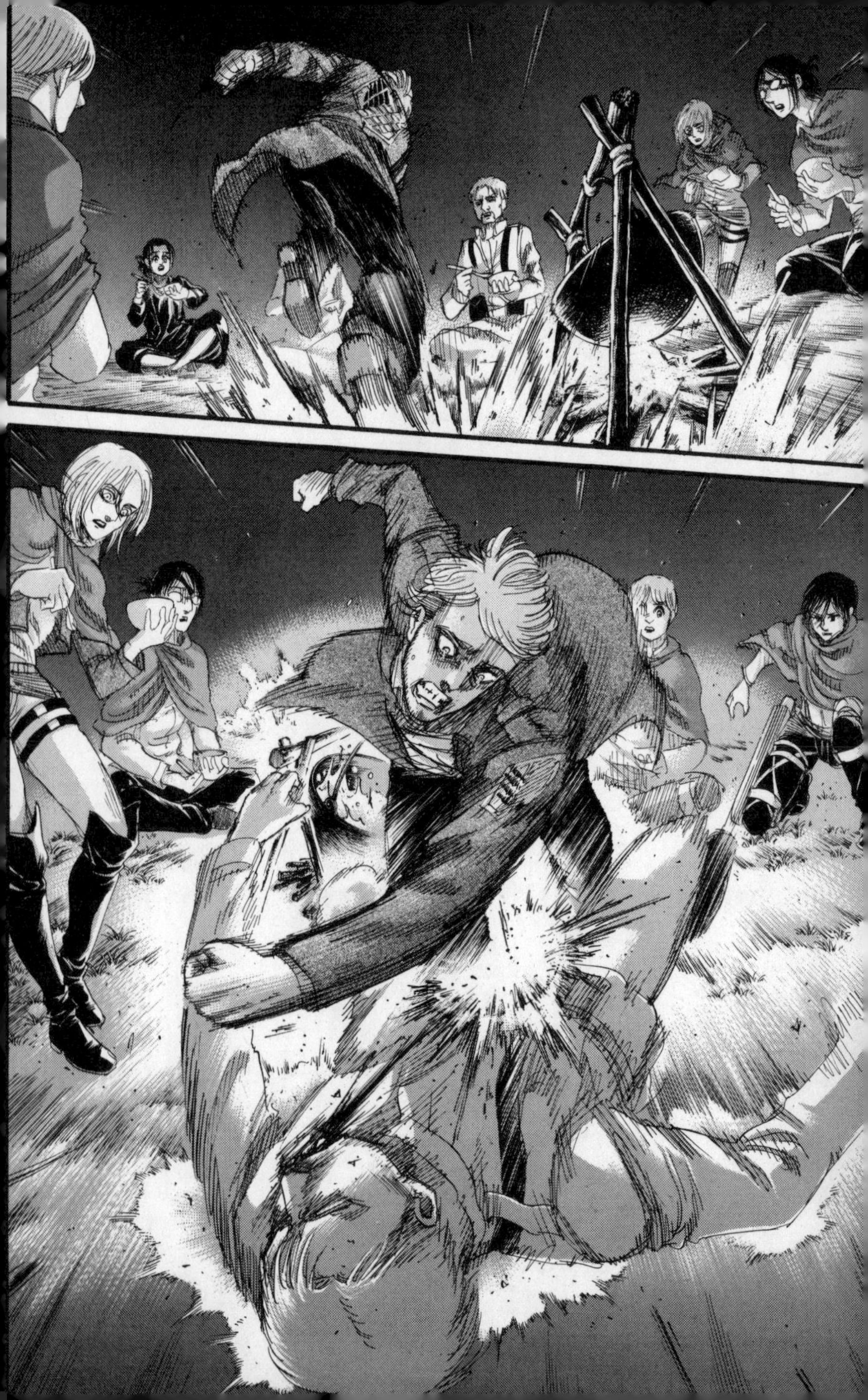

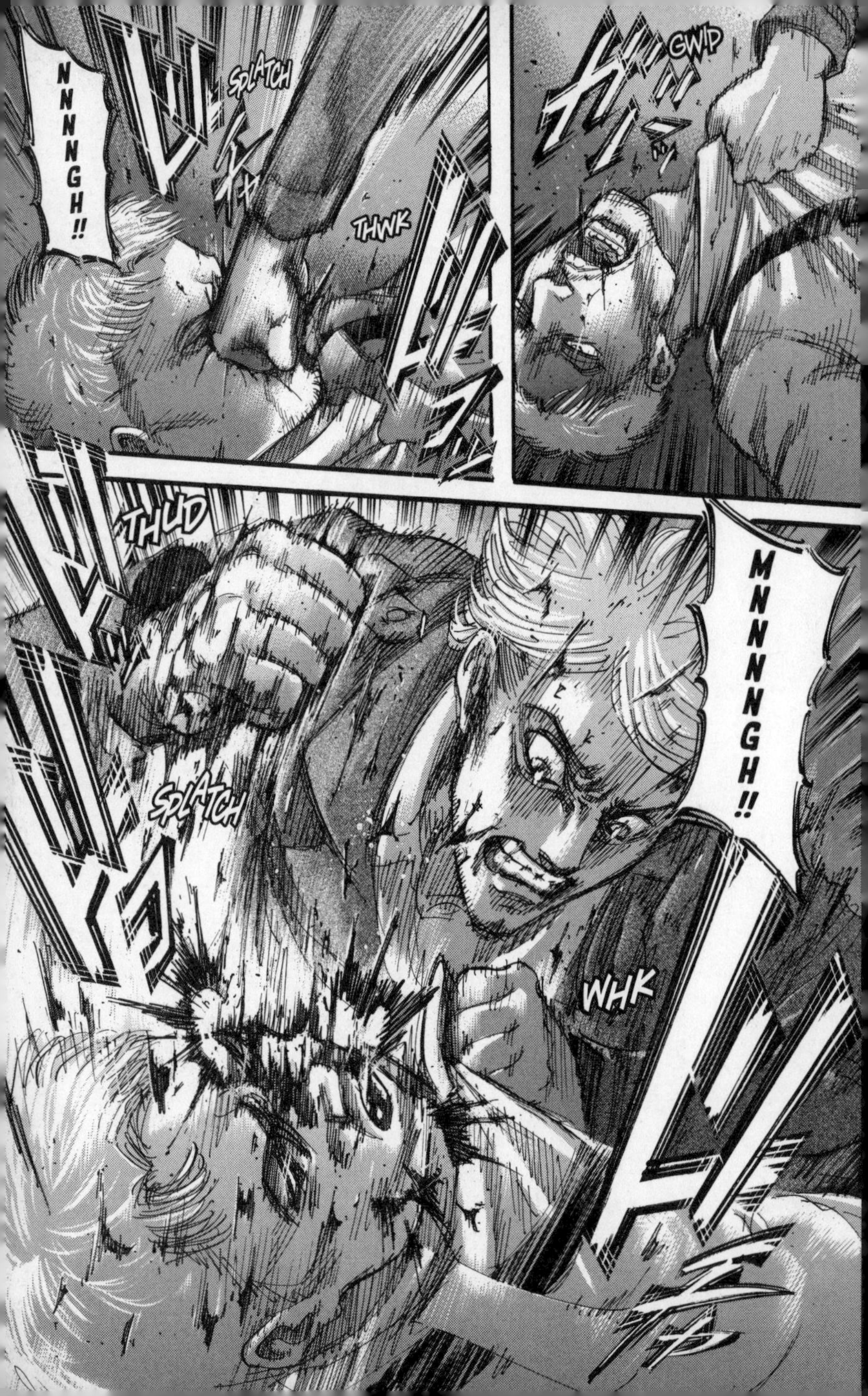
GWIP
NNNNGH!!
SPLATCH
THWK
MNNNNGH!!
THUD
WHK
SPLATCH

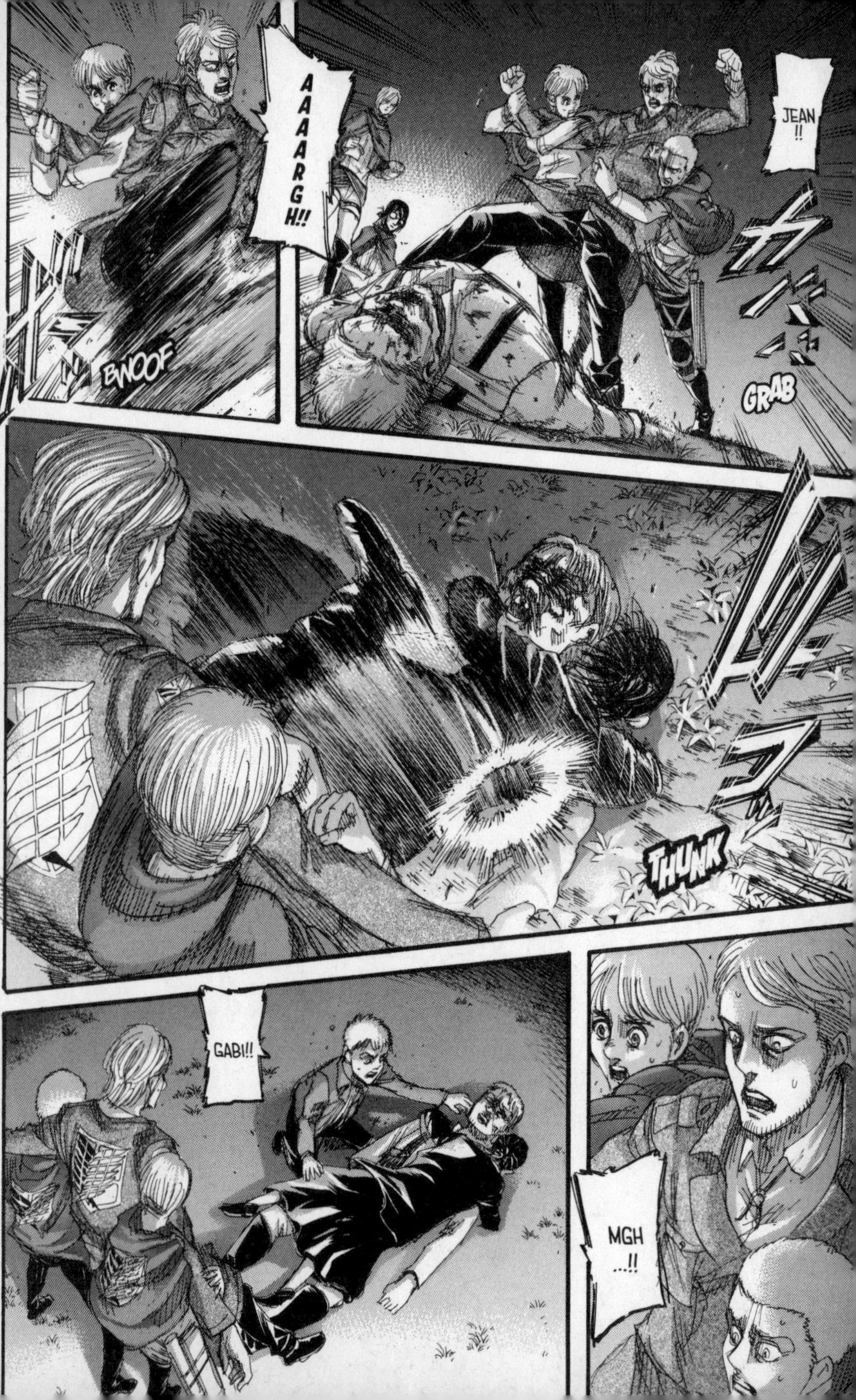
JEAN!!
GRAB
AAAARGH!!
BWOOF
THUNK
MGH...!!
GABI!!

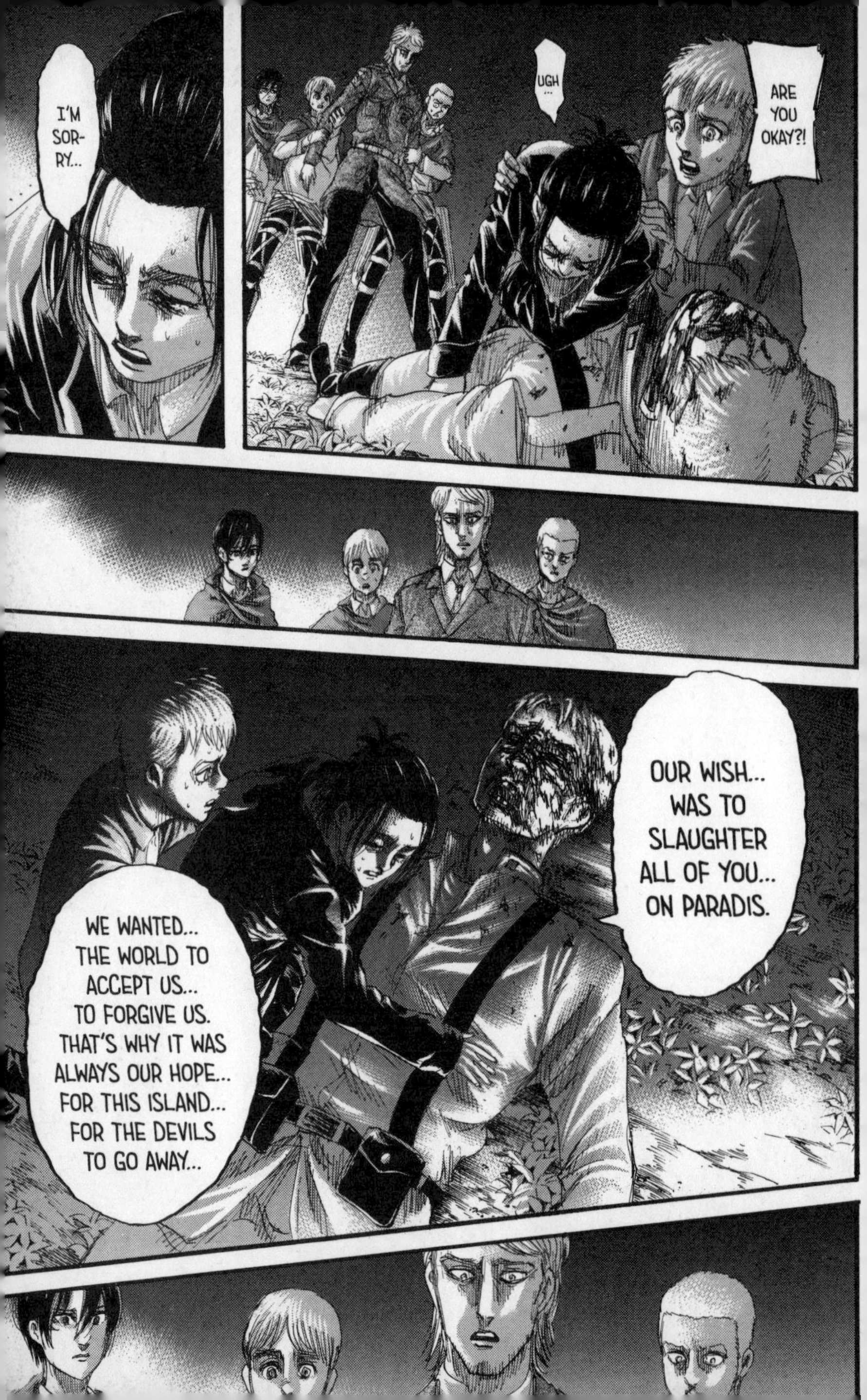
ARE YOU OKAY?!
UGH...
I'M SOR-RY...
OUR WISH... WAS TO SLAUGHTER ALL OF YOU... ON PARADIS.
WE WANTED... THE WORLD TO ACCEPT US... TO FORGIVE US. THAT'S WHY IT WAS ALWAYS OUR HOPE... FOR THIS ISLAND... FOR THE DEVILS TO GO AWAY...

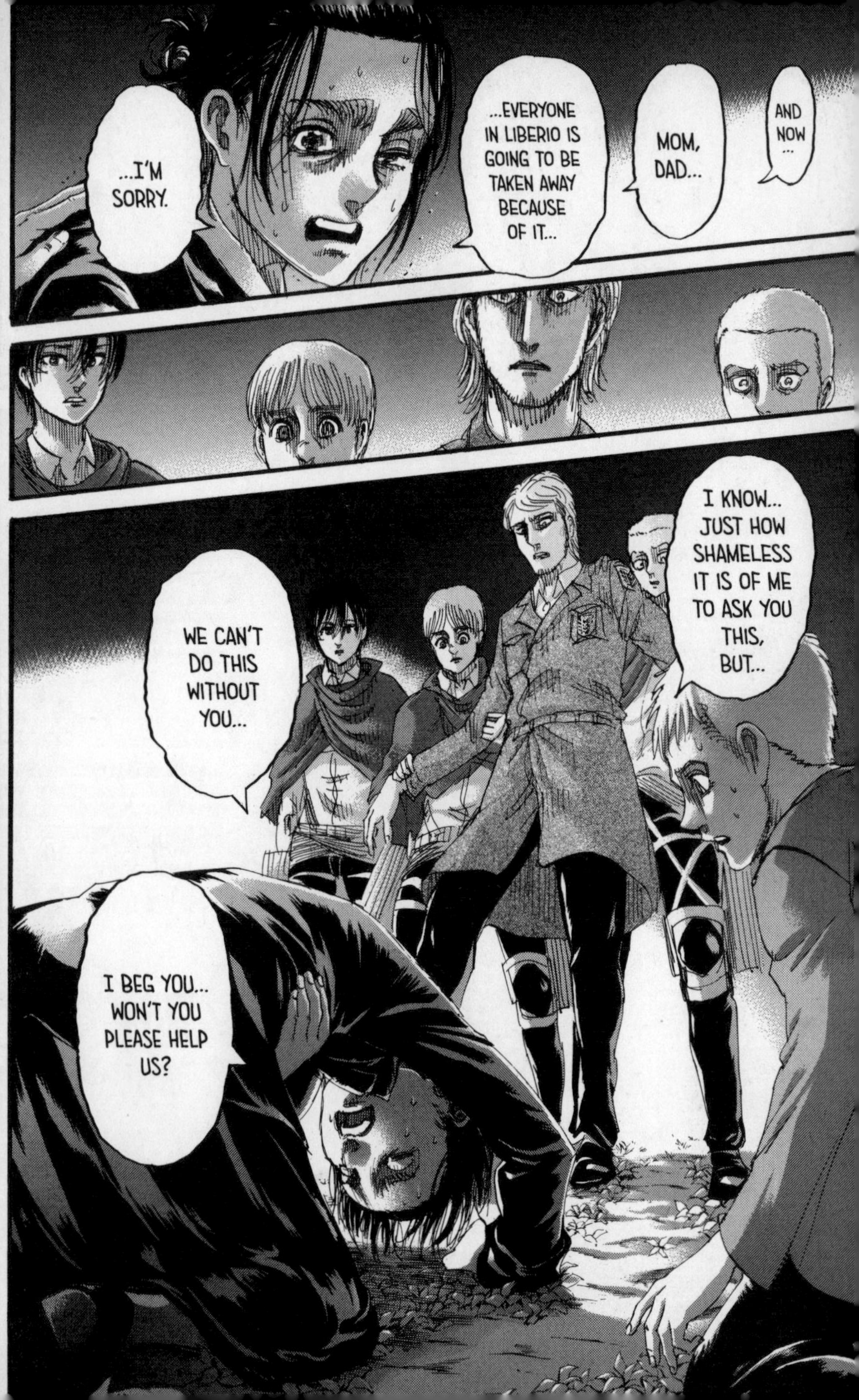
AND NOW...
MOM, DAD...
...EVERYONE IN LIBERIO IS GOING TO BE TAKEN AWAY BECAUSE OF IT...
...I'M SORRY.
I KNOW... JUST HOW SHAMELESS IT IS OF ME TO ASK YOU THIS, BUT...
WE CAN'T DO THIS WITHOUT YOU...
I BEG YOU... WON'T YOU PLEASE HELP US?

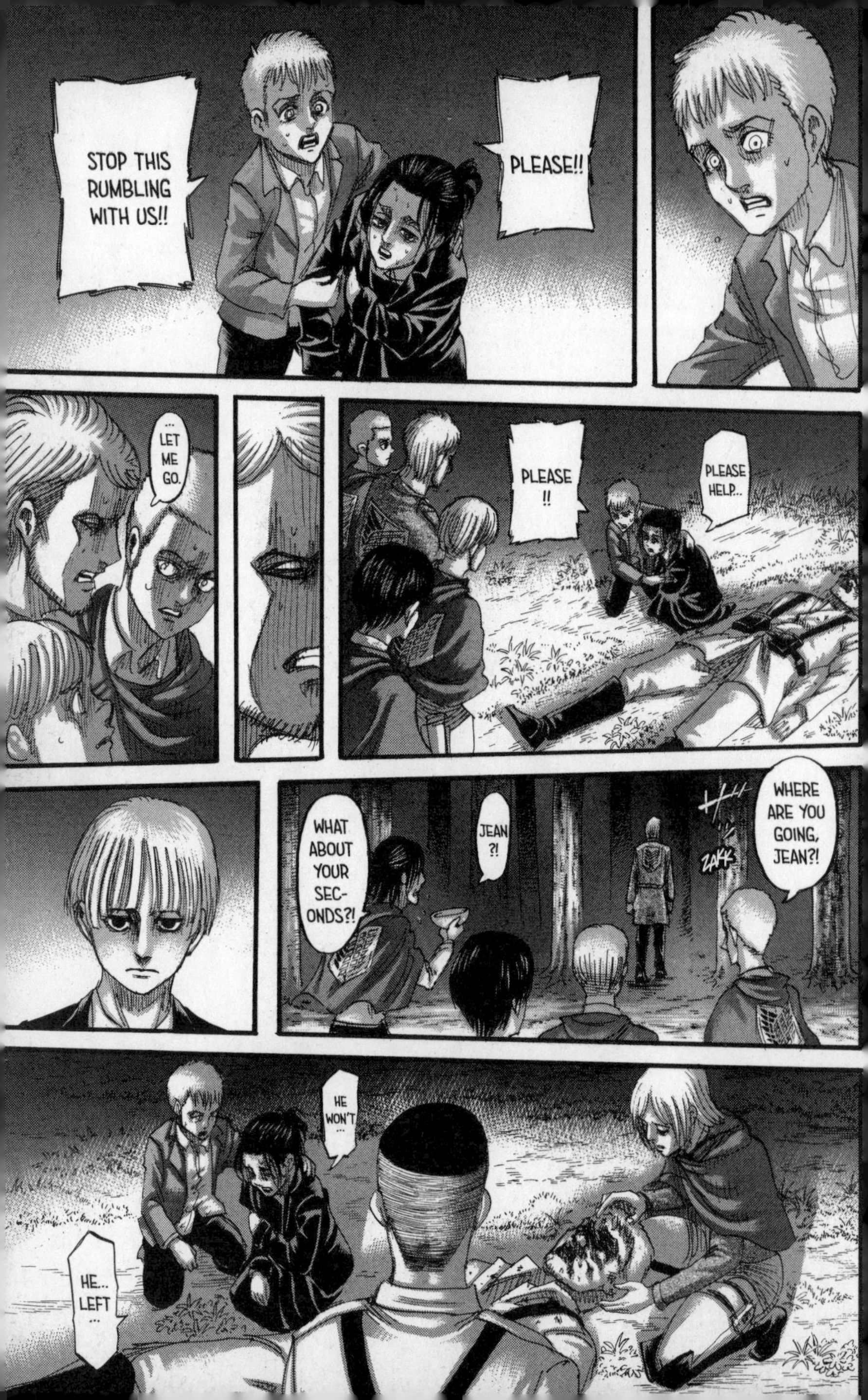
PLEASE!!
STOP THIS RUMBLING WITH US!!
PLEASE HELP..
PLEASE !!
... LET ME GO.
WHERE ARE YOU GOING, JEAN?!
ZAKK
JEAN ?!
WHAT ABOUT YOUR SEC- ONDS?!
HE WON'T ...
HE.. LEFT ...

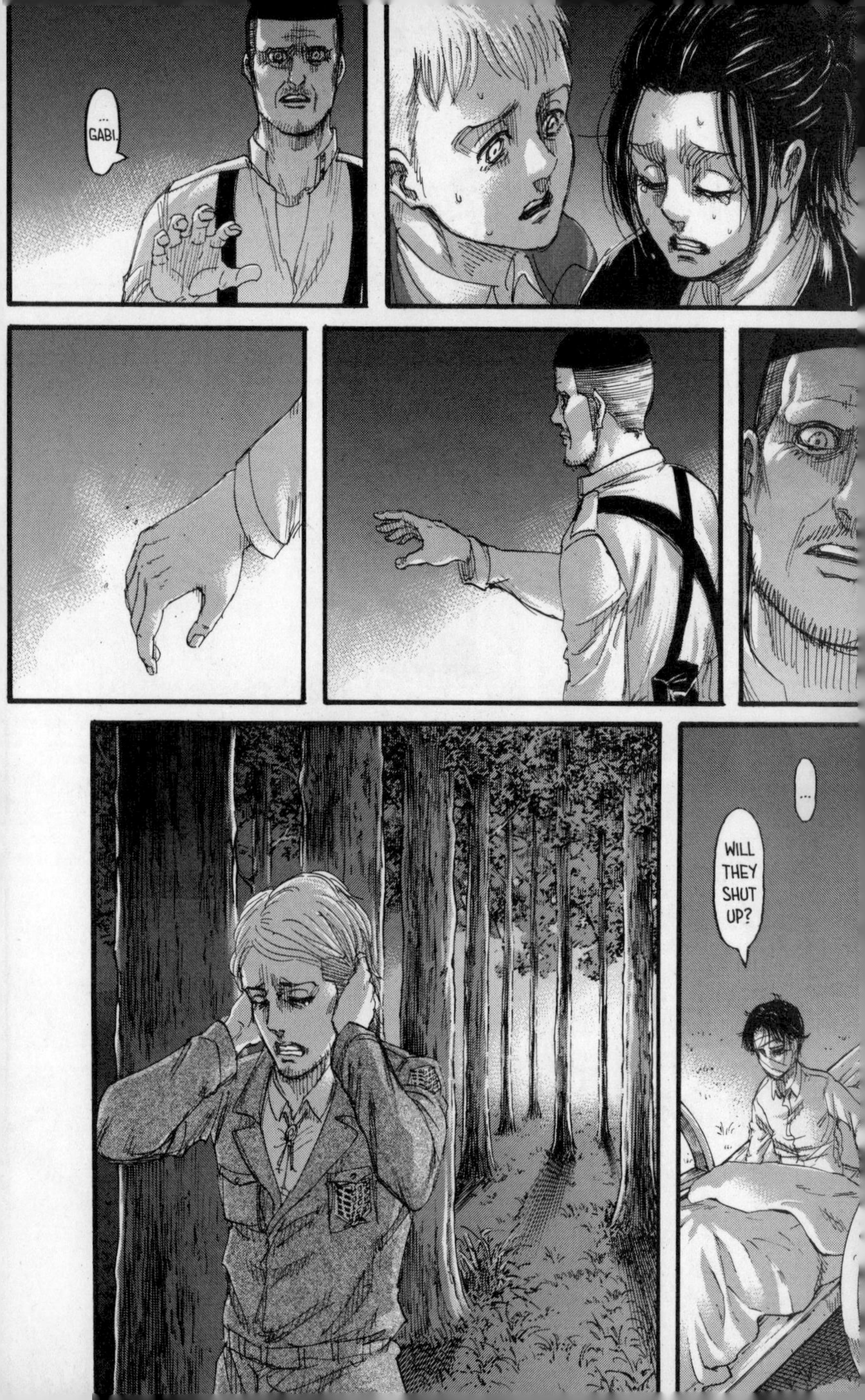
... GABI.
...
WILL THEY SHUT UP?

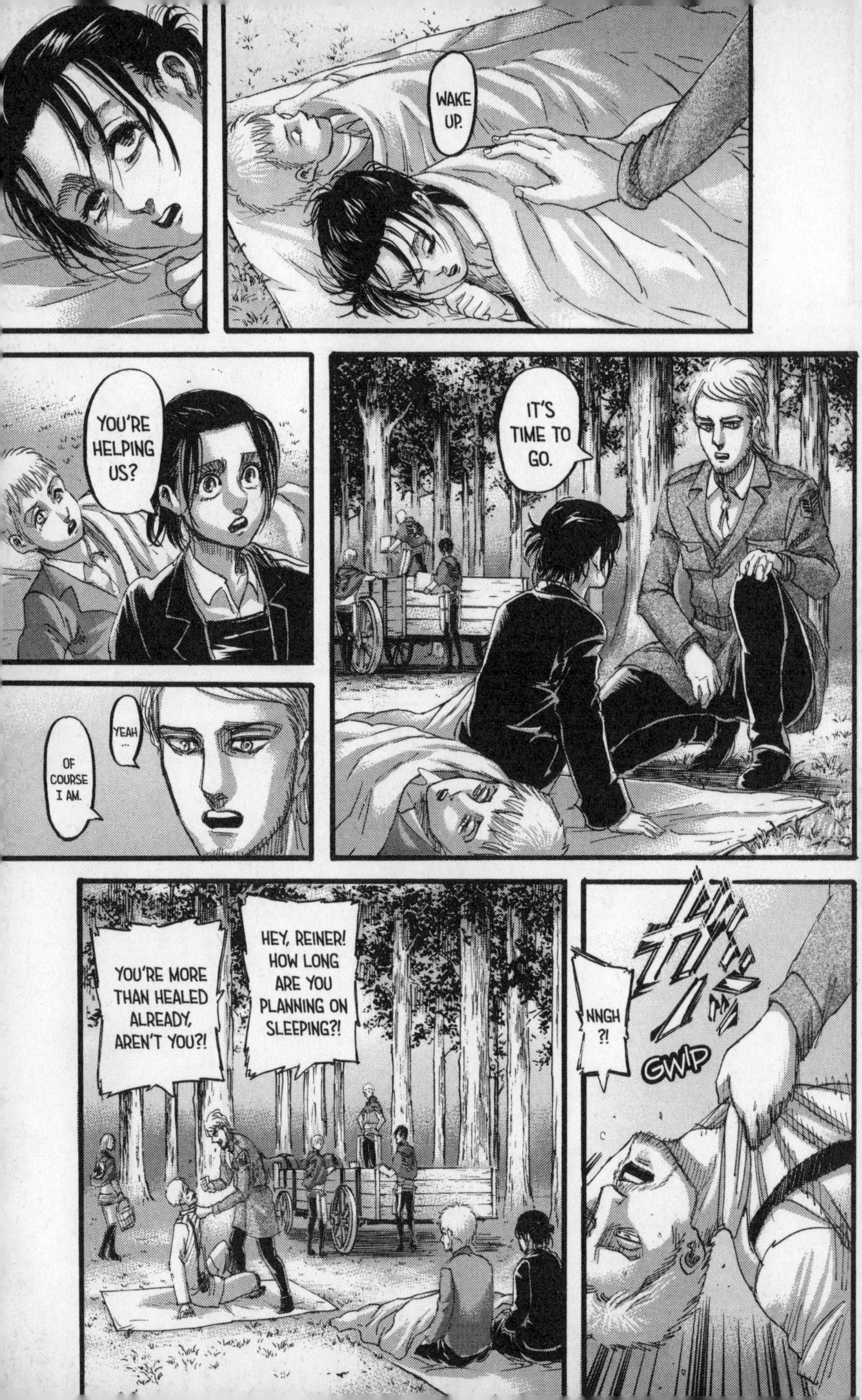
WAKE UP.
IT'S TIME TO GO.
YOU'RE HELPING US?
YEAH ...
OF COURSE I AM.
NNGH ?!
GWIP
HEY, REINER! HOW LONG ARE YOU PLANNING ON SLEEPING?!
YOU'RE MORE THAN HEALED ALREADY, AREN'T YOU?!

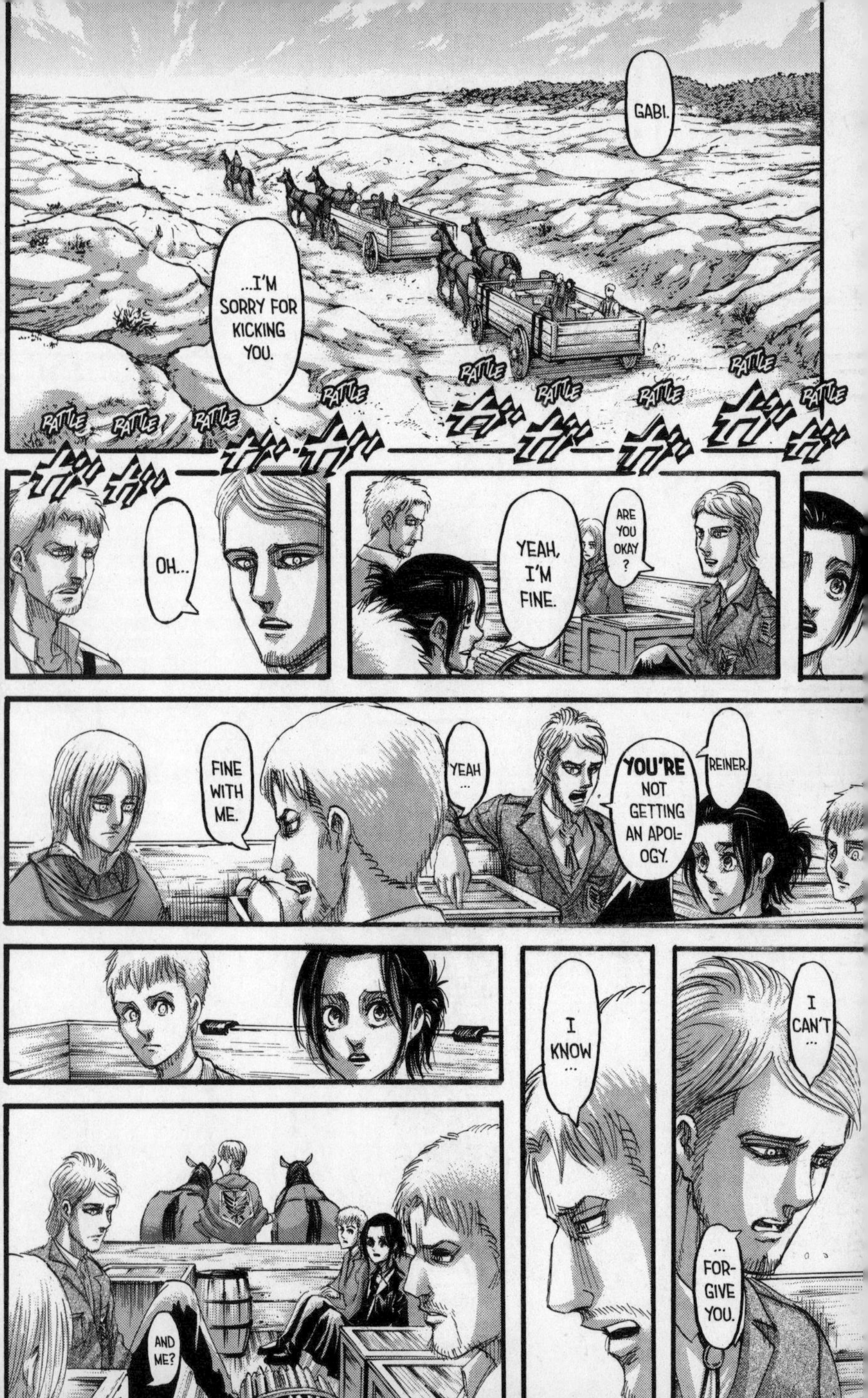
GABI.
...I'M SORRY FOR KICKING YOU.
RATTLE
RATTLE
RATTLE
RATTLE
RATTLE
RATTLE
RATTLE
RATTLE
RATTLE
ARE YOU OKAY?
YEAH, I'M FINE.
OH...
REINER.
YOU'RE NOT GETTING AN APOLOGY.
YEAH...
FINE WITH ME.
I CAN'T...
...FORGIVE YOU.
I KNOW...
AND ME?

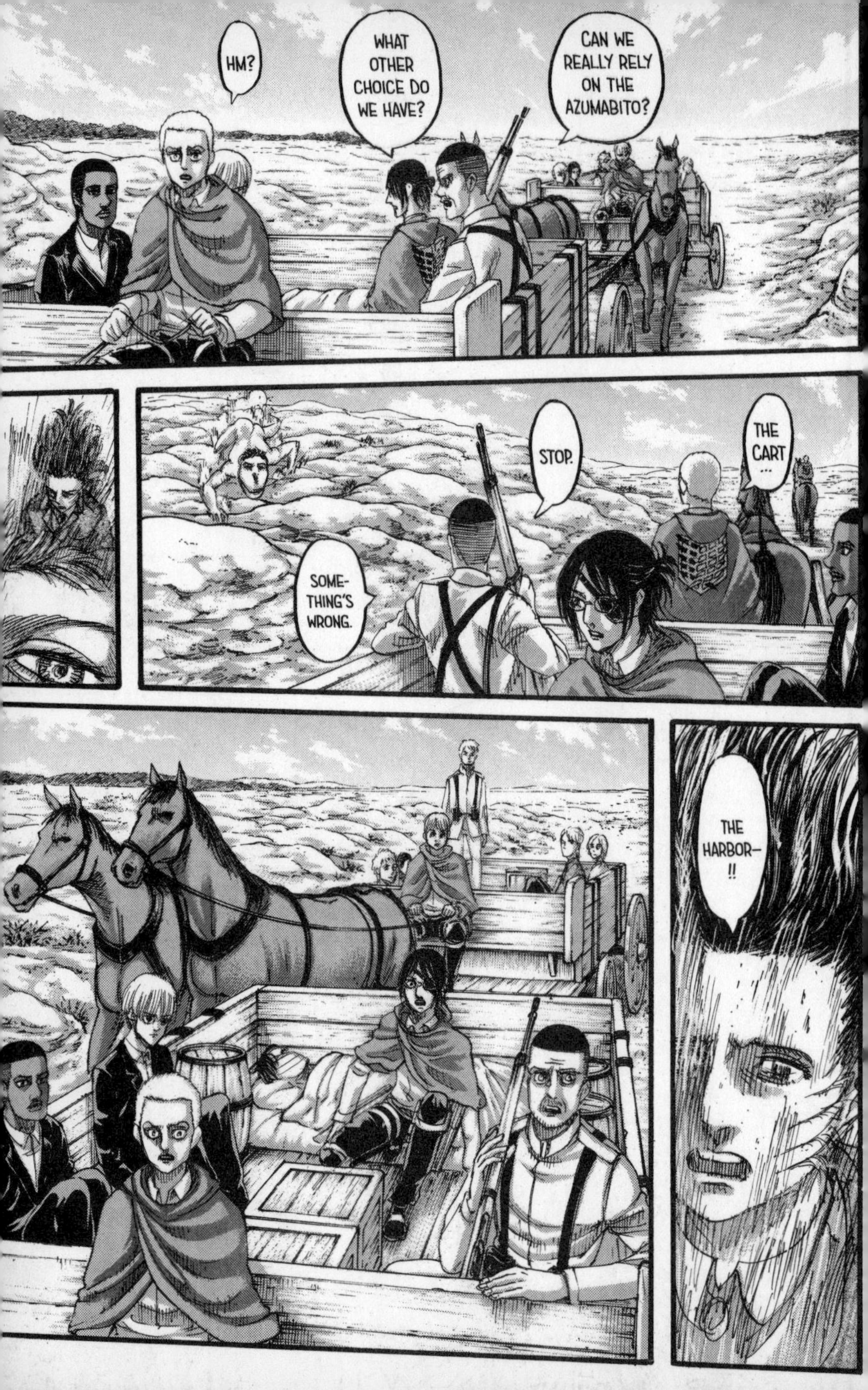
CAN WE REALLY RELY ON THE AZUMABITO?
WHAT OTHER CHOICE DO WE HAVE?
HM?
THE CART ...
STOP.
SOME-THING'S WRONG.
THE HARBOR— !!

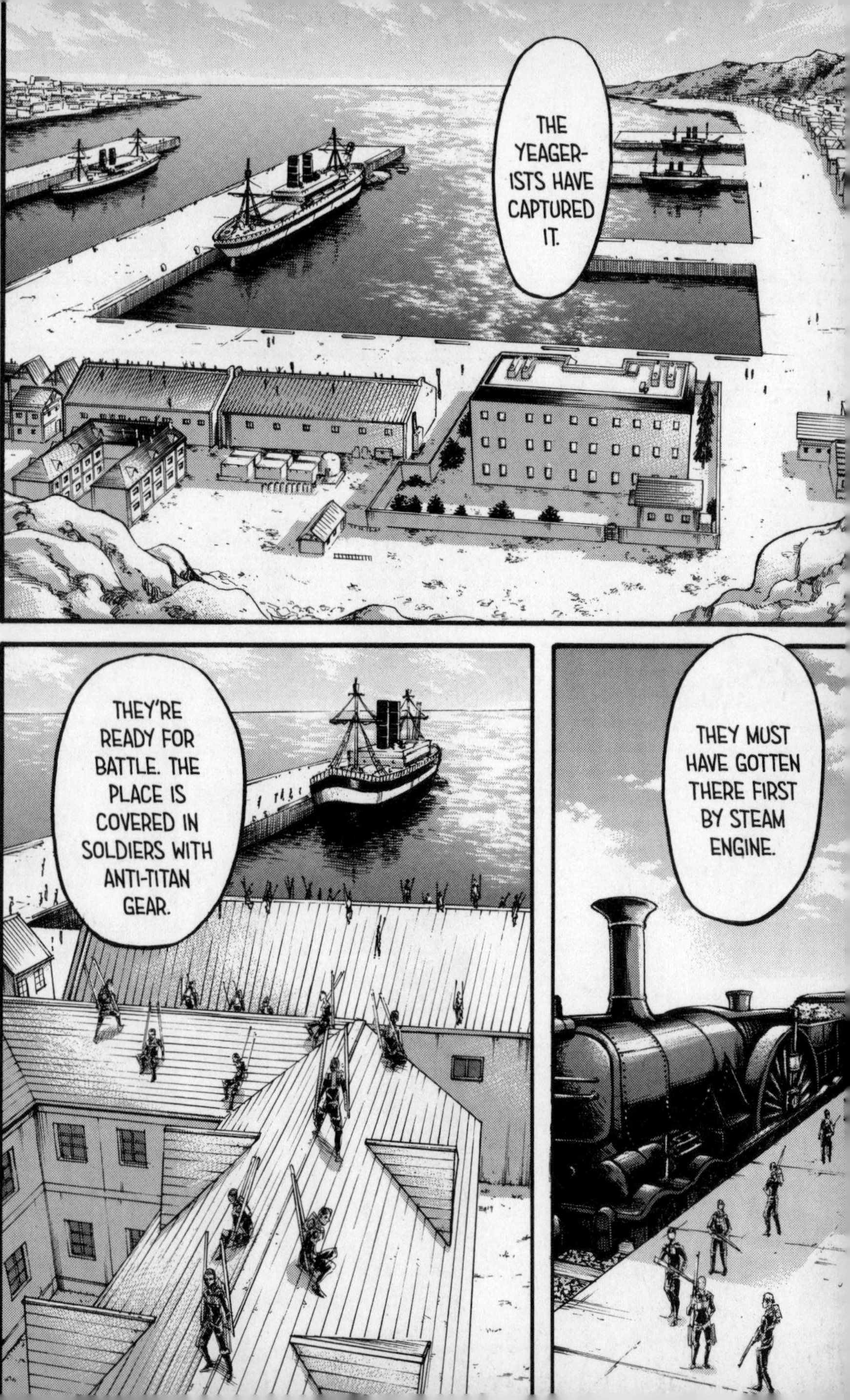
THE YEAGER-ISTS HAVE CAPTURED IT.
THEY MUST HAVE GOTTEN THERE FIRST BY STEAM ENGINE.
THEY'RE READY FOR BATTLE. THE PLACE IS COVERED IN SOLDIERS WITH ANTI-TITAN GEAR.

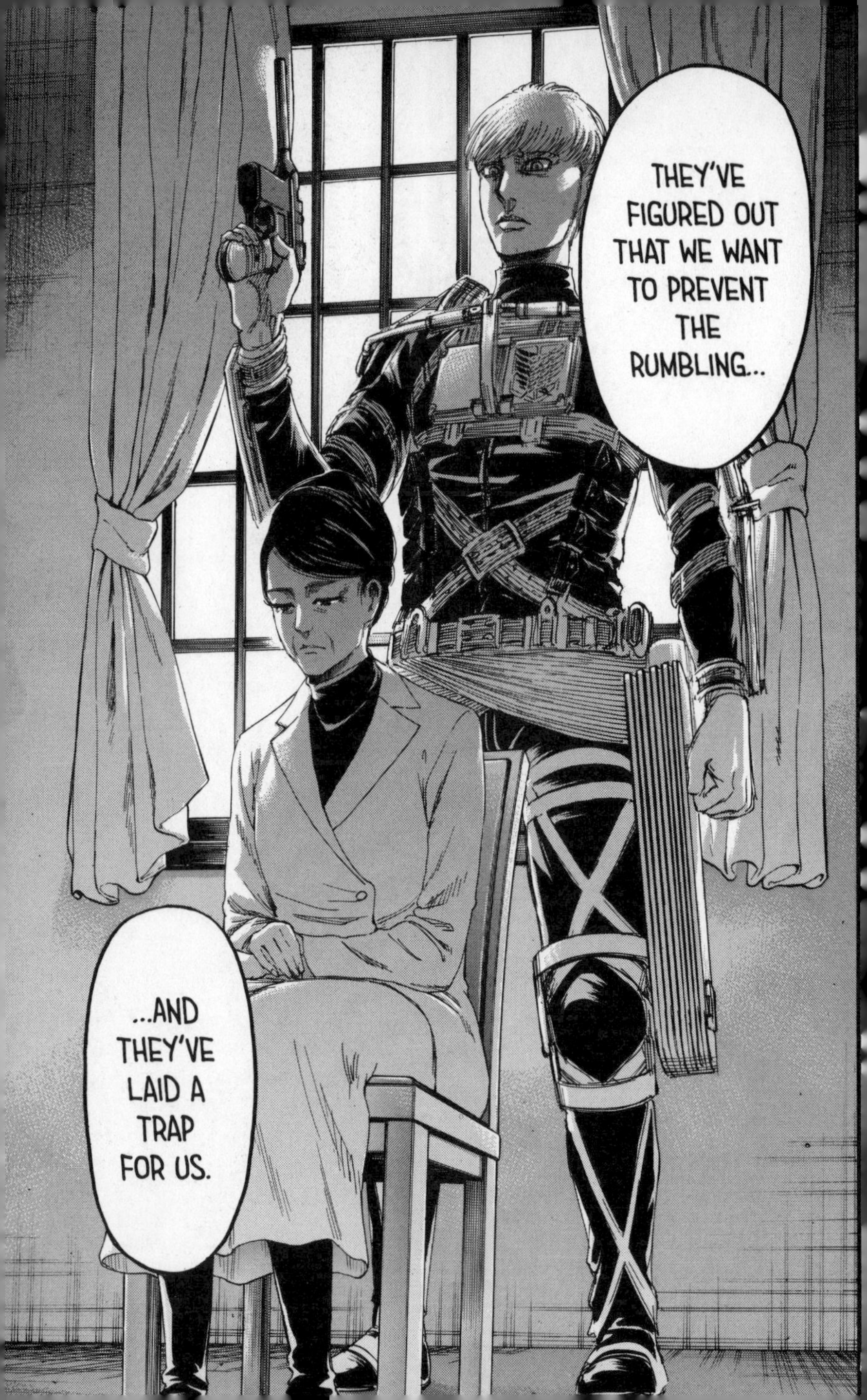
THEY'VE FIGURED OUT THAT WE WANT TO PREVENT THE RUMBLING...
...AND THEY'VE LAID A TRAP FOR US.

ATTACK on TITAN

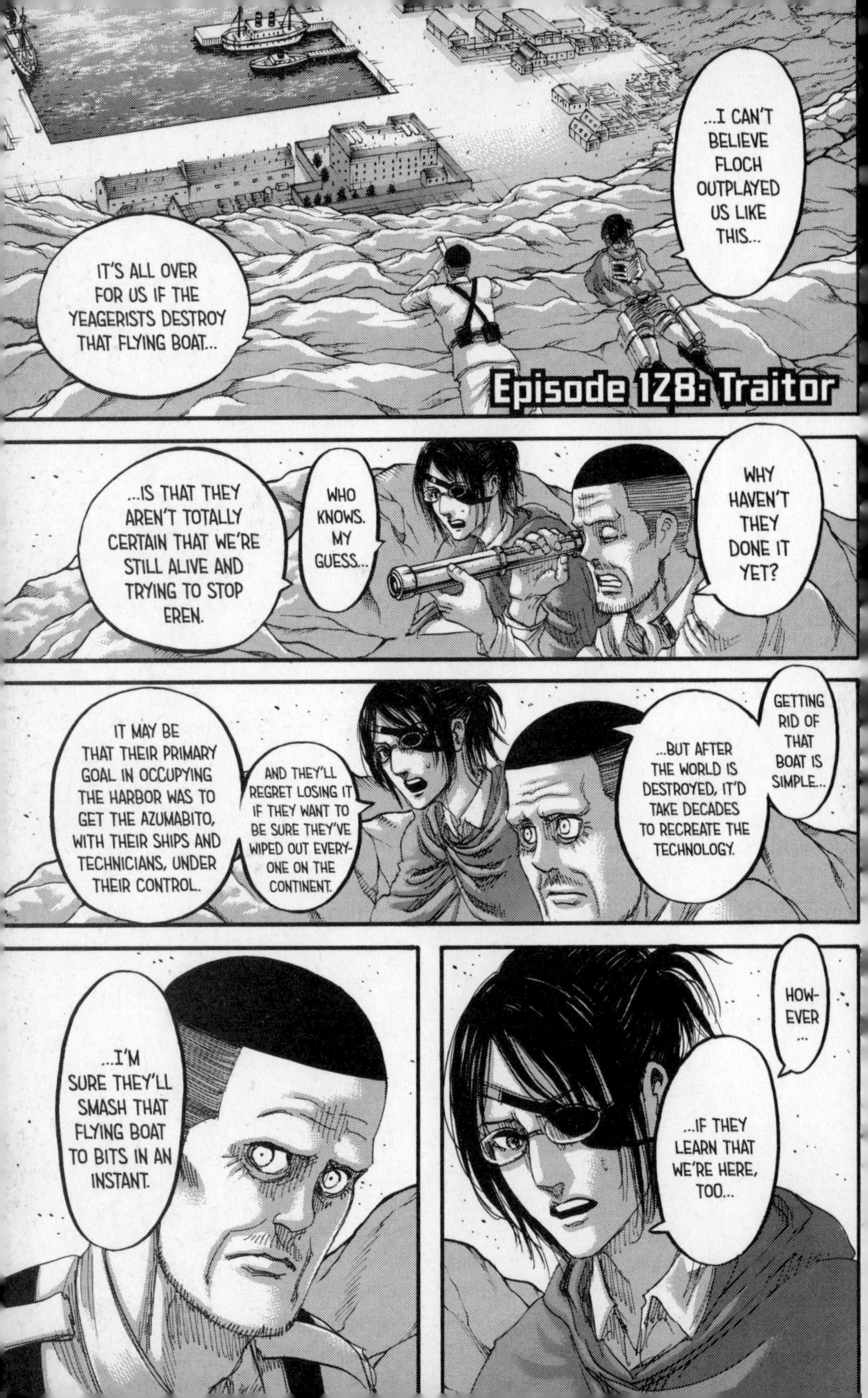
...I CAN'T BELIEVE FLOCH OUTPLAYED US LIKE THIS...
IT'S ALL OVER FOR US IF THE YEAGERISTS DESTROY THAT FLYING BOAT...
Episode 128: Traitor
WHY HAVEN'T THEY DONE IT YET?
WHO KNOWS. MY GUESS...
...IS THAT THEY AREN'T TOTALLY CERTAIN THAT WE'RE STILL ALIVE AND TRYING TO STOP EREN.
GETTING RID OF THAT BOAT IS SIMPLE...
...BUT AFTER THE WORLD IS DESTROYED, IT'D TAKE DECADES TO RECREATE THE TECHNOLOGY.
AND THEY'LL REGRET LOSING IT IF THEY WANT TO BE SURE THEY'VE WIPED OUT EVERY-ONE ON THE CONTINENT.
IT MAY BE THAT THEIR PRIMARY GOAL IN OCCUPYING THE HARBOR WAS TO GET THE AZUMABITO, WITH THEIR SHIPS AND TECHNICIANS, UNDER THEIR CONTROL.
HOW-EVER...
...IF THEY LEARN THAT WE'RE HERE, TOO...
...I'M SURE THEY'LL SMASH THAT FLYING BOAT TO BITS IN AN INSTANT.

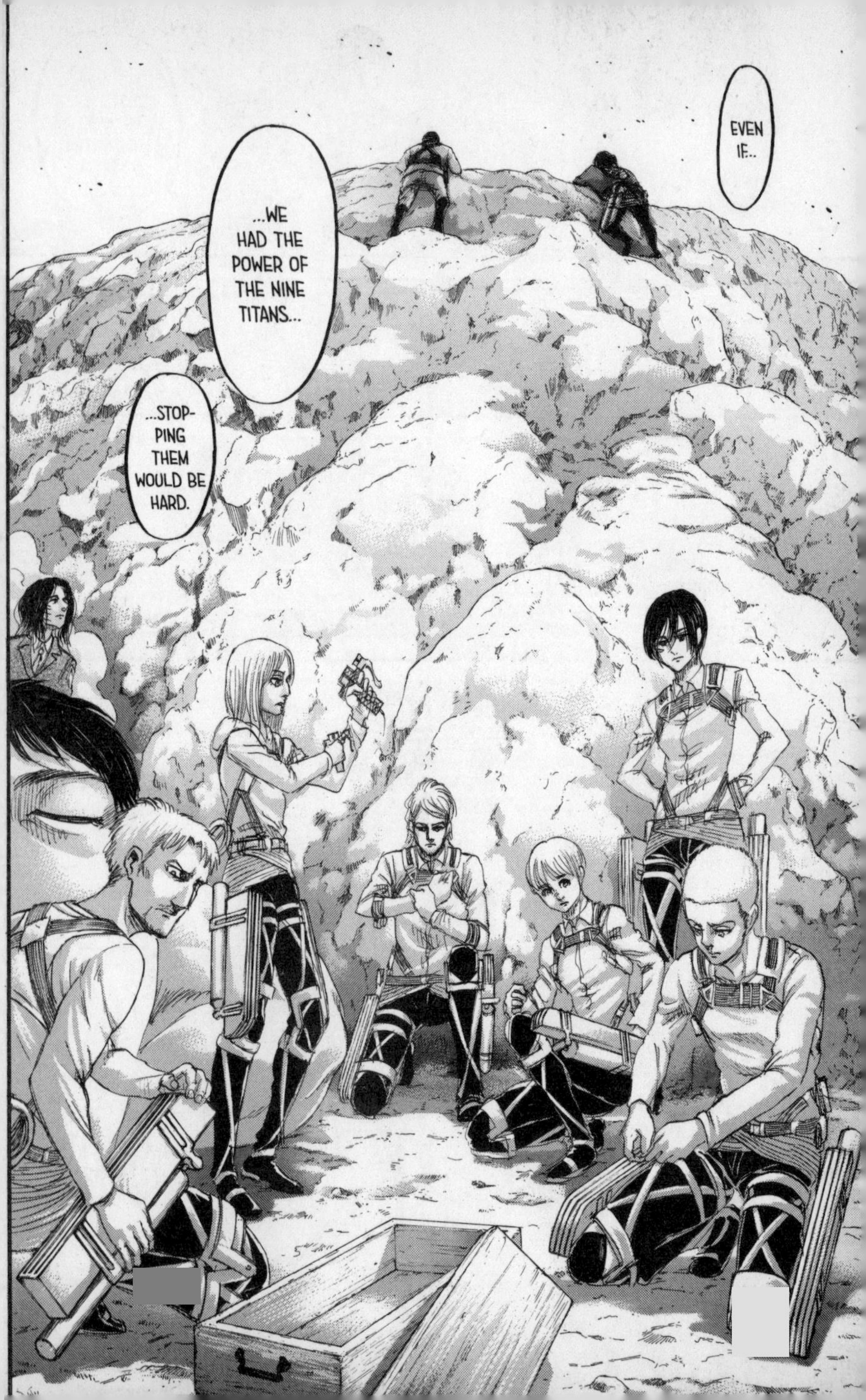
EVEN IF..
...WE HAD THE POWER OF THE NINE TITANS...
...STOP-PING THEM WOULD BE HARD.

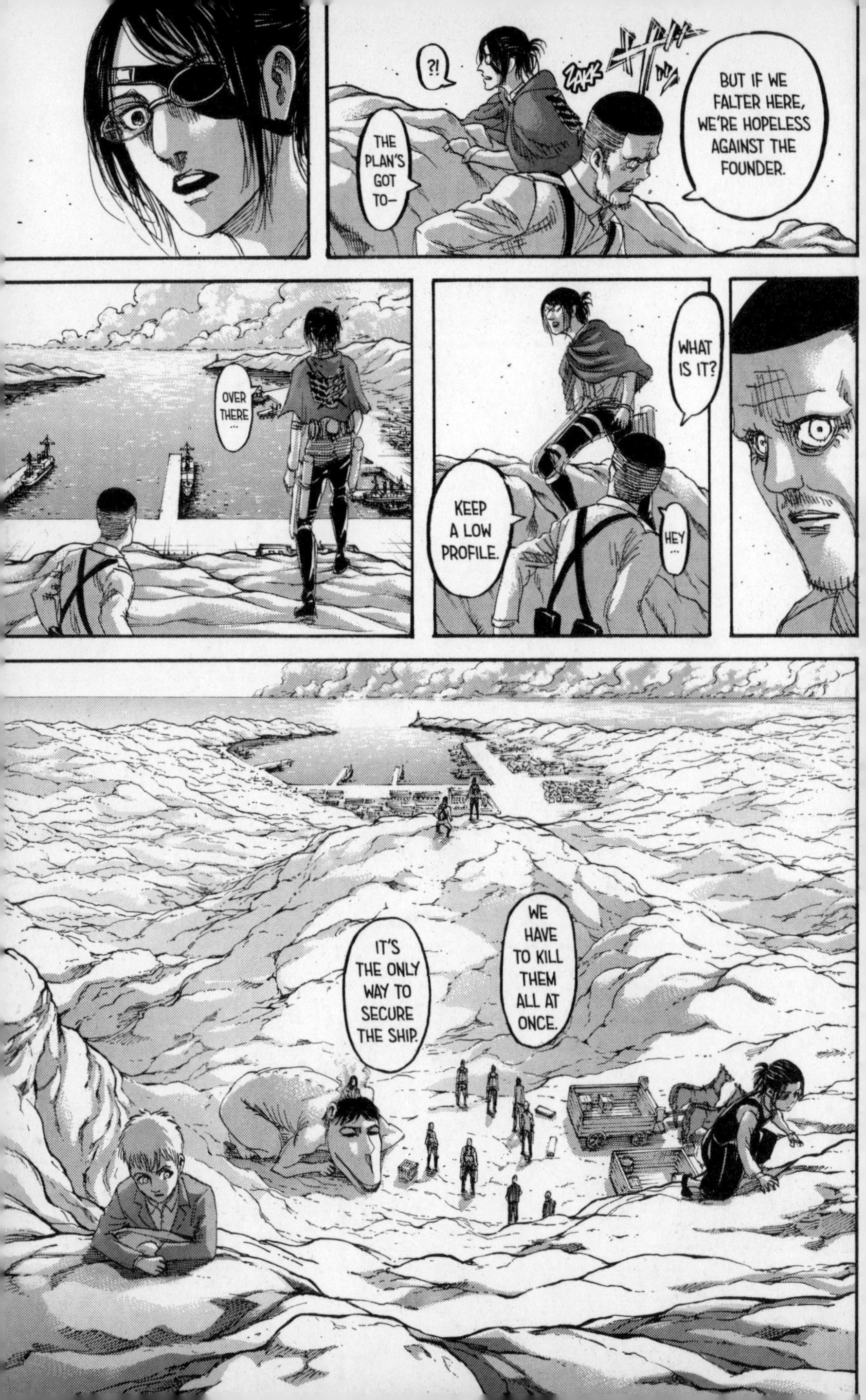
BUT IF WE FALTER HERE, WE'RE HOPELESS AGAINST THE FOUNDER.
ZAKK
?!
THE PLAN'S GOT TO—
WHAT IS IT?
HEY…
KEEP A LOW PROFILE.
OVER THERE…
WE HAVE TO KILL THEM ALL AT ONCE.
IT'S THE ONLY WAY TO SECURE THE SHIP.

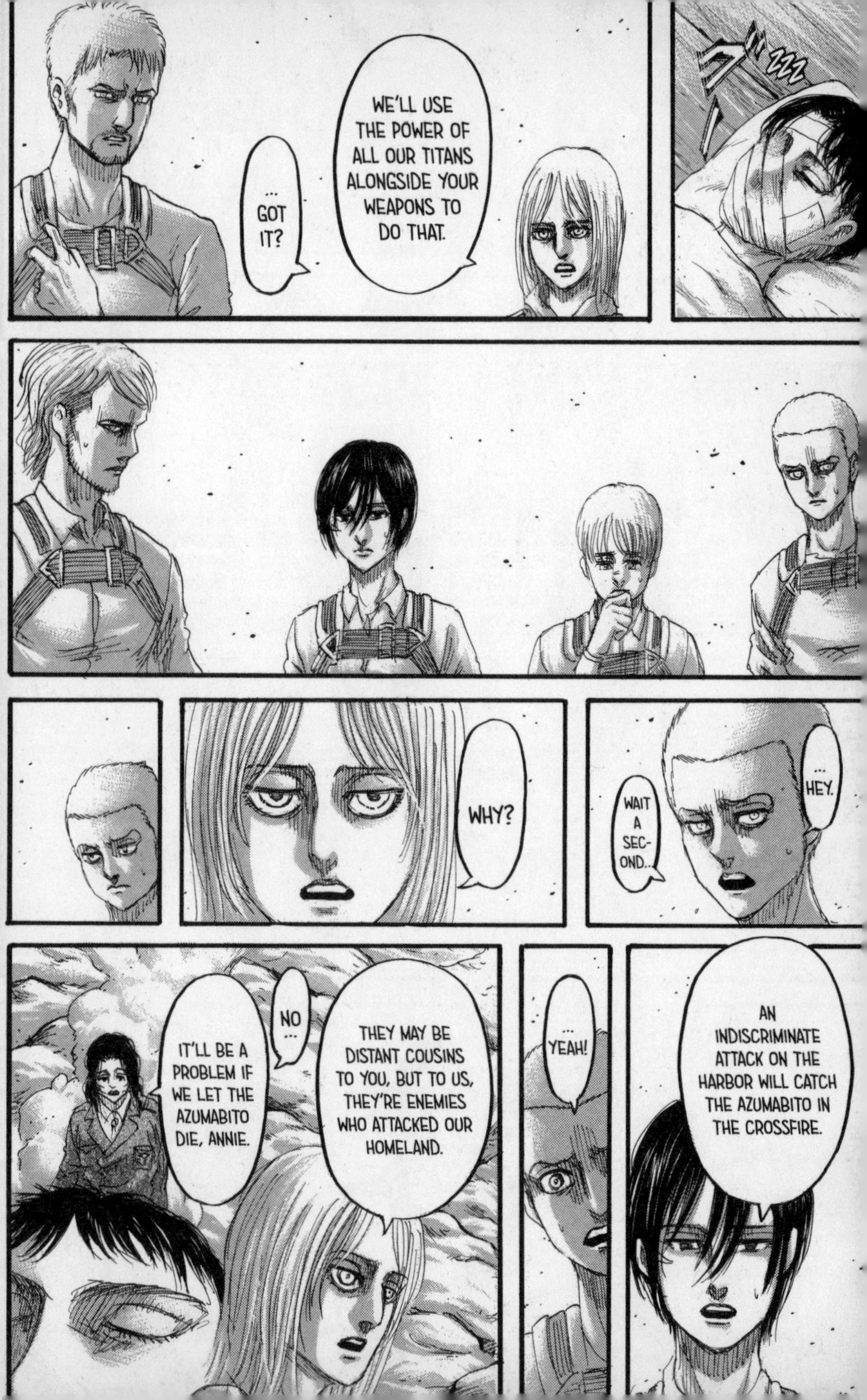
ZZZ
WE'LL USE THE POWER OF ALL OUR TITANS ALONGSIDE YOUR WEAPONS TO DO THAT.
... GOT IT?
... HEY.
WAIT A SEC-OND...
WHY?
AN INDISCRIMINATE ATTACK ON THE HARBOR WILL CATCH THE AZUMABITO IN THE CROSSFIRE.
... YEAH!
THEY MAY BE DISTANT COUSINS TO YOU, BUT TO US, THEY'RE ENEMIES WHO ATTACKED OUR HOMELAND.
NO ...
IT'LL BE A PROBLEM IF WE LET THE AZUMABITO DIE, ANNIE.

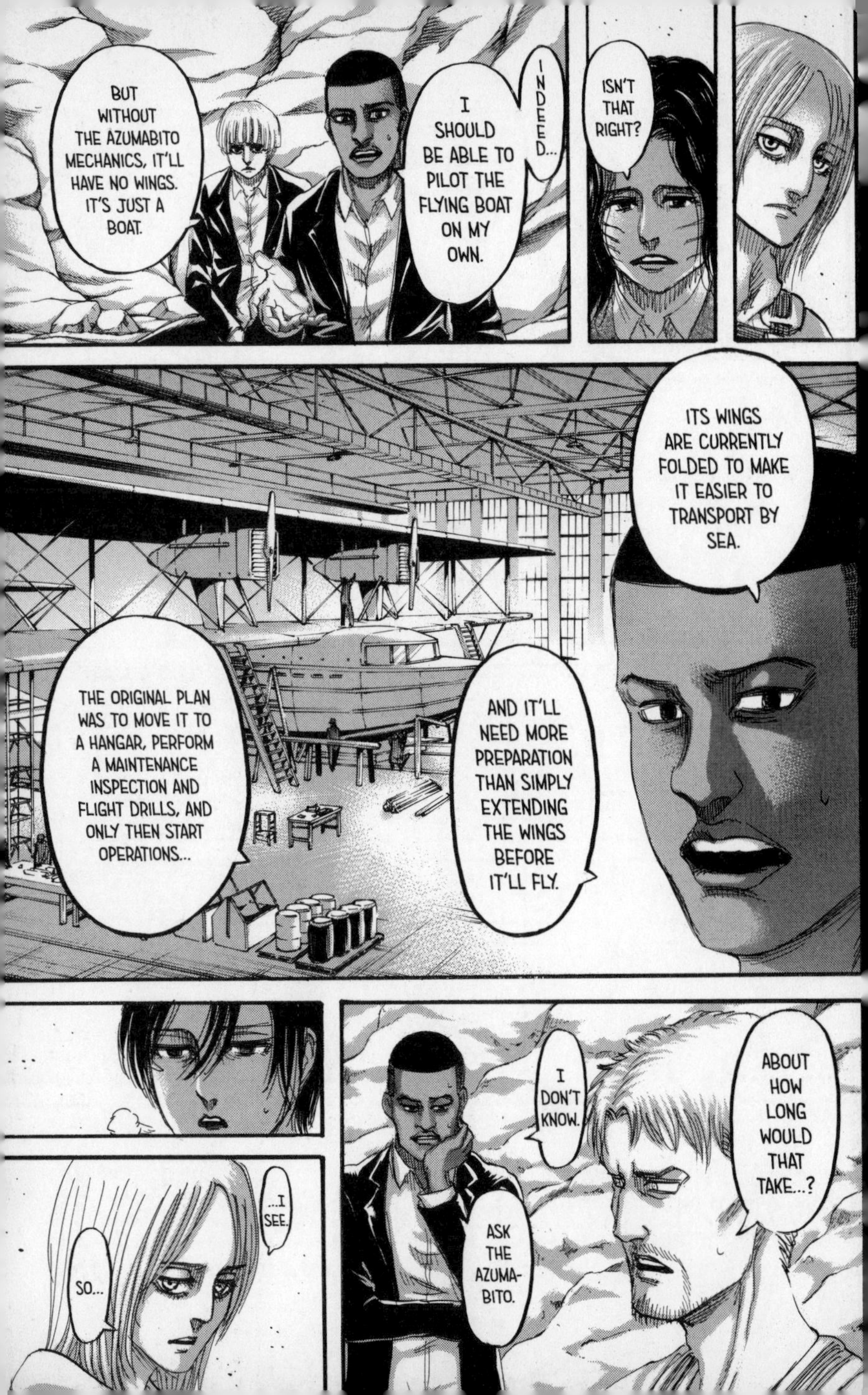
ISN'T THAT RIGHT?
INDEED...
I SHOULD BE ABLE TO PILOT THE FLYING BOAT ON MY OWN.
BUT WITHOUT THE AZUMABITO MECHANICS, IT'LL HAVE NO WINGS. IT'S JUST A BOAT.
ITS WINGS ARE CURRENTLY FOLDED TO MAKE IT EASIER TO TRANSPORT BY SEA.
AND IT'LL NEED MORE PREPARATION THAN SIMPLY EXTENDING THE WINGS BEFORE IT'LL FLY.
THE ORIGINAL PLAN WAS TO MOVE IT TO A HANGAR, PERFORM A MAINTENANCE INSPECTION AND FLIGHT DRILLS, AND ONLY THEN START OPERATIONS...
ABOUT HOW LONG WOULD THAT TAKE...?
I DON'T KNOW.
ASK THE AZUMA-BITO.
...I SEE.
SO...

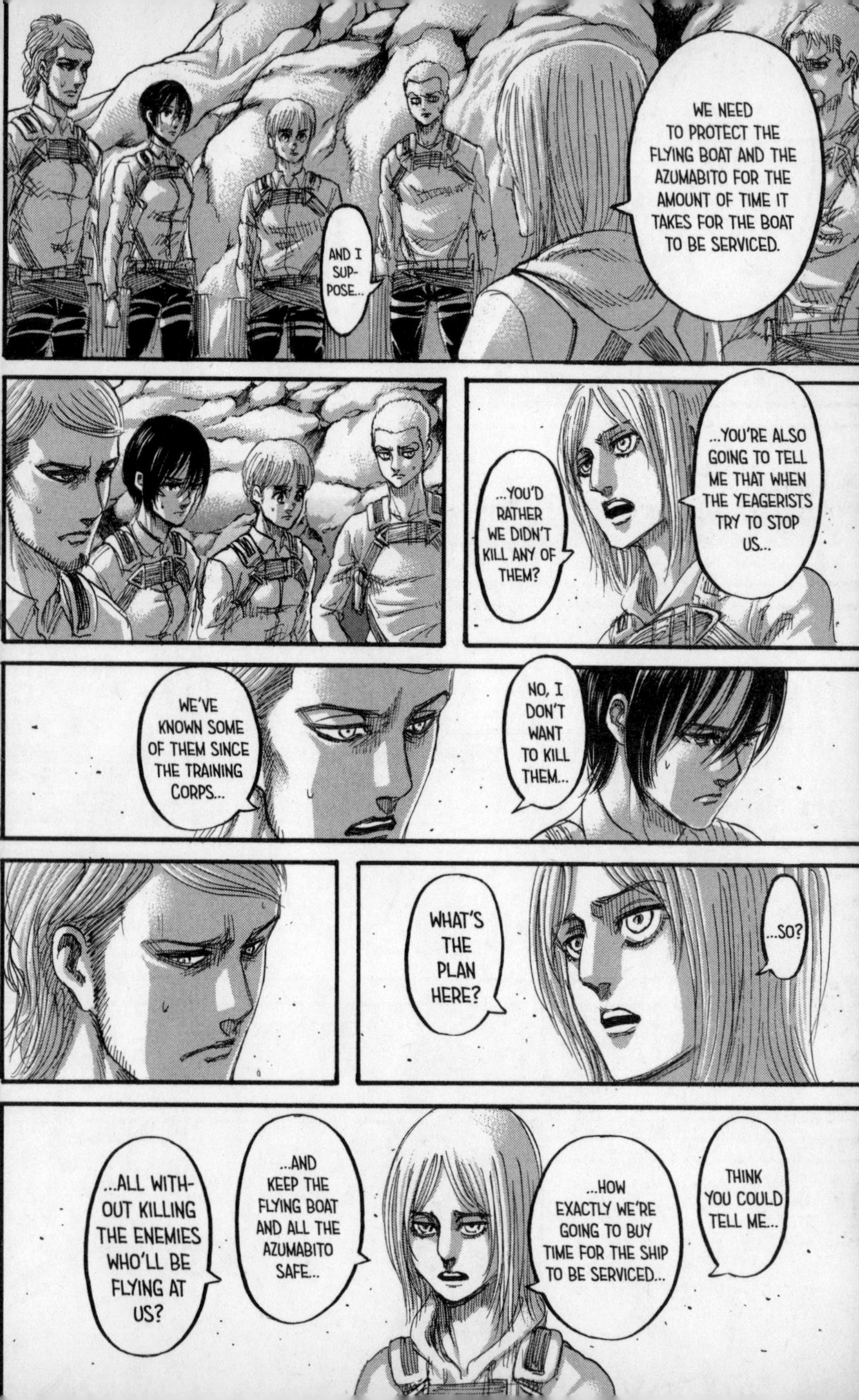
WE NEED TO PROTECT THE FLYING BOAT AND THE AZUMABITO FOR THE AMOUNT OF TIME IT TAKES FOR THE BOAT TO BE SERVICED.
AND I SUPPOSE...
...YOU'RE ALSO GOING TO TELL ME THAT WHEN THE YEAGERISTS TRY TO STOP US...
...YOU'D RATHER WE DIDN'T KILL ANY OF THEM?
NO, I DON'T WANT TO KILL THEM...
WE'VE KNOWN SOME OF THEM SINCE THE TRAINING CORPS...
...SO?
WHAT'S THE PLAN HERE?
THINK YOU COULD TELL ME...
...HOW EXACTLY WE'RE GOING TO BUY TIME FOR THE SHIP TO BE SERVICED...
...AND KEEP THE FLYING BOAT AND ALL THE AZUMABITO SAFE...
...ALL WITHOUT KILLING THE ENEMIES WHO'LL BE FLYING AT US?

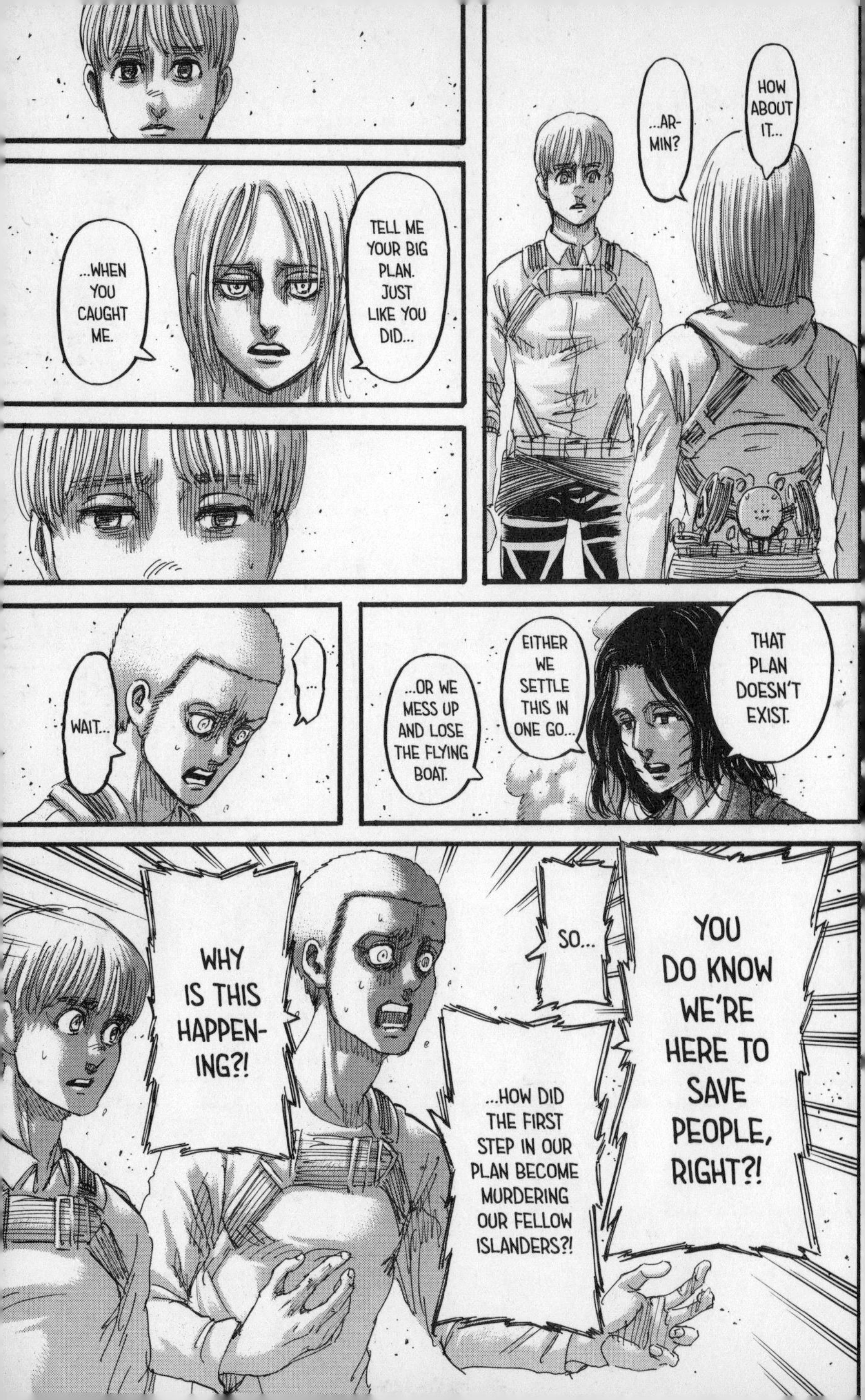
HOW ABOUT IT...
...AR-MIN?
TELL ME YOUR BIG PLAN. JUST LIKE YOU DID...
...WHEN YOU CAUGHT ME.
THAT PLAN DOESN'T EXIST.
EITHER WE SETTLE THIS IN ONE GO...
...OR WE MESS UP AND LOSE THE FLYING BOAT.
...
WAIT...
YOU DO KNOW WE'RE HERE TO SAVE PEOPLE, RIGHT?!
SO...
...HOW DID THE FIRST STEP IN OUR PLAN BECOME MURDERING OUR FELLOW ISLANDERS?!
WHY IS THIS HAPPEN-ING?!

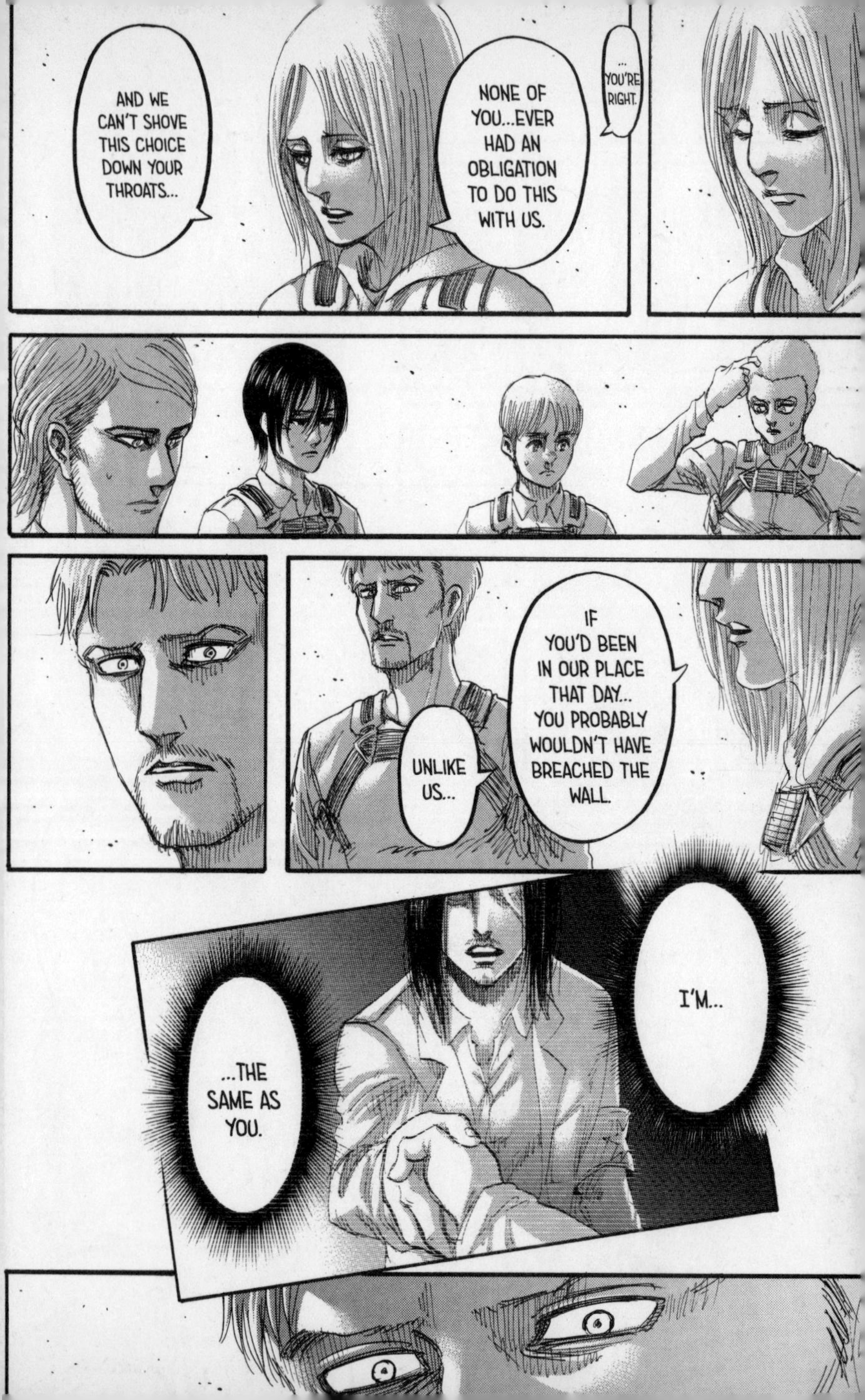
...YOU'RE RIGHT.
NONE OF YOU...EVER HAD AN OBLIGATION TO DO THIS WITH US.
AND WE CAN'T SHOVE THIS CHOICE DOWN YOUR THROATS...
IF YOU'D BEEN IN OUR PLACE THAT DAY... YOU PROBABLY WOULDN'T HAVE BREACHED THE WALL.
UNLIKE US...
I'M...
...THE SAME AS YOU.

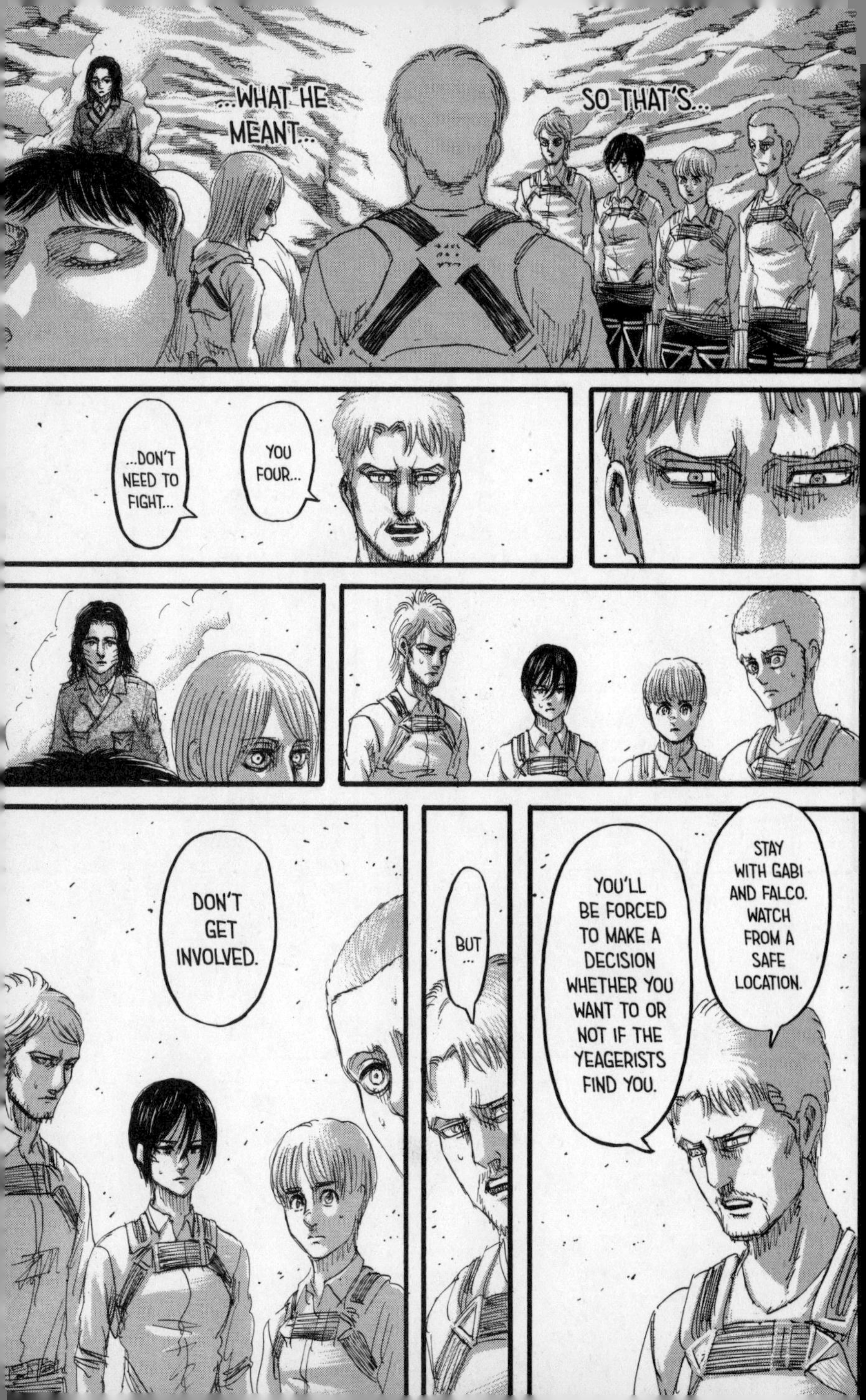
SO THAT'S...
...WHAT HE MEANT...
YOU FOUR...
...DON'T NEED TO FIGHT...
STAY WITH GABI AND FALCO. WATCH FROM A SAFE LOCATION.
YOU'LL BE FORCED TO MAKE A DECISION WHETHER YOU WANT TO OR NOT IF THE YEAGERISTS FIND YOU.
BUT ...
DON'T GET INVOLVED.

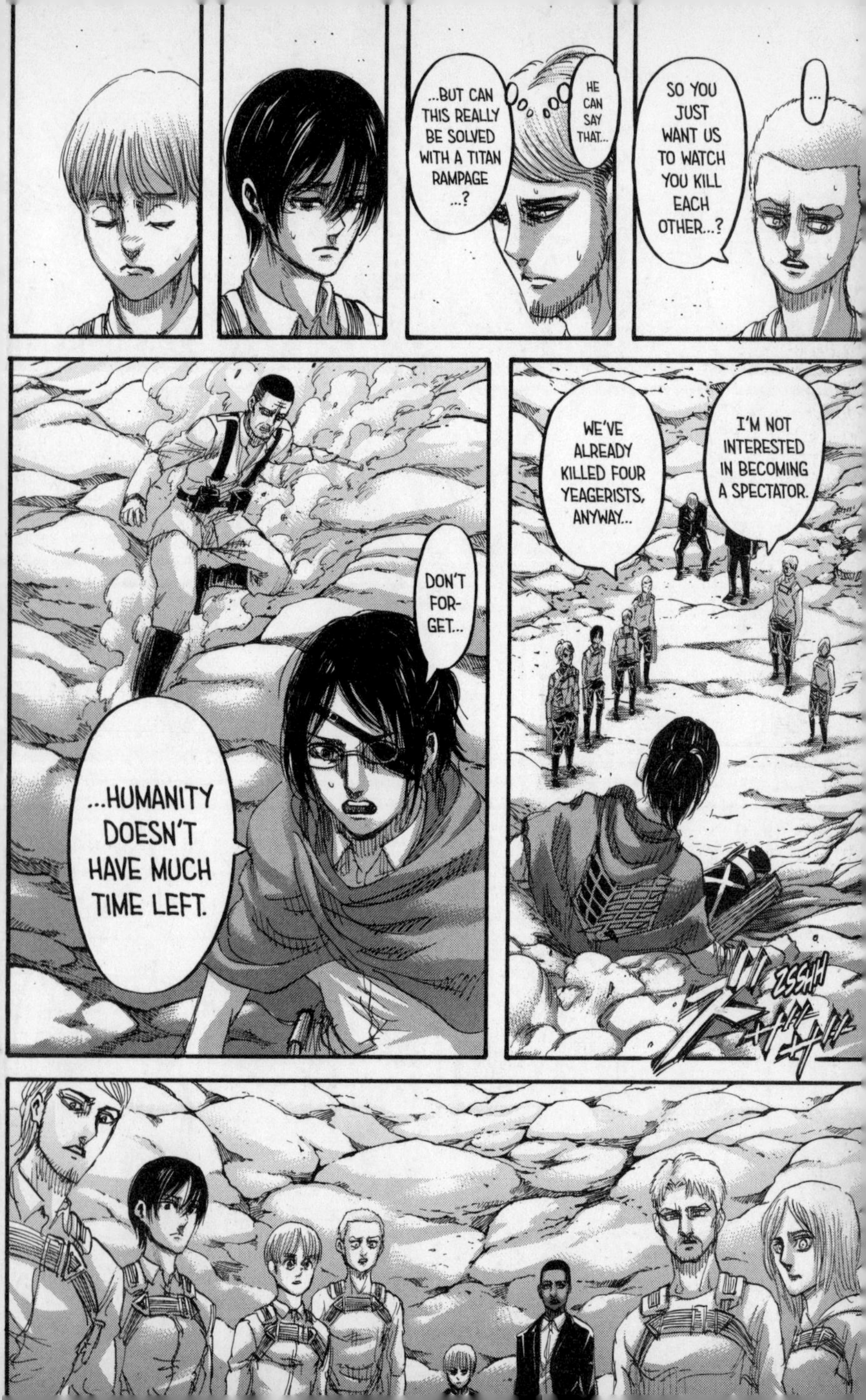
...
SO YOU JUST WANT US TO WATCH YOU KILL EACH OTHER...?
HE CAN SAY THAT...
...BUT CAN THIS REALLY BE SOLVED WITH A TITAN RAMPAGE ...?
I'M NOT INTERESTED IN BECOMING A SPECTATOR.
WE'VE ALREADY KILLED FOUR YEAGERISTS, ANYWAY...
DON'T FOR-GET...
...HUMANITY DOESN'T HAVE MUCH TIME LEFT.

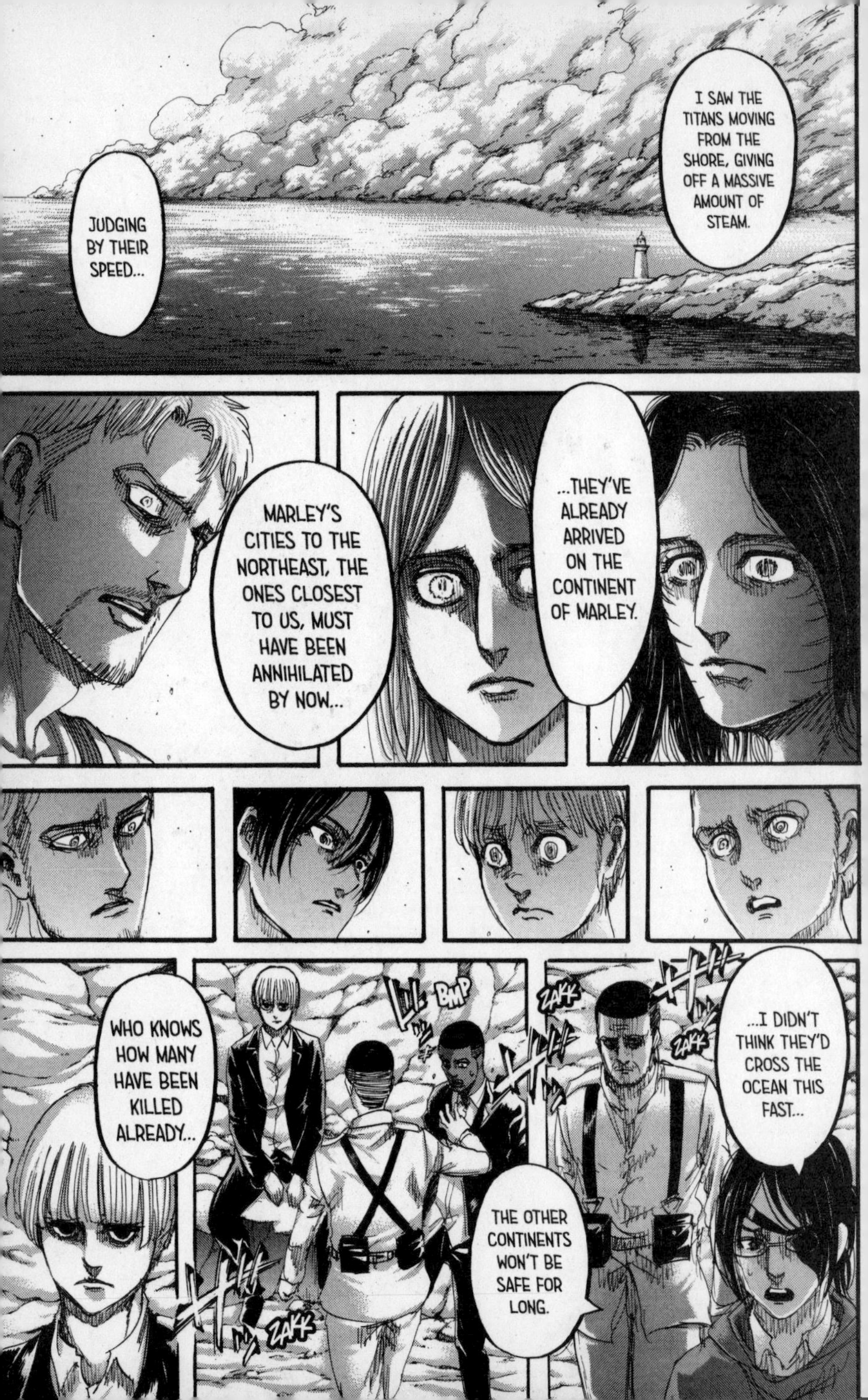
I SAW THE TITANS MOVING FROM THE SHORE, GIVING OFF A MASSIVE AMOUNT OF STEAM.
JUDGING BY THEIR SPEED...
...THEY'VE ALREADY ARRIVED ON THE CONTINENT OF MARLEY.
MARLEY'S CITIES TO THE NORTHEAST, THE ONES CLOSEST TO US, MUST HAVE BEEN ANNIHILATED BY NOW...
...I DIDN'T THINK THEY'D CROSS THE OCEAN THIS FAST...
ZAKK
ZAKK
THE OTHER CONTINENTS WON'T BE SAFE FOR LONG.
BMP
WHO KNOWS HOW MANY HAVE BEEN KILLED ALREADY...
ZAKK

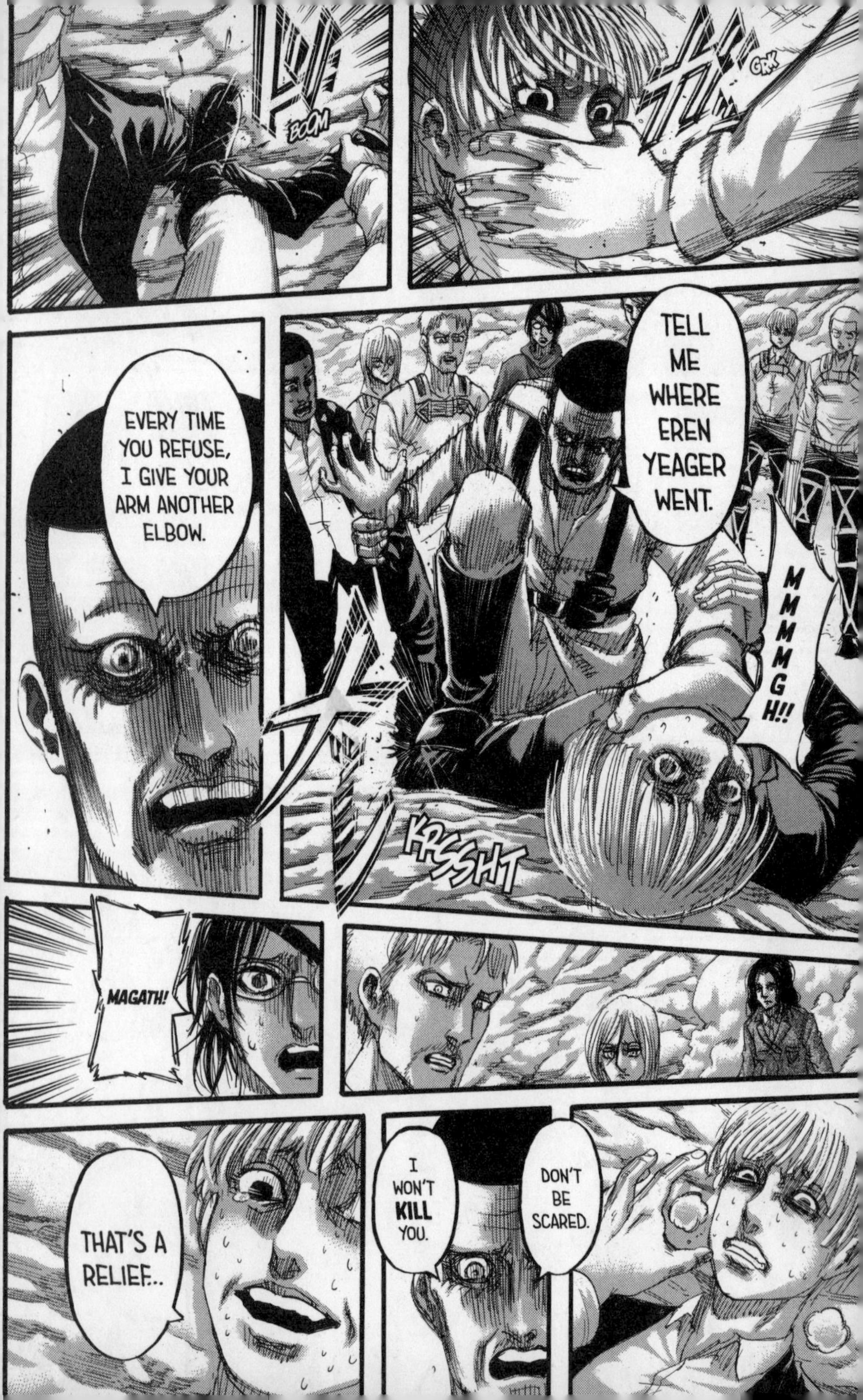
GRK
BOOM
TELL ME WHERE EREN YEAGER WENT.
MMMMMGH!!
KRSSHT
EVERY TIME YOU REFUSE, I GIVE YOUR ARM ANOTHER ELBOW.
MAGATH!
DON'T BE SCARED.
I WON'T **KILL** YOU.
THAT'S A RELIEF...

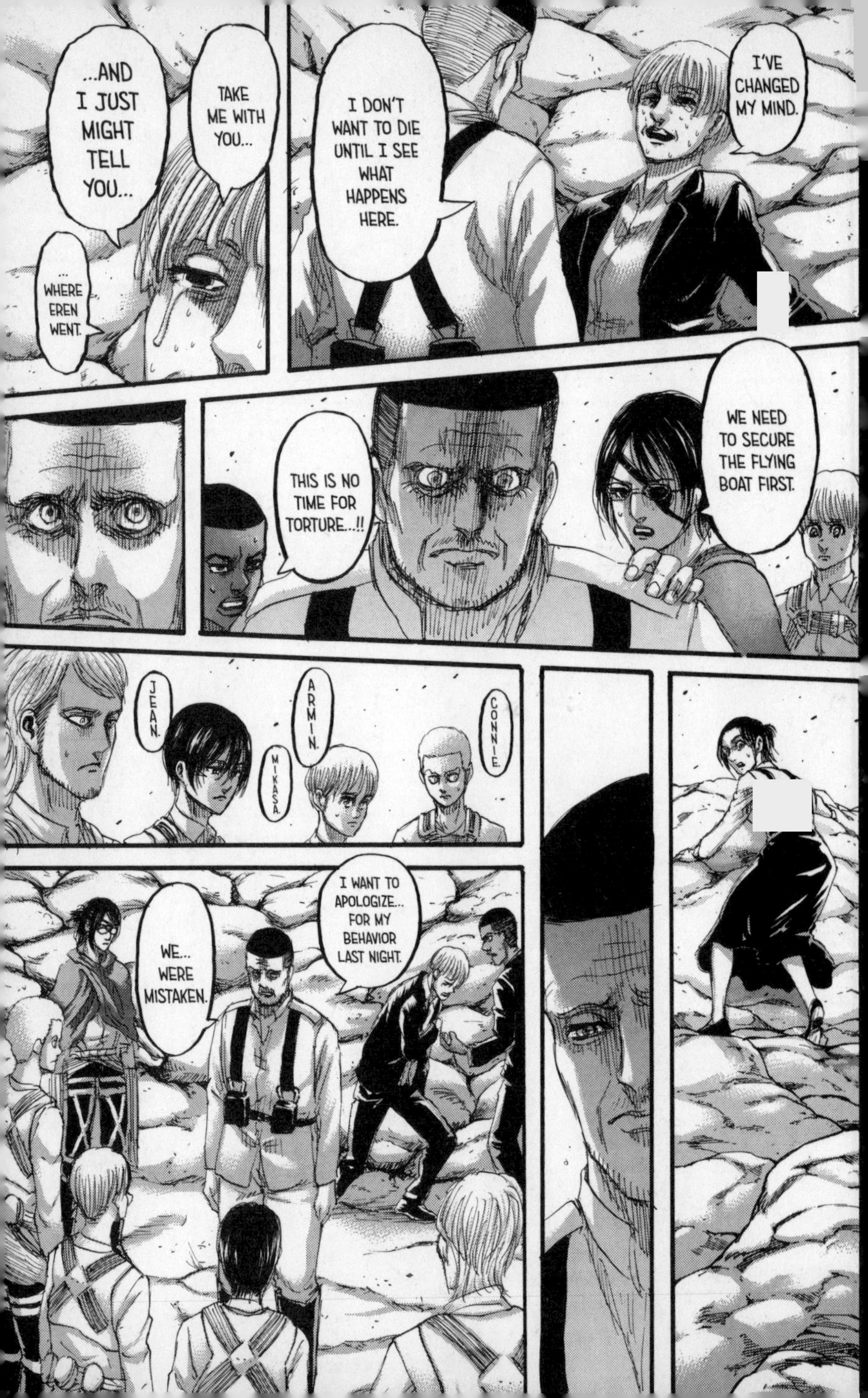
I'VE CHANGED MY MIND.
I DON'T WANT TO DIE UNTIL I SEE WHAT HAPPENS HERE.
TAKE ME WITH YOU...
...AND I JUST MIGHT TELL YOU...
...WHERE EREN WENT.
WE NEED TO SECURE THE FLYING BOAT FIRST.
THIS IS NO TIME FOR TORTURE...!!
CONNIE.
ARMIN.
MIKASA.
JEAN.
I WANT TO APOLOGIZE... FOR MY BEHAVIOR LAST NIGHT.
WE... WERE MISTAKEN.

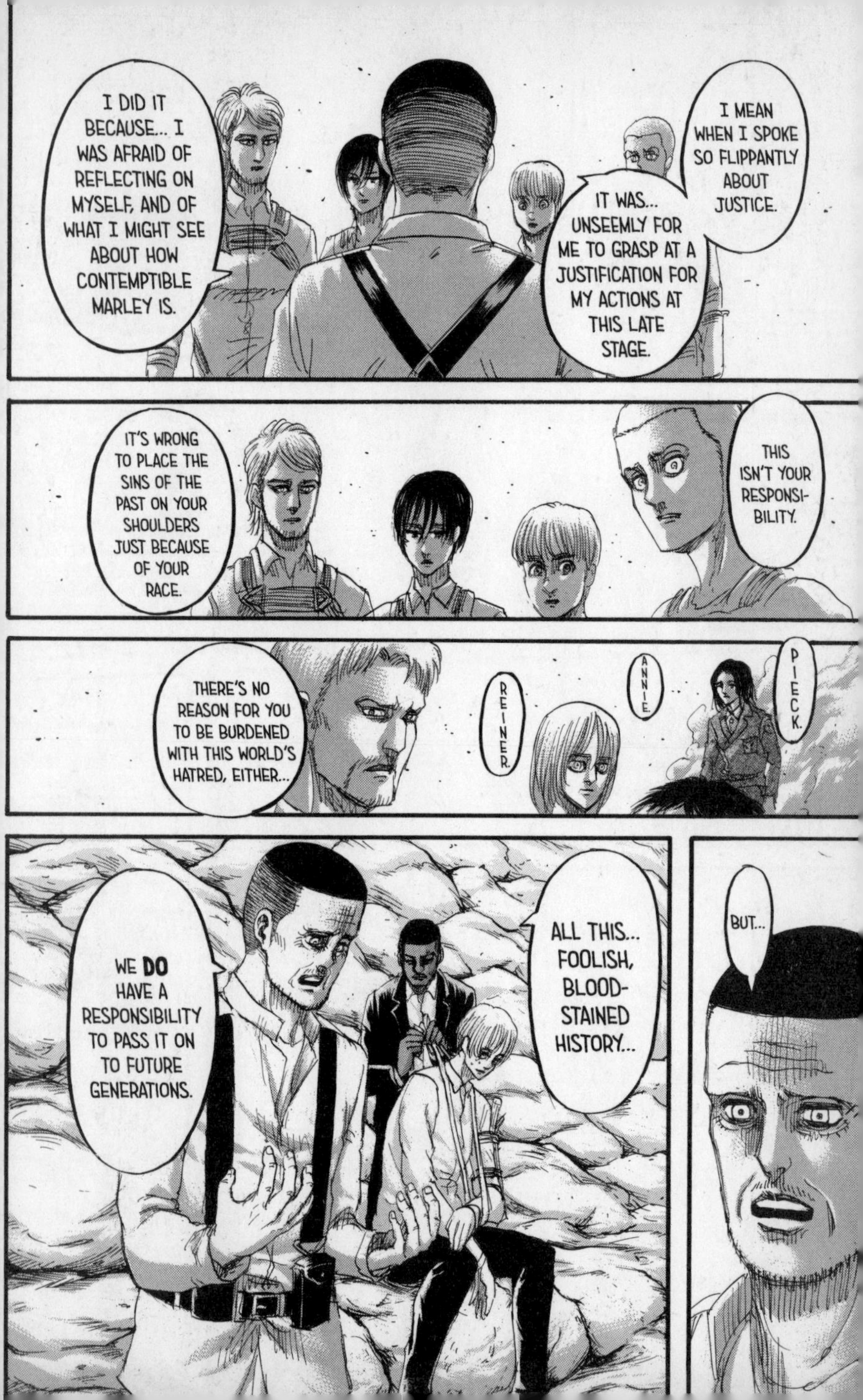
I MEAN WHEN I SPOKE SO FLIPPANTLY ABOUT JUSTICE.
IT WAS... UNSEEMLY FOR ME TO GRASP AT A JUSTIFICATION FOR MY ACTIONS AT THIS LATE STAGE.
I DID IT BECAUSE... I WAS AFRAID OF REFLECTING ON MYSELF, AND OF WHAT I MIGHT SEE ABOUT HOW CONTEMPTIBLE MARLEY IS.
THIS ISN'T YOUR RESPONSIBILITY.
IT'S WRONG TO PLACE THE SINS OF THE PAST ON YOUR SHOULDERS JUST BECAUSE OF YOUR RACE.
PIECK.
ANNIE.
REINER.
THERE'S NO REASON FOR YOU TO BE BURDENED WITH THIS WORLD'S HATRED, EITHER...
BUT...
ALL THIS... FOOLISH, BLOOD-STAINED HISTORY...
WE **DO** HAVE A RESPONSIBILITY TO PASS IT ON TO FUTURE GENERATIONS.

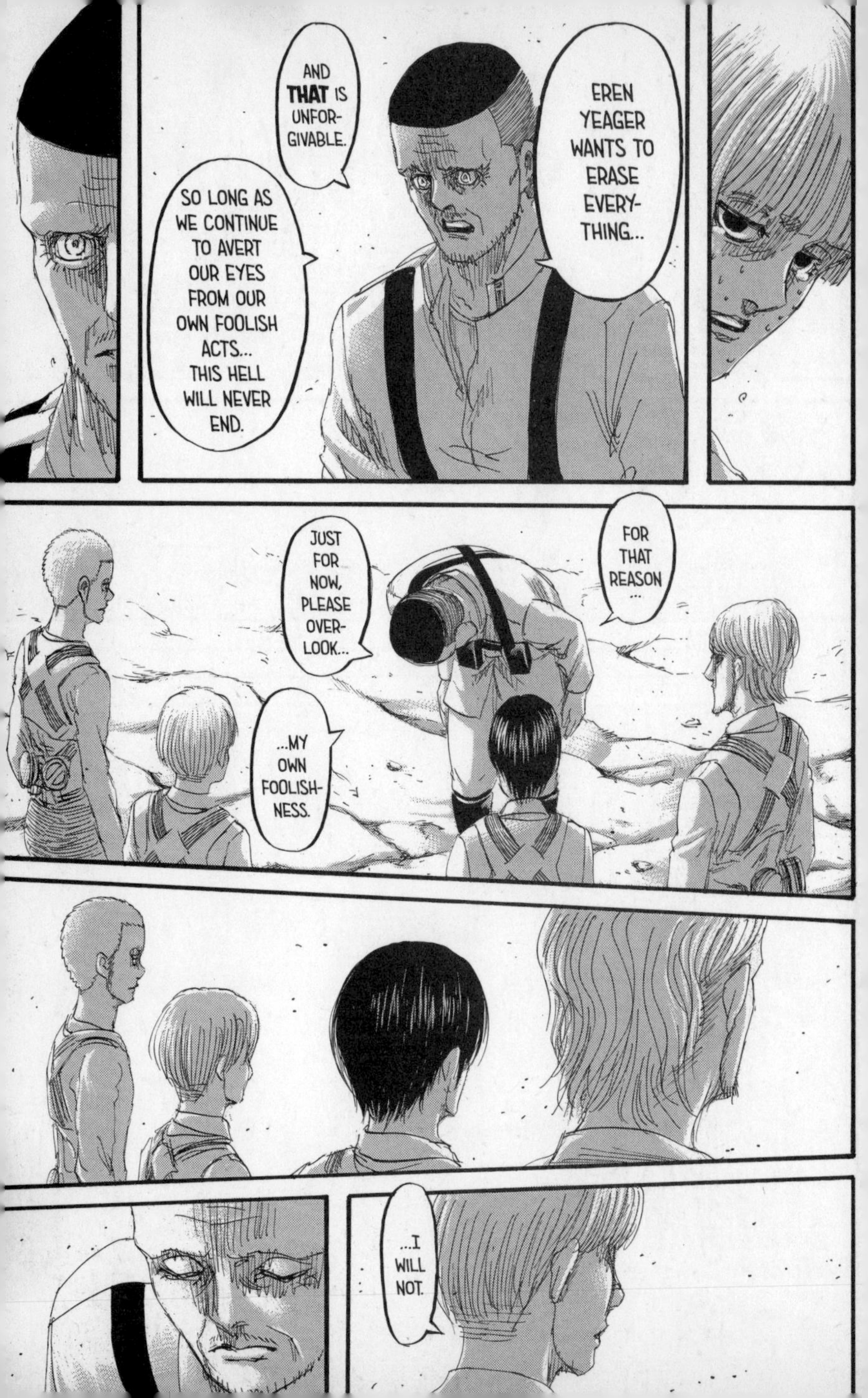
EREN YEAGER WANTS TO ERASE EVERYTHING...
AND **THAT** IS UNFORGIVABLE.
SO LONG AS WE CONTINUE TO AVERT OUR EYES FROM OUR OWN FOOLISH ACTS... THIS HELL WILL NEVER END.
FOR THAT REASON...
JUST FOR NOW, PLEASE OVERLOOK...
...MY OWN FOOLISHNESS.
...I WILL NOT.

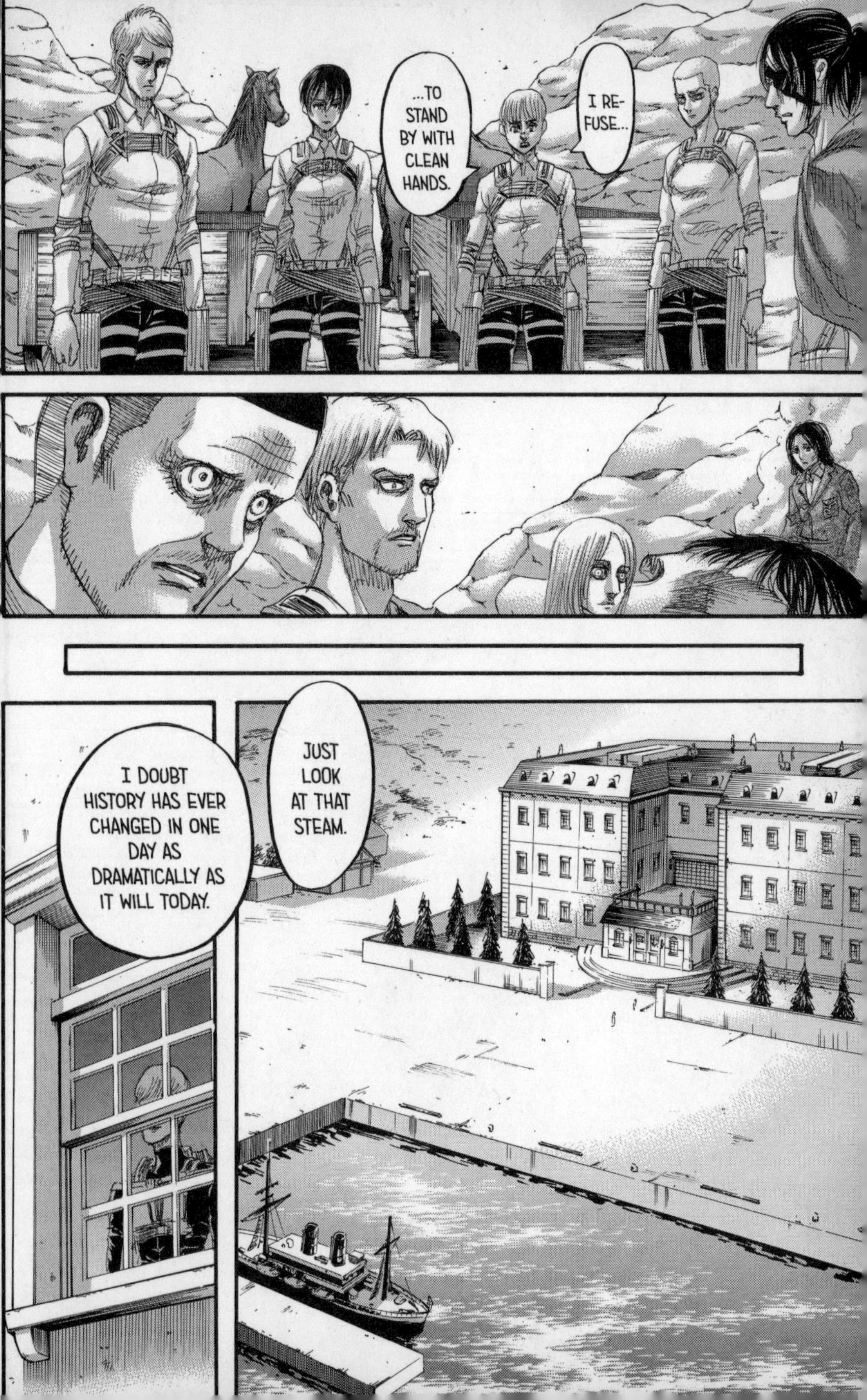
I RE-FUSE...
...TO STAND BY WITH CLEAN HANDS.
JUST LOOK AT THAT STEAM.
I DOUBT HISTORY HAS EVER CHANGED IN ONE DAY AS DRAMATICALLY AS IT WILL TODAY.

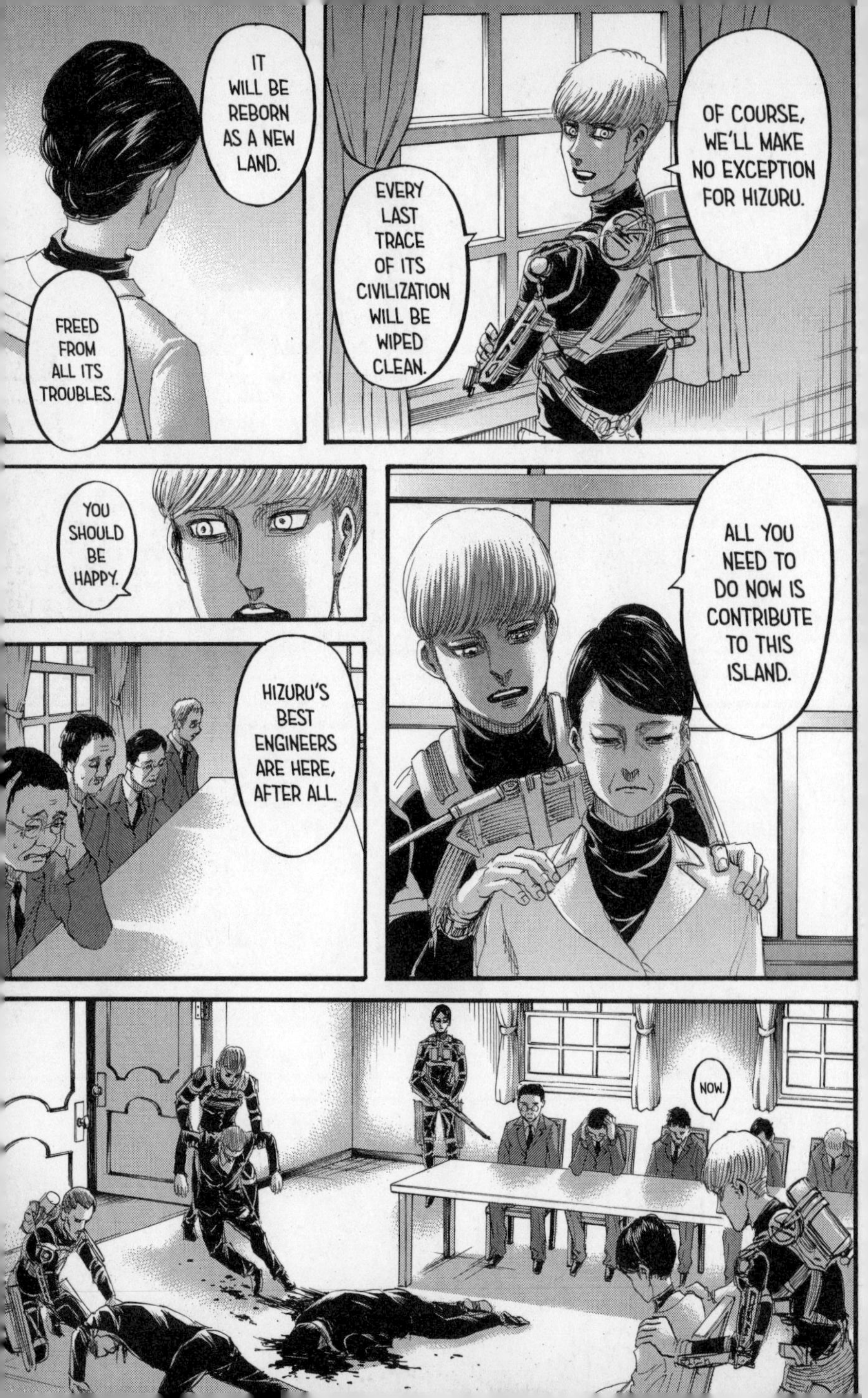
OF COURSE, WE'LL MAKE NO EXCEPTION FOR HIZURU.
EVERY LAST TRACE OF ITS CIVILIZATION WILL BE WIPED CLEAN.
IT WILL BE REBORN AS A NEW LAND.
FREED FROM ALL ITS TROUBLES.
ALL YOU NEED TO DO NOW IS CONTRIBUTE TO THIS ISLAND.
YOU SHOULD BE HAPPY.
HIZURU'S BEST ENGINEERS ARE HERE, AFTER ALL.
NOW.

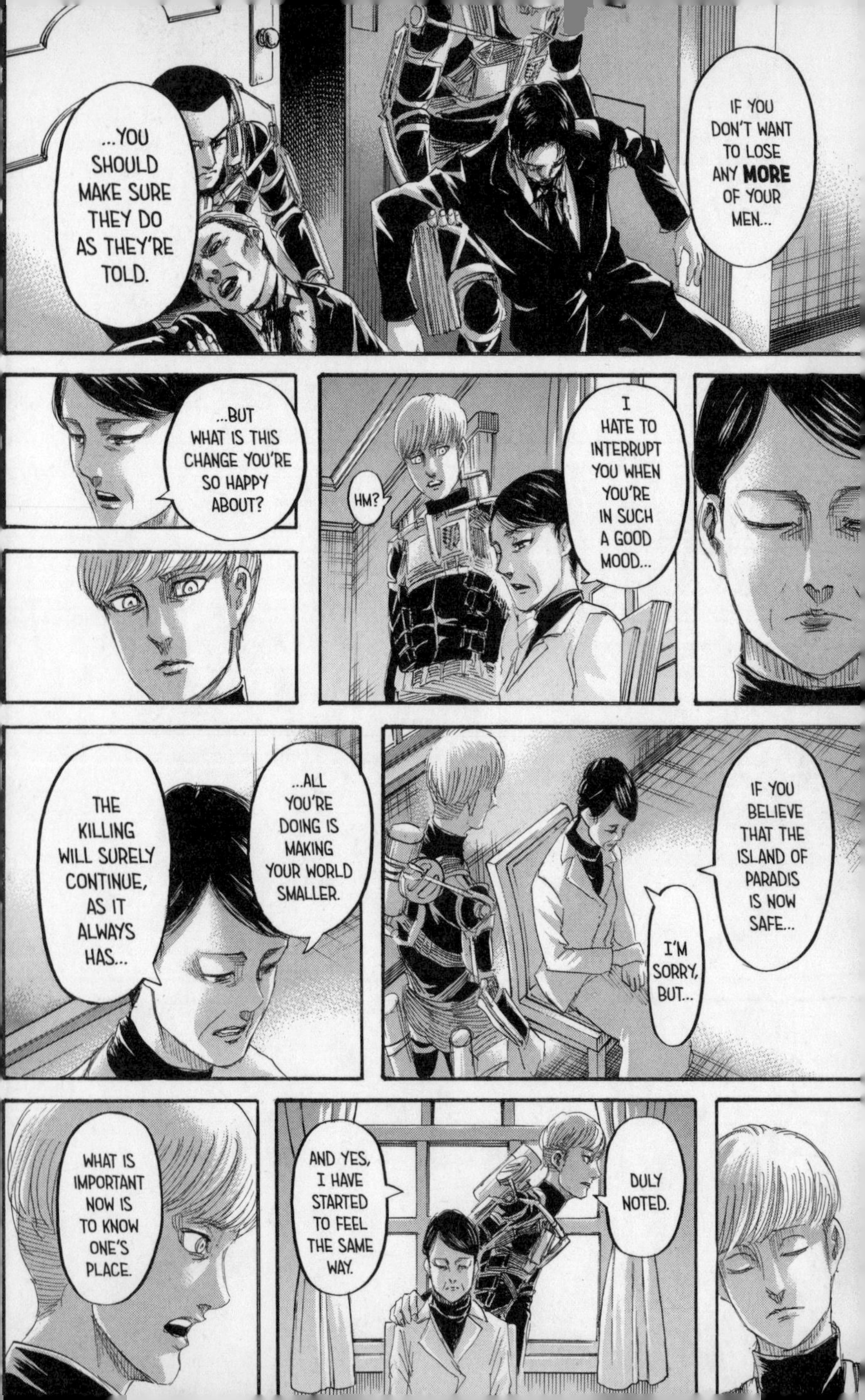
IF YOU DON'T WANT TO LOSE ANY **MORE** OF YOUR MEN...
...YOU SHOULD MAKE SURE THEY DO AS THEY'RE TOLD.
I HATE TO INTERRUPT YOU WHEN YOU'RE IN SUCH A GOOD MOOD...
HM?
...BUT WHAT IS THIS CHANGE YOU'RE SO HAPPY ABOUT?
IF YOU BELIEVE THAT THE ISLAND OF PARADIS IS NOW SAFE...
I'M SORRY, BUT...
...ALL YOU'RE DOING IS MAKING YOUR WORLD SMALLER.
THE KILLING WILL SURELY CONTINUE, AS IT ALWAYS HAS...
DULY NOTED.
AND YES, I HAVE STARTED TO FEEL THE SAME WAY.
WHAT IS IMPORTANT NOW IS TO KNOW ONE'S PLACE.

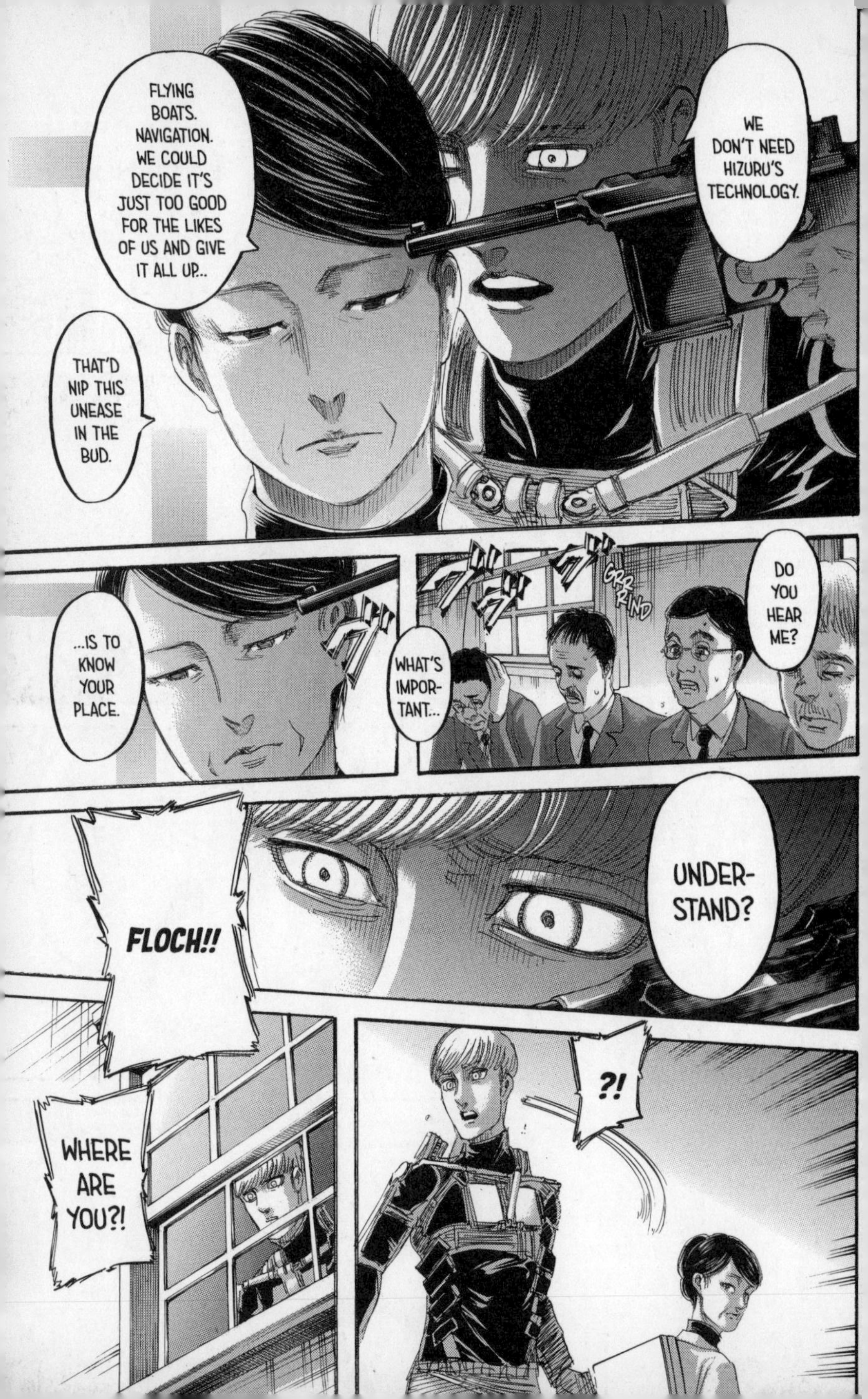
WE DON'T NEED HIZURU'S TECHNOLOGY.
FLYING BOATS. NAVIGATION. WE COULD DECIDE IT'S JUST TOO GOOD FOR THE LIKES OF US AND GIVE IT ALL UP...
THAT'D NIP THIS UNEASE IN THE BUD.
DO YOU HEAR ME?
GRRRIND
WHAT'S IMPOR-TANT...
...IS TO KNOW YOUR PLACE.
UNDER-STAND?
FLOCH!!
?!
WHERE ARE YOU?!

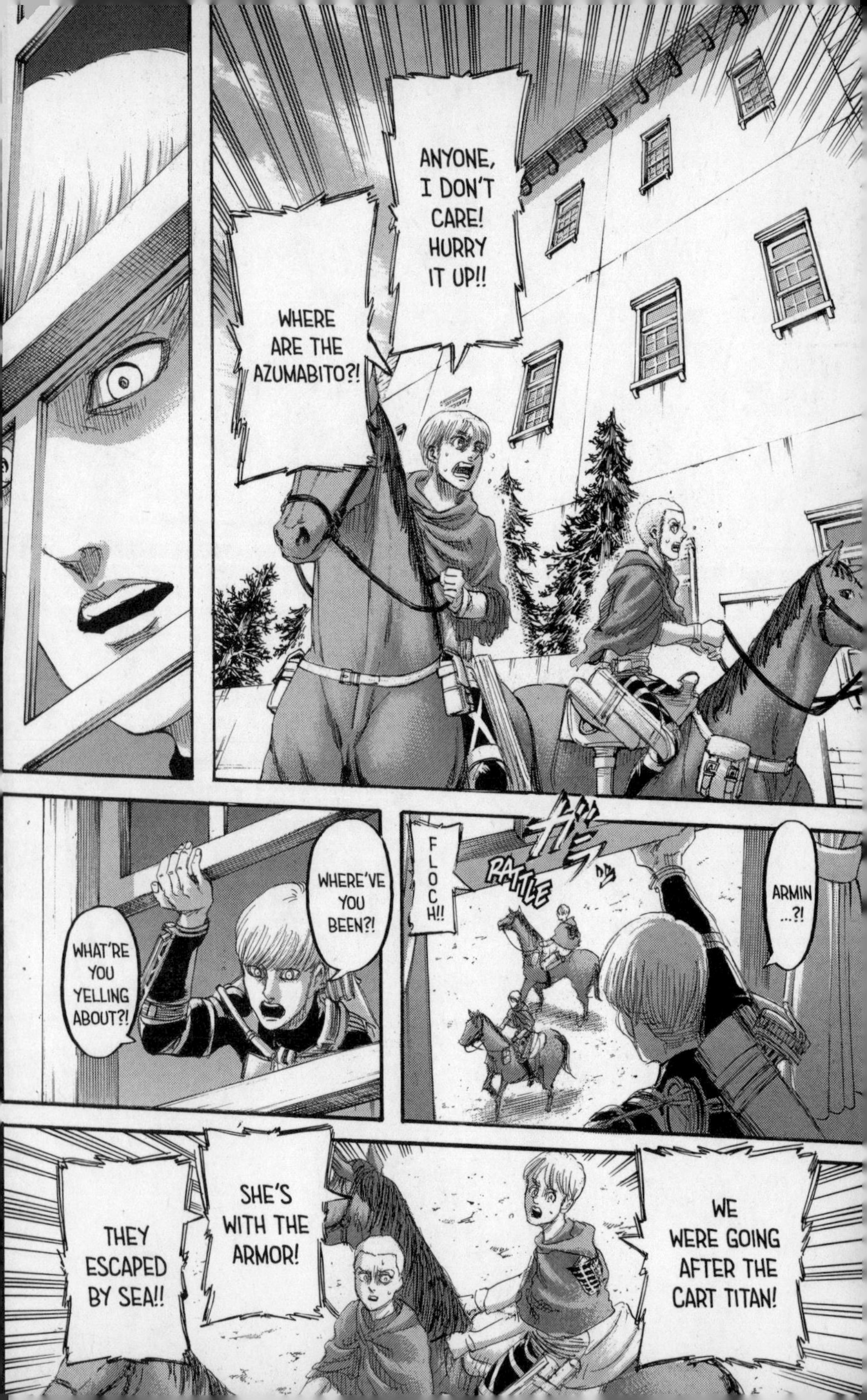
ANYONE, I DON'T CARE! HURRY IT UP!!
WHERE ARE THE AZUMABITO?!
ARMIN ...?!
RATTLE
FLOCH!!
WHERE'VE YOU BEEN?!
WHAT'RE YOU YELLING ABOUT?!
WE WERE GOING AFTER THE CART TITAN!
SHE'S WITH THE ARMOR!
THEY ESCAPED BY SEA!!

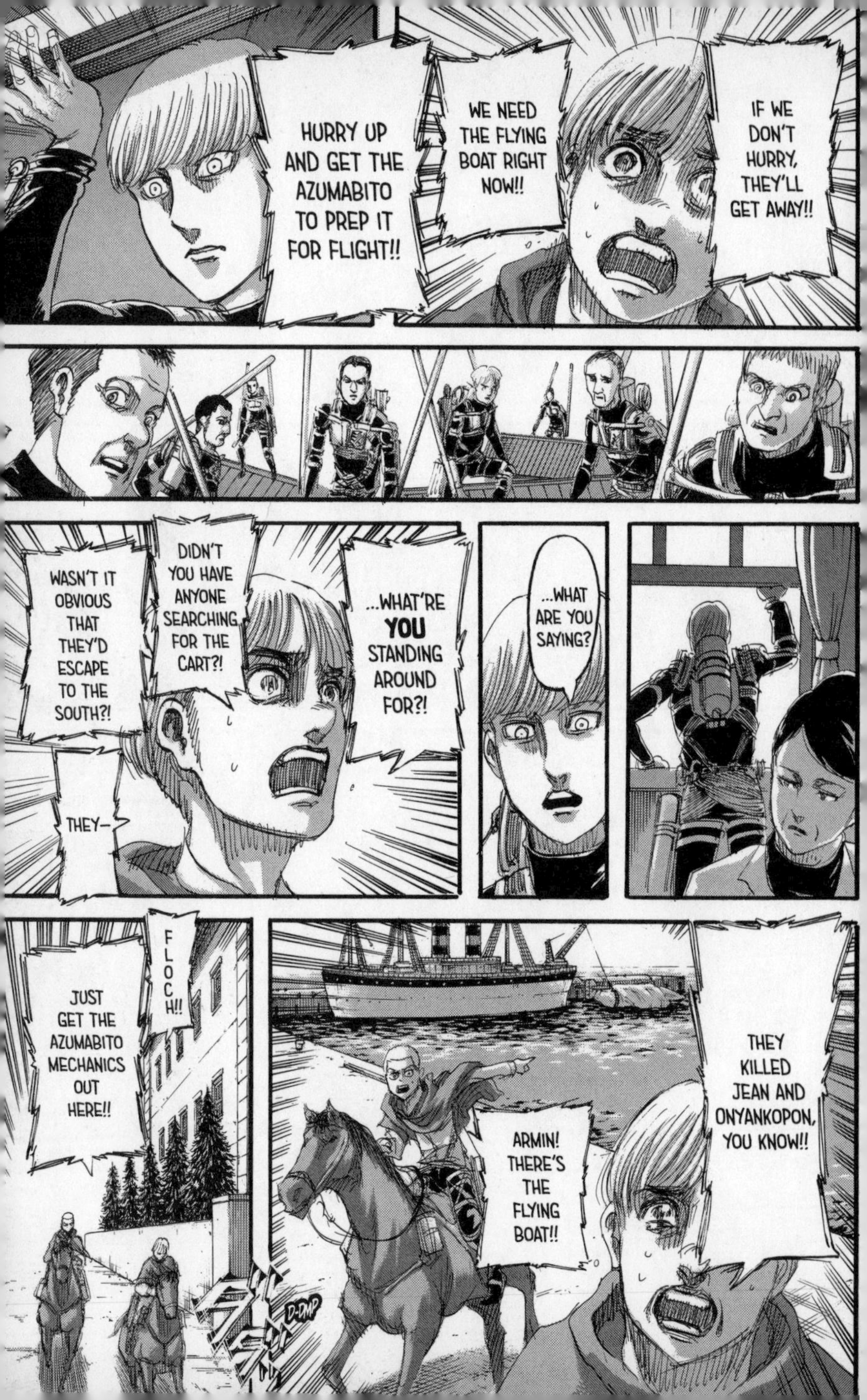
IF WE DON'T HURRY, THEY'LL GET AWAY!!
WE NEED THE FLYING BOAT RIGHT NOW!!
HURRY UP AND GET THE AZUMABITO TO PREP IT FOR FLIGHT!!
...WHAT ARE YOU SAYING?
...WHAT'RE YOU STANDING AROUND FOR?!
DIDN'T YOU HAVE ANYONE SEARCHING FOR THE CART?!
WASN'T IT OBVIOUS THAT THEY'D ESCAPE TO THE SOUTH?!
THEY—
THEY KILLED JEAN AND ONYANKOPON, YOU KNOW!!
ARMIN! THERE'S THE FLYING BOAT!!
D-DMP
FLOCH!!
JUST GET THE AZUMABITO MECHANICS OUT HERE!!

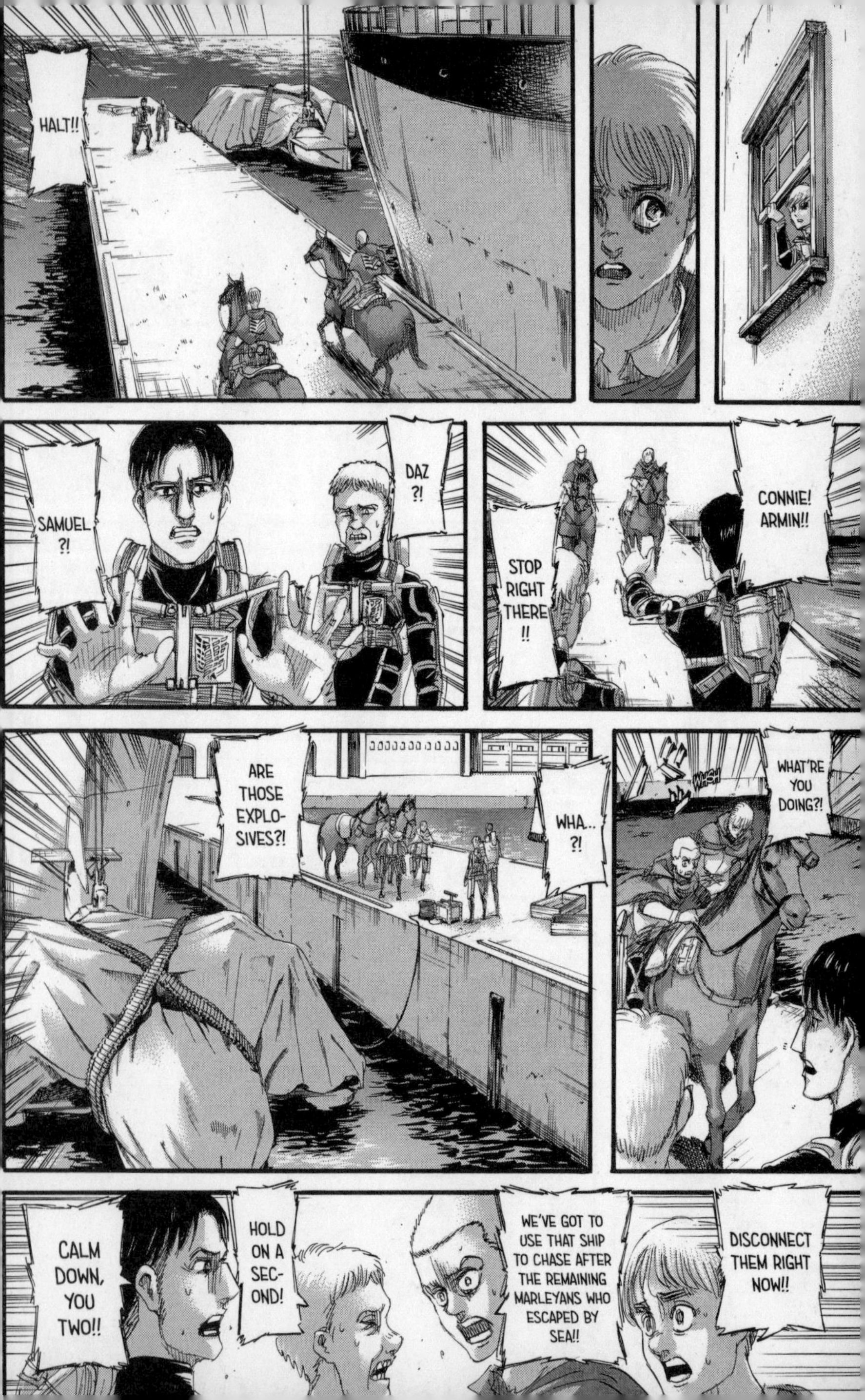
HALT!!
CONNIE! ARMIN!!
STOP RIGHT THERE !!
DAZ ?!
SAMUEL ?!
WHSH
WHAT'RE YOU DOING?!
WHA... ?!
ARE THOSE EXPLO- SIVES?!
DISCONNECT THEM RIGHT NOW!!
WE'VE GOT TO USE THAT SHIP TO CHASE AFTER THE REMAINING MARLEYANS WHO ESCAPED BY SEA!!
HOLD ON A SEC- OND!
CALM DOWN, YOU TWO!!

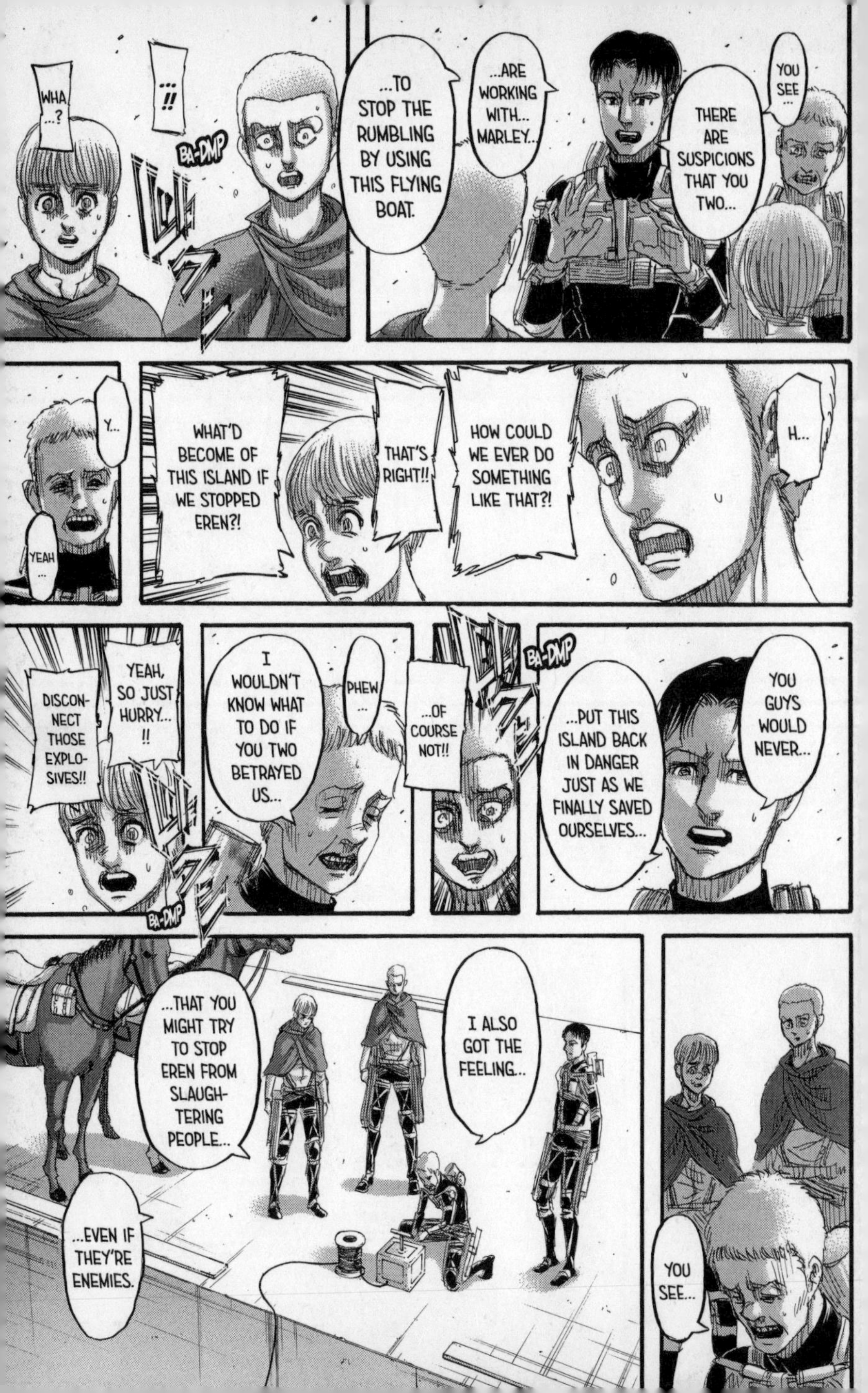

YOU SEE...
THERE ARE SUSPICIONS THAT YOU TWO...
...ARE WORKING WITH... MARLEY...
...TO STOP THE RUMBLING BY USING THIS FLYING BOAT.
...!!
BA-DMP
WHA...?
H...
HOW COULD WE EVER DO SOMETHING LIKE THAT?!
THAT'S RIGHT!!
WHAT'D BECOME OF THIS ISLAND IF WE STOPPED EREN?!
Y...
YEAH...
YOU GUYS WOULD NEVER...
...PUT THIS ISLAND BACK IN DANGER JUST AS WE FINALLY SAVED OURSELVES...
BA-DMP
...OF COURSE NOT!!
PHEW...
I WOULDN'T KNOW WHAT TO DO IF YOU TWO BETRAYED US...
YEAH, SO JUST HURRY...!!
DISCON-NECT THOSE EXPLO-SIVES!!
BA-DMP
YOU SEE...
I ALSO GOT THE FEELING...
...THAT YOU MIGHT TRY TO STOP EREN FROM SLAUGH-TERING PEOPLE...
...EVEN IF THEY'RE ENEMIES.

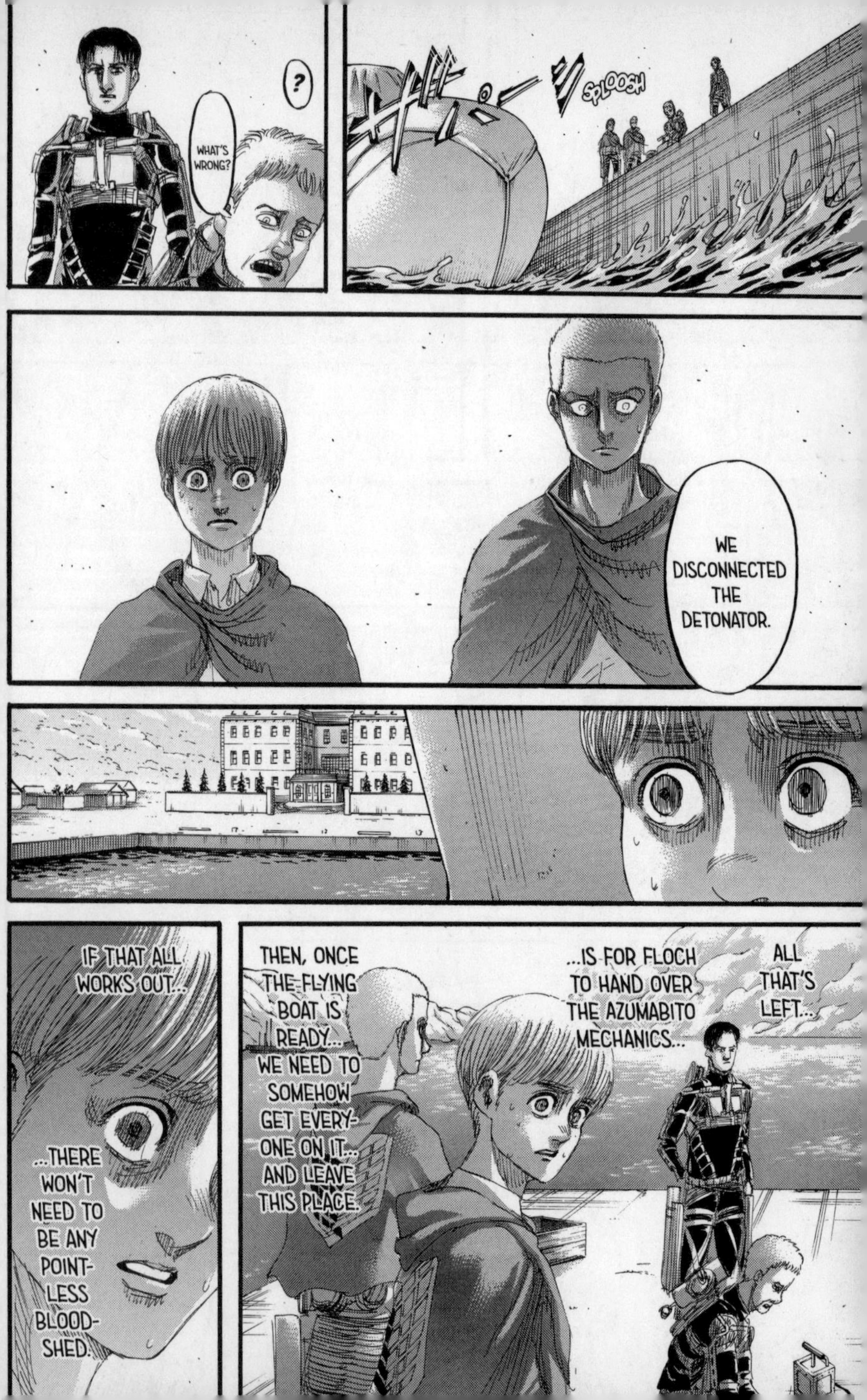
SPLOOSH
?
WHAT'S WRONG?
WE DISCONNECTED THE DETONATOR.
ALL THAT'S LEFT...
...IS FOR FLOCH TO HAND OVER THE AZUMABITO MECHANICS...
THEN, ONCE THE FLYING BOAT IS READY... WE NEED TO SOMEHOW GET EVERYONE ON IT... AND LEAVE THIS PLACE.
IF THAT ALL WORKS OUT...
...THERE WON'T NEED TO BE ANY POINTLESS BLOODSHED.

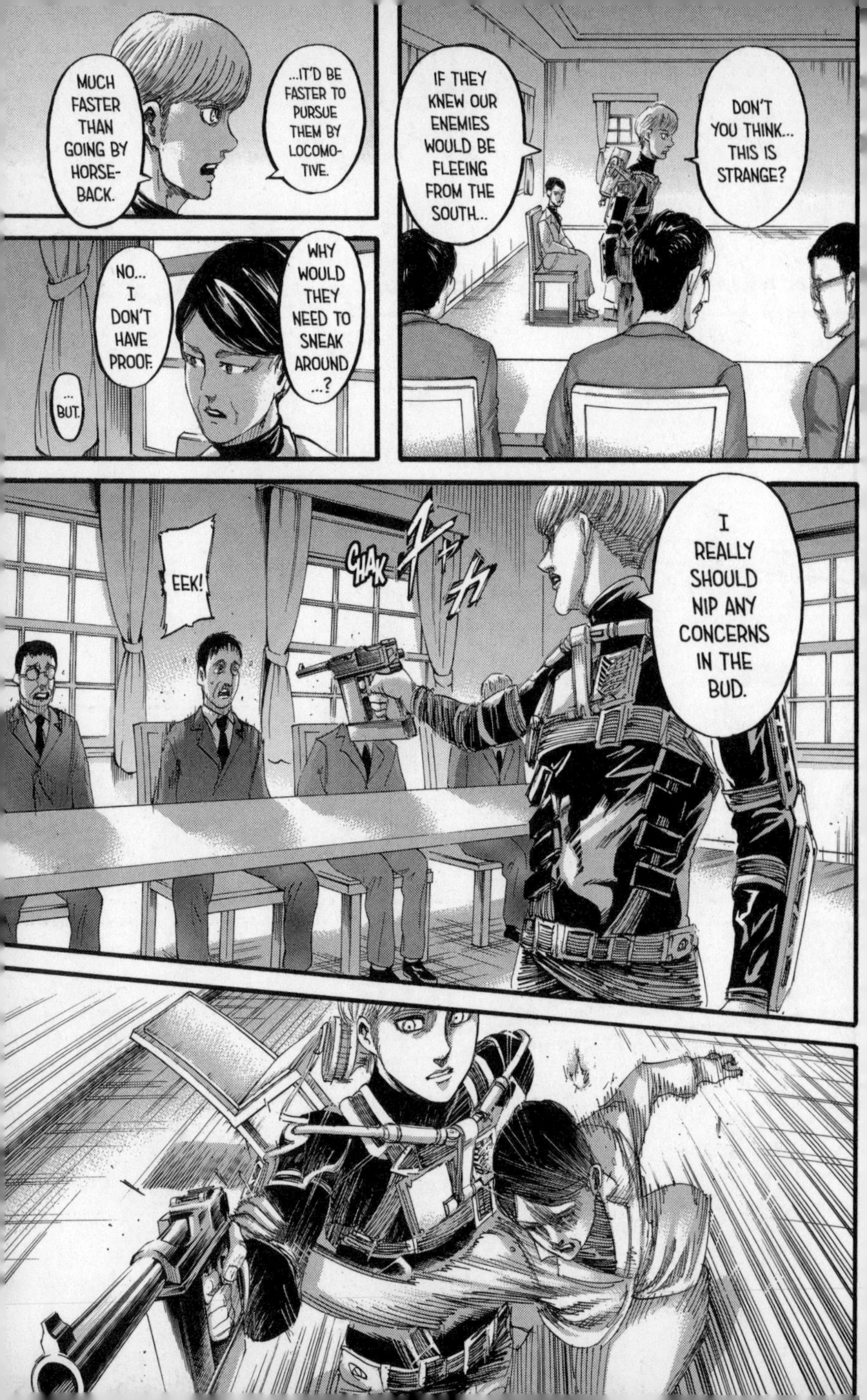
DON'T YOU THINK... THIS IS STRANGE?
IF THEY KNEW OUR ENEMIES WOULD BE FLEEING FROM THE SOUTH...
...IT'D BE FASTER TO PURSUE THEM BY LOCOMOTIVE.
MUCH FASTER THAN GOING BY HORSE-BACK.
WHY WOULD THEY NEED TO SNEAK AROUND ...?
NO... I DON'T HAVE PROOF.
... BUT.
I REALLY SHOULD NIP ANY CONCERNS IN THE BUD.
CHAK
EEK!

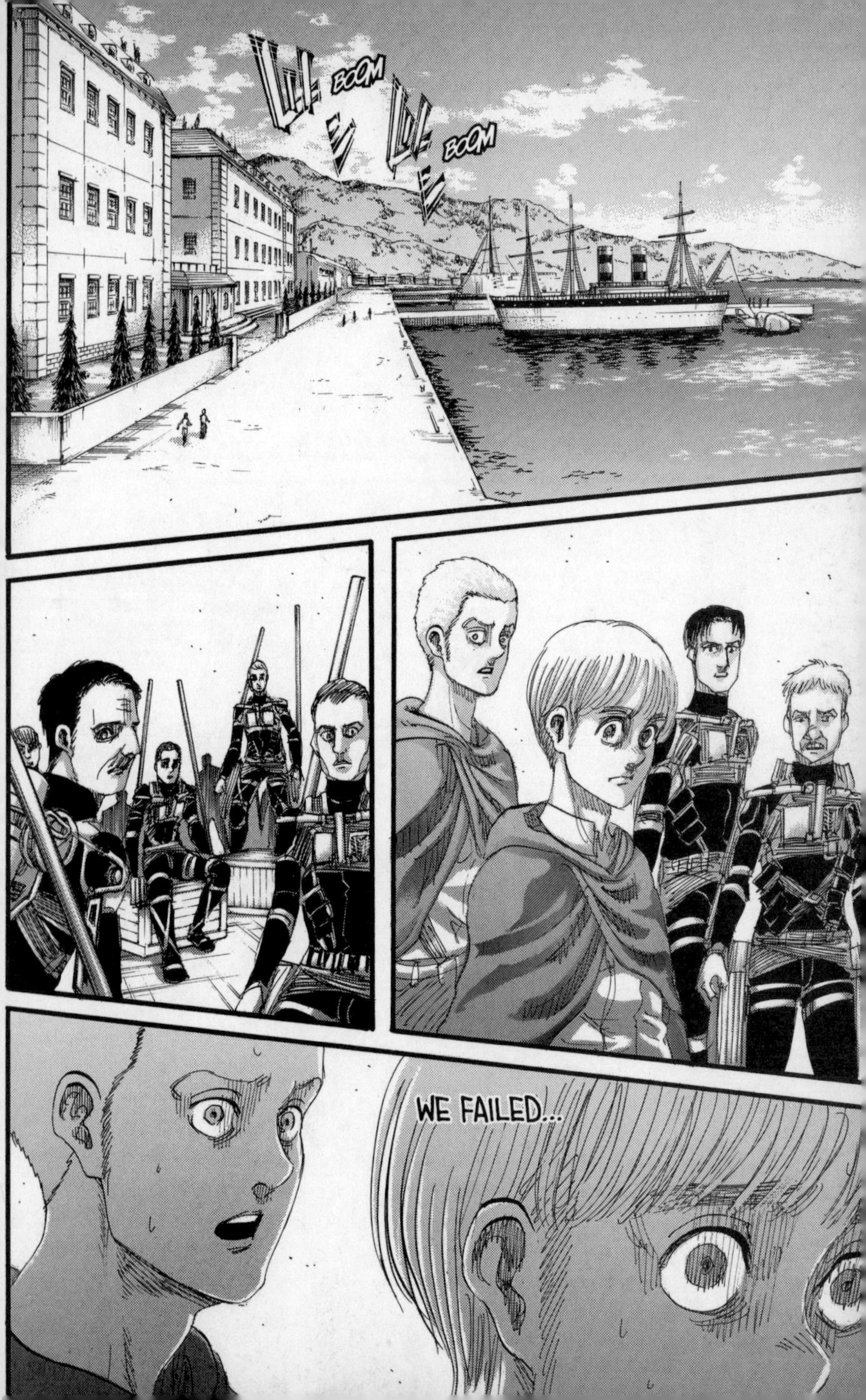
BOOM
BOOM
WE FAILED...

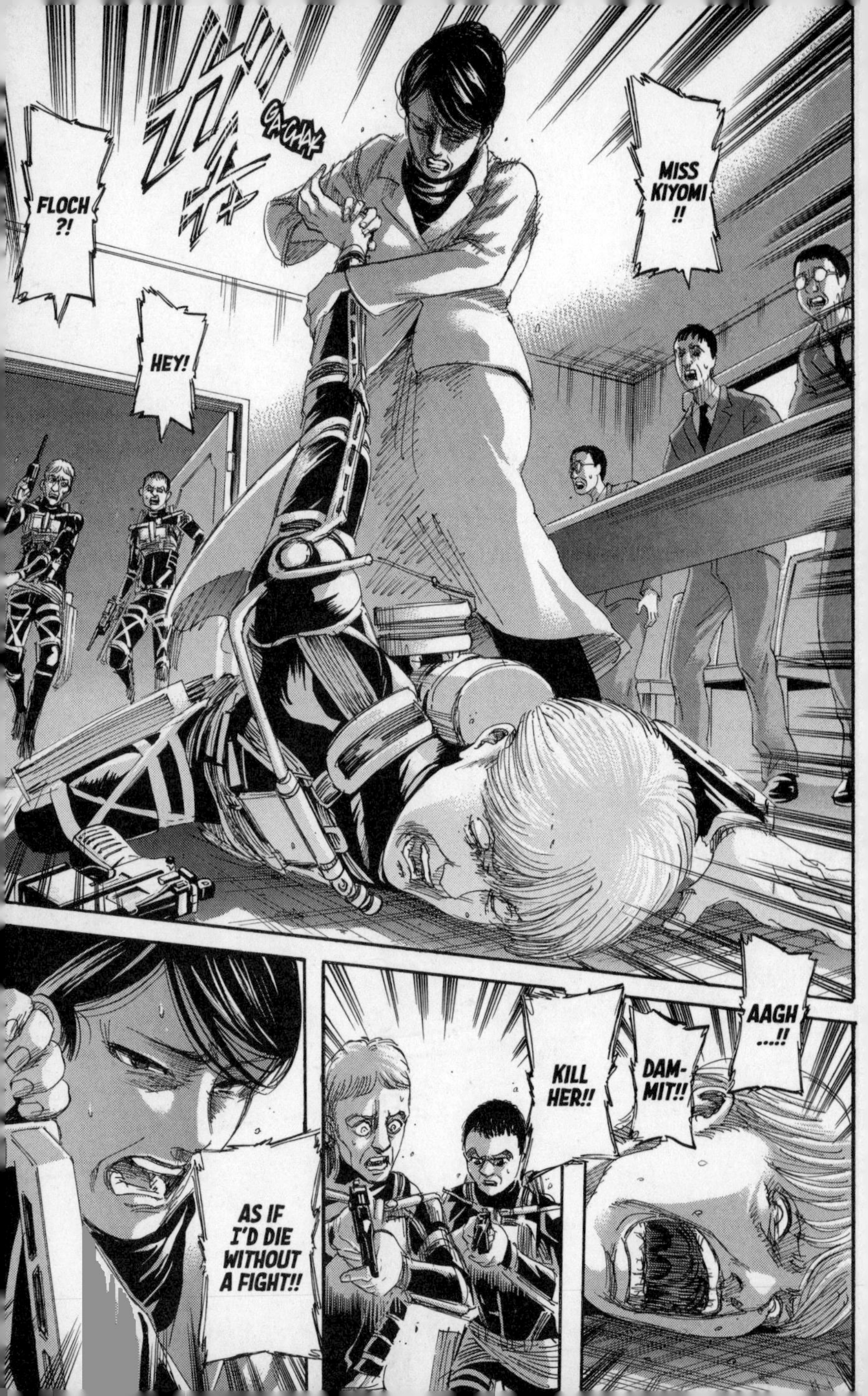
MISS KIYOMI!!
GA-CHA
FLOCH?!
HEY!
AAGH...!!
DAM-MIT!!
KILL HER!!
AS IF I'D DIE WITHOUT A FIGHT!!

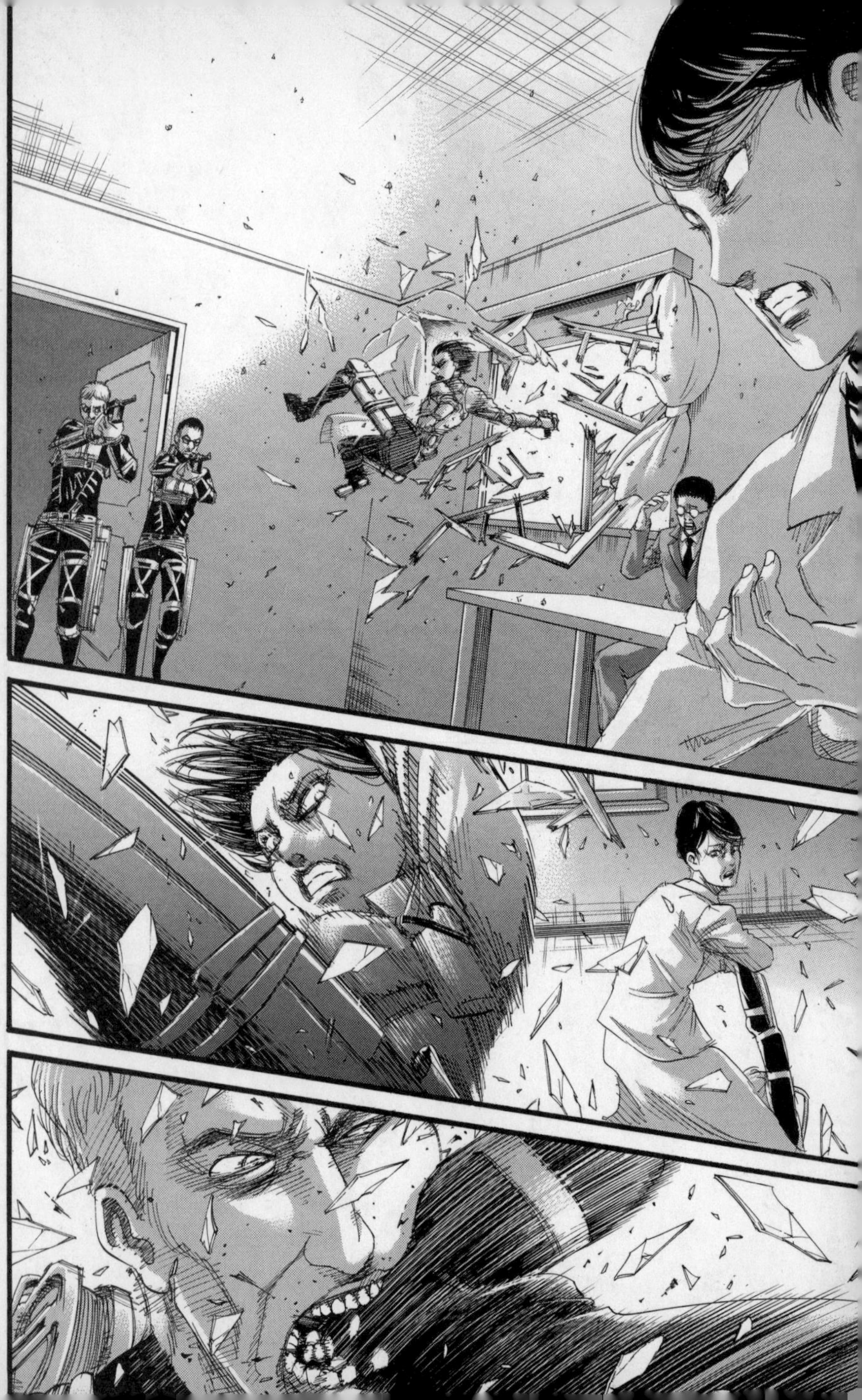

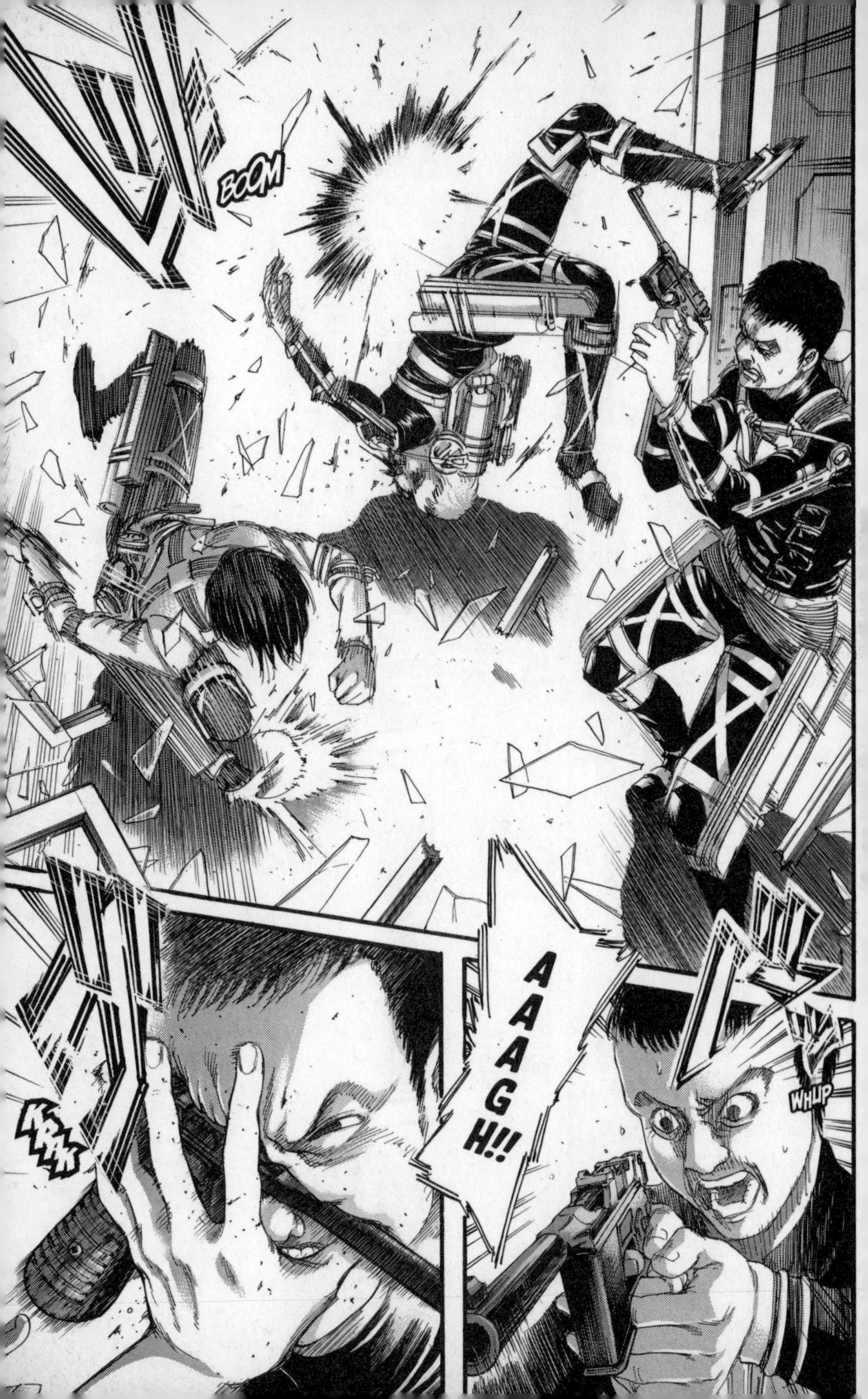
BOOM
WHUP
AAAAGH!!
KRAK

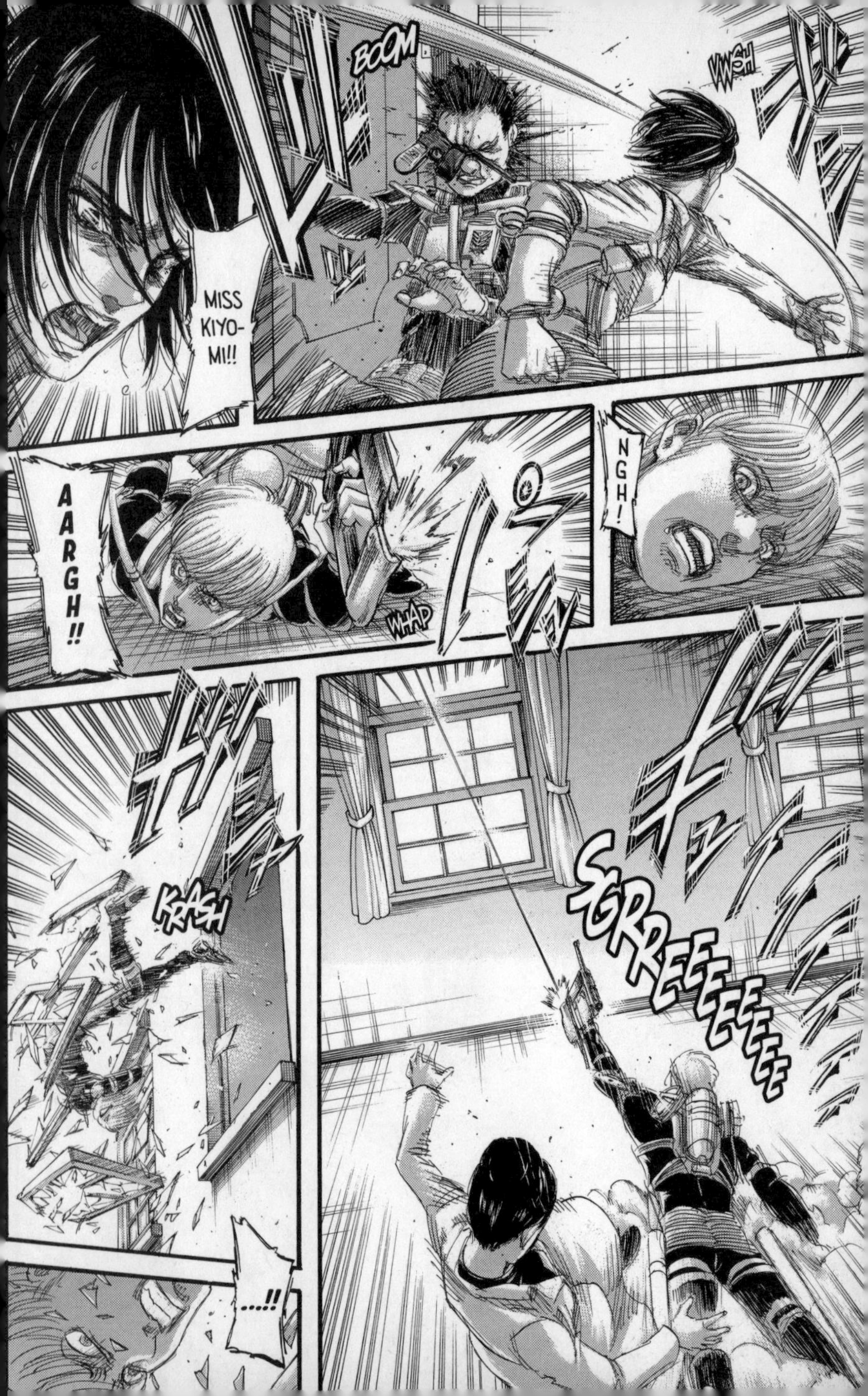
VWSH
BOOM
MISS KIYOMI!!
NGH!
AARGH!!
WHAP
SCREEEEEEEE
KRASH
...!!

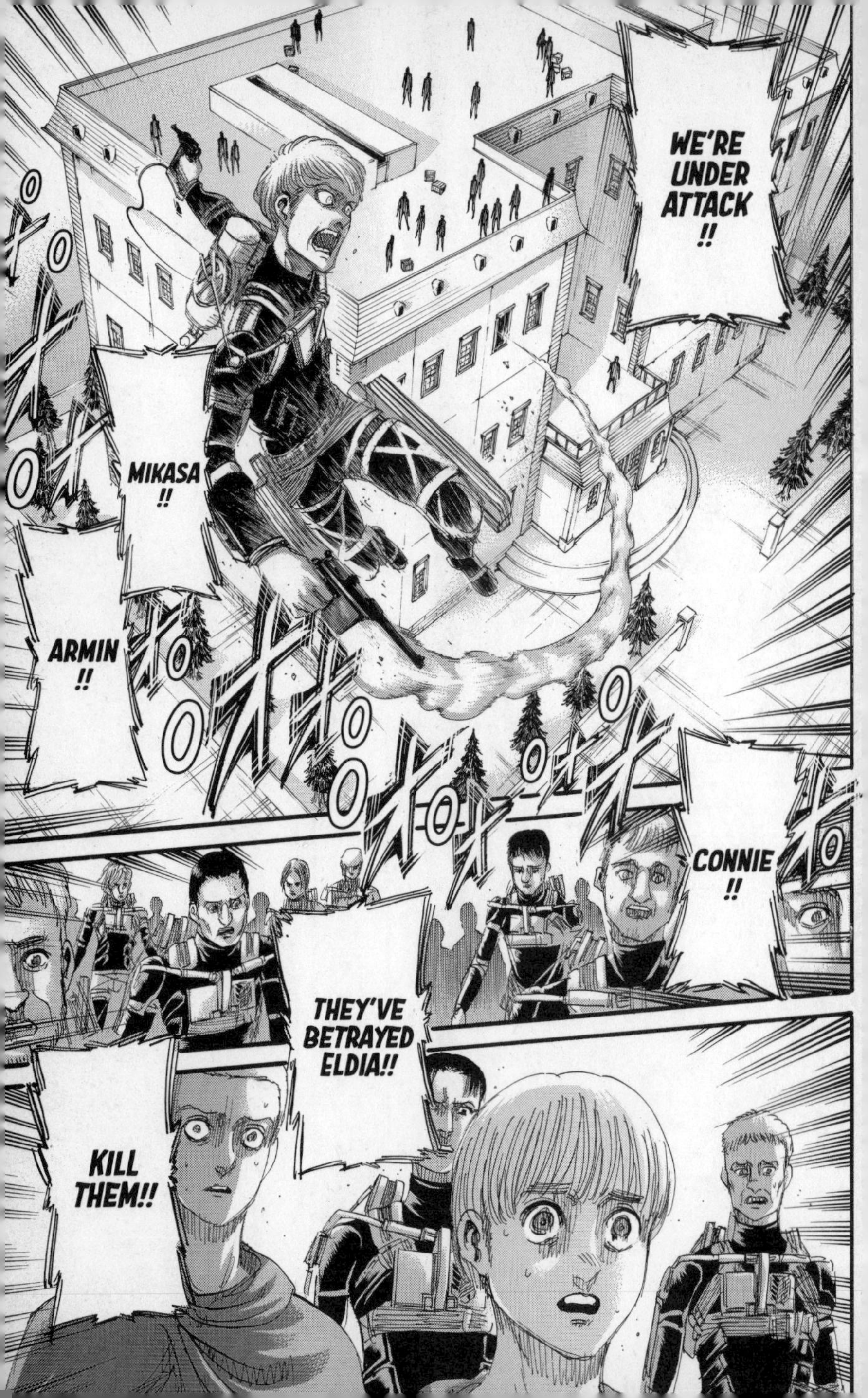
WE'RE UNDER ATTACK !!
MIKASA !!
ARMIN !!
CONNIE !!
THEY'VE BETRAYED ELDIA!!
KILL THEM!!

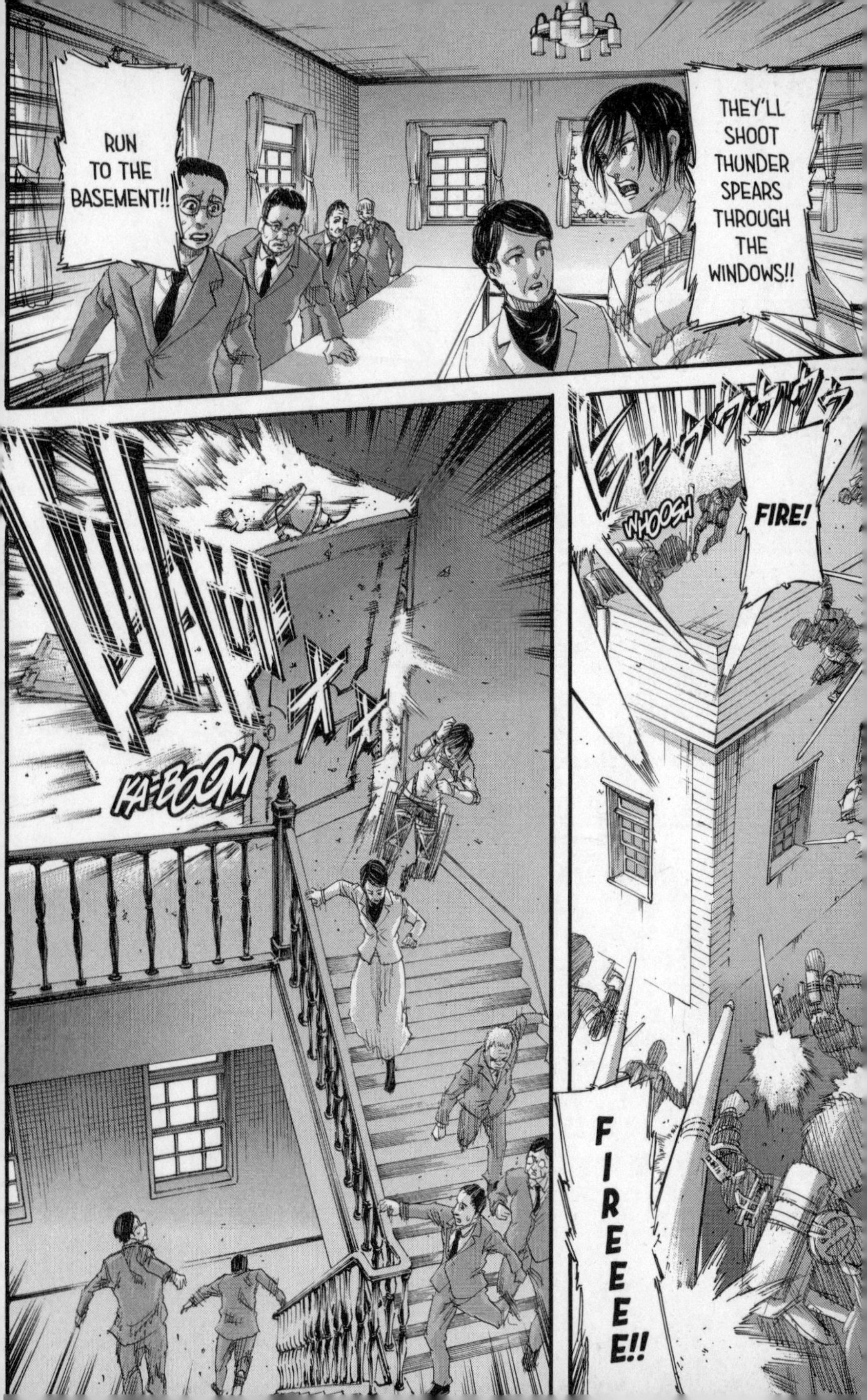
THEY'LL SHOOT THUNDER SPEARS THROUGH THE WINDOWS!!
RUN TO THE BASEMENT!!
FIRE!
WHOOSH
FIREEEE!!
KA-BOOM

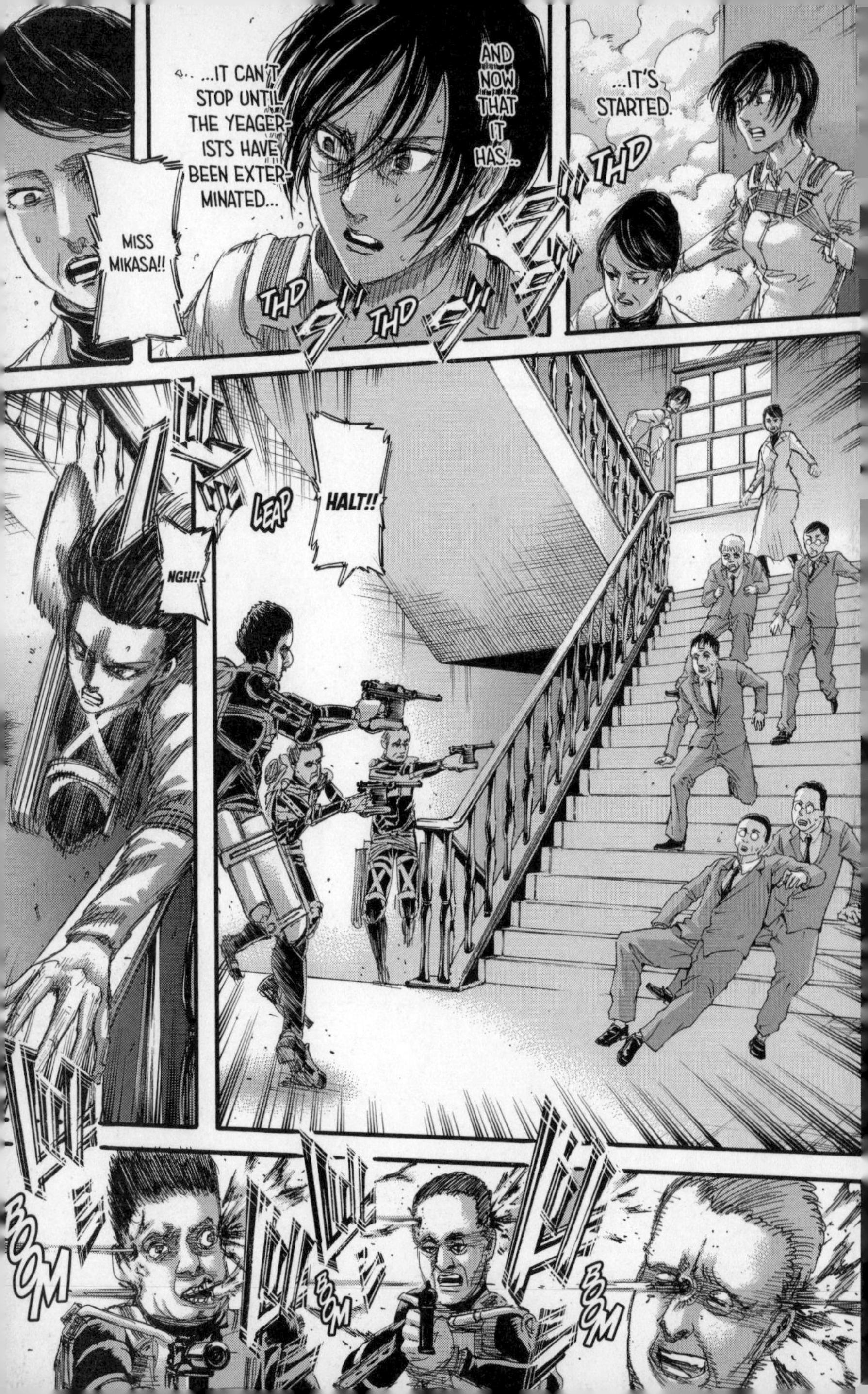
...IT'S STARTED.
THD
AND NOW THAT IT HAS...
...IT CAN'T STOP UNTIL THE YEAGERISTS HAVE BEEN EXTERMINATED...
THD
THD
MISS MIKASA!!
HALT!!
LEAP
NGH!!
BOOM
BOOM
BOOM

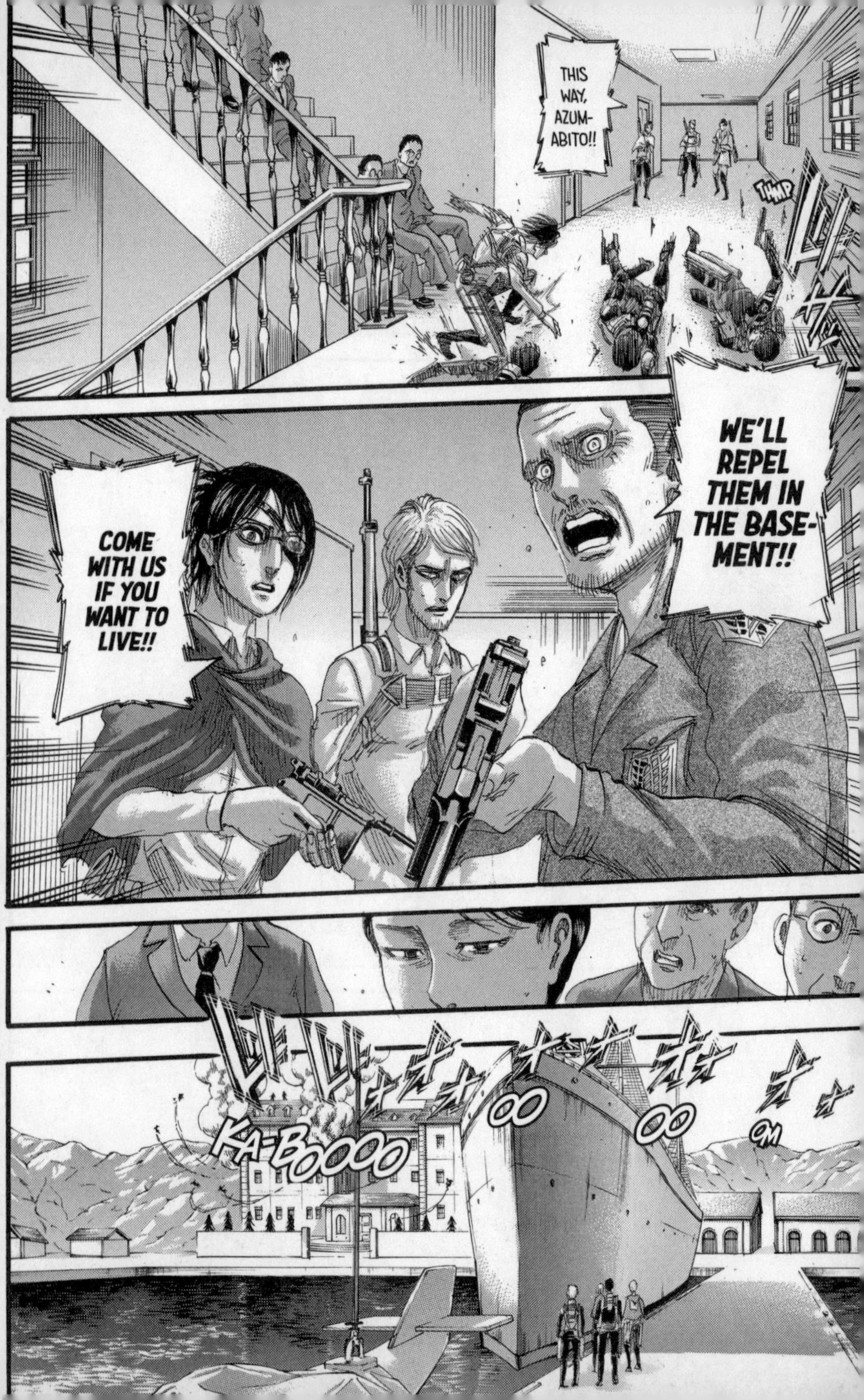
THIS WAY, AZUM-ABITO!!
THMP
WE'LL REPEL THEM IN THE BASE-MENT!!
COME WITH US IF YOU WANT TO LIVE!!
KA-BOOOOO
OOOO
OM

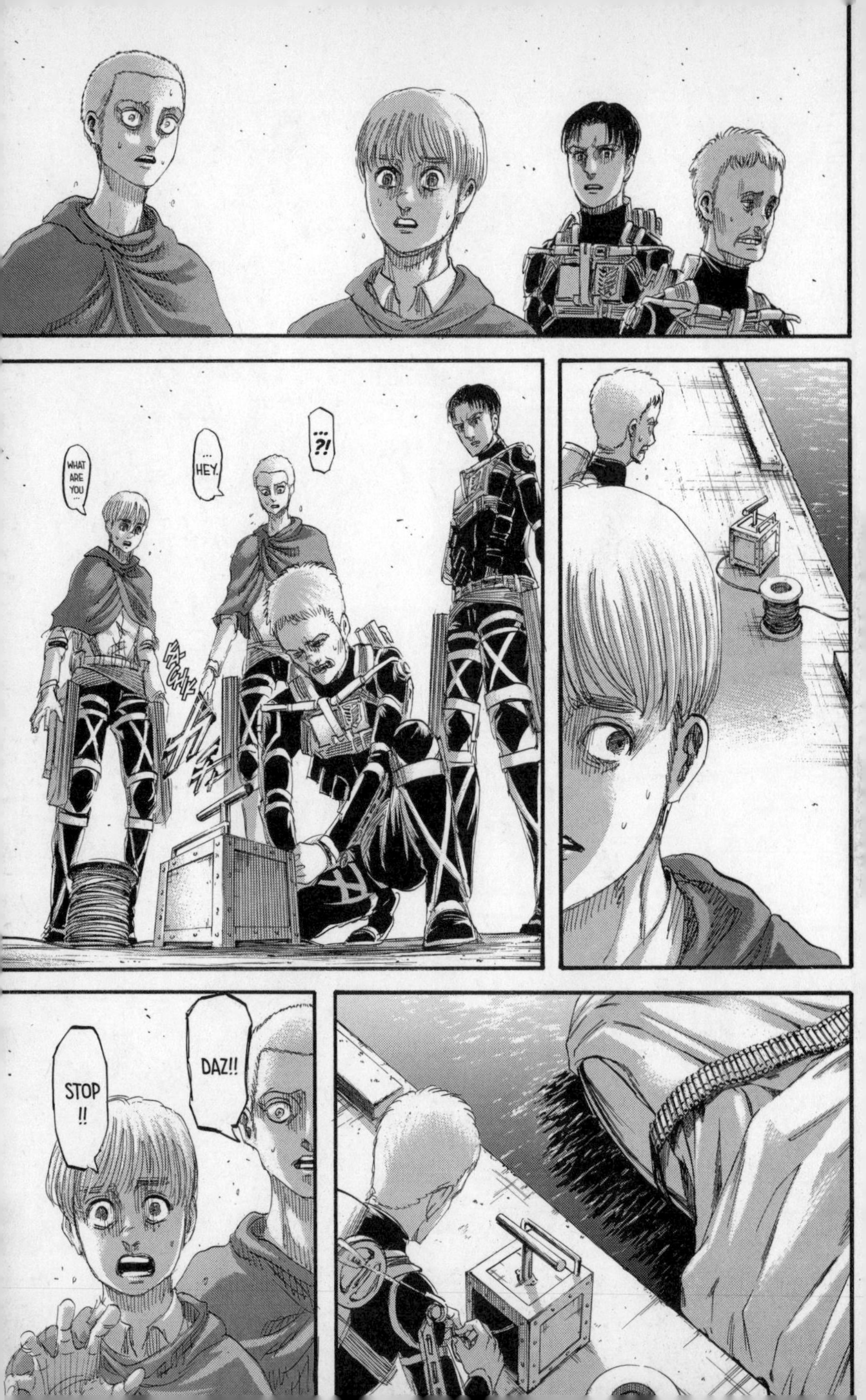
...?!
... HEY.
WHAT ARE YOU ...
DAZ!!
STOP !!

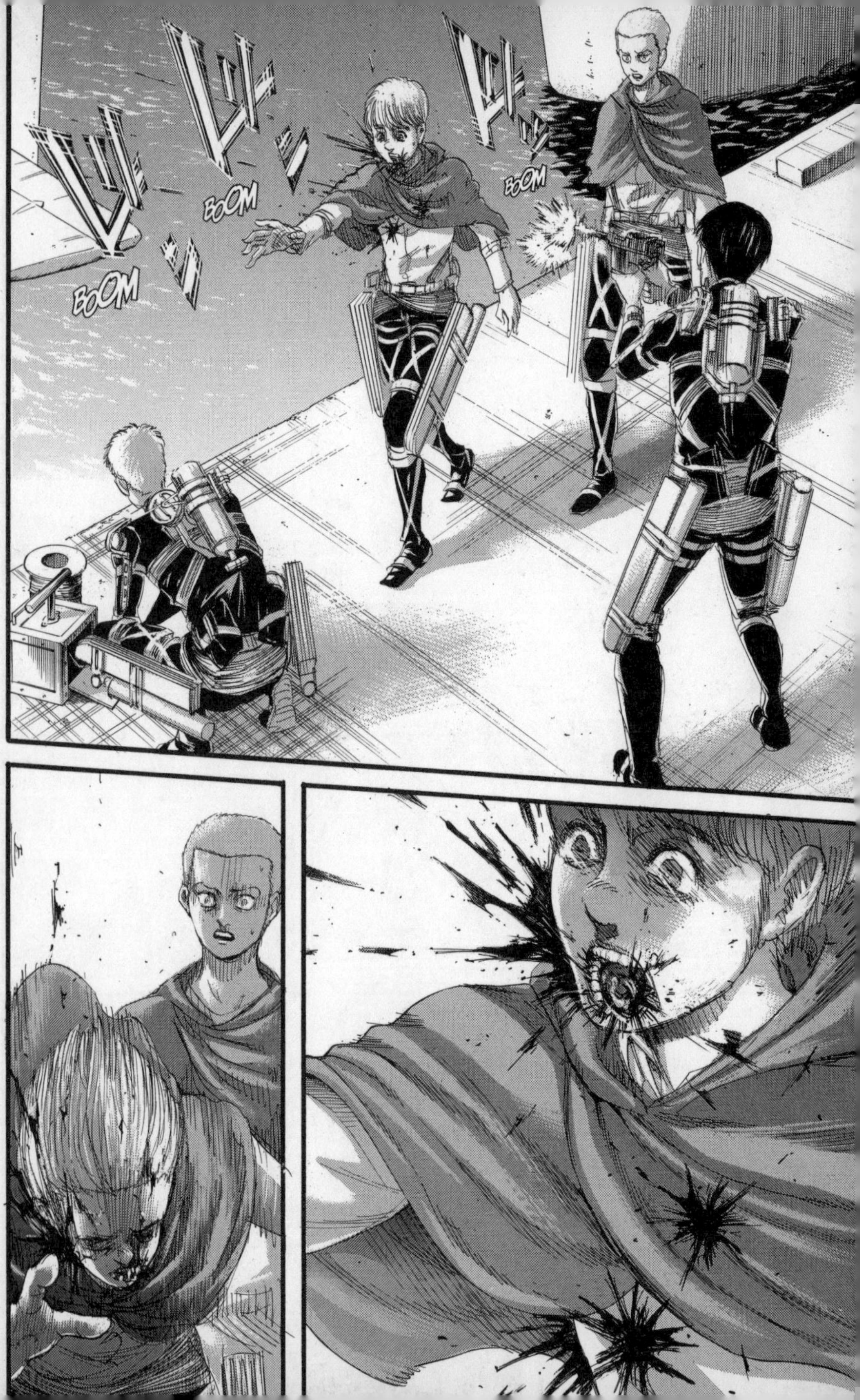
BOOM
BOOM
BOOM

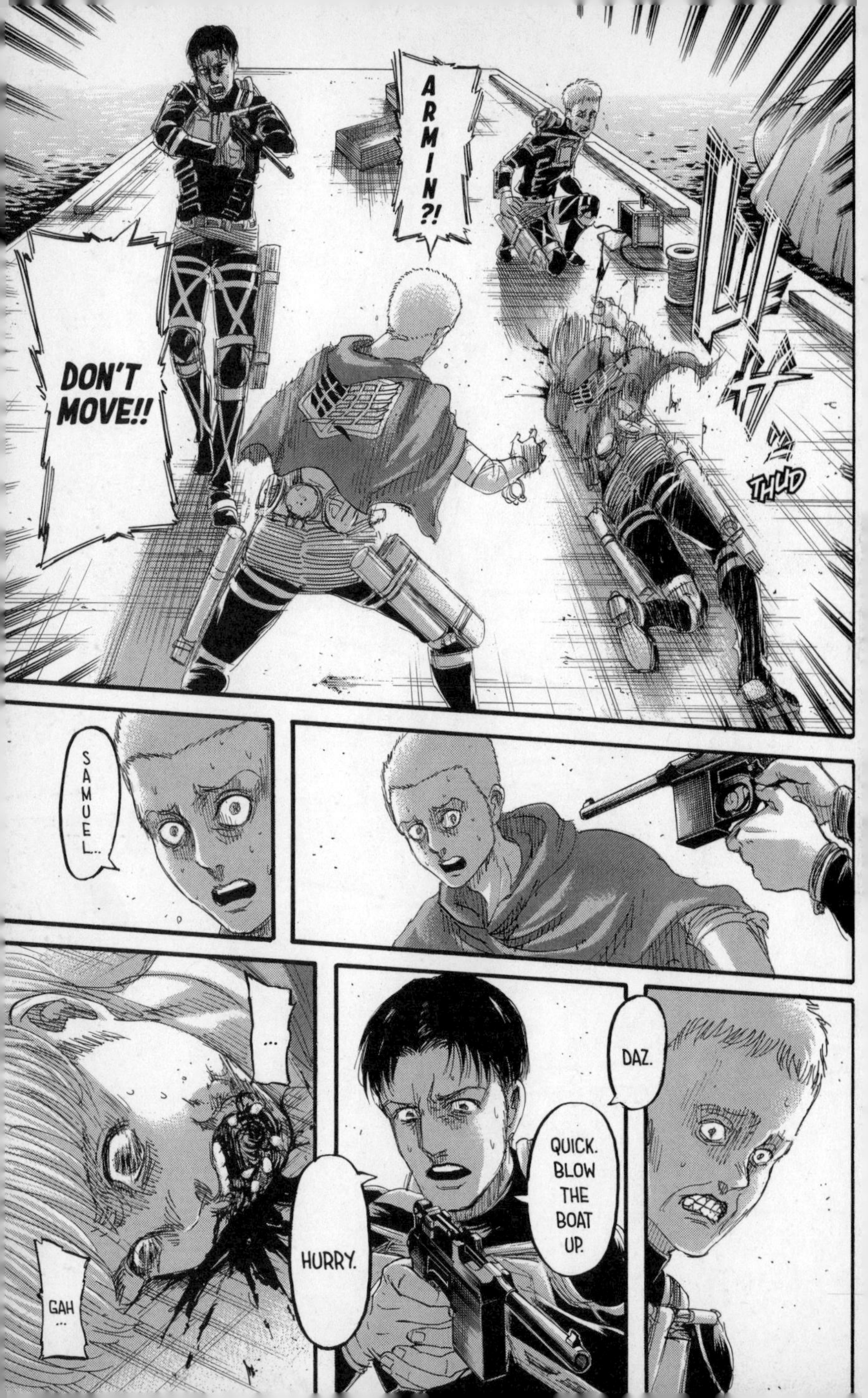
ARMIN?!
THUD
DON'T MOVE!!
SAMUEL...
DAZ.
QUICK. BLOW THE BOAT UP.
HURRY.
...
GAH ...

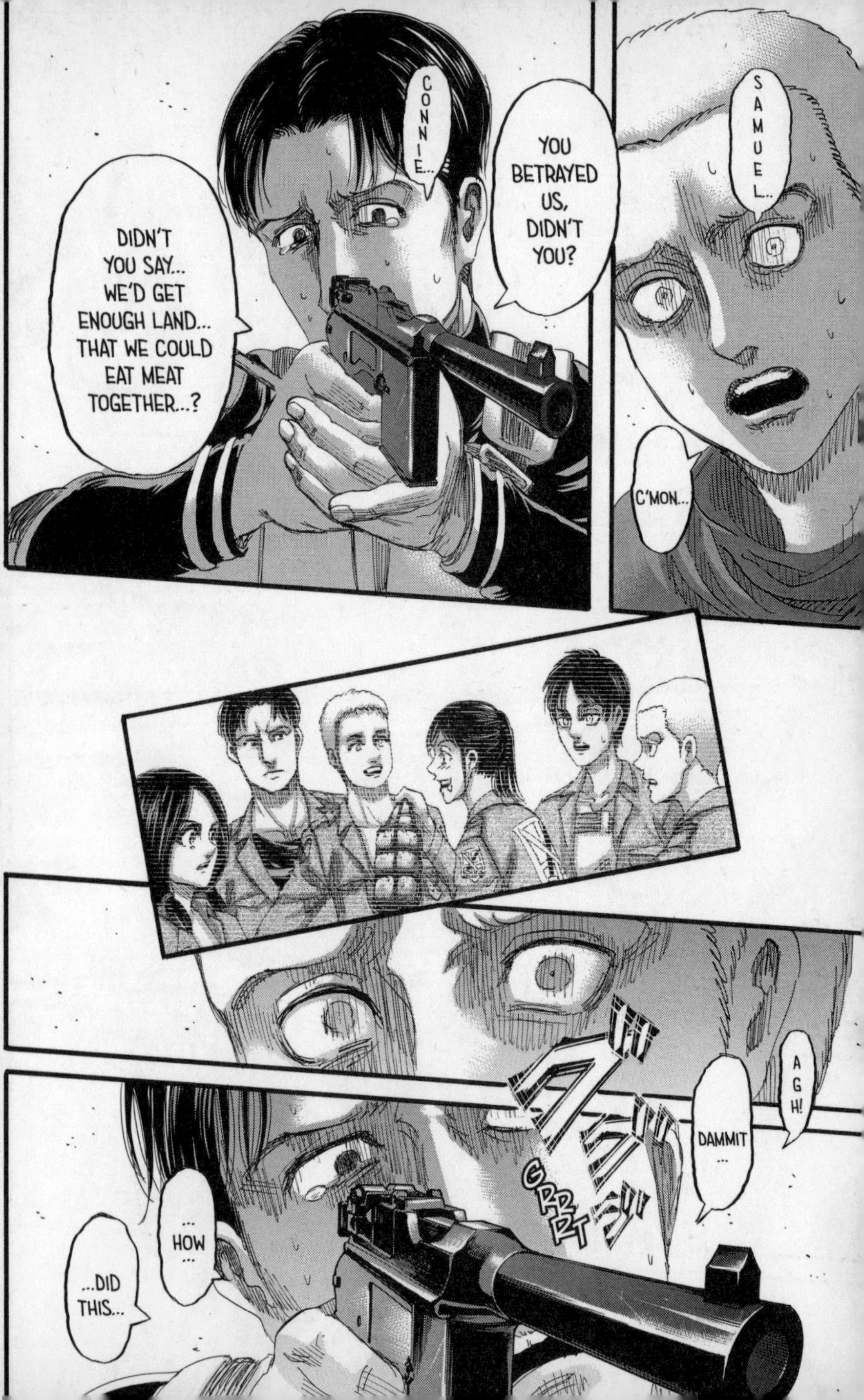
SAMUEL..
C'MON...
CONNIE..
YOU BETRAYED US, DIDN'T YOU?
DIDN'T YOU SAY... WE'D GET ENOUGH LAND... THAT WE COULD EAT MEAT TOGETHER...?
AGH!
DAMMIT ...
GRRRT
... HOW ...
...DID THIS...

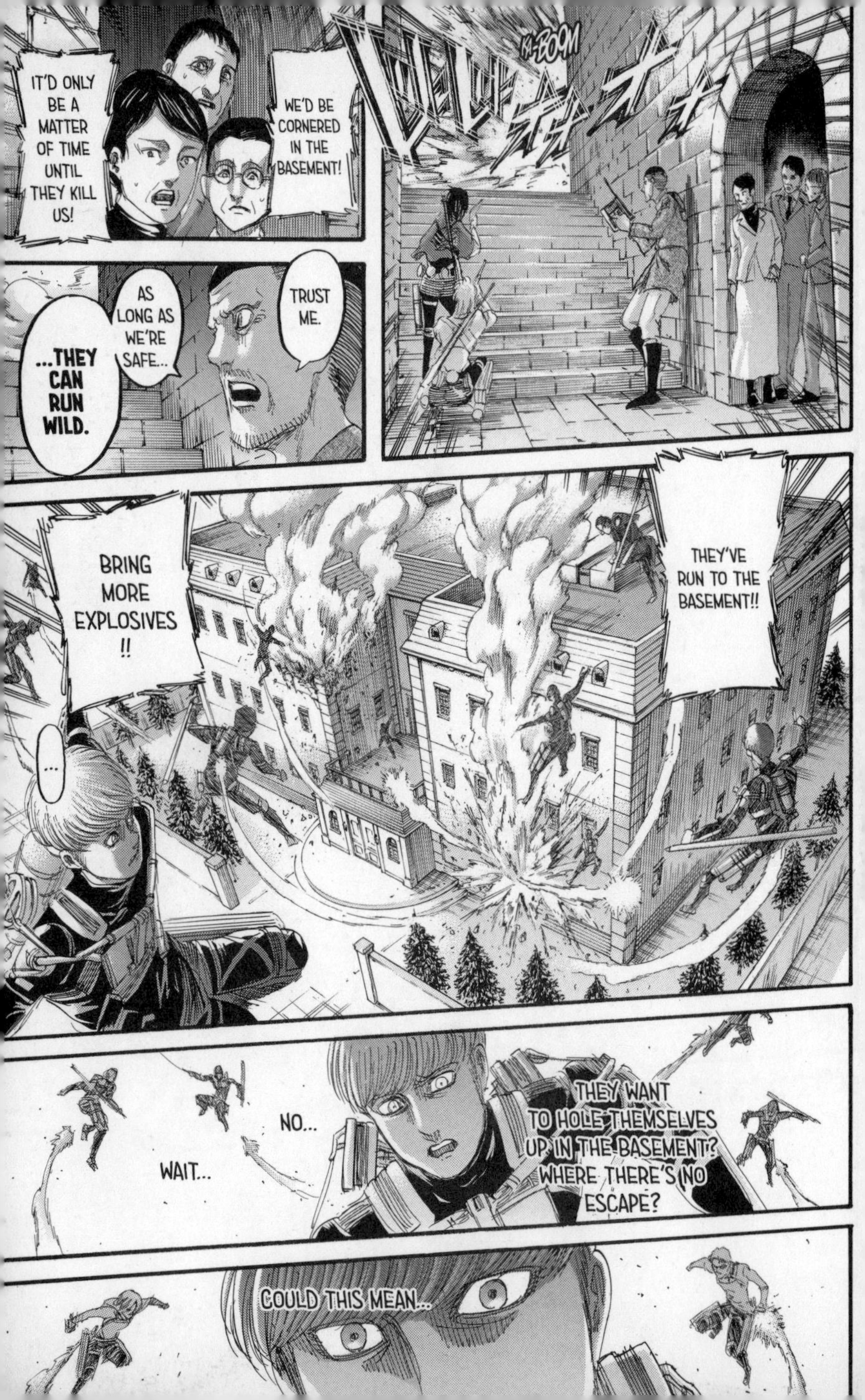
KA-BOOM
WE'D BE CORNERED IN THE BASEMENT!
IT'D ONLY BE A MATTER OF TIME UNTIL THEY KILL US!
TRUST ME.
AS LONG AS WE'RE SAFE...
...THEY CAN RUN WILD.
THEY'VE RUN TO THE BASEMENT!!
BRING MORE EXPLOSIVES !!
...
THEY WANT TO HOLE THEMSELVES UP IN THE BASEMENT? WHERE THERE'S NO ESCAPE?
NO...
WAIT...
COULD THIS MEAN...

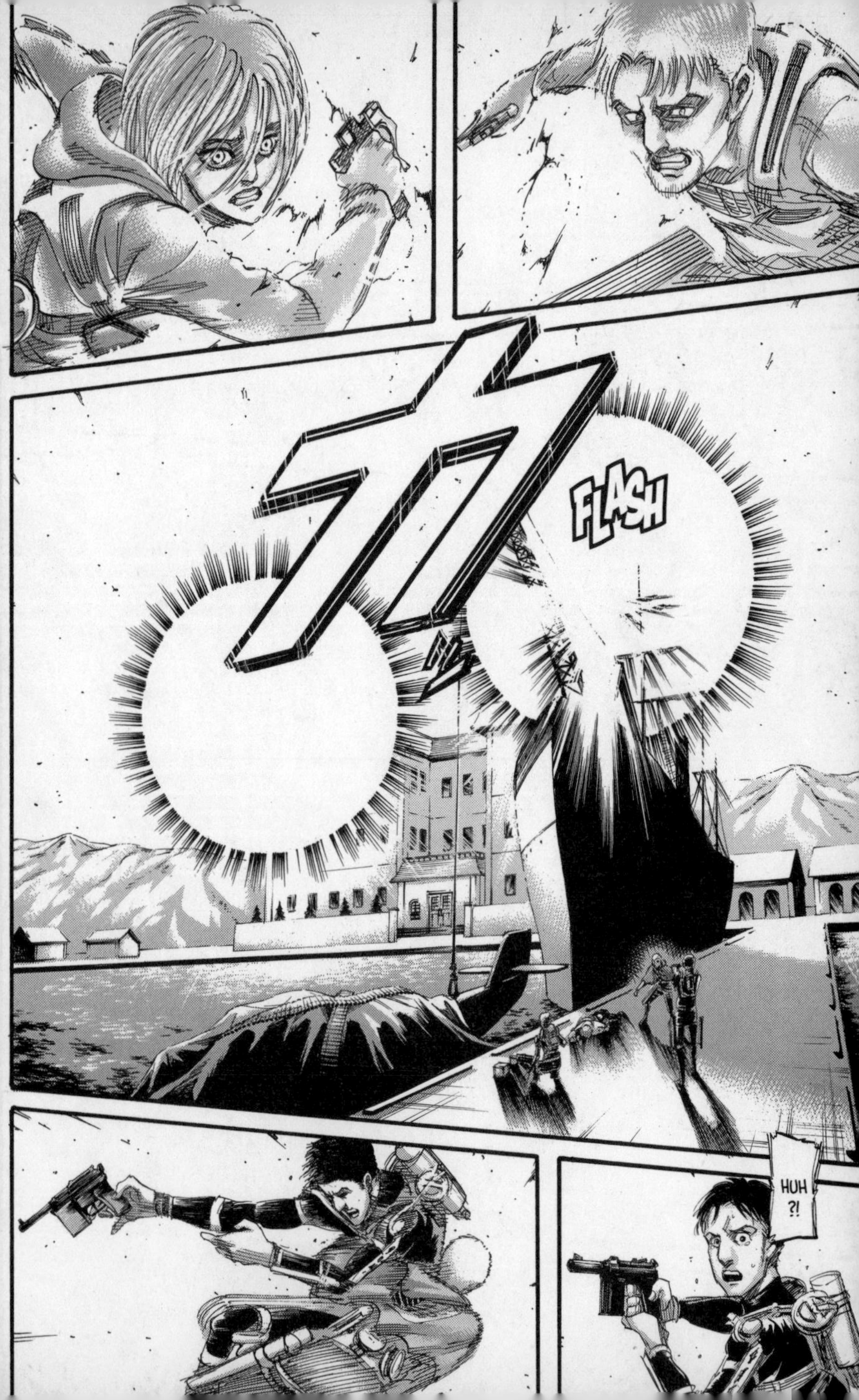
カッ
FLASH
HUH ?!

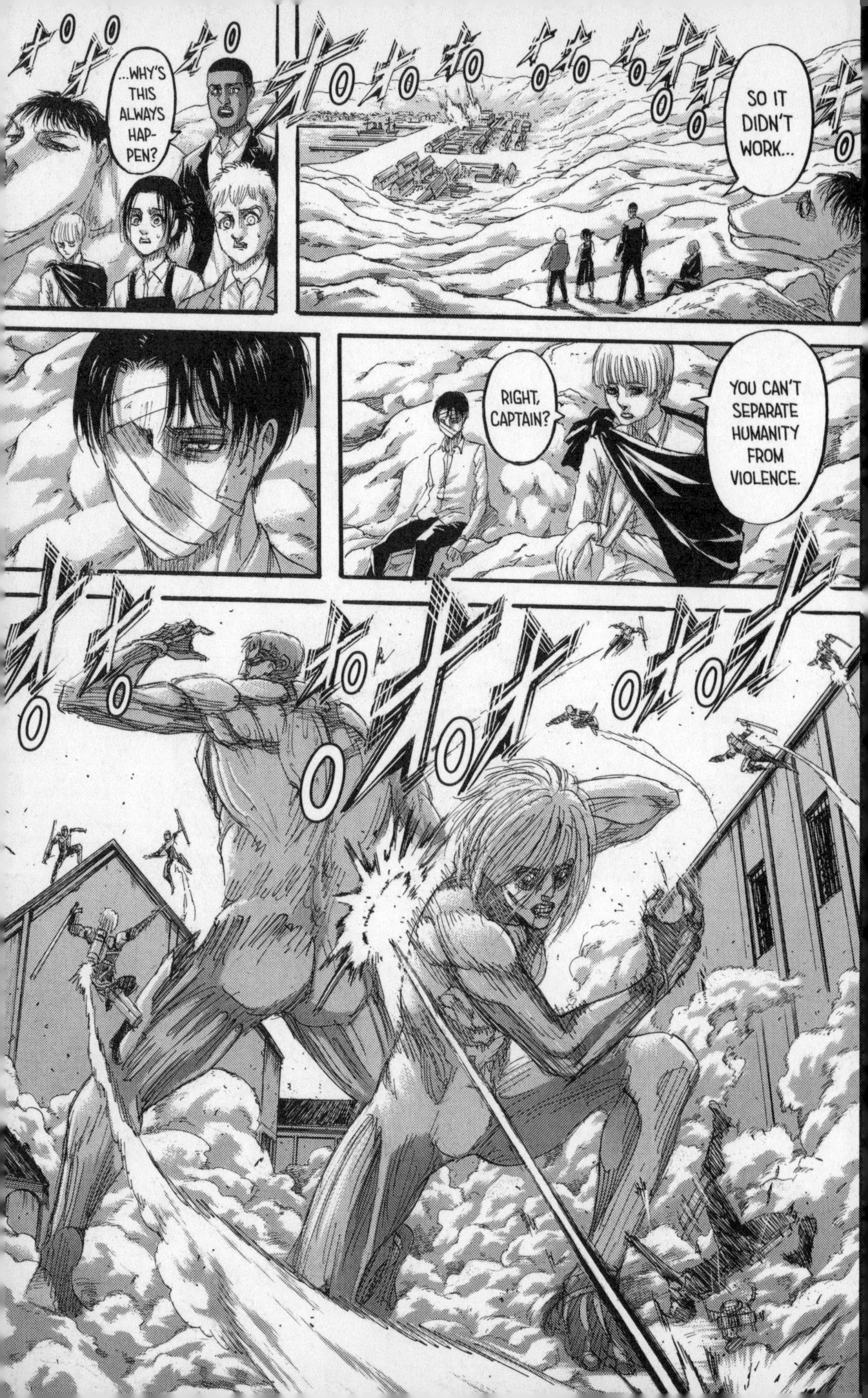
SO IT DIDN'T WORK...
...WHY'S THIS ALWAYS HAP-PEN?
YOU CAN'T SEPARATE HUMANITY FROM VIOLENCE.
RIGHT, CAPTAIN?

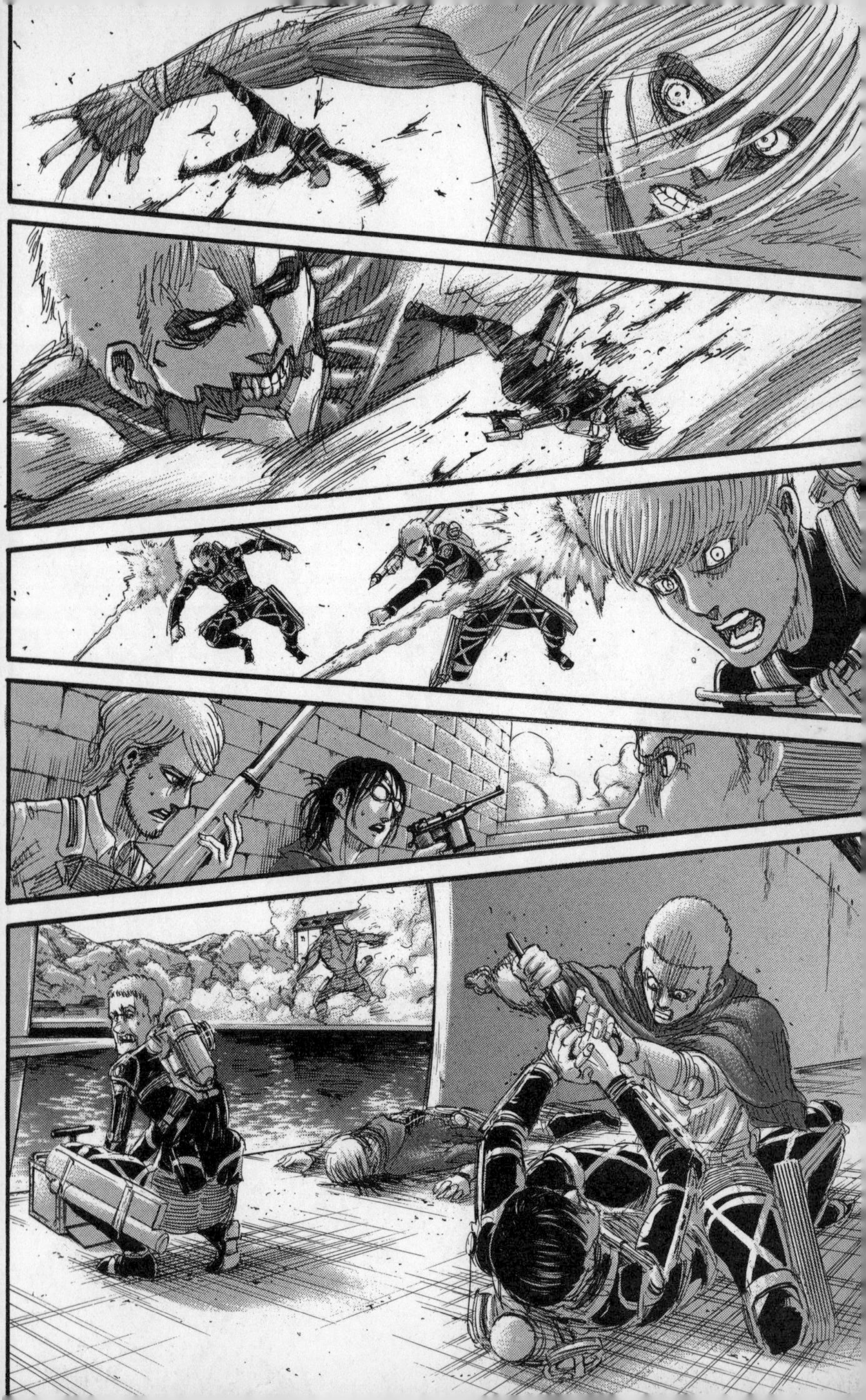

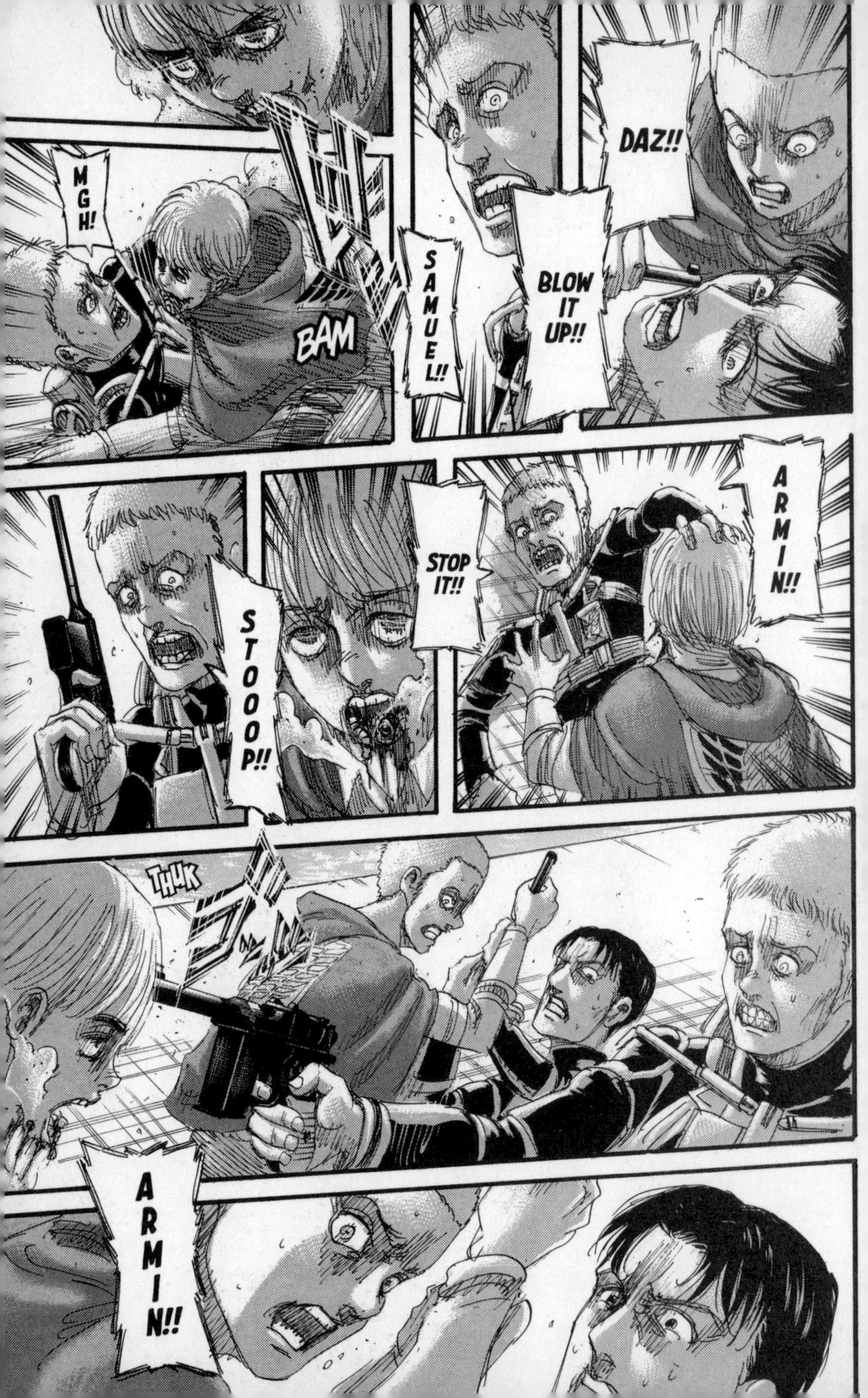
DAZ!!
BLOW IT UP!!
SAMUEL!!
MGH!
BAM
ARMIN!!
STOP IT!!
STOOOOP!!
THUK
ARMIN!!

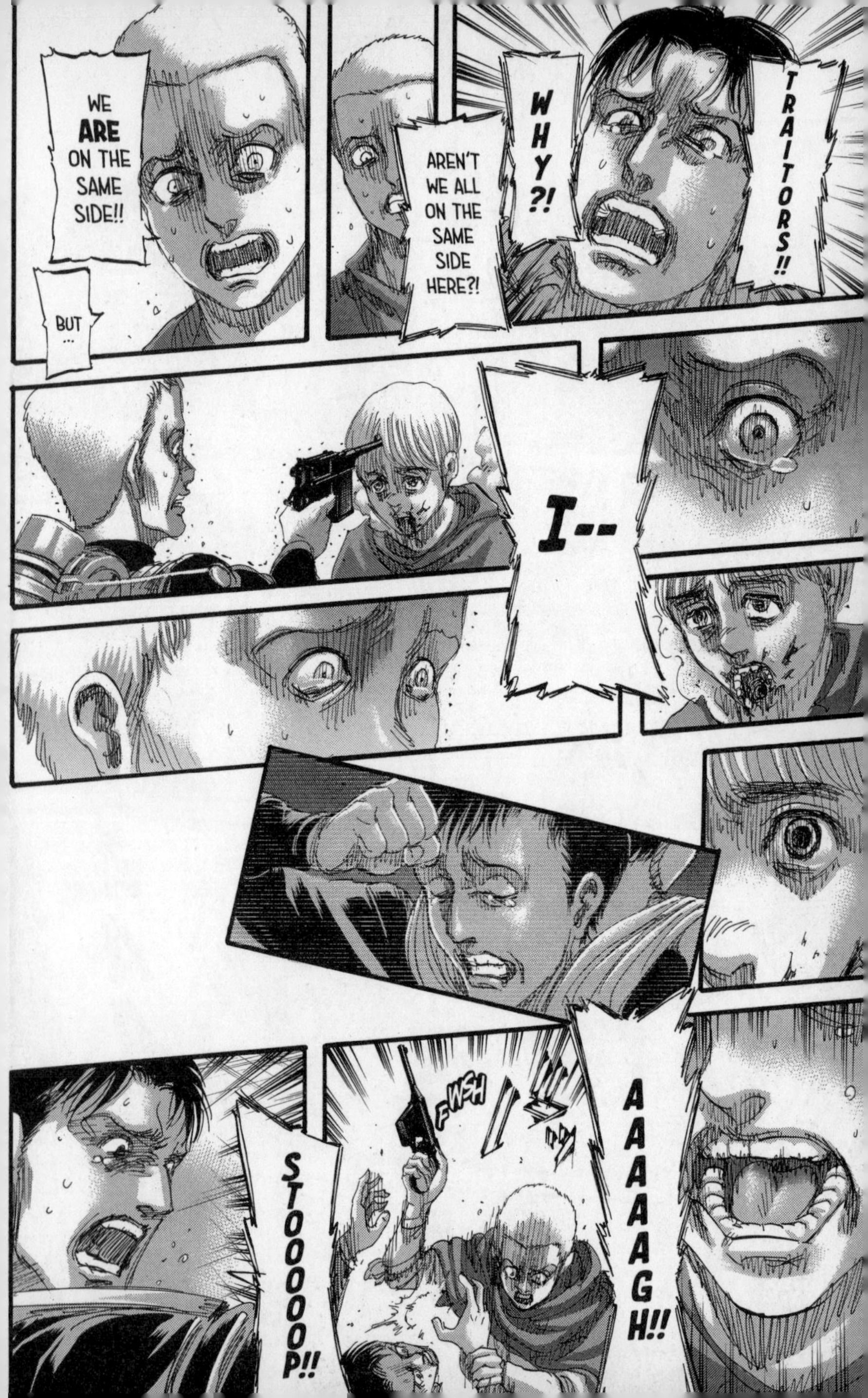
TRAITORS!!
WHY?!
AREN'T WE ALL ON THE SAME SIDE HERE?!
WE **ARE** ON THE SAME SIDE!!
BUT ...
I--
AAAAAAGH!!
FWSH
STOOOOOOP!!

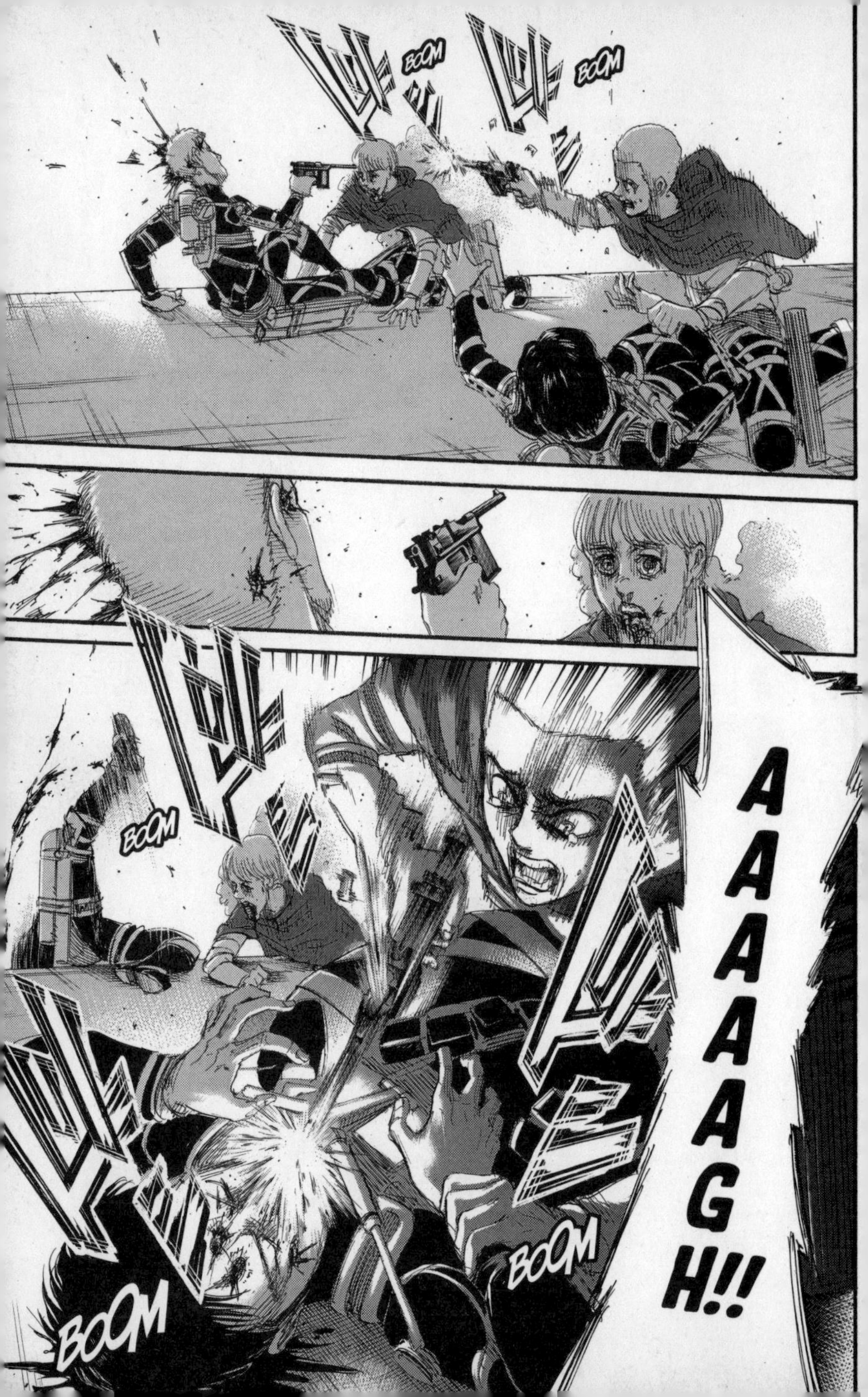
BOOM
BOOM
AAAAAAAGH!!
BOOM
BOOM
BOOM

ATTACK on TITAN

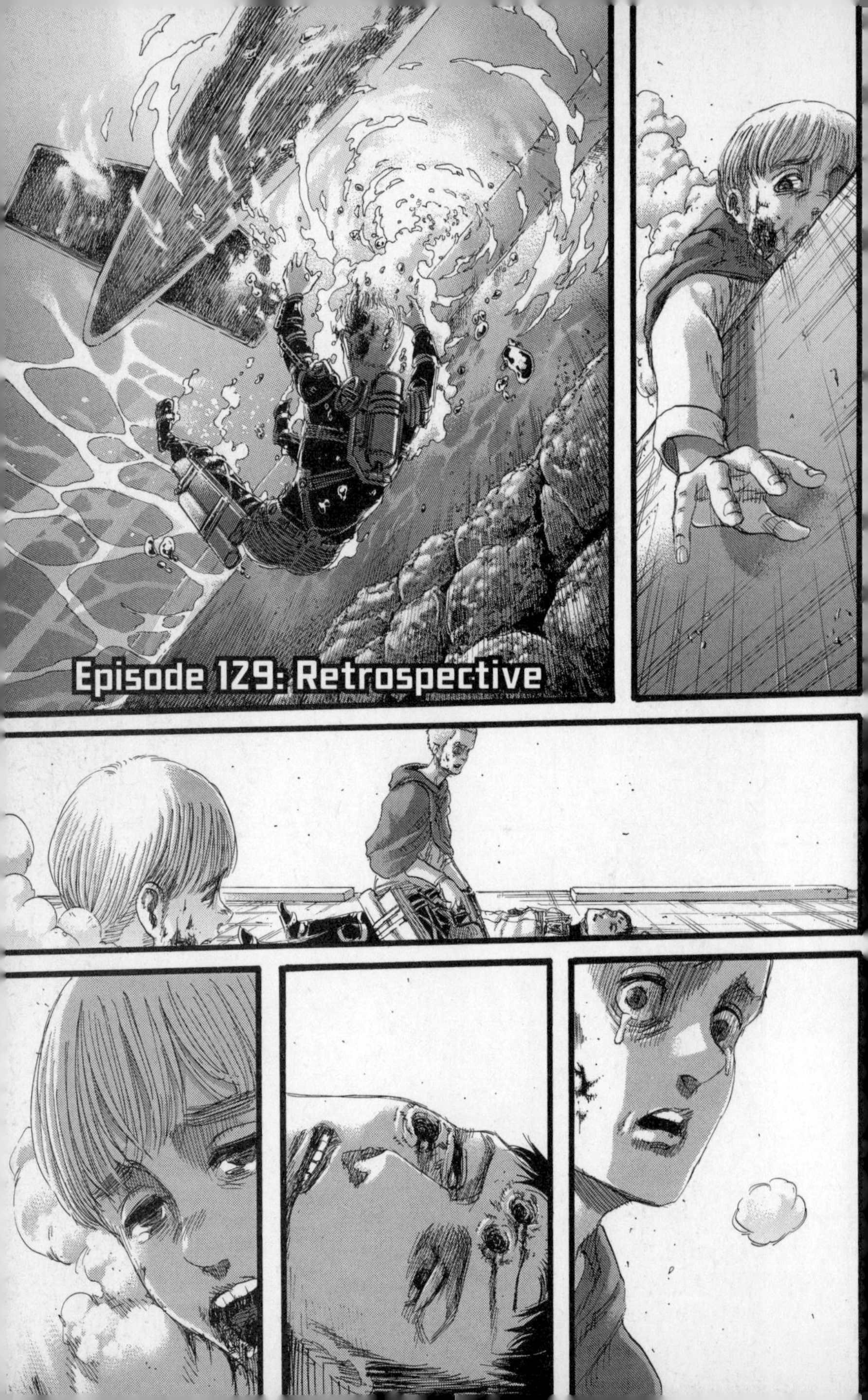
Episode 129: Retrospective

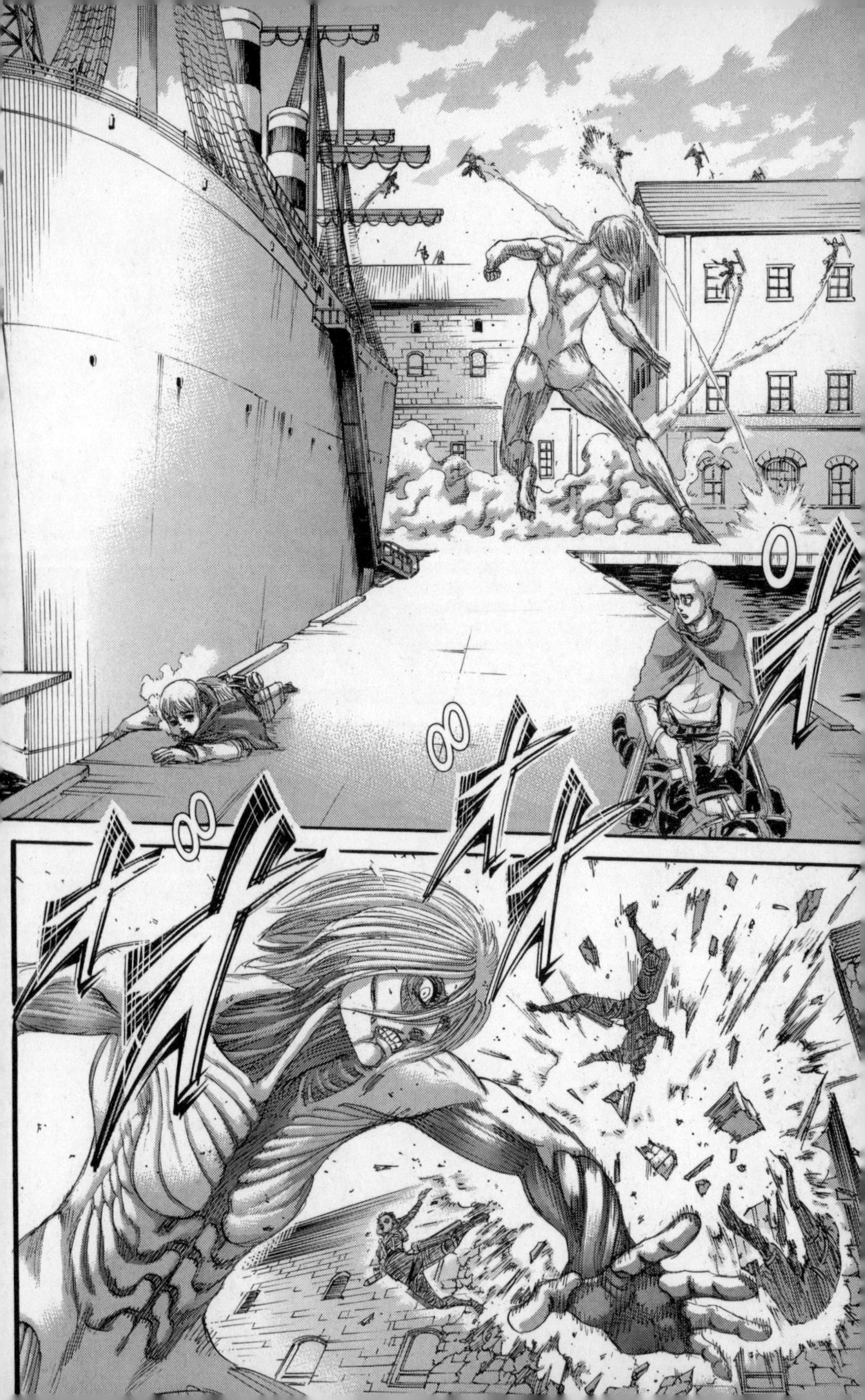

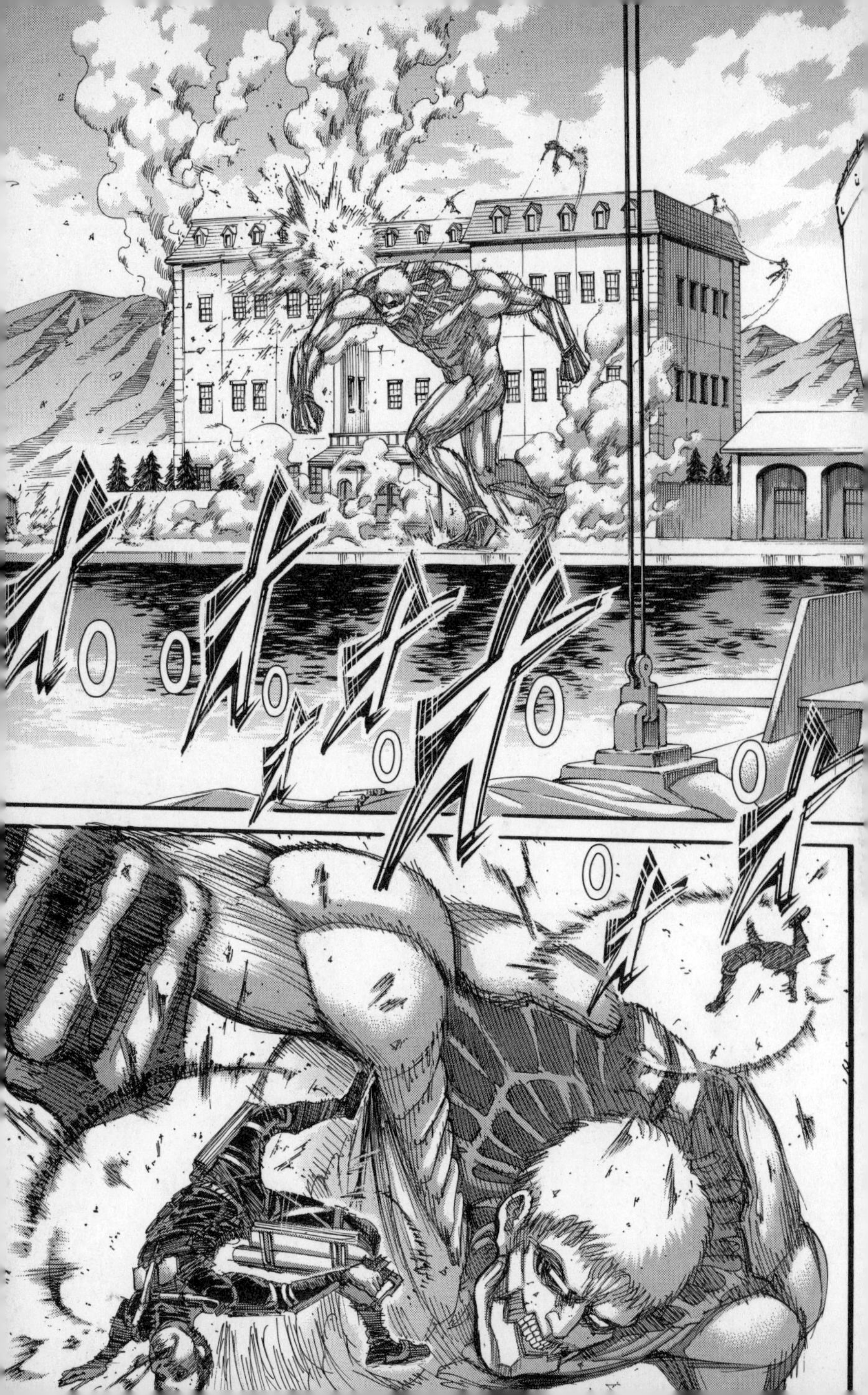

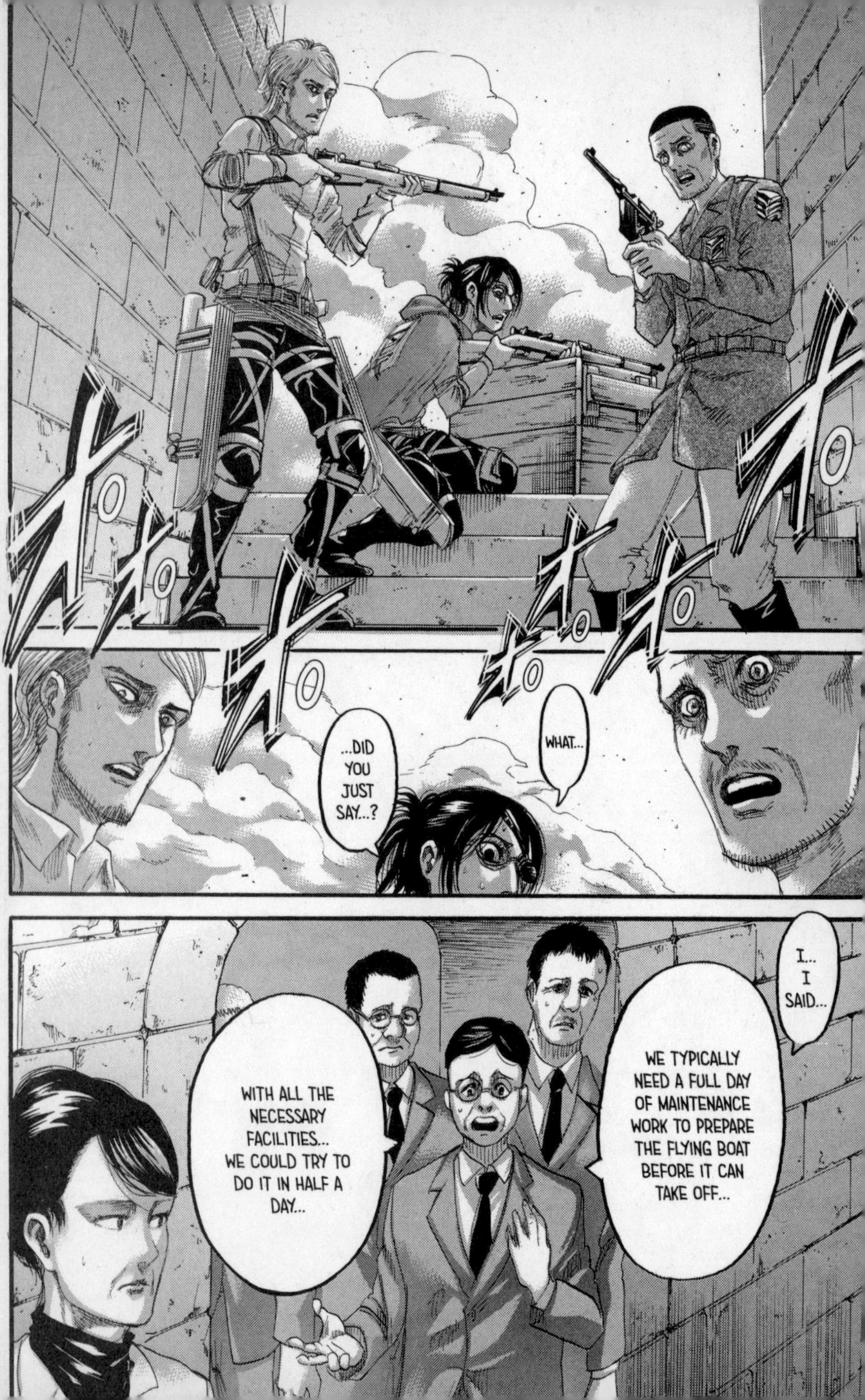
WHAT...
...DID YOU JUST SAY...?
I... I SAID...
WE TYPICALLY NEED A FULL DAY OF MAINTENANCE WORK TO PREPARE THE FLYING BOAT BEFORE IT CAN TAKE OFF...
WITH ALL THE NECESSARY FACILITIES... WE COULD TRY TO DO IT IN HALF A DAY...

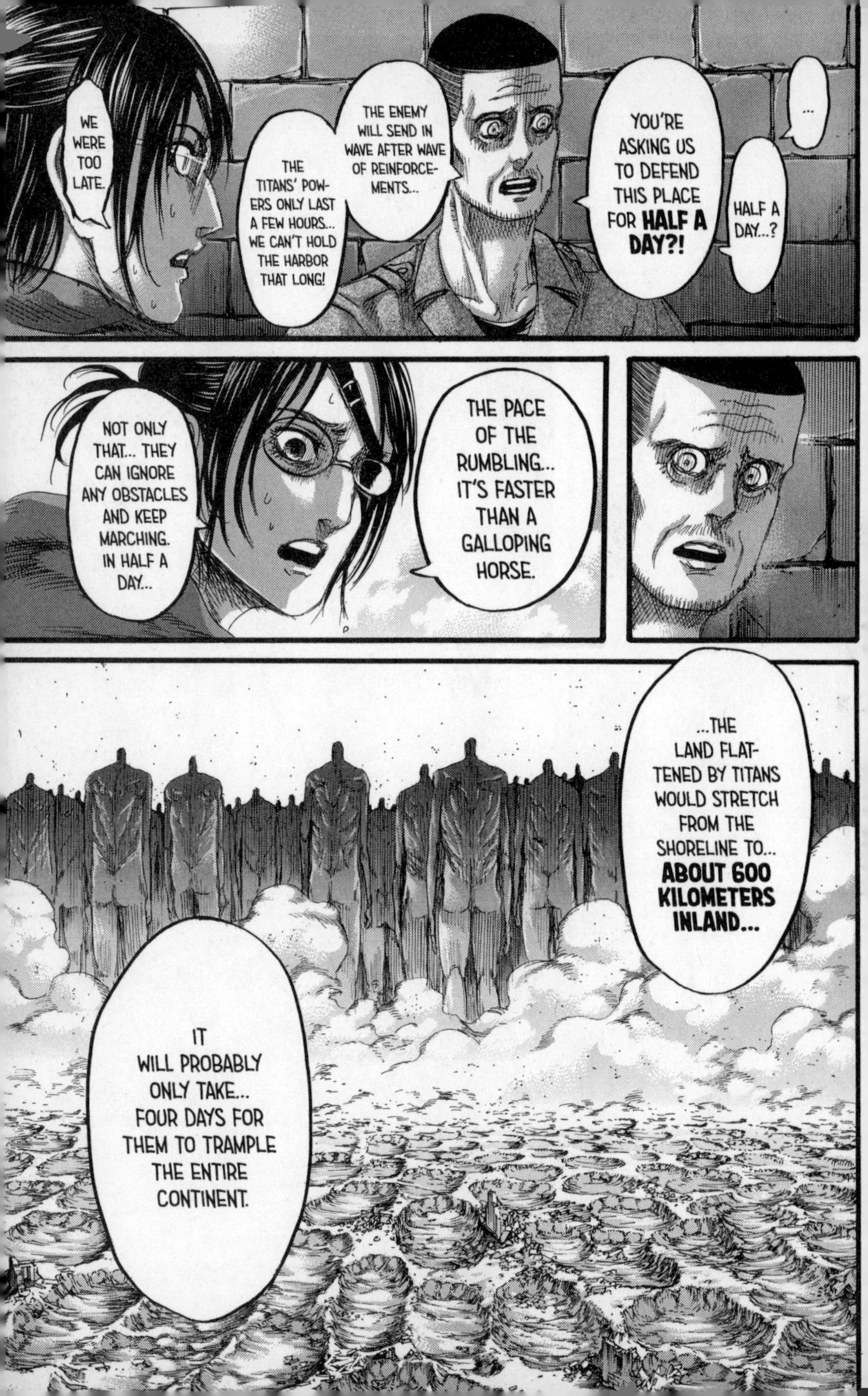
...
HALF A DAY...?
YOU'RE ASKING US TO DEFEND THIS PLACE FOR HALF A DAY?!
THE ENEMY WILL SEND IN WAVE AFTER WAVE OF REINFORCEMENTS...
THE TITANS' POWERS ONLY LAST A FEW HOURS... WE CAN'T HOLD THE HARBOR THAT LONG!
WE WERE TOO LATE.
THE PACE OF THE RUMBLING... IT'S FASTER THAN A GALLOPING HORSE.
NOT ONLY THAT... THEY CAN IGNORE ANY OBSTACLES AND KEEP MARCHING. IN HALF A DAY...
...THE LAND FLATTENED BY TITANS WOULD STRETCH FROM THE SHORELINE TO... ABOUT 600 KILOMETERS INLAND...
IT WILL PROBABLY ONLY TAKE... FOUR DAYS FOR THEM TO TRAMPLE THE ENTIRE CONTINENT.

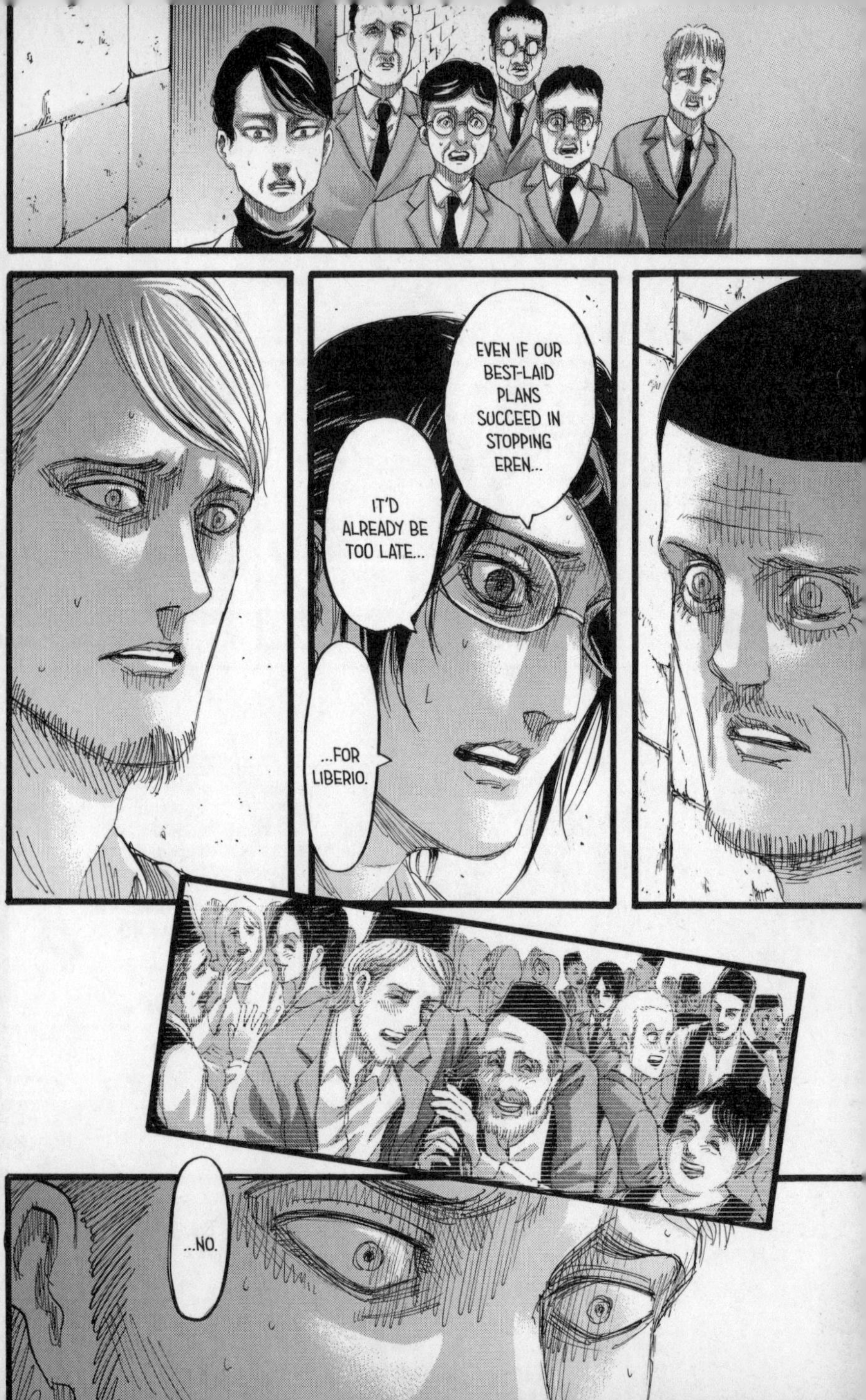
EVEN IF OUR BEST-LAID PLANS SUCCEED IN STOPPING EREN...
IT'D ALREADY BE TOO LATE...
...FOR LIBERIO.
...NO.

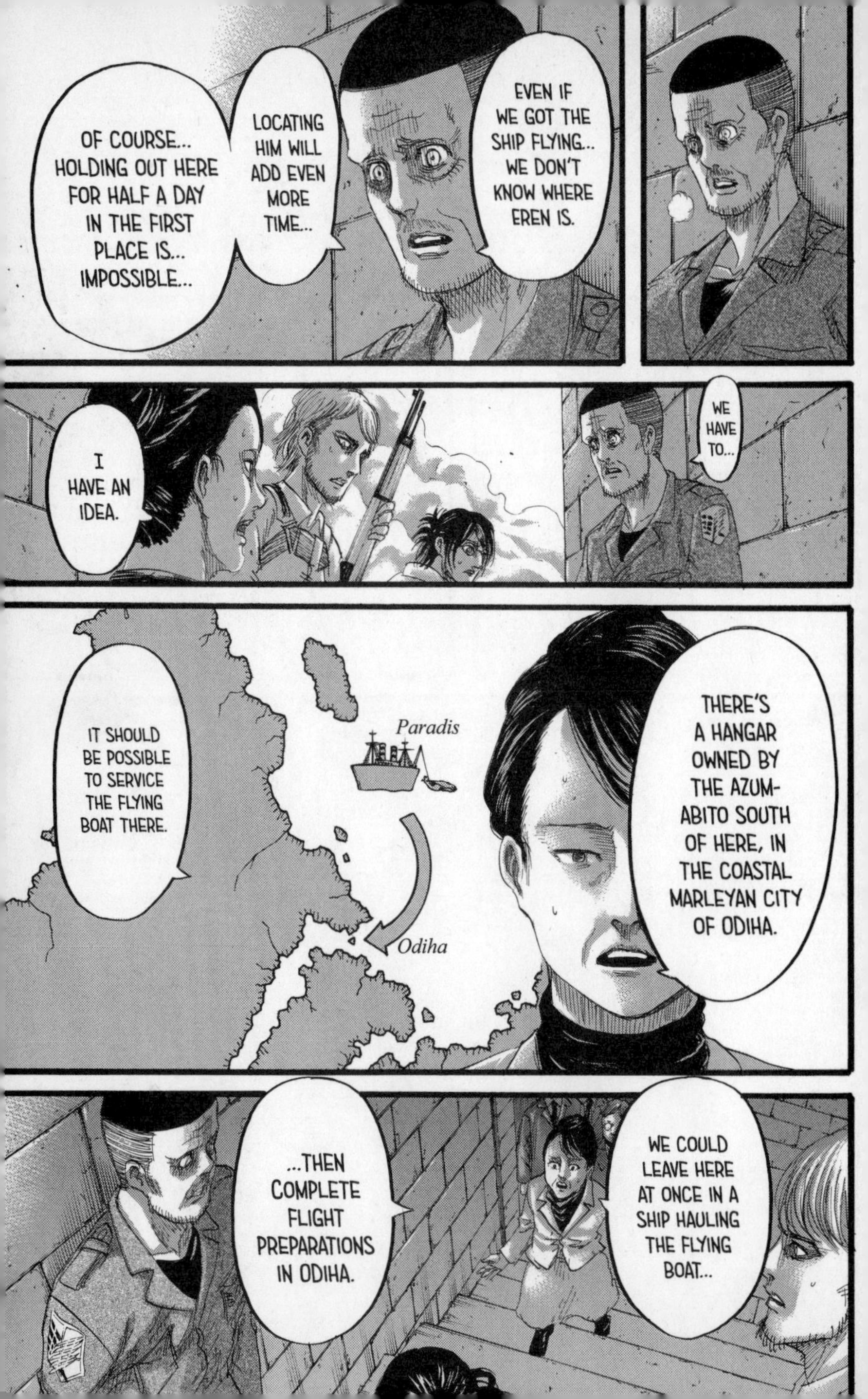
EVEN IF WE GOT THE SHIP FLYING... WE DON'T KNOW WHERE EREN IS.
LOCATING HIM WILL ADD EVEN MORE TIME...
OF COURSE... HOLDING OUT HERE FOR HALF A DAY IN THE FIRST PLACE IS... IMPOSSIBLE...
WE HAVE TO...
I HAVE AN IDEA.
THERE'S A HANGAR OWNED BY THE AZUMABITO SOUTH OF HERE, IN THE COASTAL MARLEYAN CITY OF ODIHA.
Paradis
Odiha
IT SHOULD BE POSSIBLE TO SERVICE THE FLYING BOAT THERE.
WE COULD LEAVE HERE AT ONCE IN A SHIP HAULING THE FLYING BOAT...
...THEN COMPLETE FLIGHT PREPARATIONS IN ODIHA.

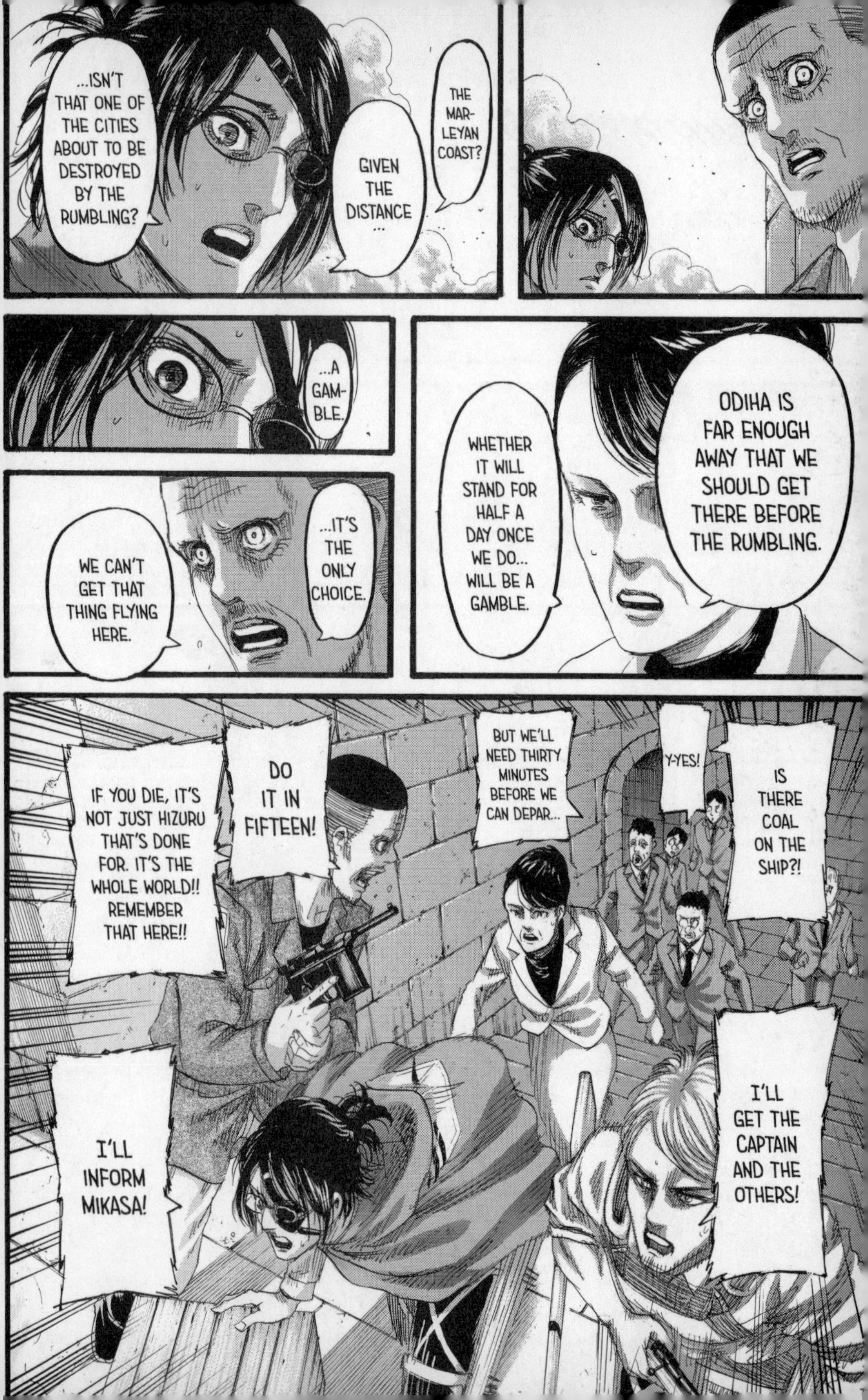
THE MAR-LEYAN COAST?
GIVEN THE DISTANCE ...
...ISN'T THAT ONE OF THE CITIES ABOUT TO BE DESTROYED BY THE RUMBLING?
ODIHA IS FAR ENOUGH AWAY THAT WE SHOULD GET THERE BEFORE THE RUMBLING.
WHETHER IT WILL STAND FOR HALF A DAY ONCE WE DO... WILL BE A GAMBLE.
...A GAM-BLE.
...IT'S THE ONLY CHOICE.
WE CAN'T GET THAT THING FLYING HERE.
IS THERE COAL ON THE SHIP?!
Y-YES!
BUT WE'LL NEED THIRTY MINUTES BEFORE WE CAN DEPAR...
DO IT IN FIFTEEN!
IF YOU DIE, IT'S NOT JUST HIZURU THAT'S DONE FOR. IT'S THE WHOLE WORLD!! REMEMBER THAT HERE!!
I'LL GET THE CAPTAIN AND THE OTHERS!
I'LL INFORM MIKASA!

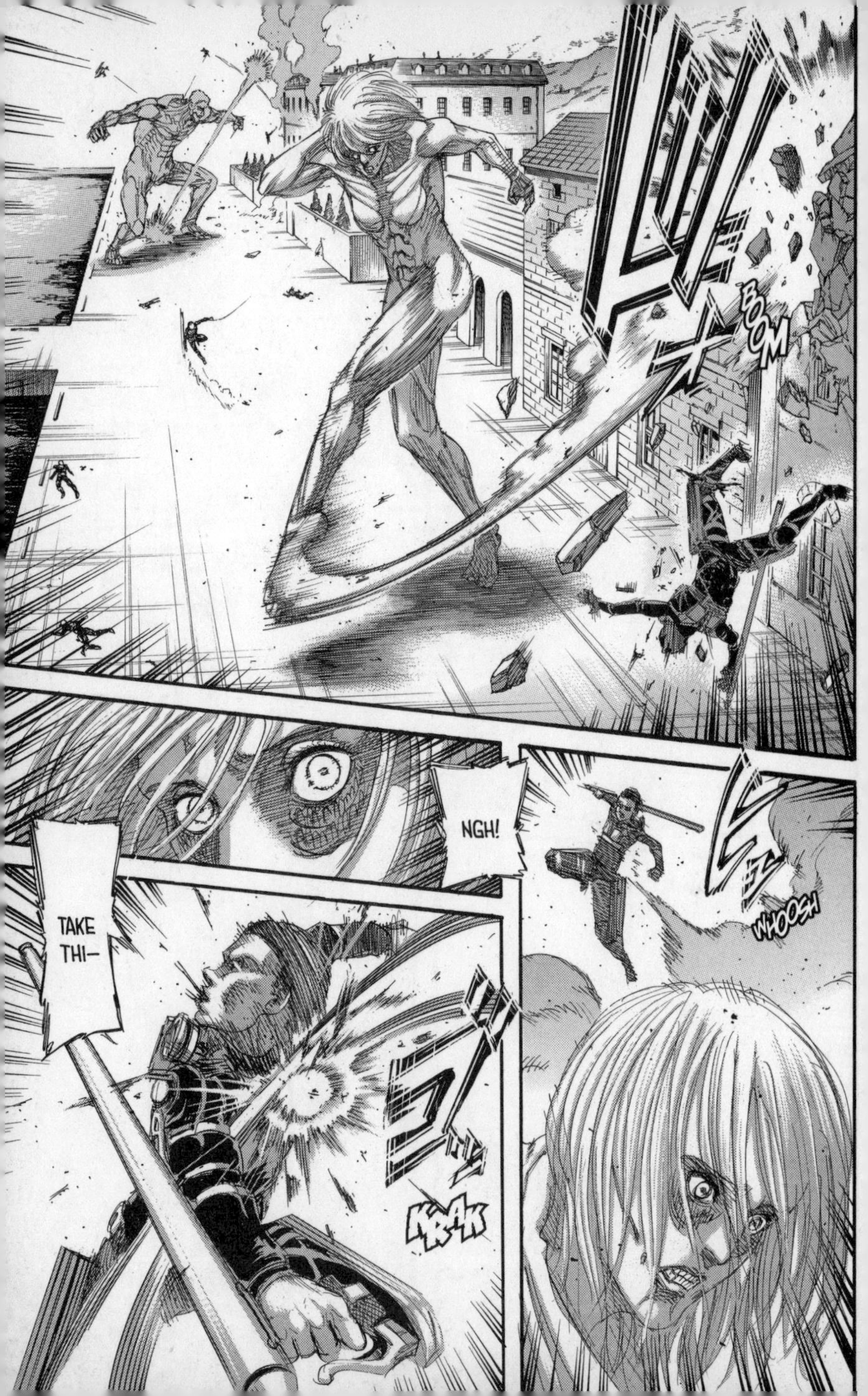
BOOM
WHOOSH
NGH!
TAKE THI-
KRAK

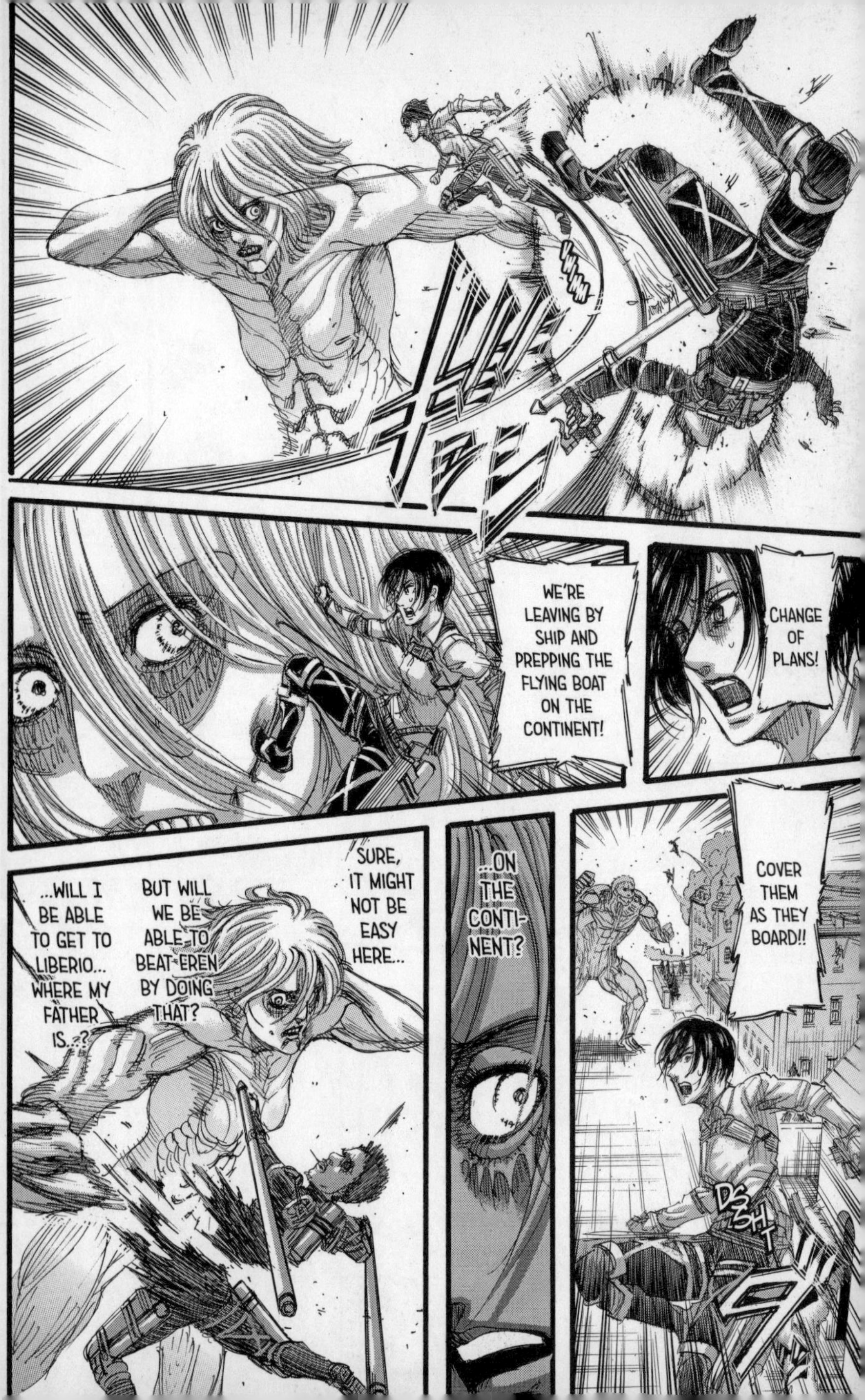
CHANGE OF PLANS!
WE'RE LEAVING BY SHIP AND PREPPING THE FLYING BOAT ON THE CONTINENT!
COVER THEM AS THEY BOARD!!
...ON THE CONTI-NENT?
SURE, IT MIGHT NOT BE EASY HERE...
BUT WILL WE BE ABLE TO BEAT EREN BY DOING THAT?
...WILL I BE ABLE TO GET TO LIBERIO... WHERE MY FATHER IS...?

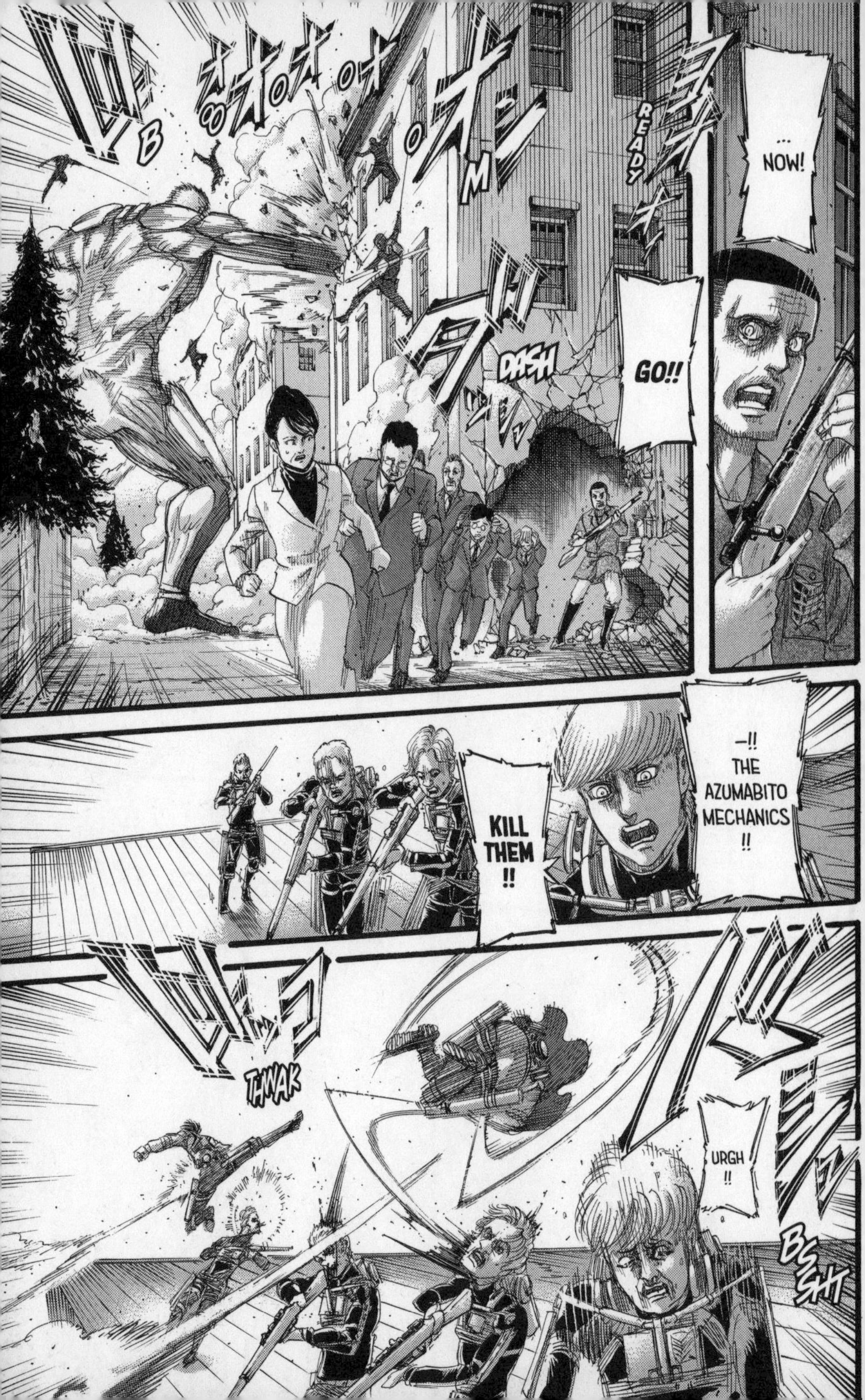
... NOW!
READY
B
M
GO!!
DASH
–!! THE AZUMABITO MECHANICS !!
KILL THEM !!
URGH !!
BSHT
THWAK

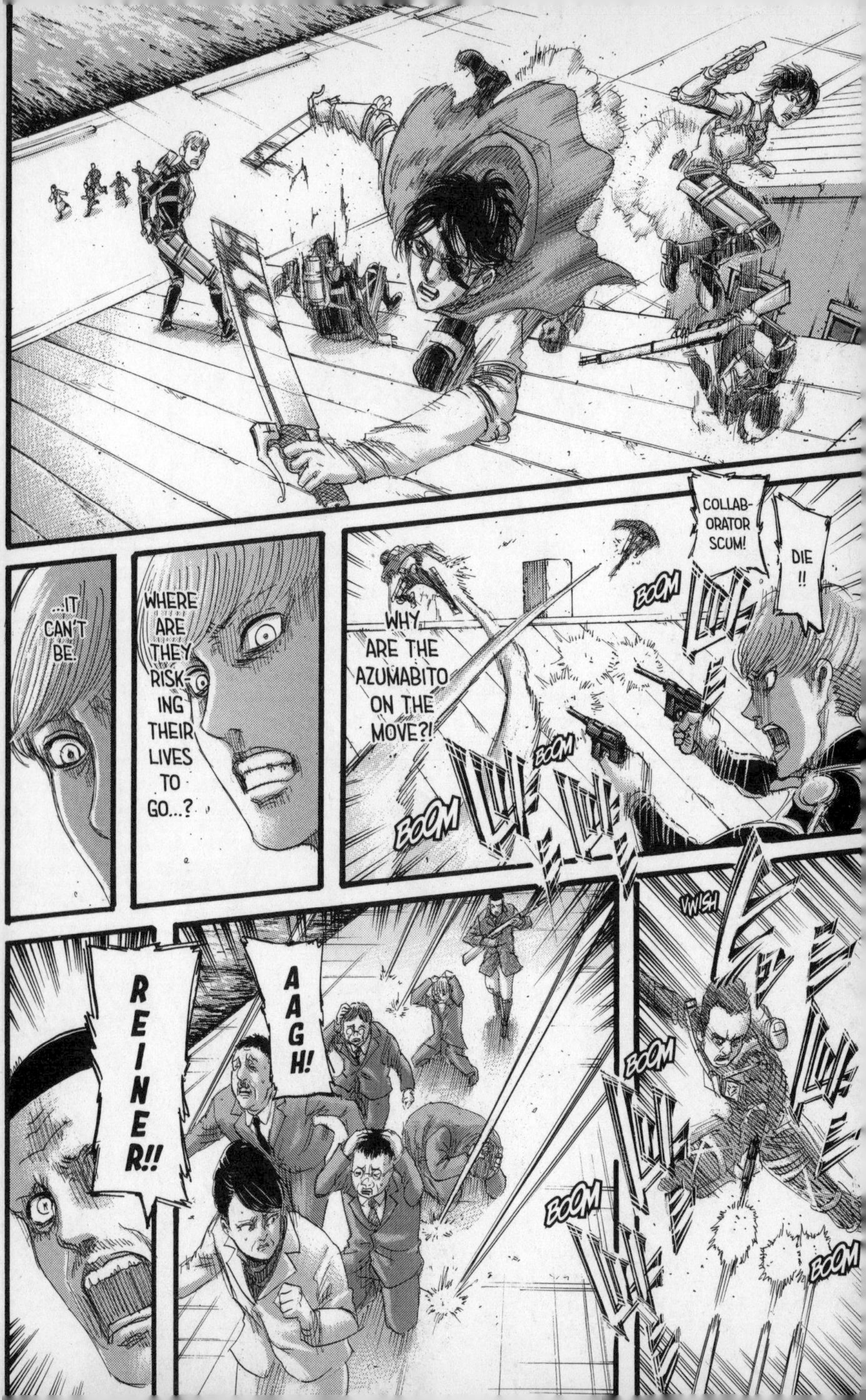
COLLAB-ORATOR SCUM!
DIE!!
BOOM
WHY ARE THE AZUMABITO ON THE MOVE?!
BOOM
BOOM
WHERE ARE THEY RISK-ING THEIR LIVES TO GO...?
...IT CAN'T BE.
VWISH
BOOM
BOOM
BOOM
AAGH!
REINER!!

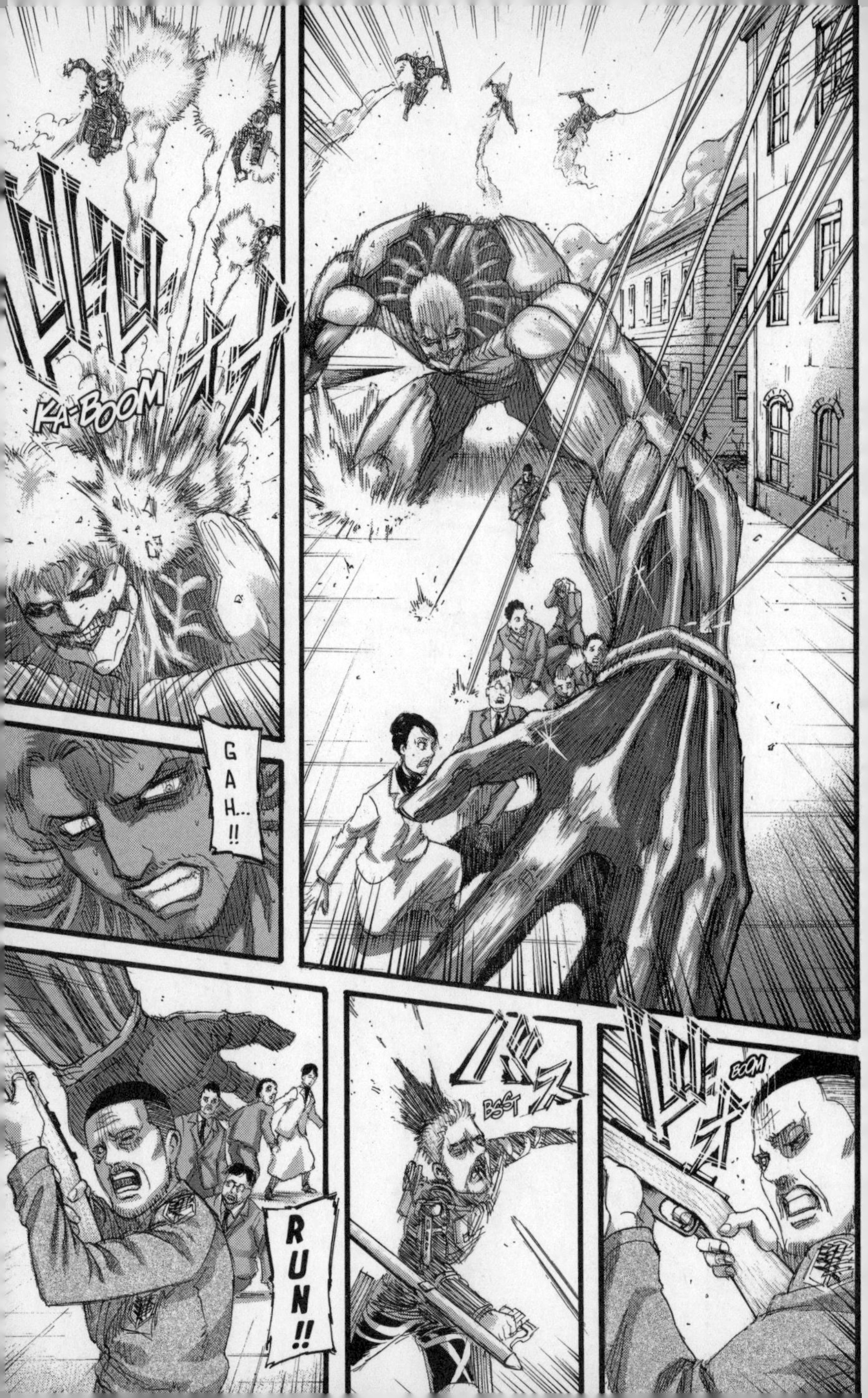
KA-BOOM
GAH...!!
BOOM
BSST
RUN!!

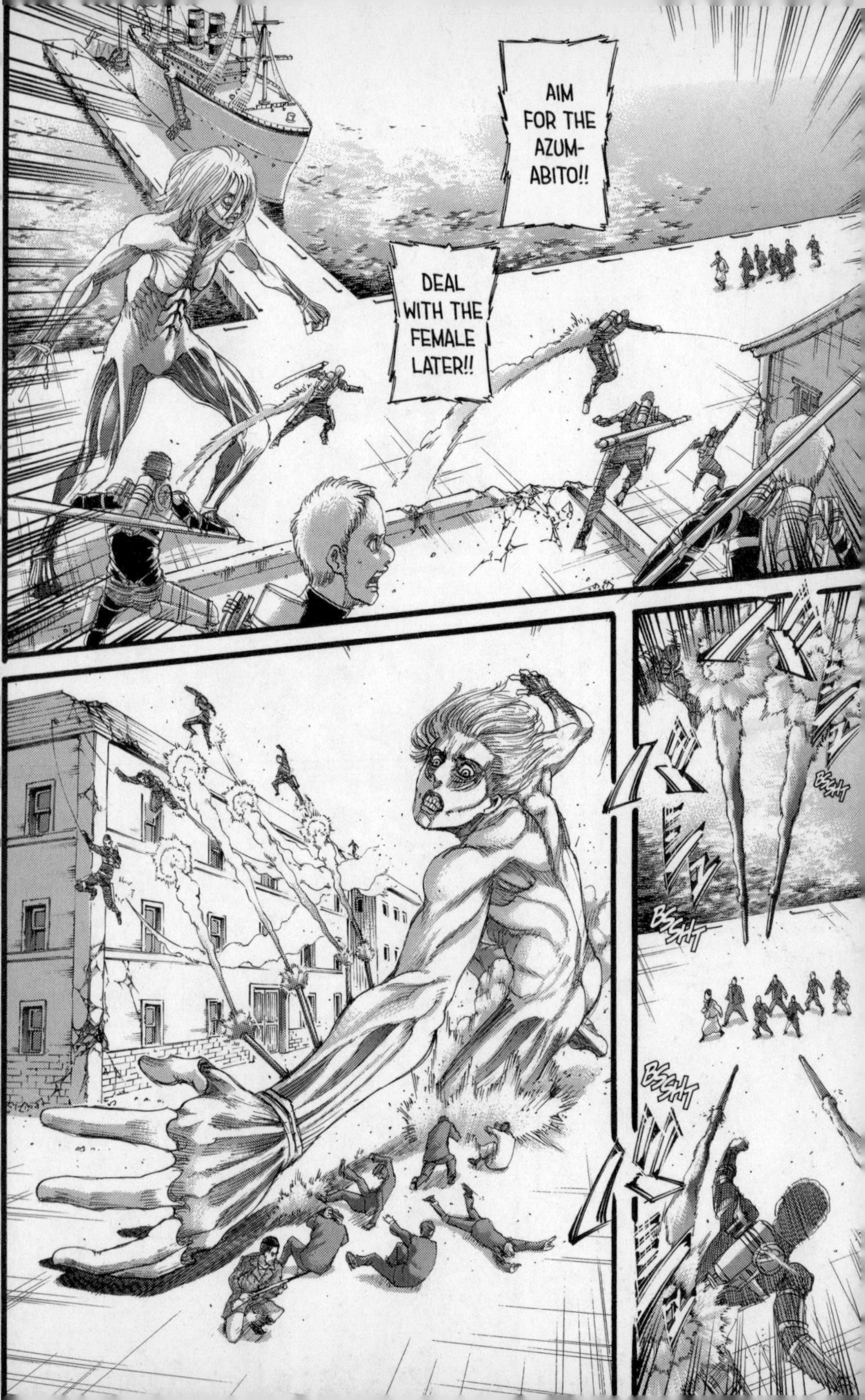
AIM FOR THE AZUM-ABITO!!
DEAL WITH THE FEMALE LATER!!
BSSHT
BSSHT
BSSHT

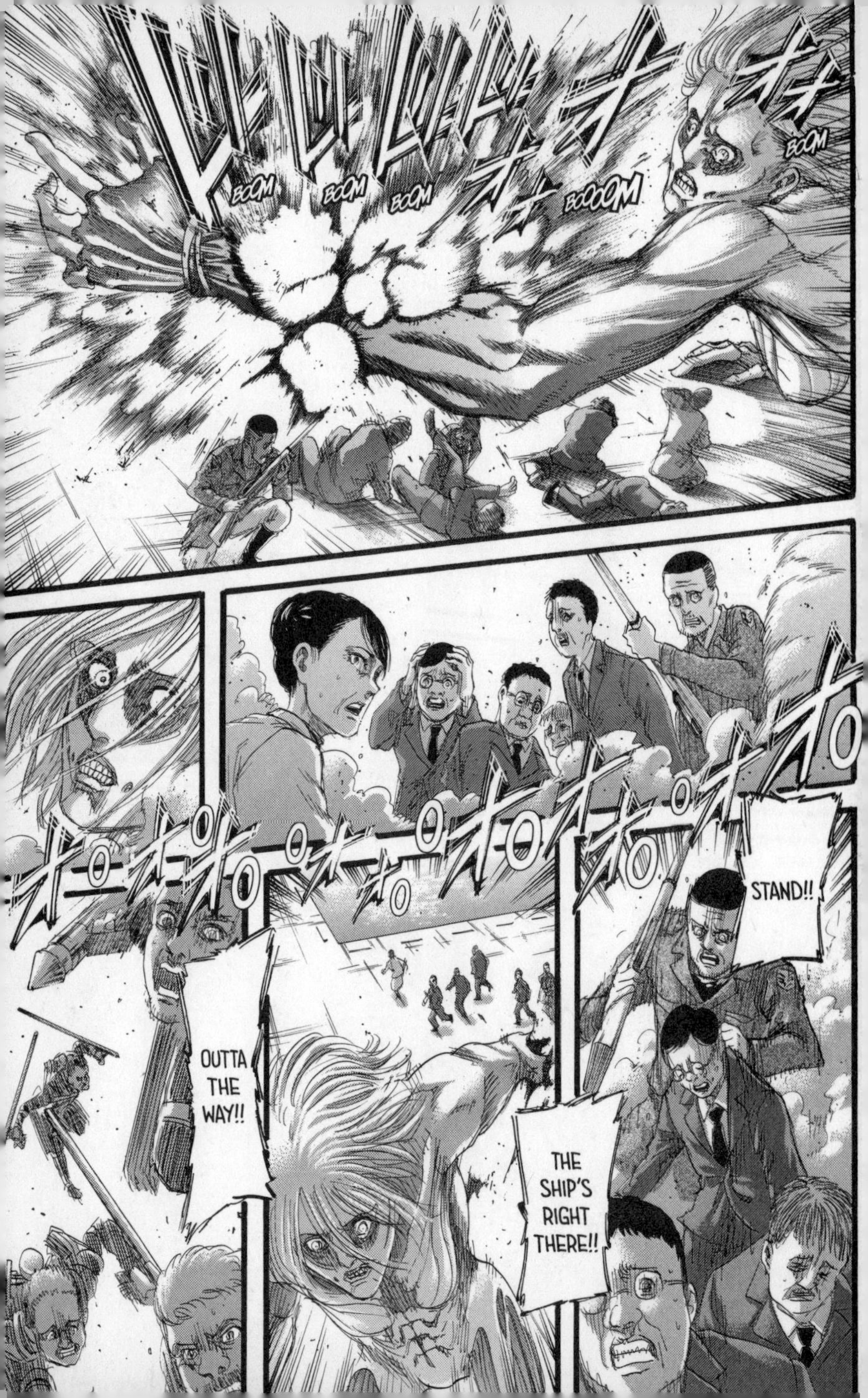
BOOM
BOOOOM
BOOM
BOOM
BOOM
STAND!!
THE SHIP'S RIGHT THERE!!
OUTTA THE WAY!!

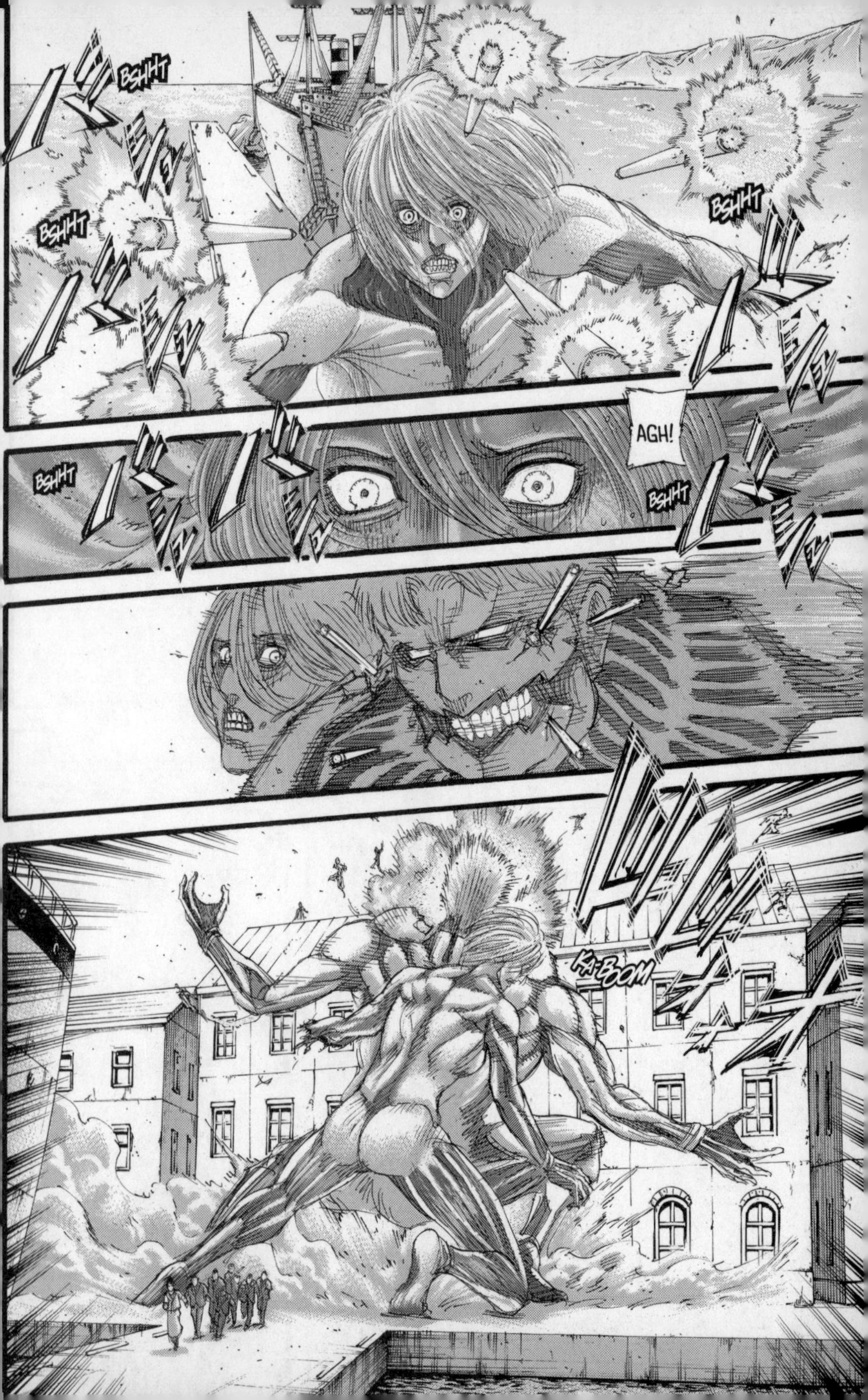
BSHHT
BSHHT
BSHHT
AGH!
BSHHT
BSHHT
KA-BOOM

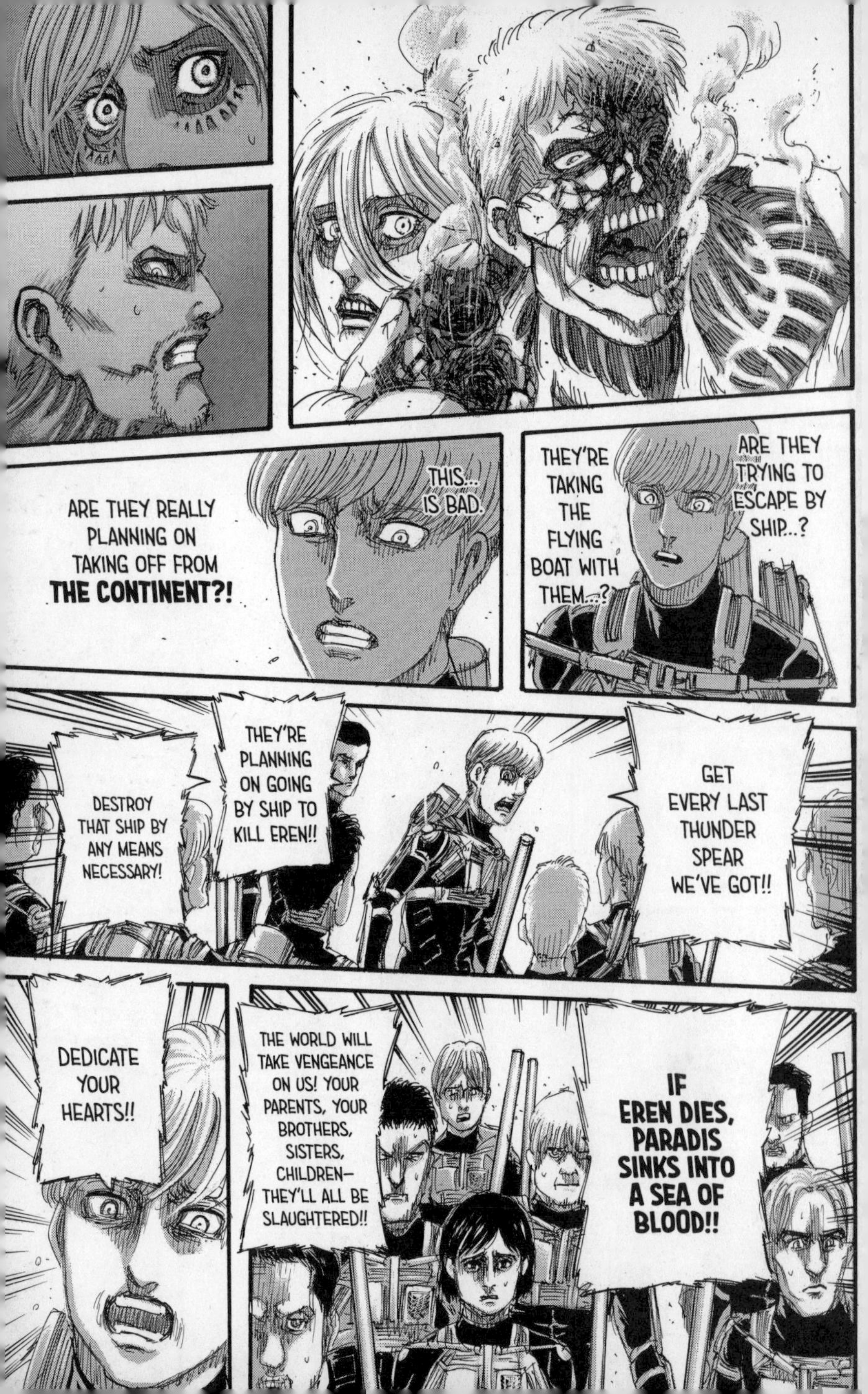

ARE THEY TRYING TO ESCAPE BY SHIP...?
THEY'RE TAKING THE FLYING BOAT WITH THEM...?
THIS... IS BAD.
ARE THEY REALLY PLANNING ON TAKING OFF FROM **THE CONTINENT?!**
GET EVERY LAST THUNDER SPEAR WE'VE GOT!!
THEY'RE PLANNING ON GOING BY SHIP TO KILL EREN!!
DESTROY THAT SHIP BY ANY MEANS NECESSARY!
IF EREN DIES, PARADIS SINKS INTO A SEA OF BLOOD!!
THE WORLD WILL TAKE VENGEANCE ON US! YOUR PARENTS, YOUR BROTHERS, SISTERS, CHILDREN— THEY'LL ALL BE SLAUGHTERED!!
DEDICATE YOUR HEARTS!!

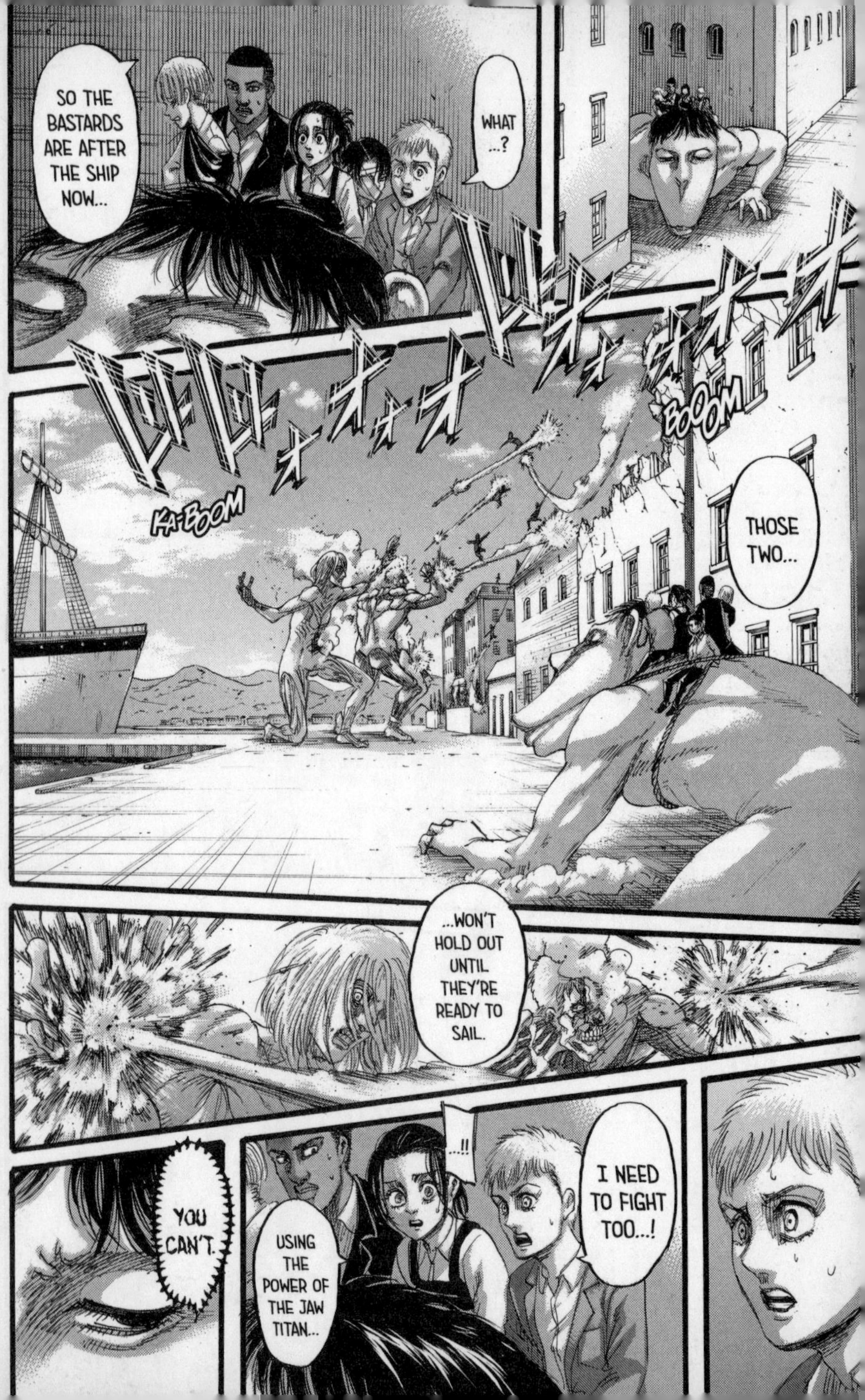

WHAT ...?
SO THE BASTARDS ARE AFTER THE SHIP NOW...
BOOOM
THOSE TWO...
KA-BOOM
...WON'T HOLD OUT UNTIL THEY'RE READY TO SAIL.
I NEED TO FIGHT TOO...!
...!!
USING THE POWER OF THE JAW TITAN...
YOU CAN'T.

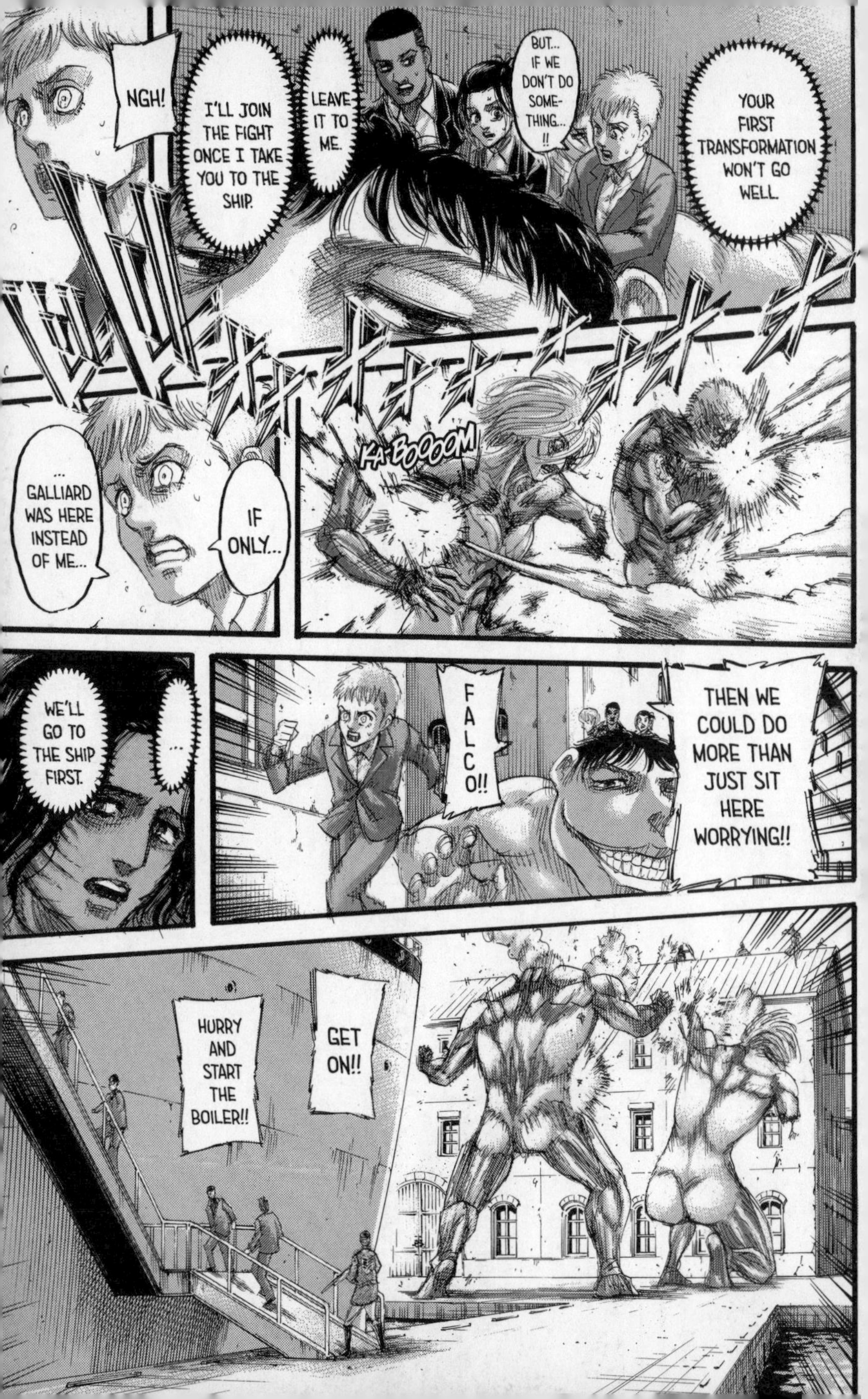
YOUR FIRST TRANSFORMATION WON'T GO WELL.
BUT... IF WE DON'T DO SOME-THING... !!
LEAVE IT TO ME.
I'LL JOIN THE FIGHT ONCE I TAKE YOU TO THE SHIP.
NGH!
KA-BOOOOM
IF ONLY...
... GALLIARD WAS HERE INSTEAD OF ME...
THEN WE COULD DO MORE THAN JUST SIT HERE WORRYING!!
FALCO!!
...
WE'LL GO TO THE SHIP FIRST.
GET ON!!
HURRY AND START THE BOILER!!

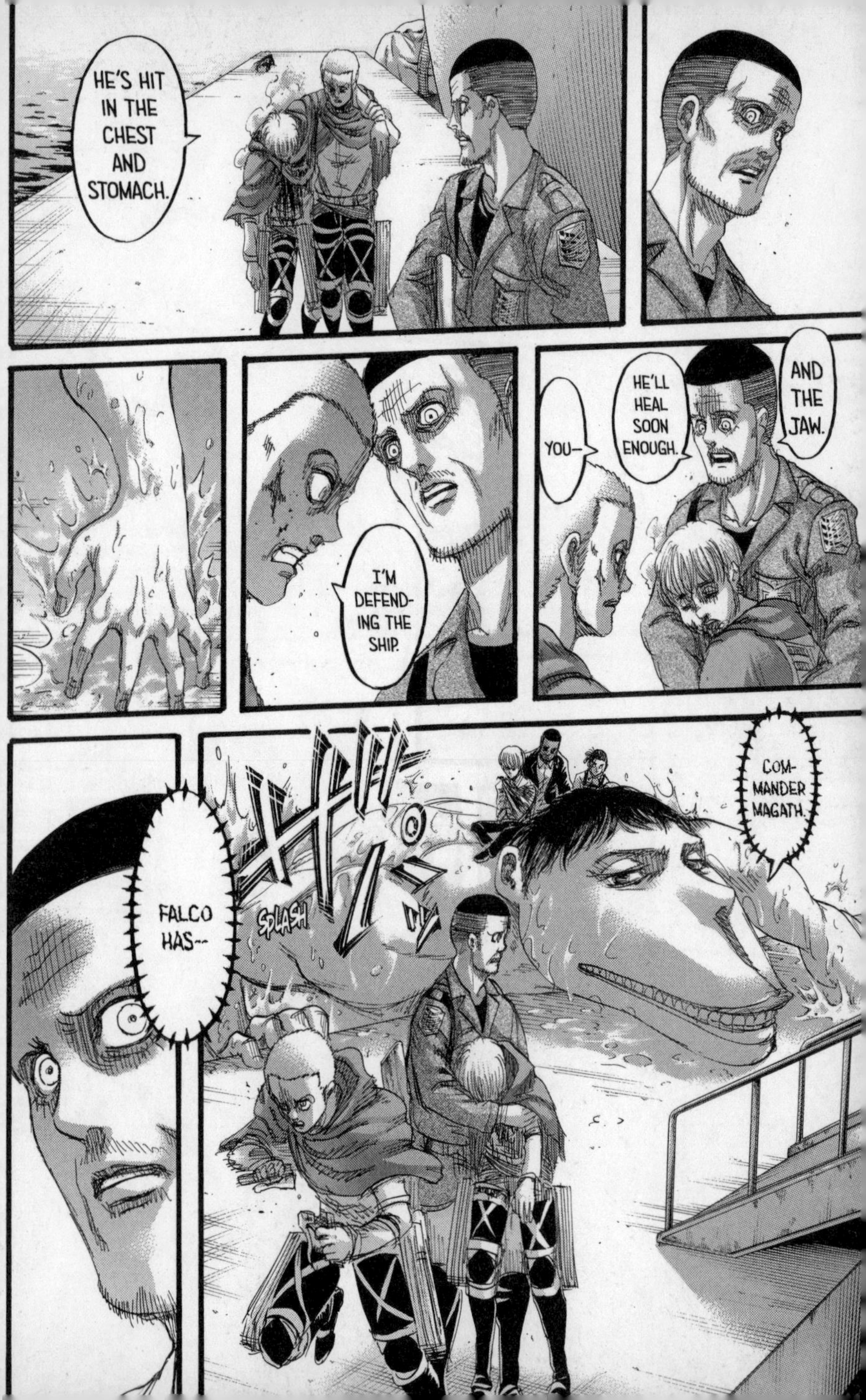
HE'S HIT IN THE CHEST AND STOMACH.
AND THE JAW.
HE'LL HEAL SOON ENOUGH.
YOU—
I'M DEFEND-ING THE SHIP.
COM-MANDER MAGATH.
SPLASH
FALCO HAS--

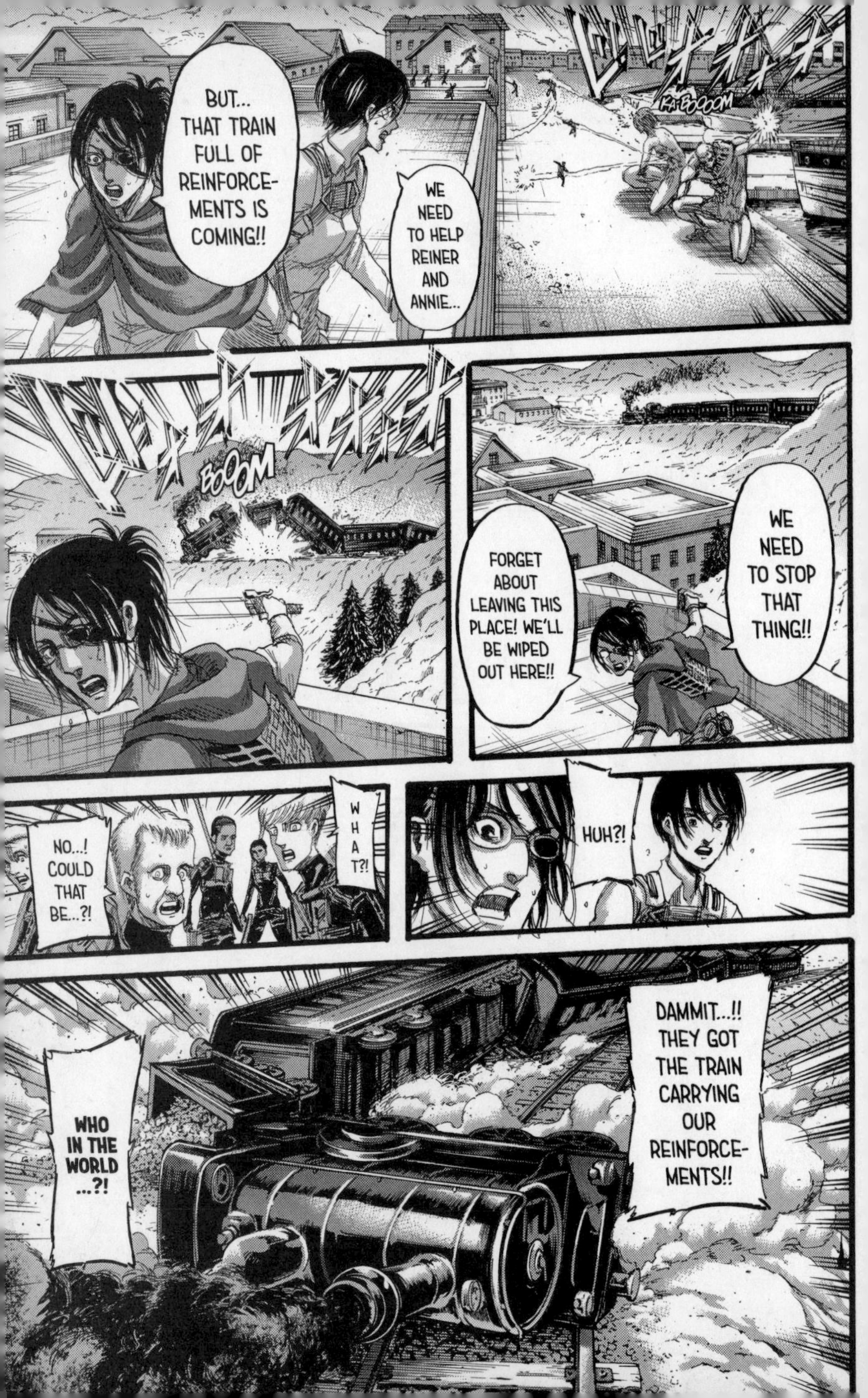
KA-BOOOM
WE NEED TO HELP REINER AND ANNIE...
BUT... THAT TRAIN FULL OF REINFORCEMENTS IS COMING!!
WE NEED TO STOP THAT THING!!
FORGET ABOUT LEAVING THIS PLACE! WE'LL BE WIPED OUT HERE!!
BOOOM
HUH?!
WHAT?!
NO...! COULD THAT BE...?!
DAMMIT...!! THEY GOT THE TRAIN CARRYING OUR REINFORCEMENTS!!
WHO IN THE WORLD ...?!

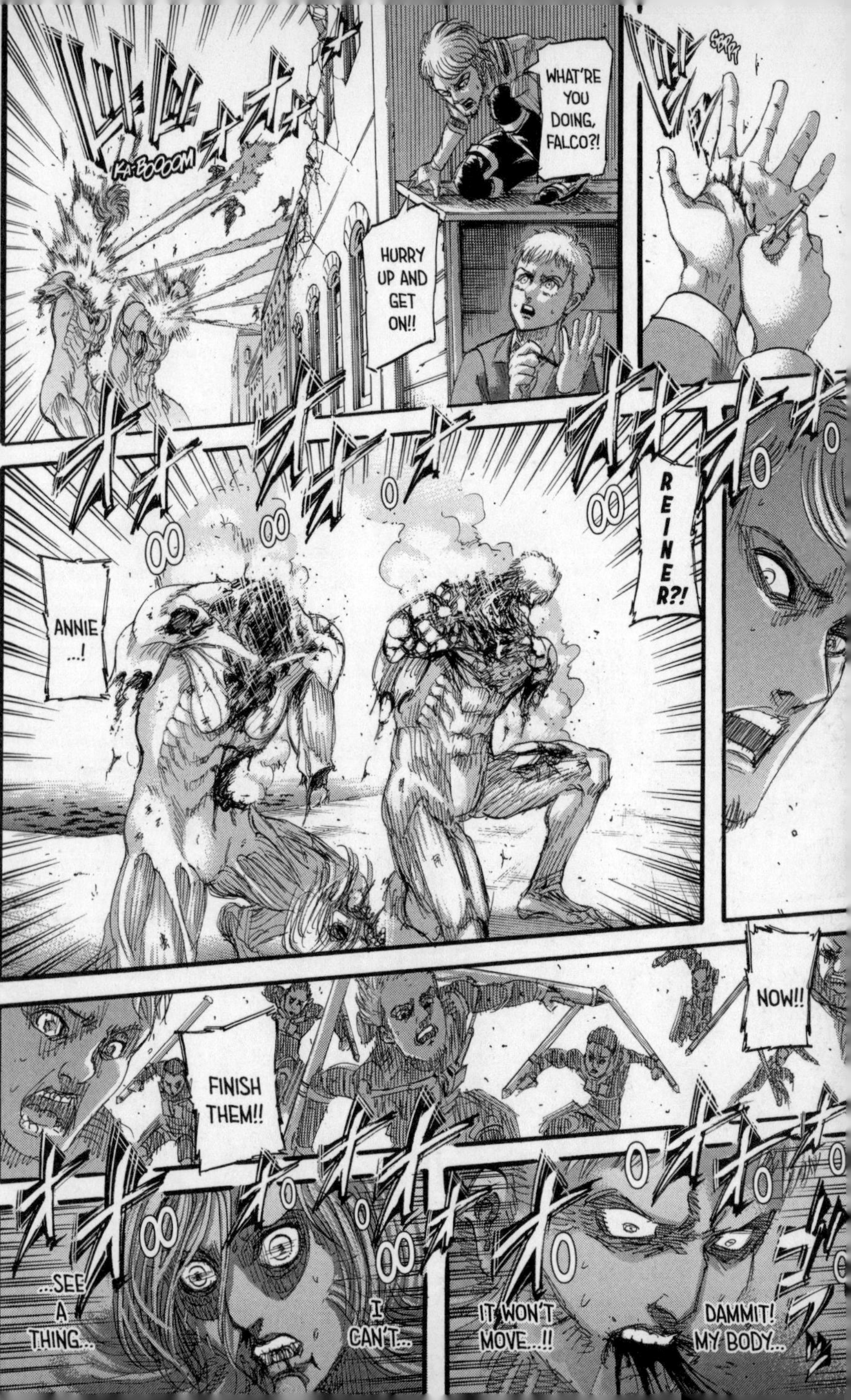
WHAT'RE YOU DOING, FALCO?!
HURRY UP AND GET ON!!
KA-BOOOOM
REINER?!
ANNIE ...!
NOW!!
FINISH THEM!!
DAMMIT! MY BODY...
IT WON'T MOVE...!!
I CAN'T...
...SEE A THING...

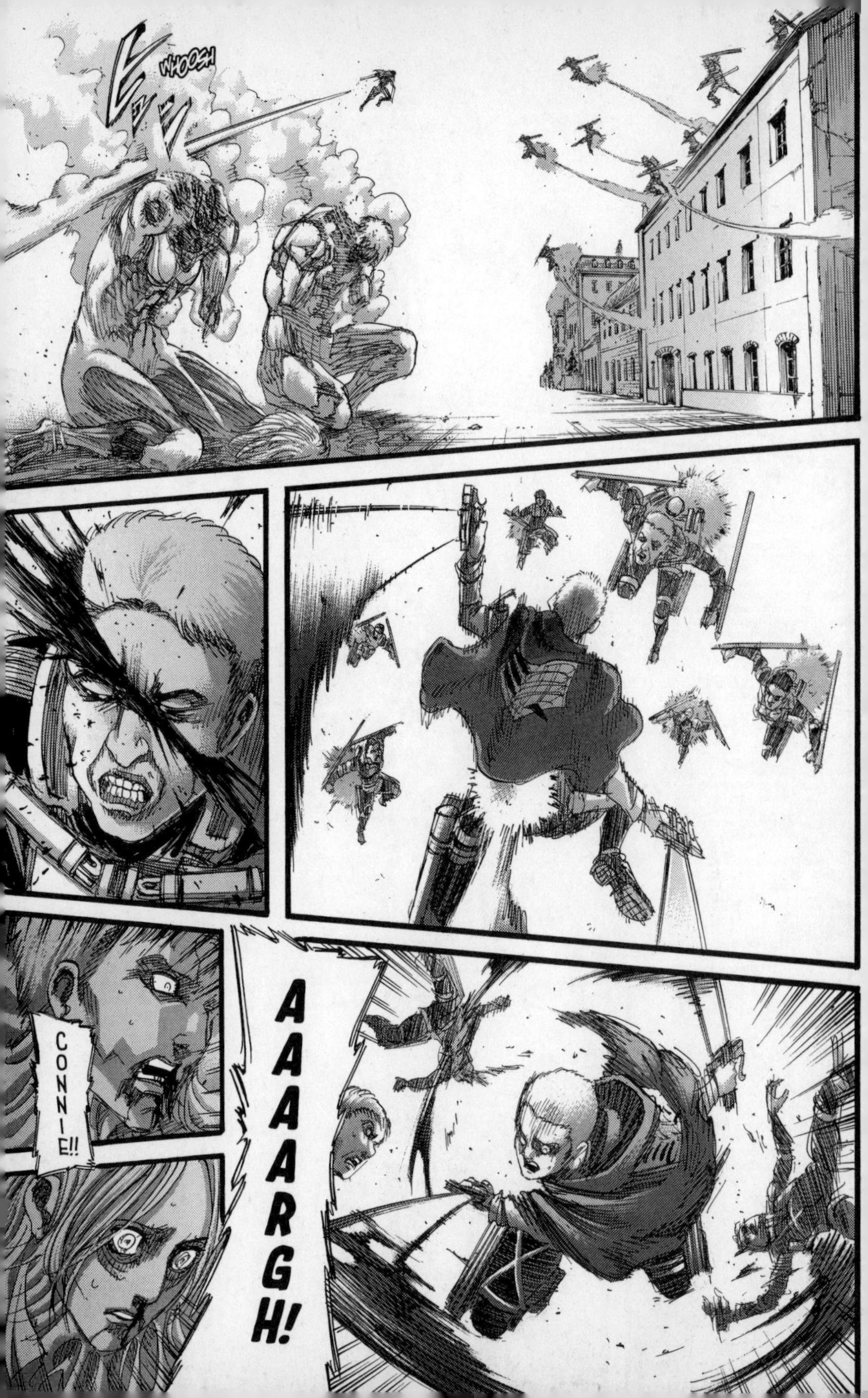
WHOOSH
AAAAARGH!
CONNIE!!

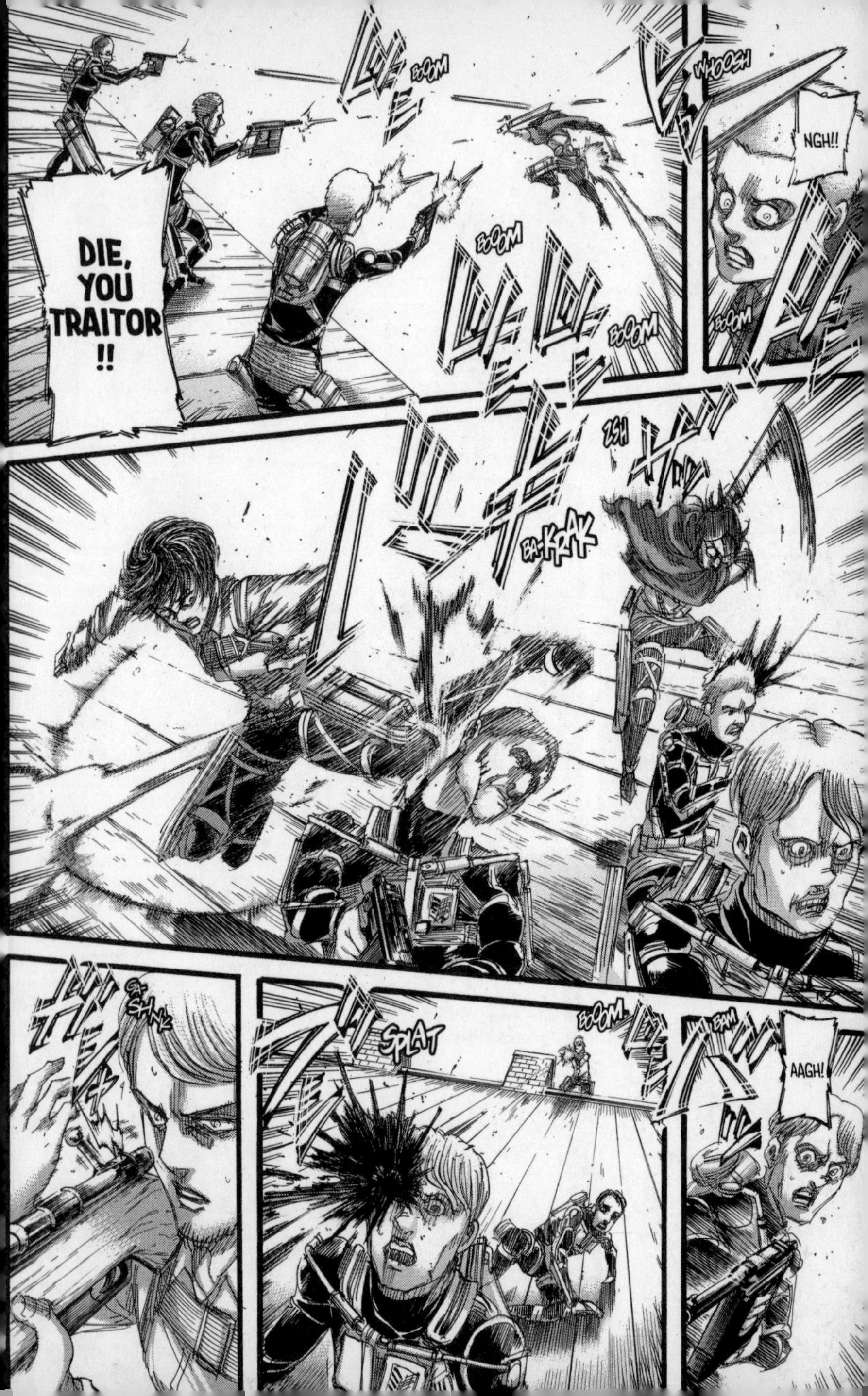
WHOOSH
NGH!!
BOOOM
BOOOM
BOOOM
BOOOM
DIE, YOU TRAITOR!!
ZSH
BA-KRAK
BAM
AAGH!
BOOOM
SPLAT
GA-SHNK

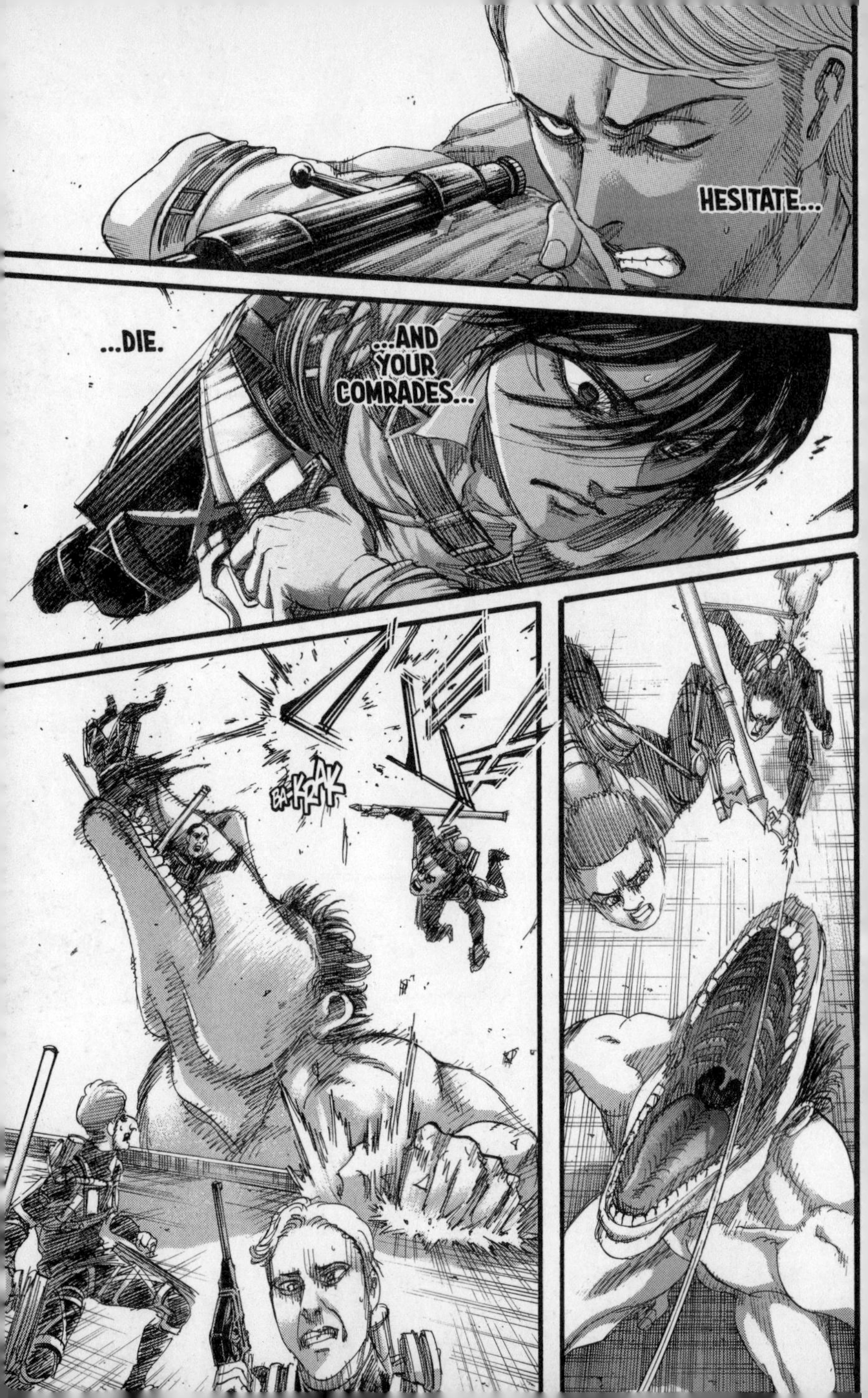
HESITATE...
...AND YOUR COMRADES...
...DIE.
BA-KRAK

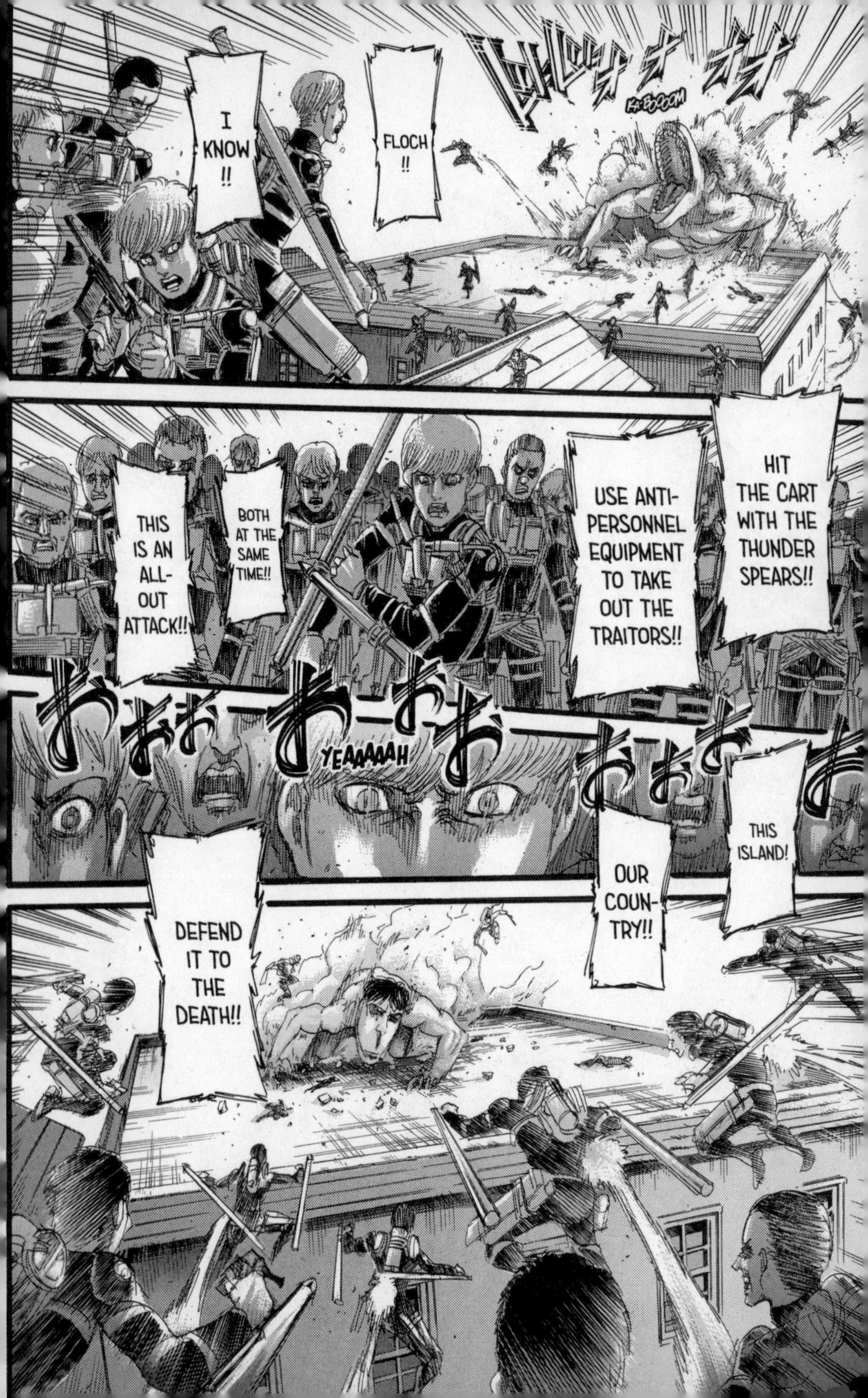
KA-BOOOM
FLOCH!!
I KNOW!!
HIT THE CART WITH THE THUNDER SPEARS!!
USE ANTI-PERSONNEL EQUIPMENT TO TAKE OUT THE TRAITORS!!
BOTH AT THE SAME TIME!!
THIS IS AN ALL-OUT ATTACK!!
YEAAAAAH
THIS ISLAND!
OUR COUNTRY!!
DEFEND IT TO THE DEATH!!

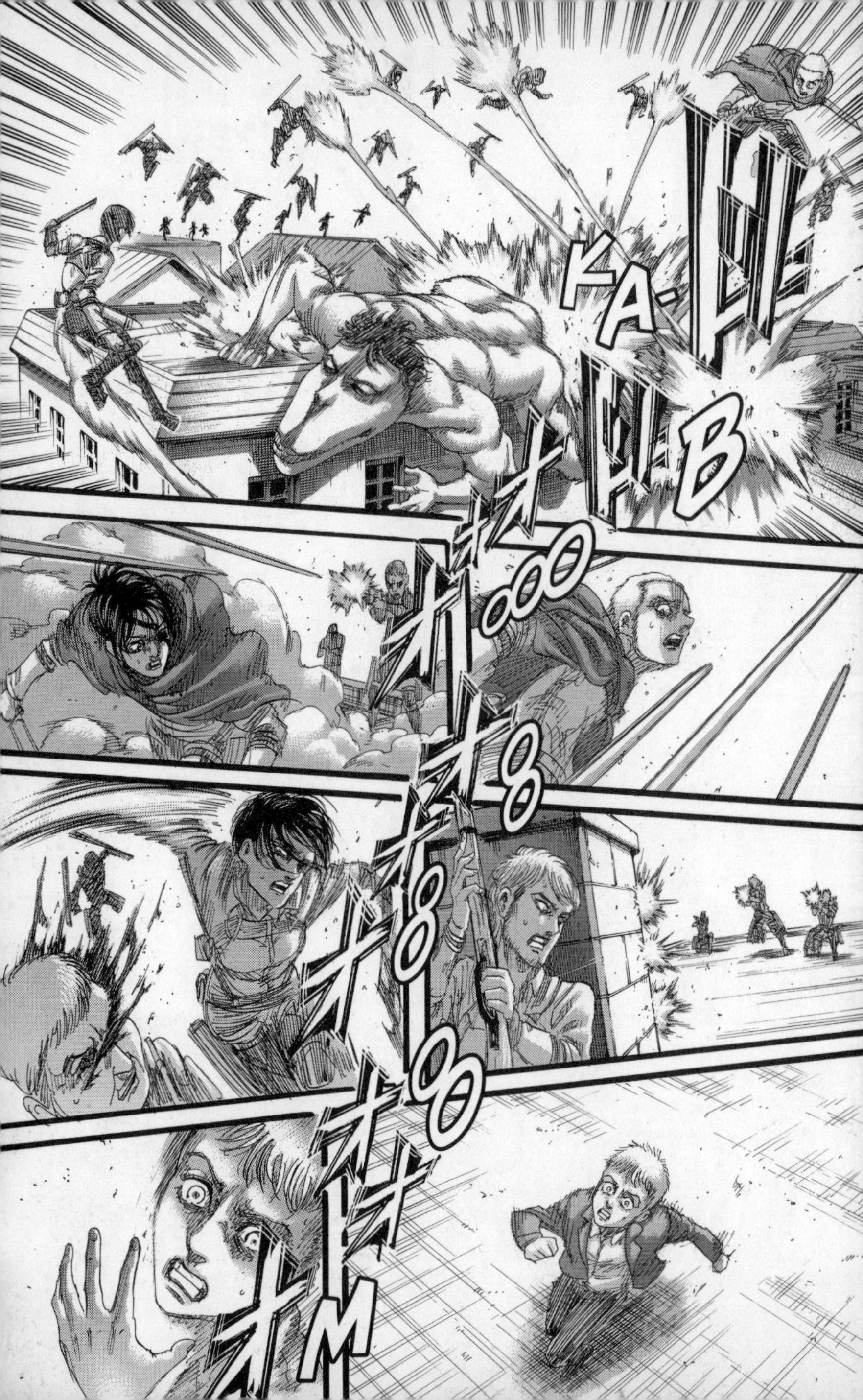
KA-BOOOOOOOOOM

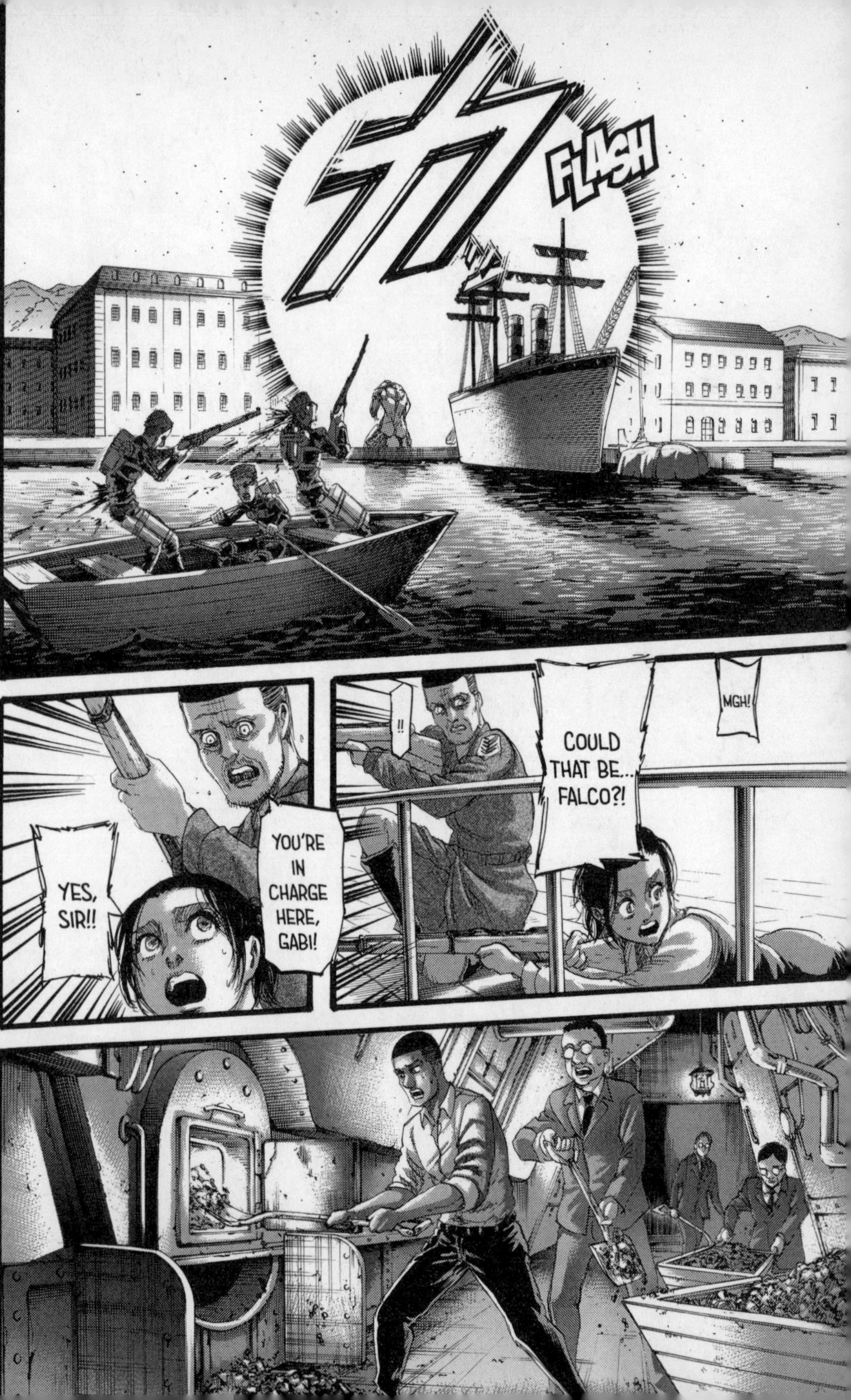
FLASH
MGH!
COULD THAT BE... FALCO?!
!!
YOU'RE IN CHARGE HERE, GABI!
YES, SIR!!

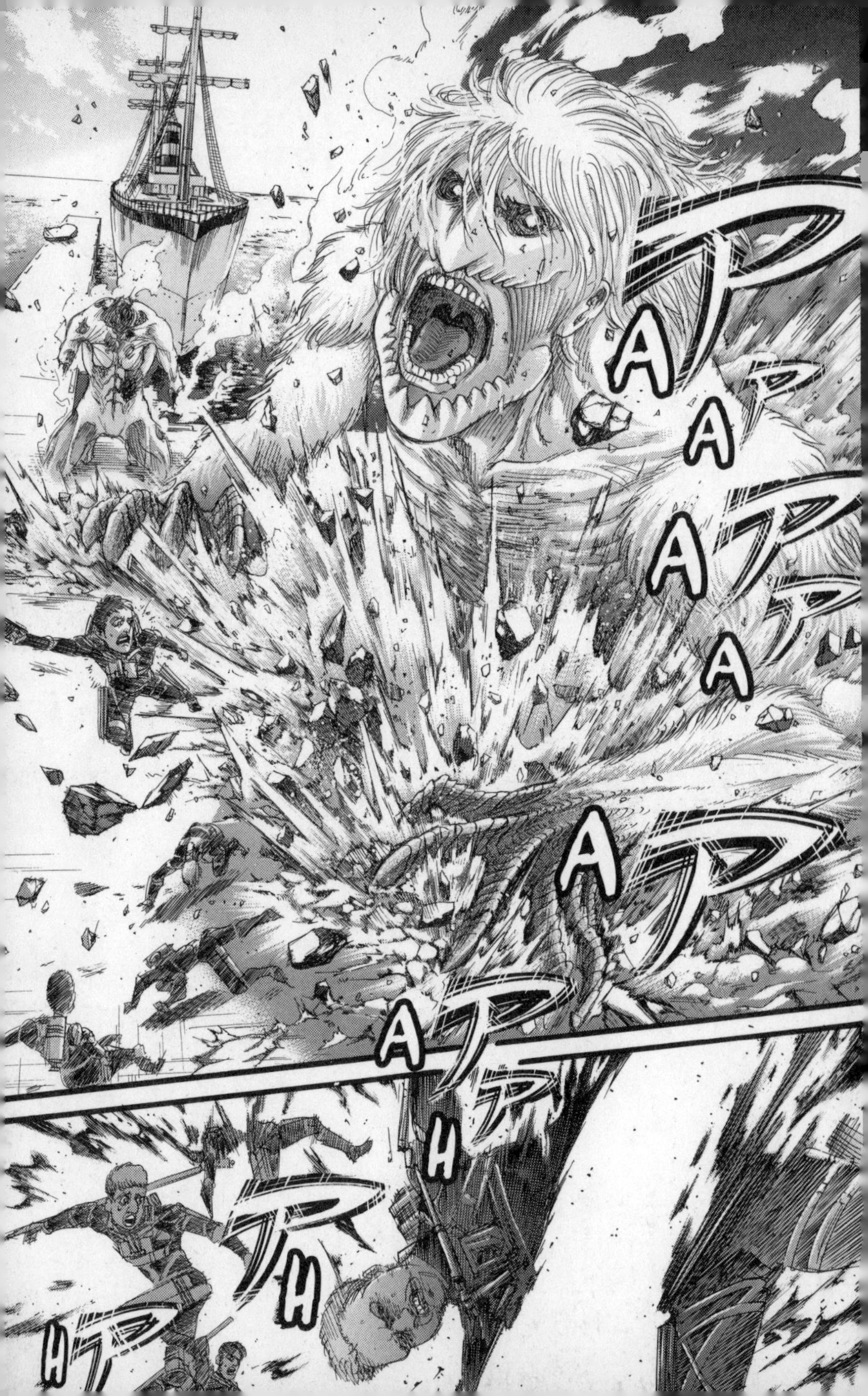
A A A A A A
H H H

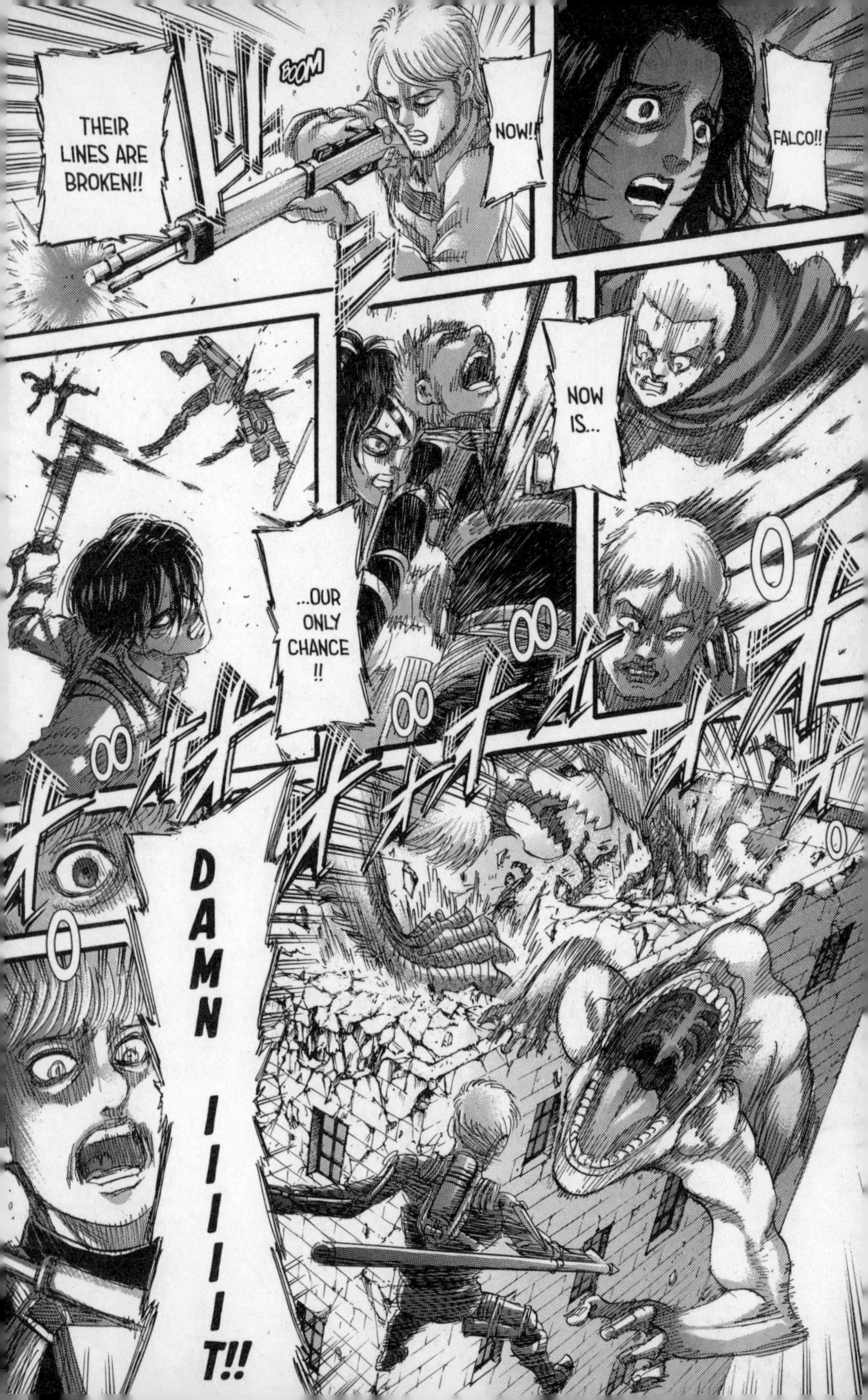
FALCO!!
BOOM
NOW!!
THEIR LINES ARE BROKEN!!
NOW IS...
...OUR ONLY CHANCE !!
DAMN IIIIIT!!

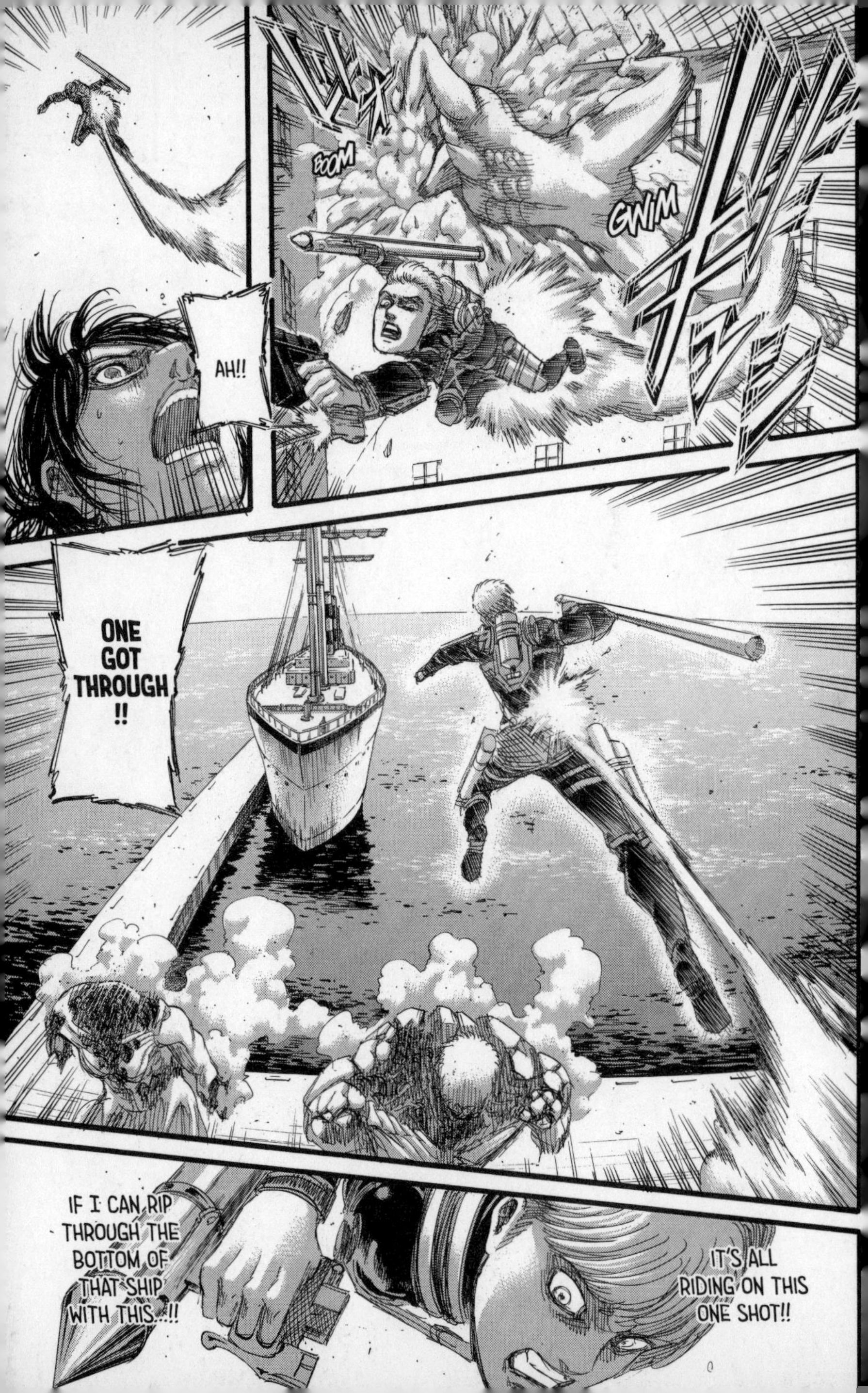
BOOM
GWIM
AH!!
ONE GOT THROUGH!!
IT'S ALL RIDING ON THIS ONE SHOT!!
IF I CAN RIP THROUGH THE BOTTOM OF THAT SHIP WITH THIS...!!

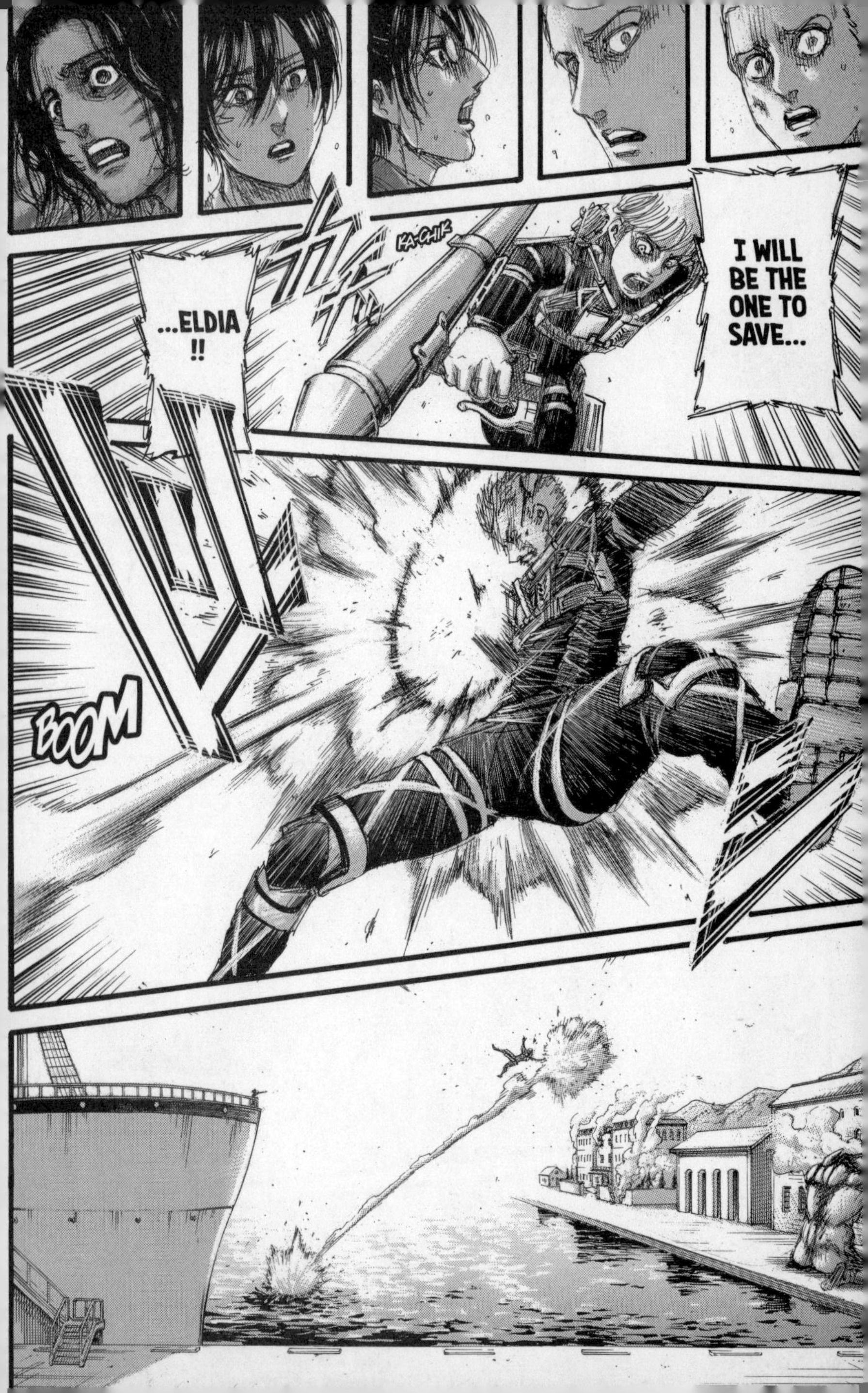

I WILL BE THE ONE TO SAVE...
KA-CHIK
...ELDIA !!
BOOM

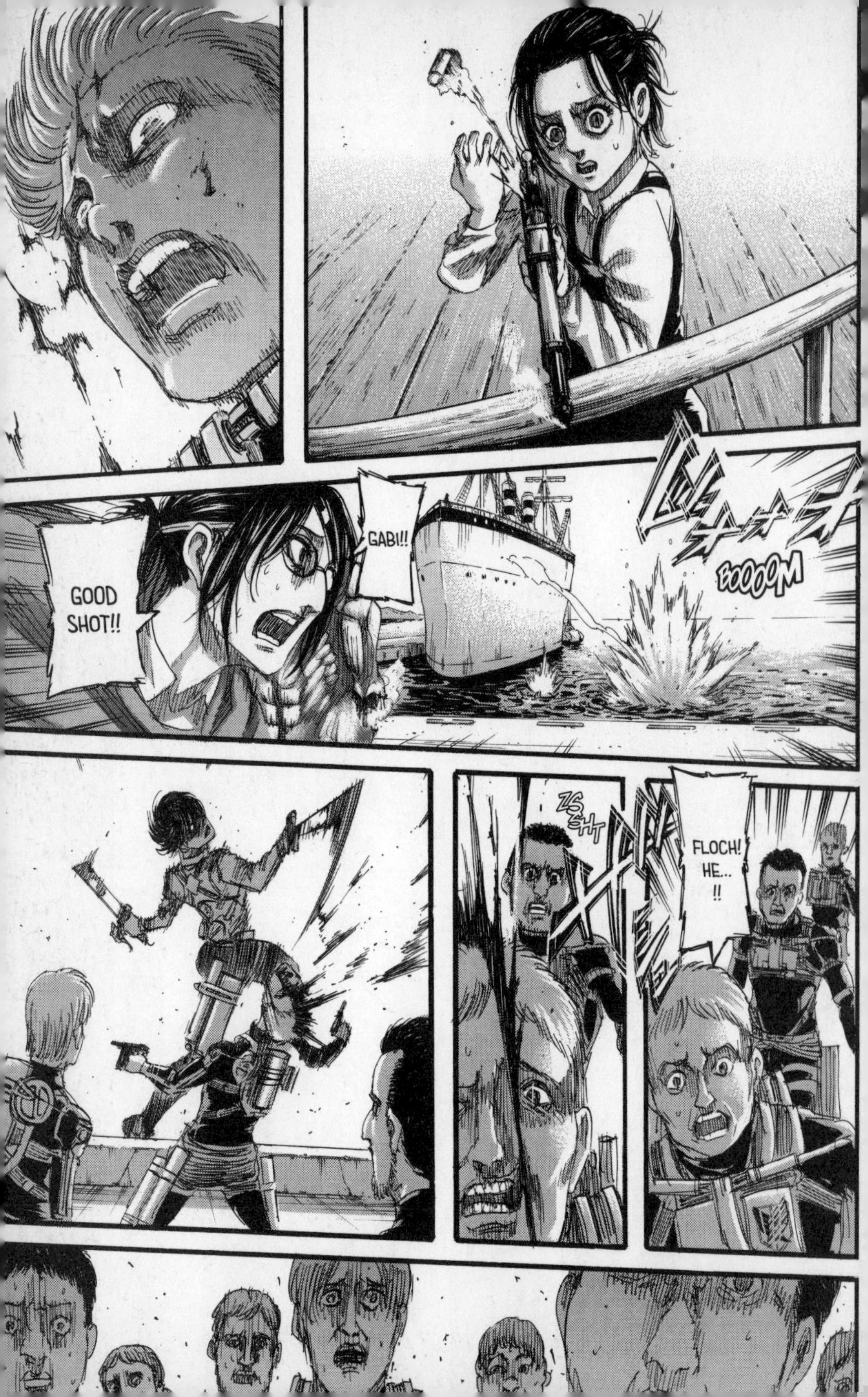
BOOOOM
GABI!!
GOOD SHOT!!
FLOCH! HE... !!
ZSHT

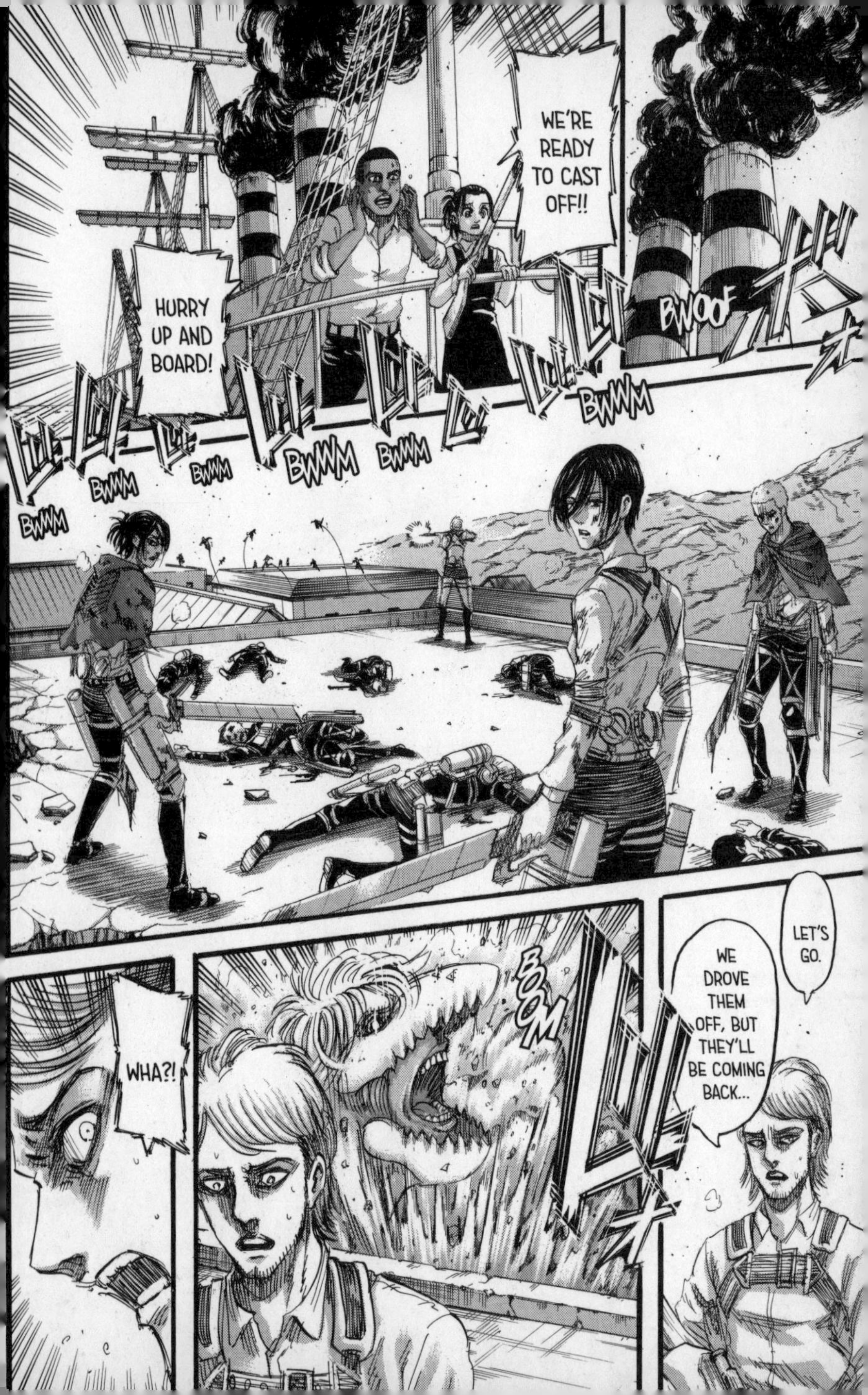
WE'RE READY TO CAST OFF!!
BWOOF
BWMM
HURRY UP AND BOARD!
BWMM
BWMM
BWMM
BWMM
BWMM
LET'S GO.
WE DROVE THEM OFF, BUT THEY'LL BE COMING BACK...
BOOM
WHA?!

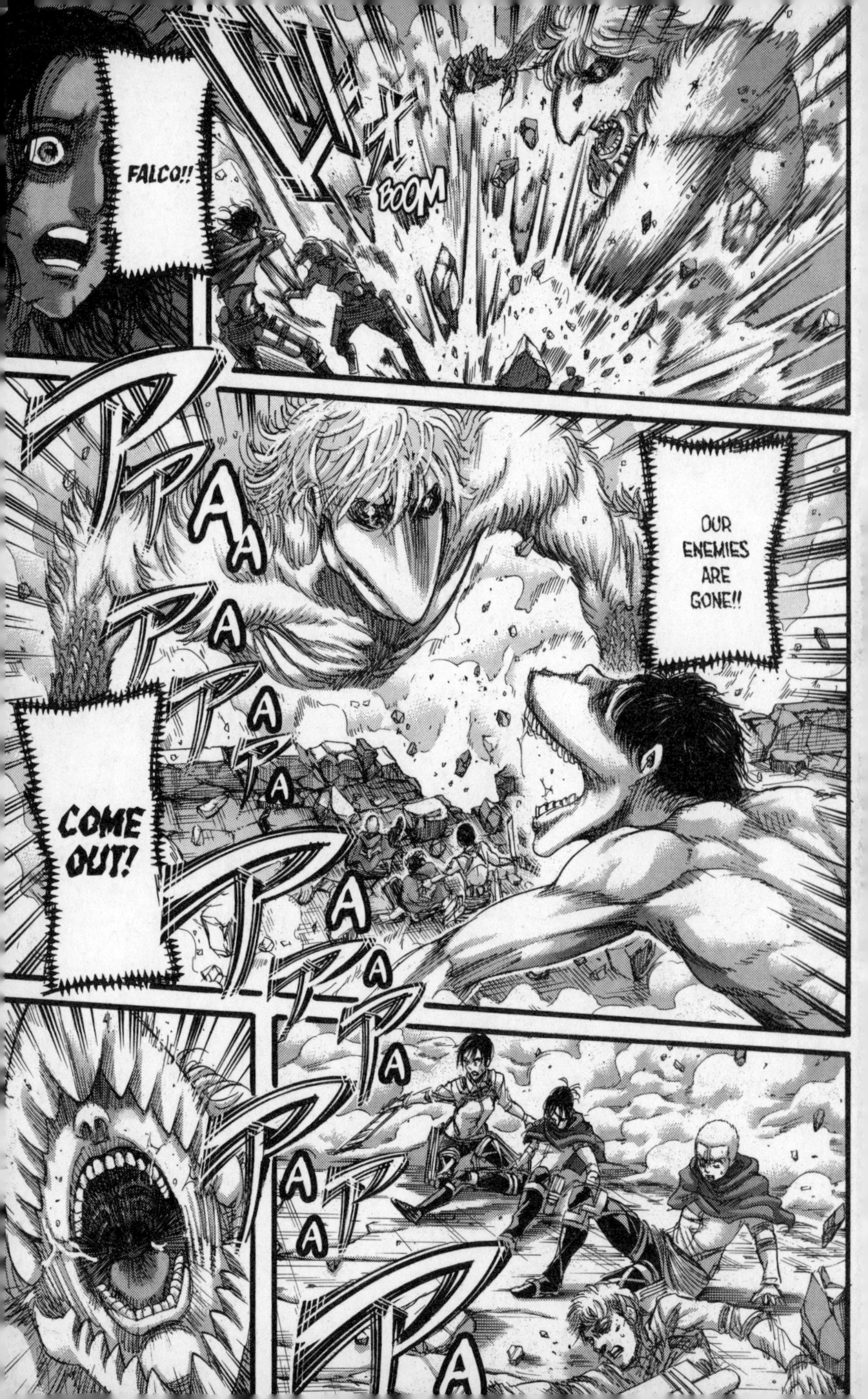
BOOM
FALCO!!
OUR ENEMIES ARE GONE!!
COME OUT!
AAAAAAAAAAAAA

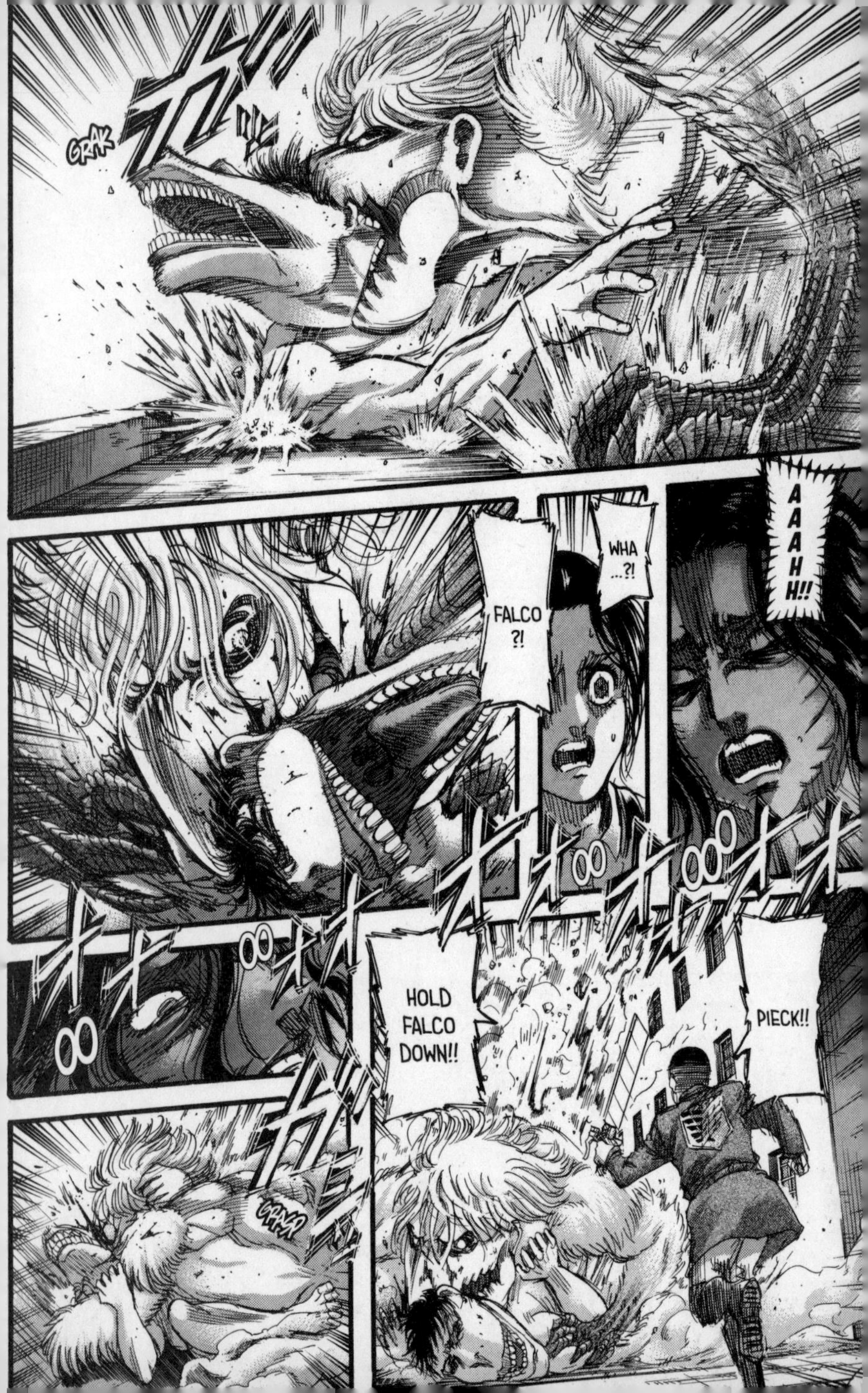
GRAK
AAAAH!!
WHA ...?!
FALCO ?!
PIECK!!
HOLD FALCO DOWN!!
GRASP

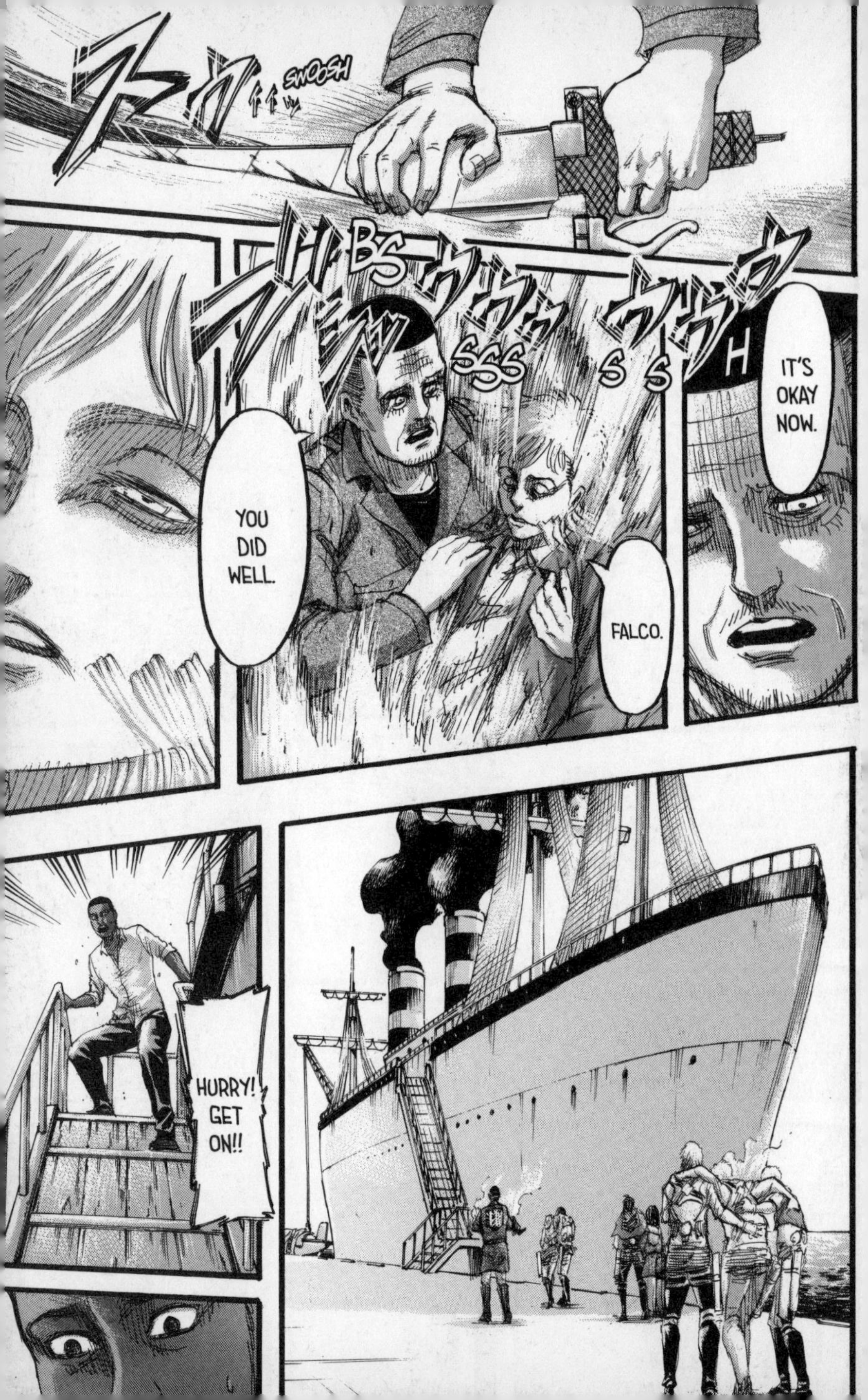
SWOOSH
IT'S OKAY NOW.
YOU DID WELL.
FALCO.
HURRY! GET ON!!

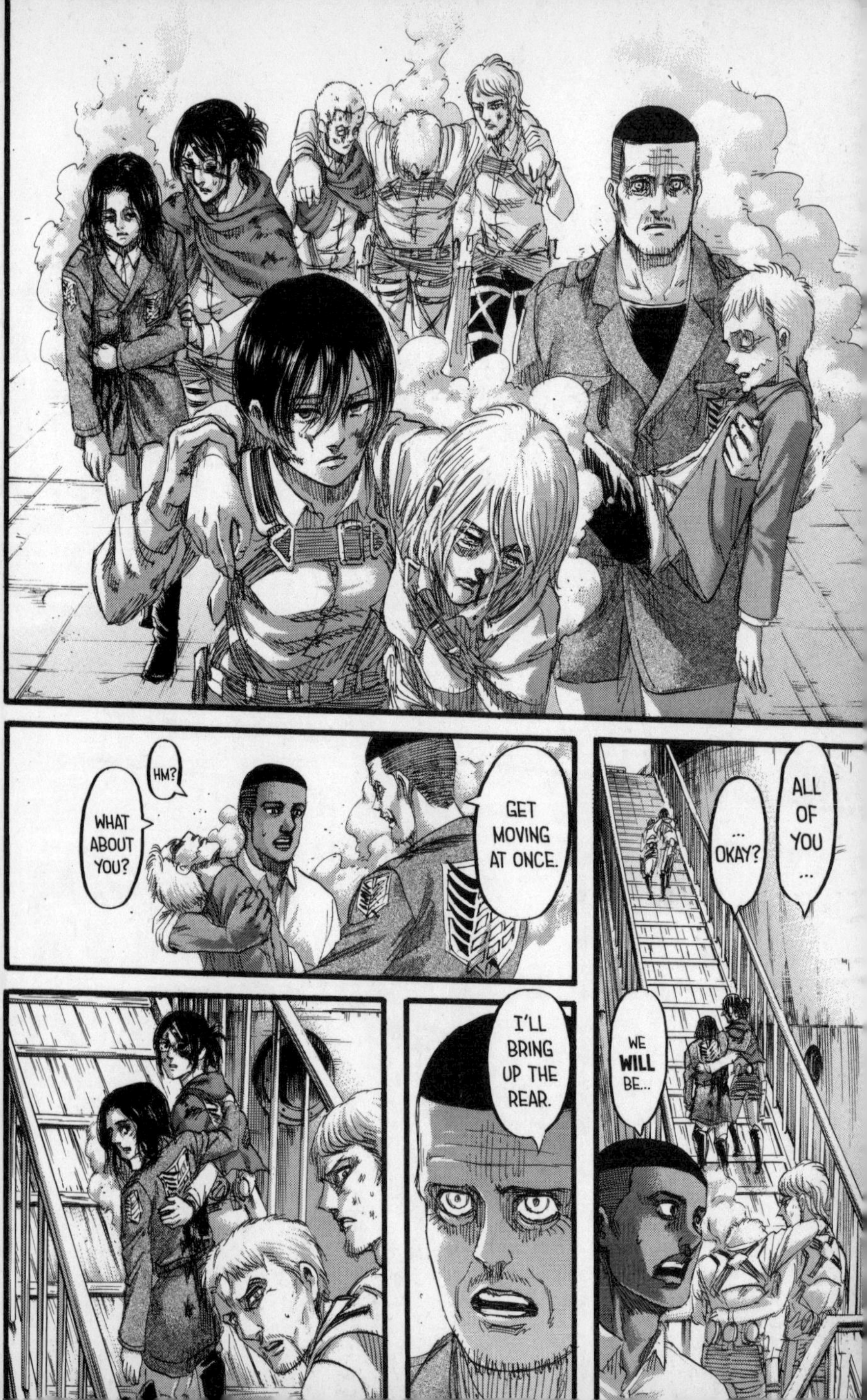
ALL OF YOU ...
... OKAY?
WE WILL BE...
GET MOVING AT ONCE.
HM?
WHAT ABOUT YOU?
I'LL BRING UP THE REAR.

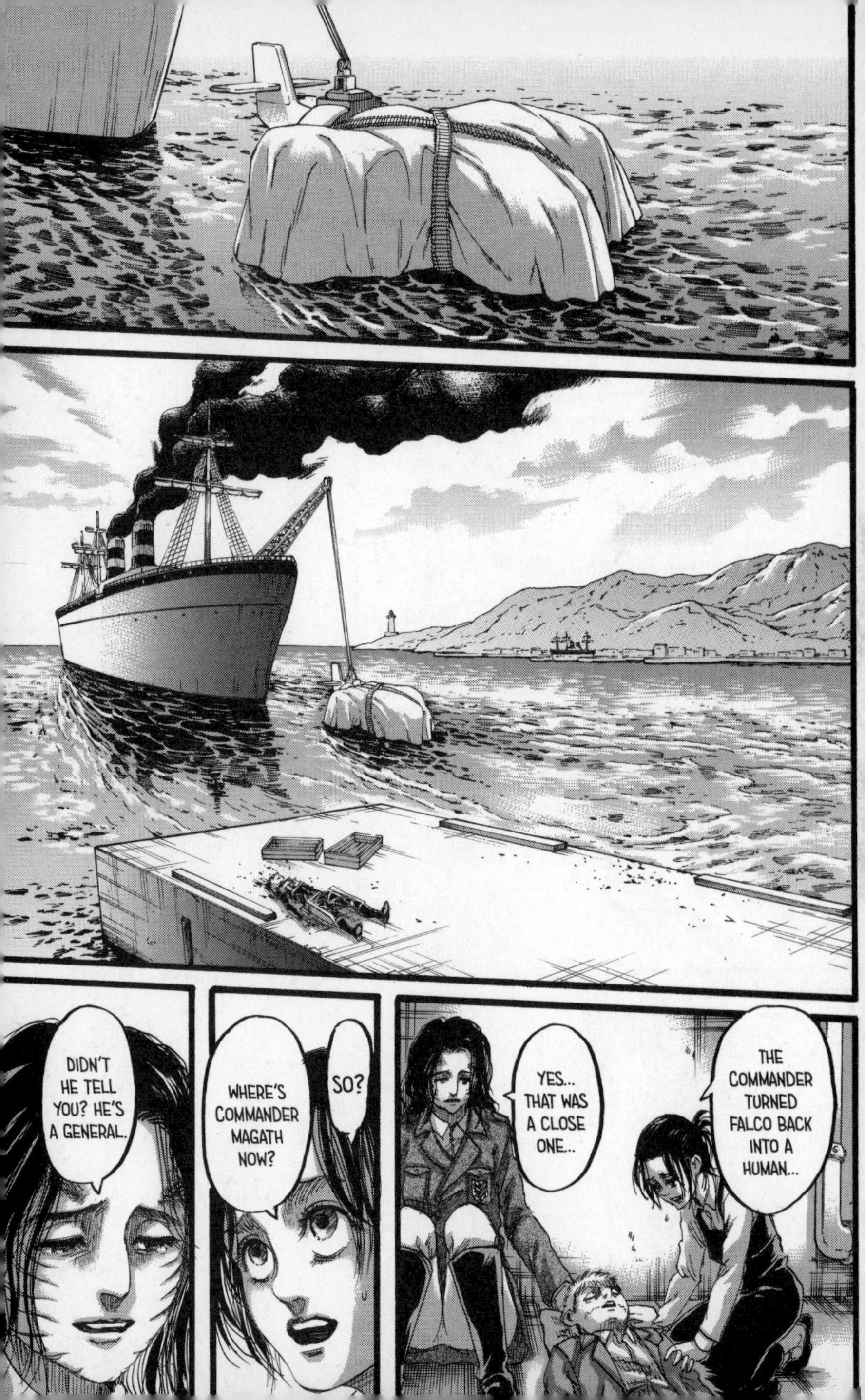
THE COMMANDER TURNED FALCO BACK INTO A HUMAN...
YES... THAT WAS A CLOSE ONE...
SO?
WHERE'S COMMANDER MAGATH NOW?
DIDN'T HE TELL YOU? HE'S A GENERAL.

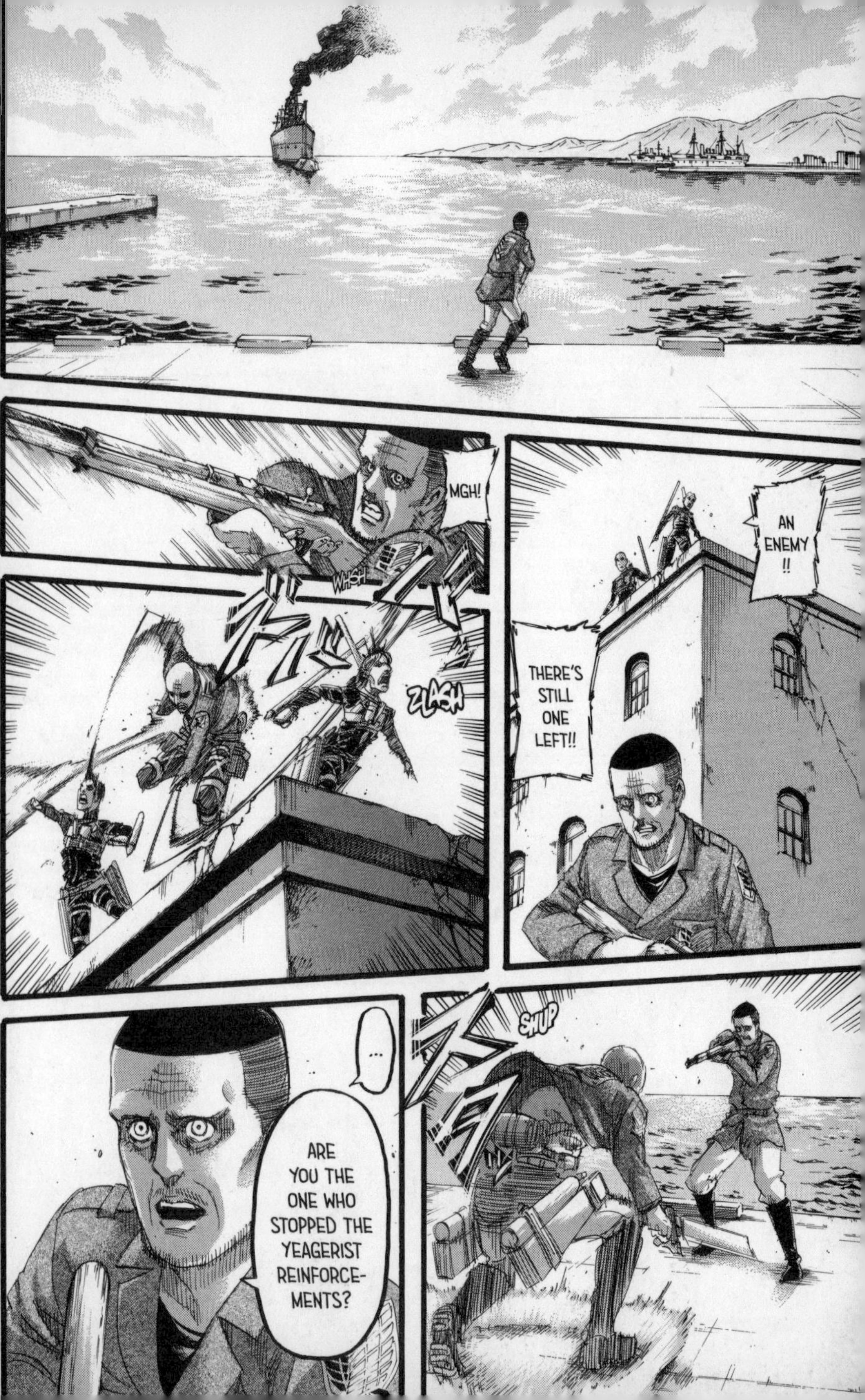
AN ENEMY !!
THERE'S STILL ONE LEFT!!
MGH!
WHSH
ZLASH
SHUP
...
ARE YOU THE ONE WHO STOPPED THE YEAGERIST REINFORCE-MENTS?

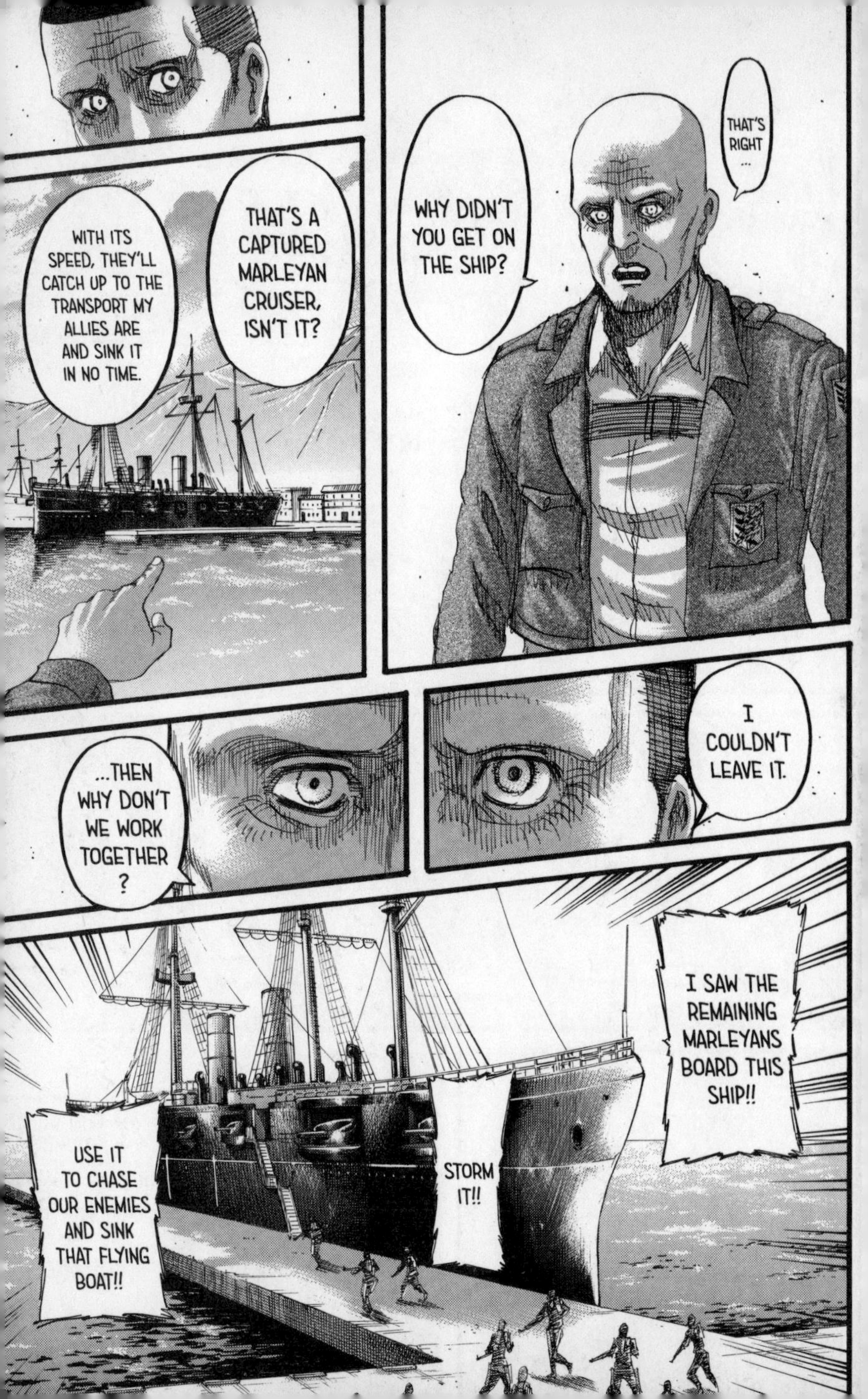
THAT'S RIGHT ...
WHY DIDN'T YOU GET ON THE SHIP?
THAT'S A CAPTURED MARLEYAN CRUISER, ISN'T IT?
WITH ITS SPEED, THEY'LL CATCH UP TO THE TRANSPORT MY ALLIES ARE AND SINK IT IN NO TIME.
I COULDN'T LEAVE IT.
...THEN WHY DON'T WE WORK TOGETHER ?
I SAW THE REMAINING MARLEYANS BOARD THIS SHIP!!
STORM IT!!
USE IT TO CHASE OUR ENEMIES AND SINK THAT FLYING BOAT!!

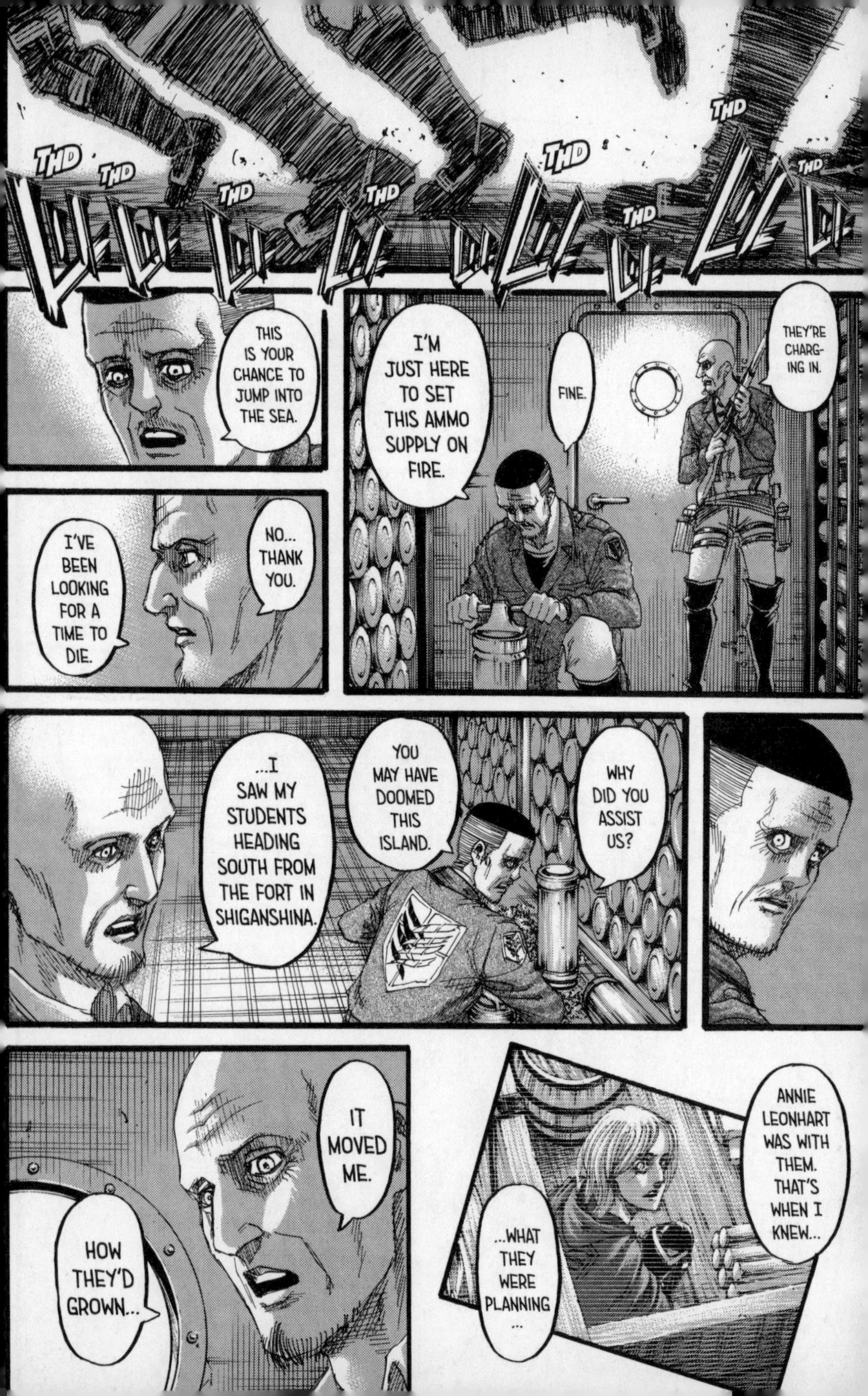
THD
THD
THD
THD
THD
THD
THD
THD
THEY'RE CHARG-ING IN.
FINE.
I'M JUST HERE TO SET THIS AMMO SUPPLY ON FIRE.
THIS IS YOUR CHANCE TO JUMP INTO THE SEA.
NO... THANK YOU.
I'VE BEEN LOOKING FOR A TIME TO DIE.
WHY DID YOU ASSIST US?
YOU MAY HAVE DOOMED THIS ISLAND.
...I SAW MY STUDENTS HEADING SOUTH FROM THE FORT IN SHIGANSHINA.
ANNIE LEONHART WAS WITH THEM. THAT'S WHEN I KNEW...
...WHAT THEY WERE PLANNING...
IT MOVED ME.
HOW THEY'D GROWN...

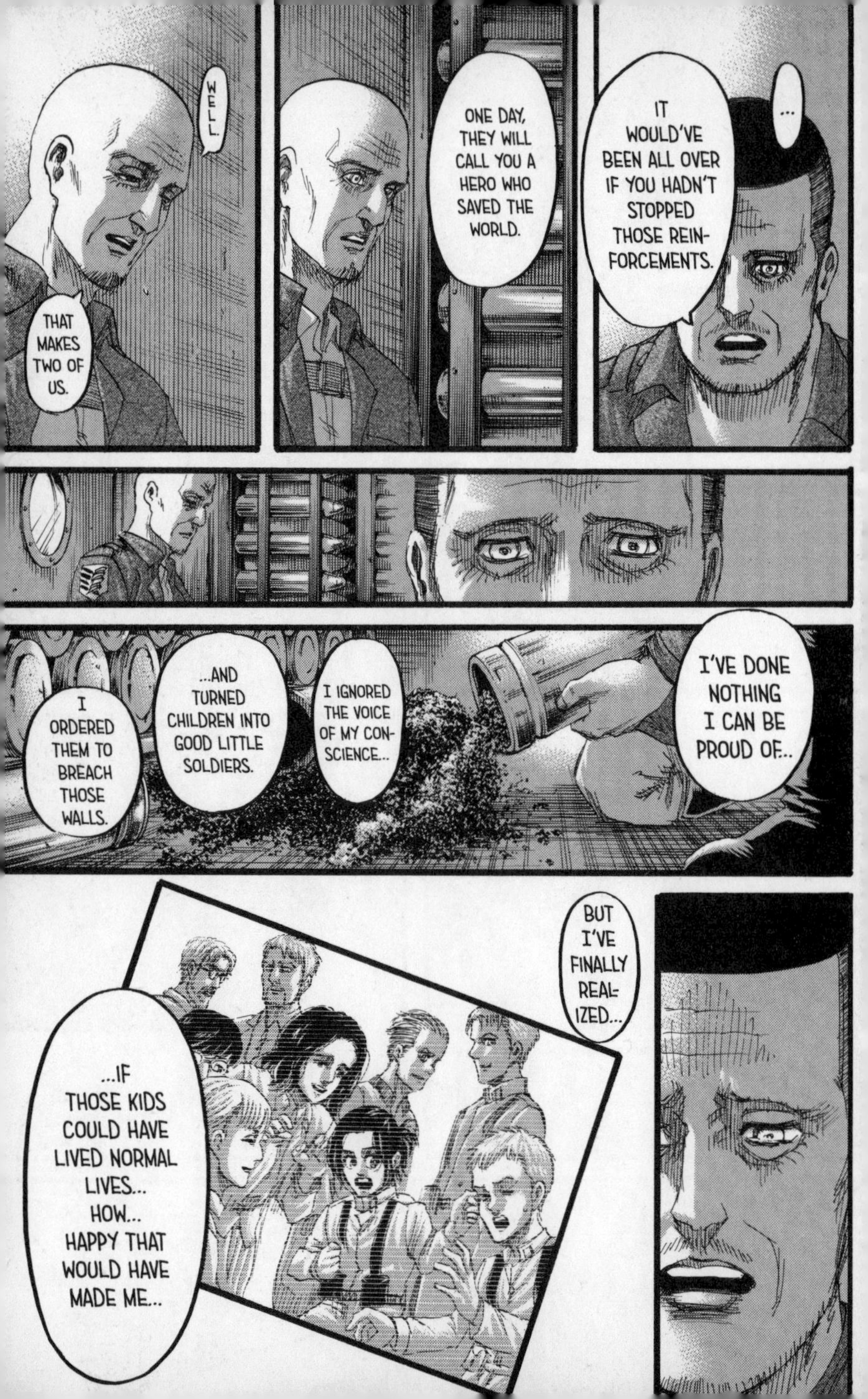
...
IT WOULD'VE BEEN ALL OVER IF YOU HADN'T STOPPED THOSE REIN-FORCEMENTS.
ONE DAY, THEY WILL CALL YOU A HERO WHO SAVED THE WORLD.
WELL.
THAT MAKES TWO OF US.
I'VE DONE NOTHING I CAN BE PROUD OF...
I IGNORED THE VOICE OF MY CON-SCIENCE...
...AND TURNED CHILDREN INTO GOOD LITTLE SOLDIERS.
I ORDERED THEM TO BREACH THOSE WALLS.
BUT I'VE FINALLY REAL-IZED...
...IF THOSE KIDS COULD HAVE LIVED NORMAL LIVES... HOW... HAPPY THAT WOULD HAVE MADE ME...

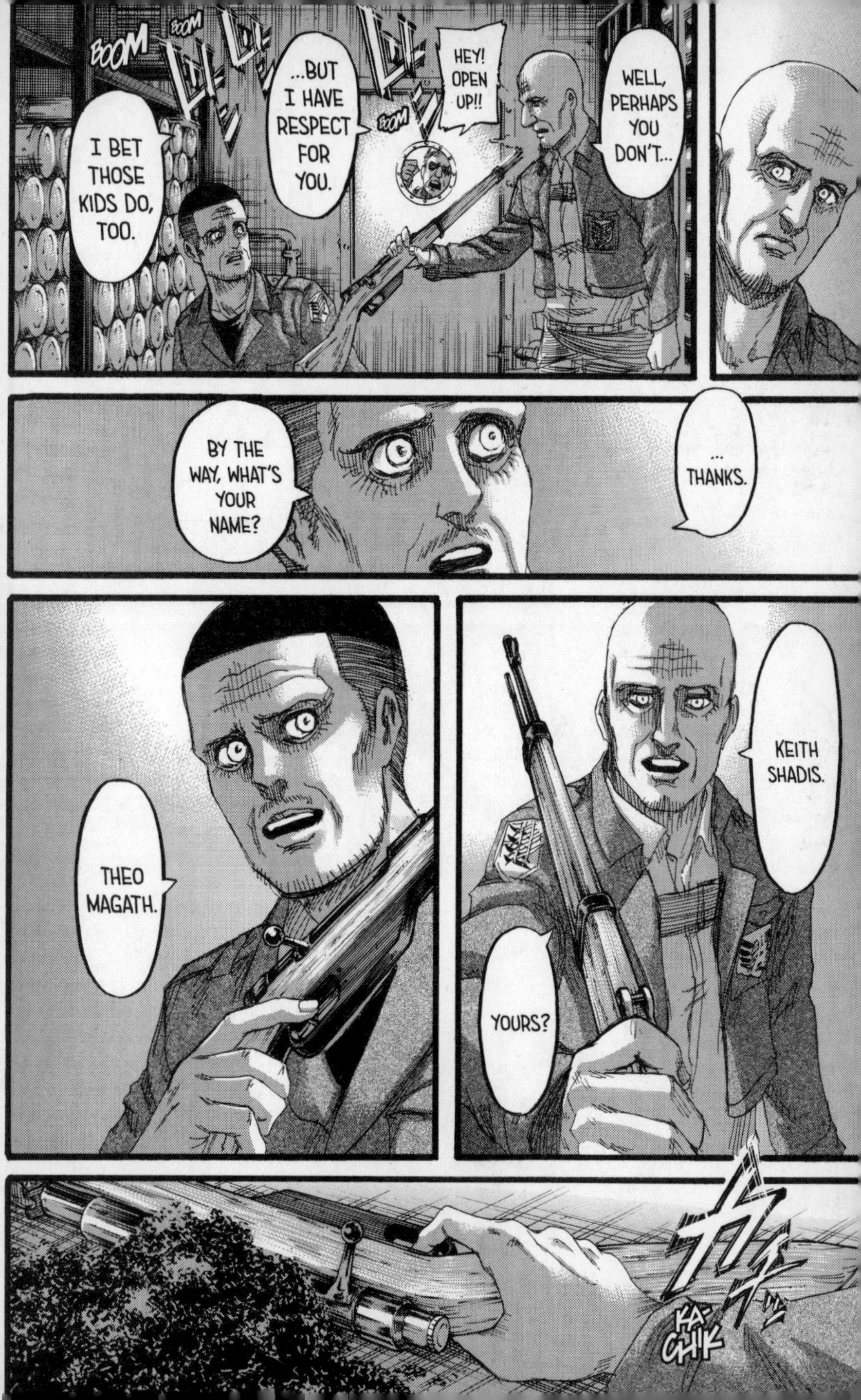
WELL, PERHAPS YOU DON'T...
HEY! OPEN UP!!
BOOM
...BUT I HAVE RESPECT FOR YOU.
BOOM
BOOM
I BET THOSE KIDS DO, TOO.
... THANKS.
BY THE WAY, WHAT'S YOUR NAME?
KEITH SHADIS.
YOURS?
THEO MAGATH.
KA-CHIK

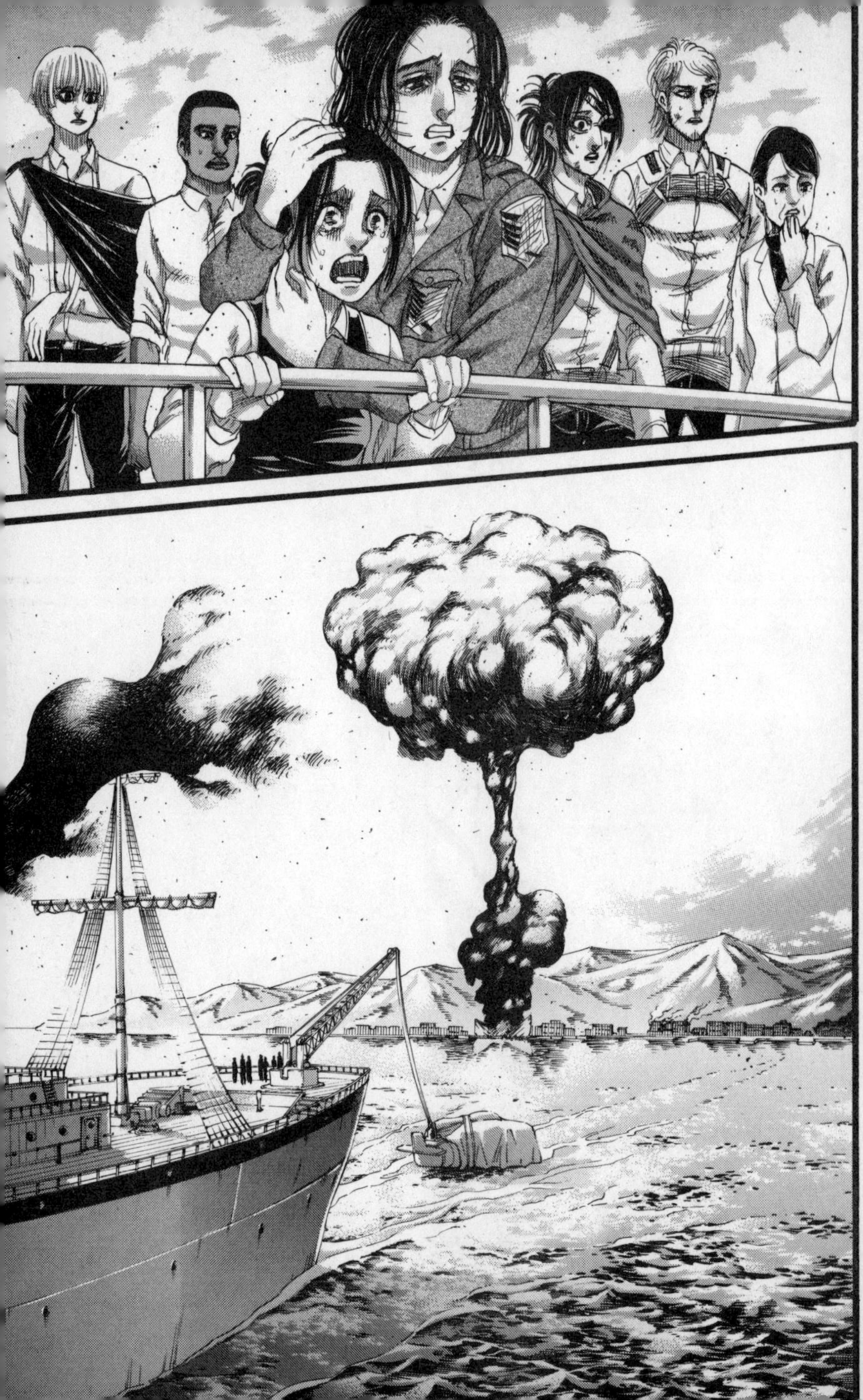

ATTACK on TITAN

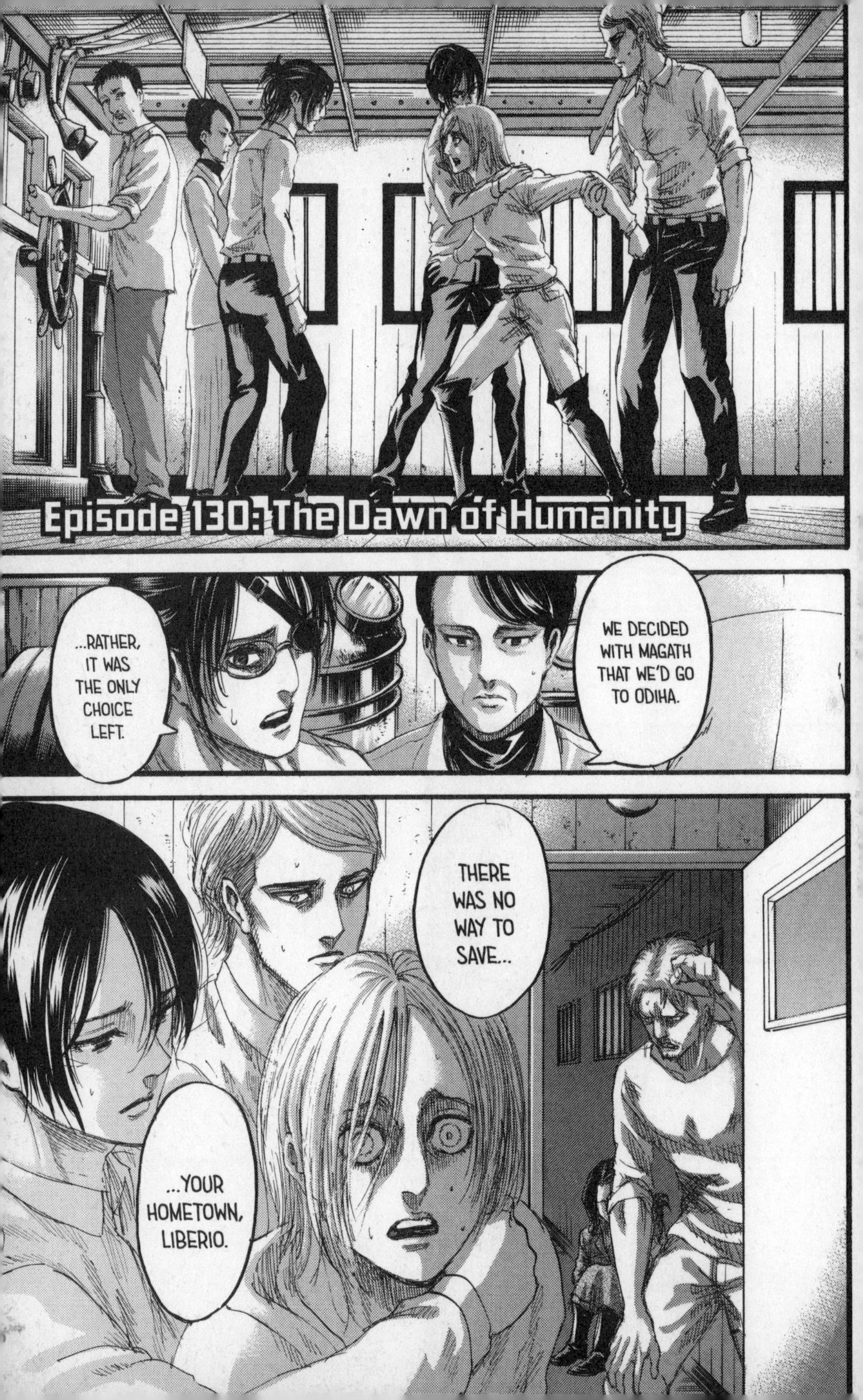
Episode 130: The Dawn of Humanity
WE DECIDED WITH MAGATH THAT WE'D GO TO ODIHA.
...RATHER, IT WAS THE ONLY CHOICE LEFT.
THERE WAS NO WAY TO SAVE...
...YOUR HOMETOWN, LIBERIO.

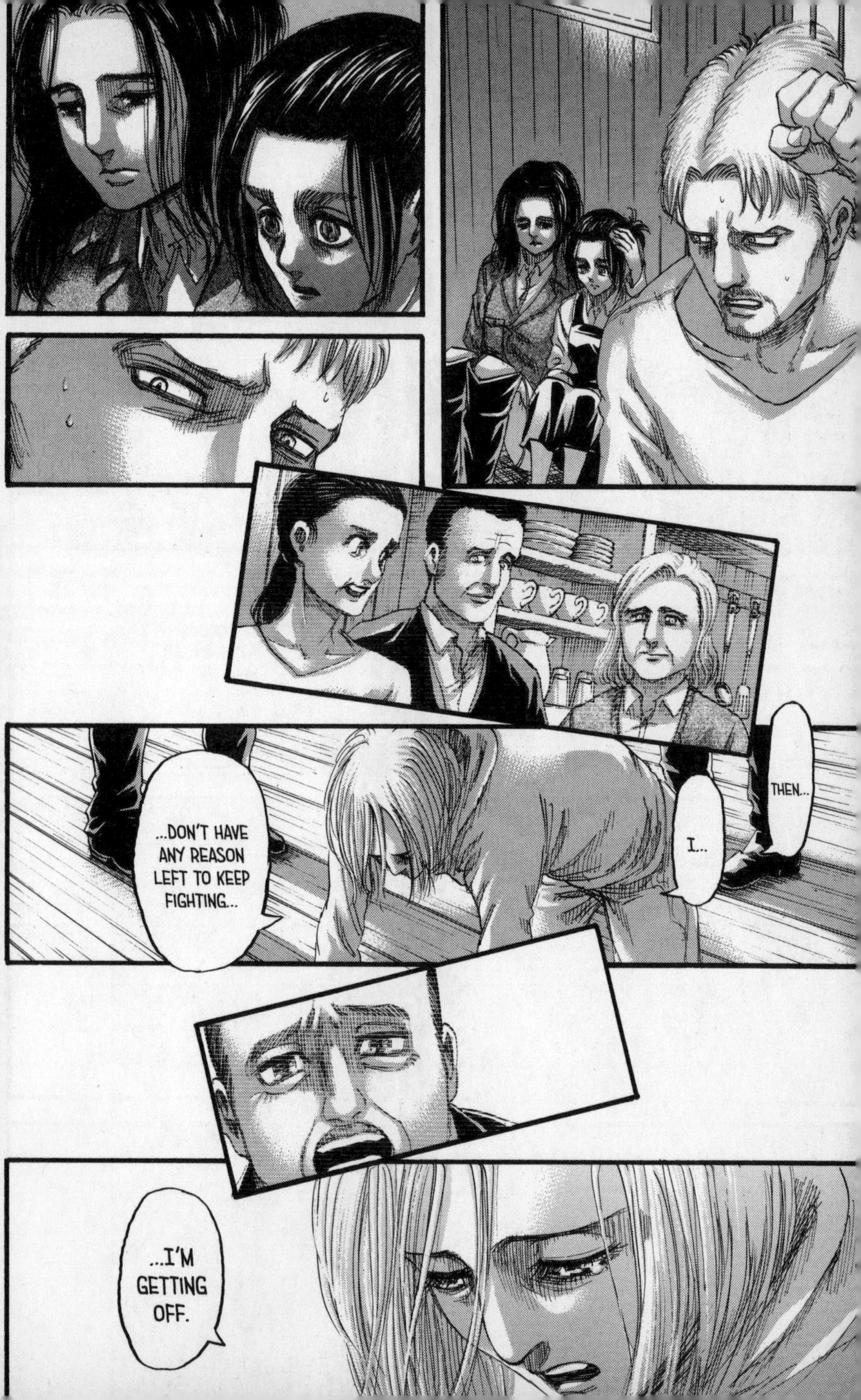
THEN...
I...
...DON'T HAVE ANY REASON LEFT TO KEEP FIGHTING...
...I'M GETTING OFF.

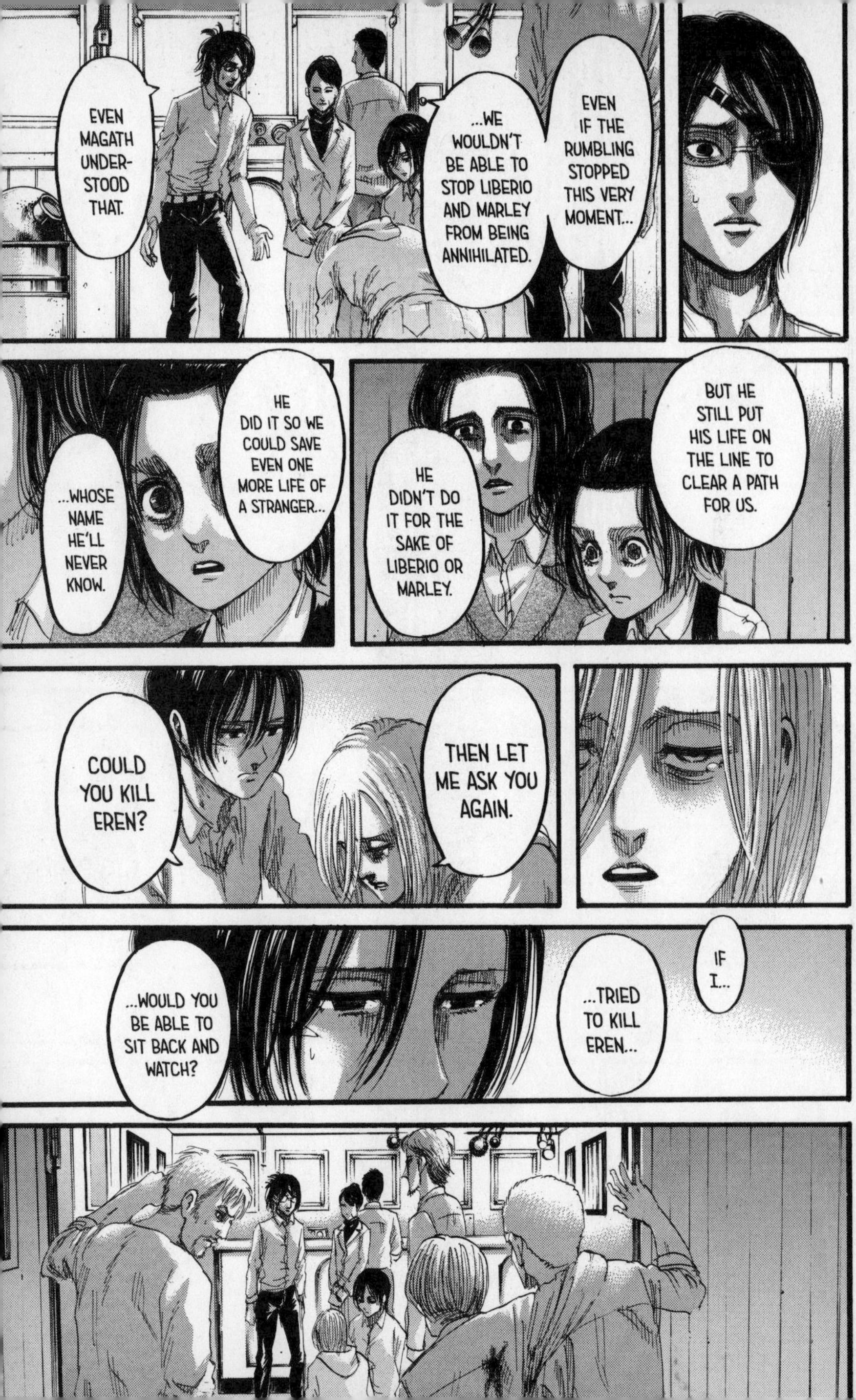
EVEN IF THE RUMBLING STOPPED THIS VERY MOMENT...
...WE WOULDN'T BE ABLE TO STOP LIBERIO AND MARLEY FROM BEING ANNIHILATED.
EVEN MAGATH UNDER-STOOD THAT.
BUT HE STILL PUT HIS LIFE ON THE LINE TO CLEAR A PATH FOR US.
HE DIDN'T DO IT FOR THE SAKE OF LIBERIO OR MARLEY.
HE DID IT SO WE COULD SAVE EVEN ONE MORE LIFE OF A STRANGER...
...WHOSE NAME HE'LL NEVER KNOW.
THEN LET ME ASK YOU AGAIN.
COULD YOU KILL EREN?
IF I...
...TRIED TO KILL EREN...
...WOULD YOU BE ABLE TO SIT BACK AND WATCH?

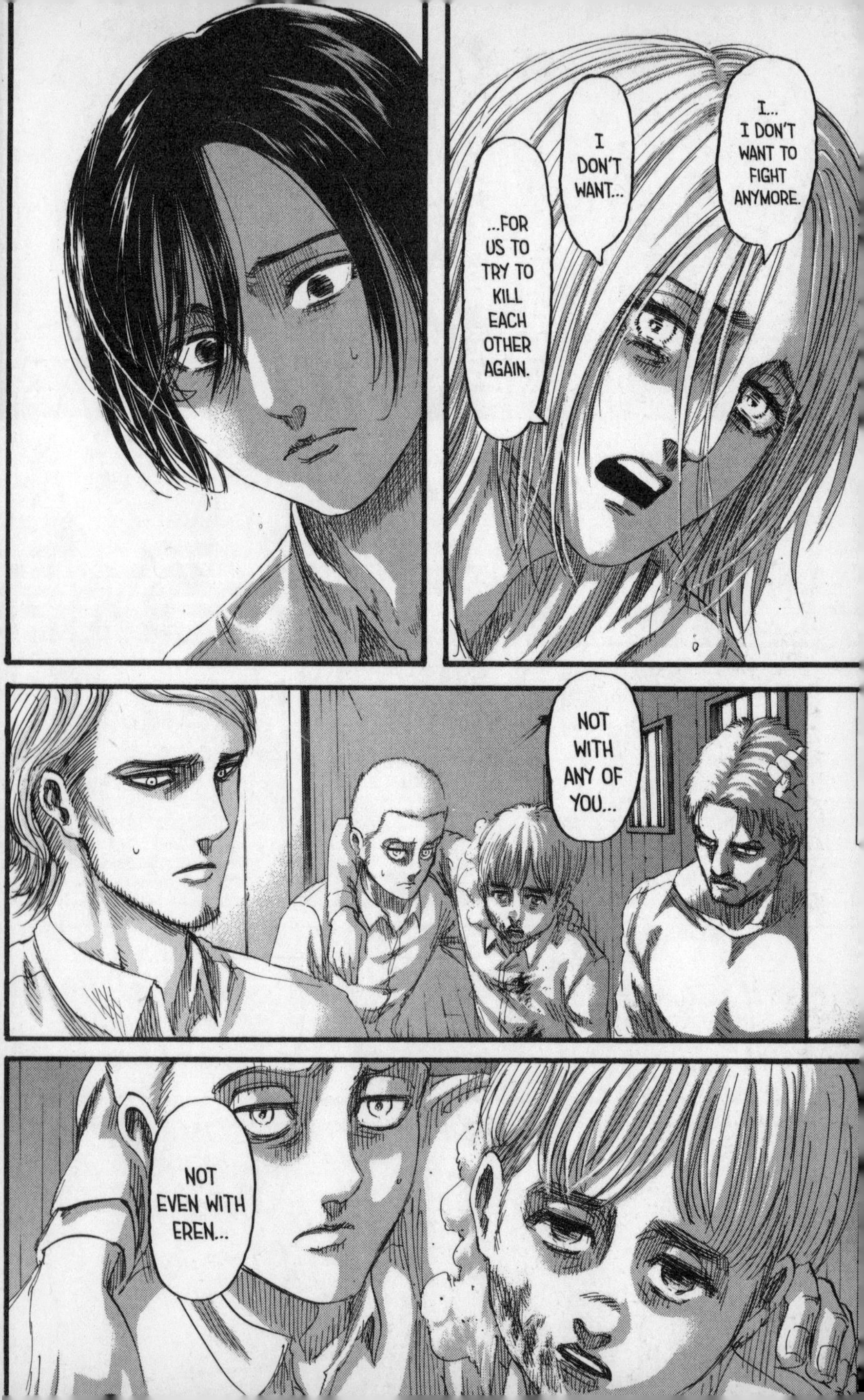
I... I DON'T WANT TO FIGHT ANYMORE.
I DON'T WANT...
...FOR US TO TRY TO KILL EACH OTHER AGAIN.
NOT WITH ANY OF YOU...
NOT EVEN WITH EREN...

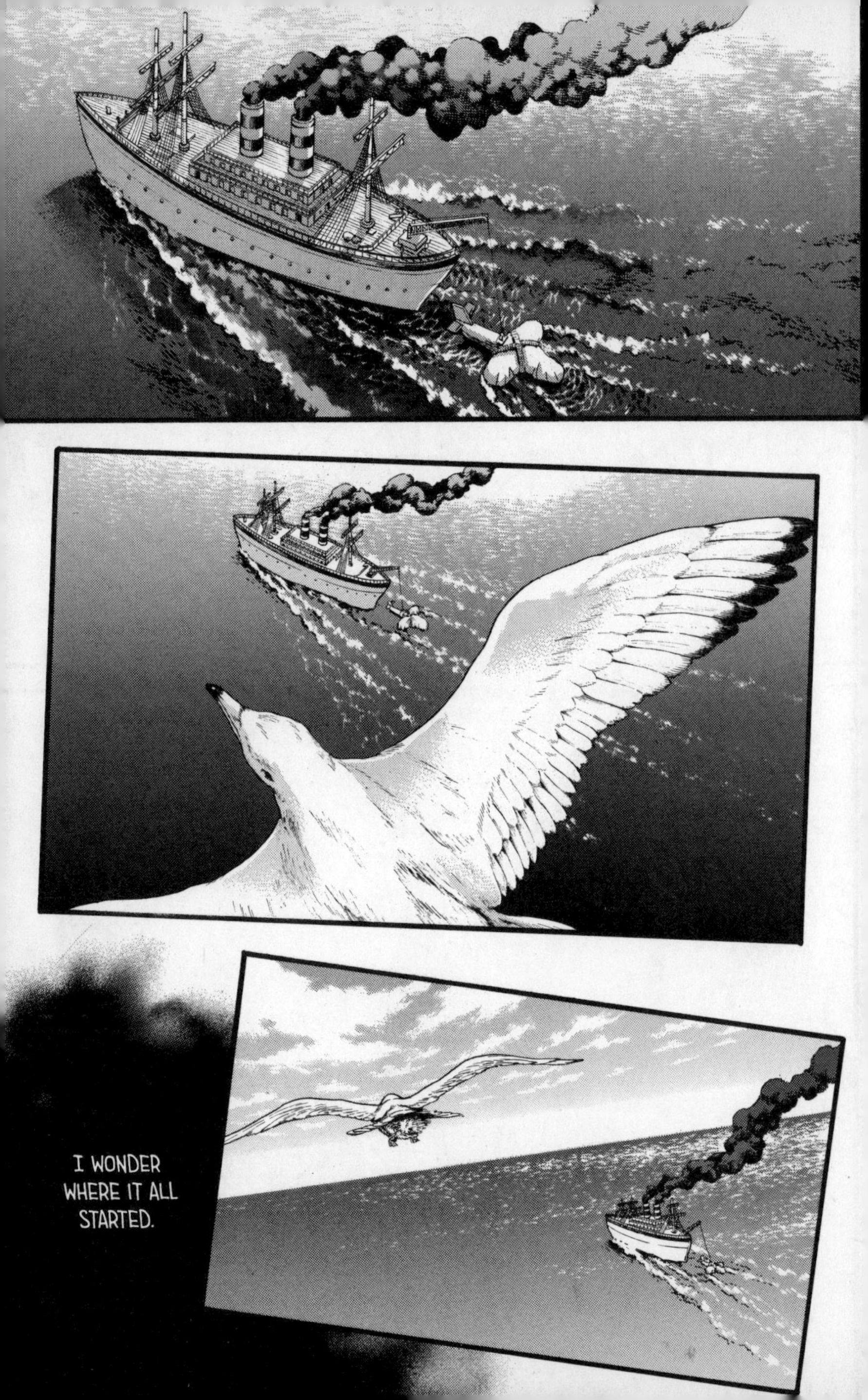
I WONDER WHERE IT ALL STARTED.

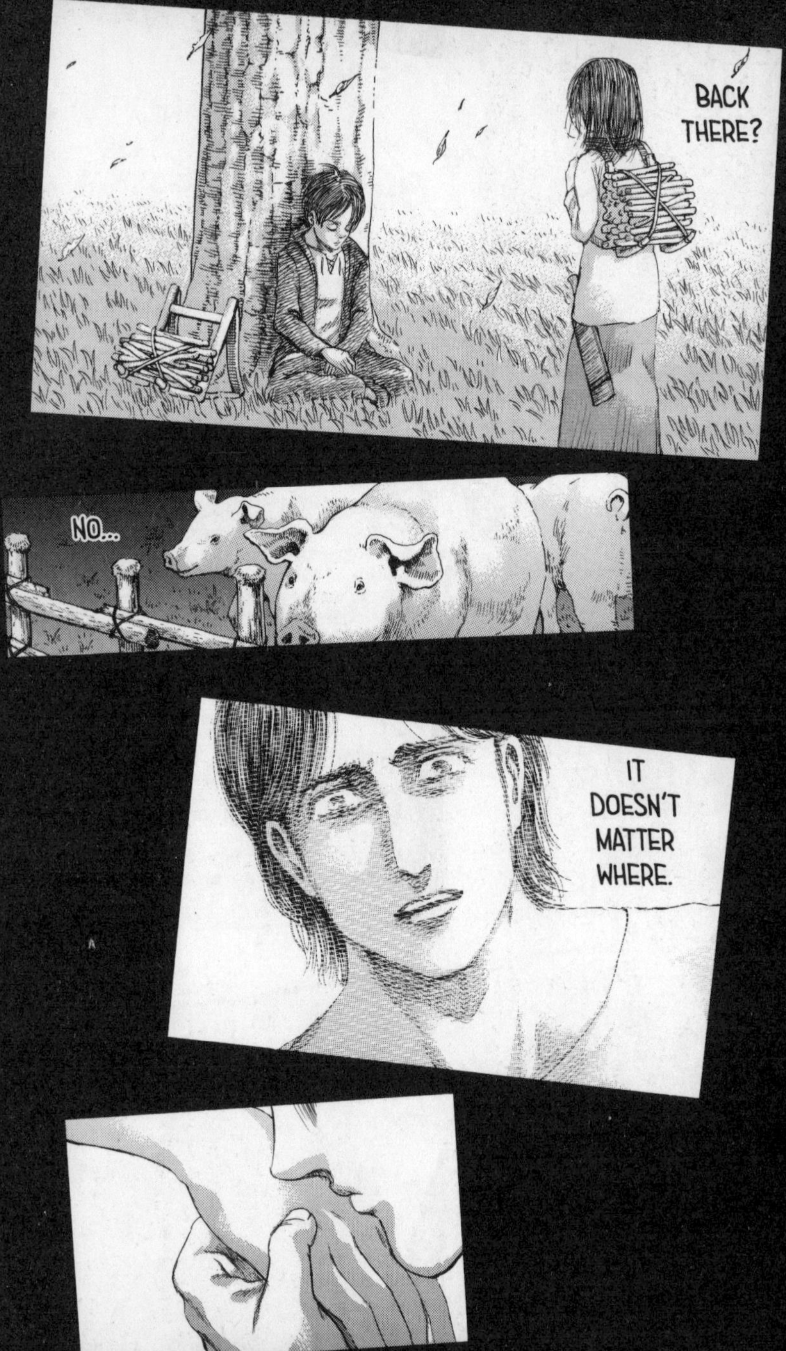
BACK THERE?
NO...
IT DOESN'T MATTER WHERE.

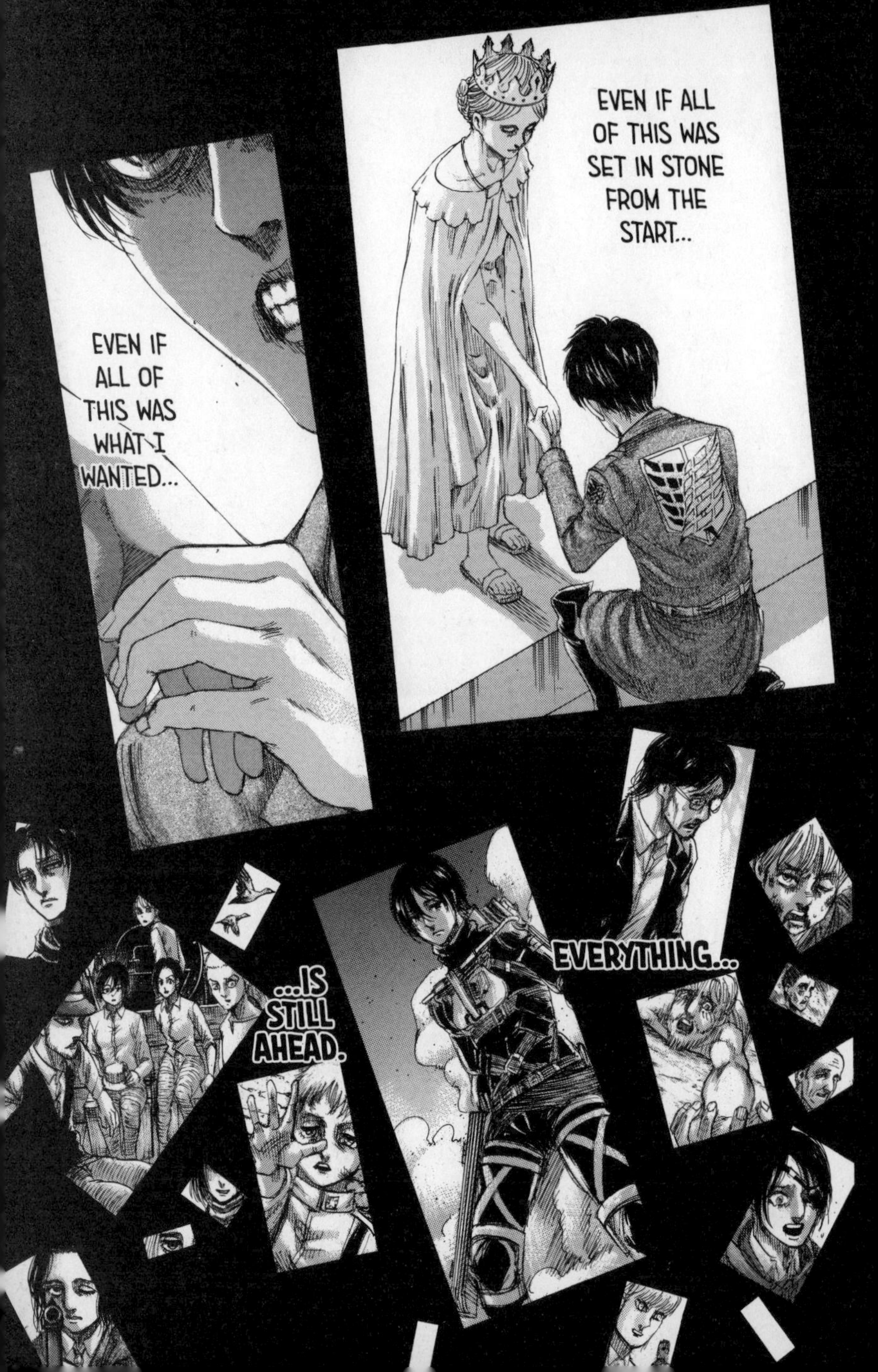
EVEN IF ALL OF THIS WAS SET IN STONE FROM THE START...
EVEN IF ALL OF THIS WAS WHAT I WANTED...
EVERYTHING...
...IS STILL AHEAD.

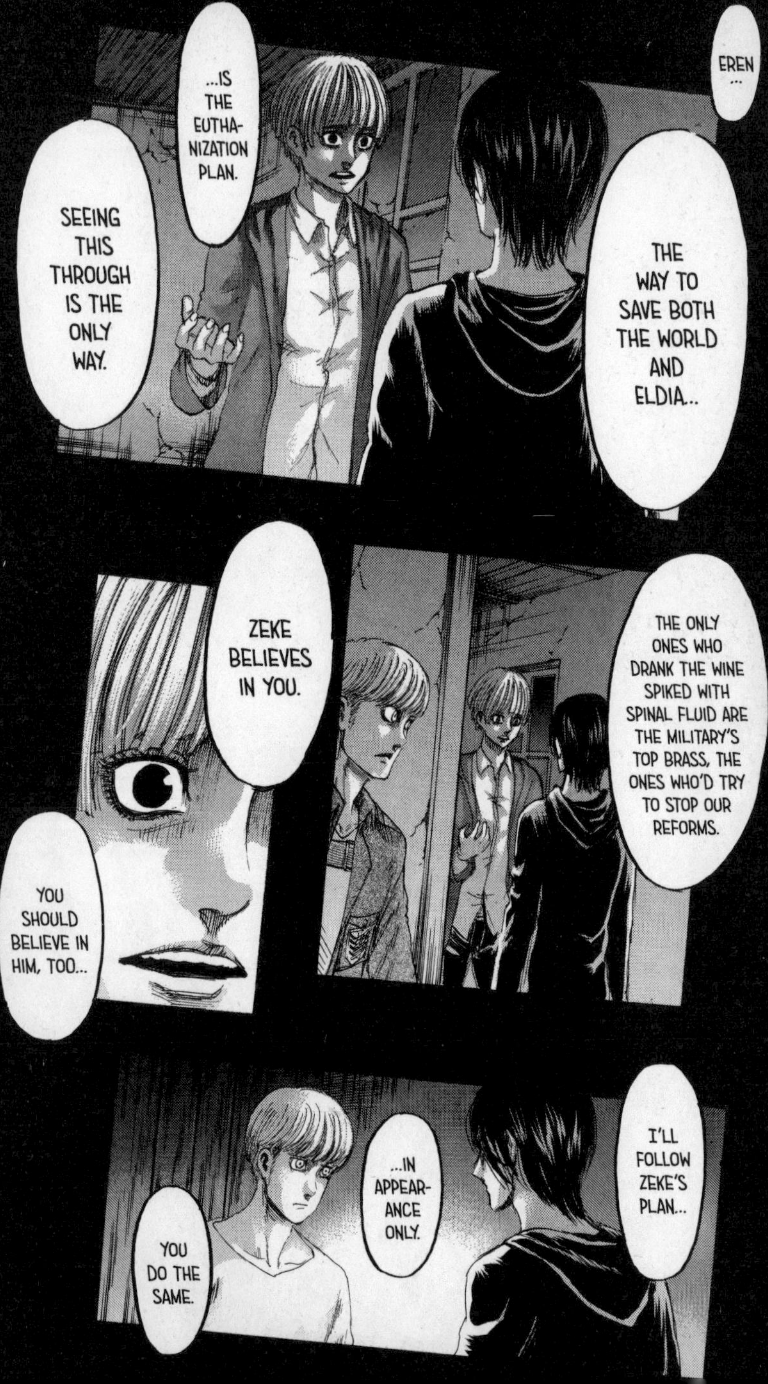
EREN ...
THE WAY TO SAVE BOTH THE WORLD AND ELDIA...
...IS THE EUTHANIZATION PLAN.
SEEING THIS THROUGH IS THE ONLY WAY.
THE ONLY ONES WHO DRANK THE WINE SPIKED WITH SPINAL FLUID ARE THE MILITARY'S TOP BRASS, THE ONES WHO'D TRY TO STOP OUR REFORMS.
ZEKE BELIEVES IN YOU.
YOU SHOULD BELIEVE IN HIM, TOO...
I'LL FOLLOW ZEKE'S PLAN...
...IN APPEARANCE ONLY.
YOU DO THE SAME.

...WHAT WILL PRETENDING...

...TO FOLLOW ZEKE ACHIEVE?

THE MILITARY POLICE BRIGADE IS MOVING FORWARD WITH A PLAN TO TURN YOU INTO A TITAN AND FEED ZEKE TO YOU NOW THAT HE'S HERE ON THE ISLAND.

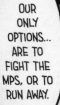

OUR ONLY OPTIONS... ARE TO FIGHT THE MPS, OR TO RUN AWAY.

...YOU KNOW I HAVEN'T REALLY JUST BEEN TENDING TO CATTLE ALL THIS TIME.

THERE'S NO NEED TO FIGHT OR RUN.

I KNOW.

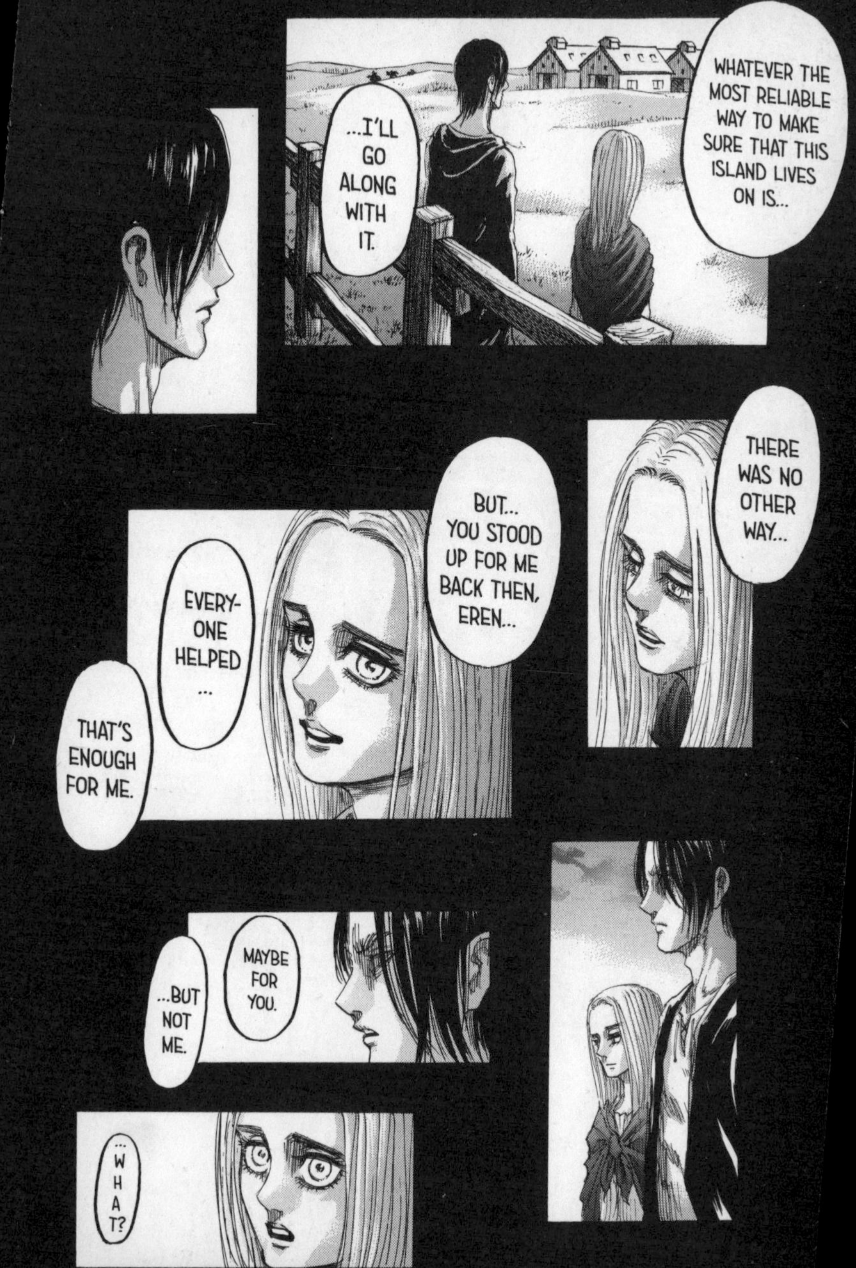
WHATEVER THE MOST RELIABLE WAY TO MAKE SURE THAT THIS ISLAND LIVES ON IS...
...I'LL GO ALONG WITH IT.
THERE WAS NO OTHER WAY...
BUT... YOU STOOD UP FOR ME BACK THEN, EREN...
EVERY-ONE HELPED ...
THAT'S ENOUGH FOR ME.
MAYBE FOR YOU.
...BUT NOT ME.
...WHAT?

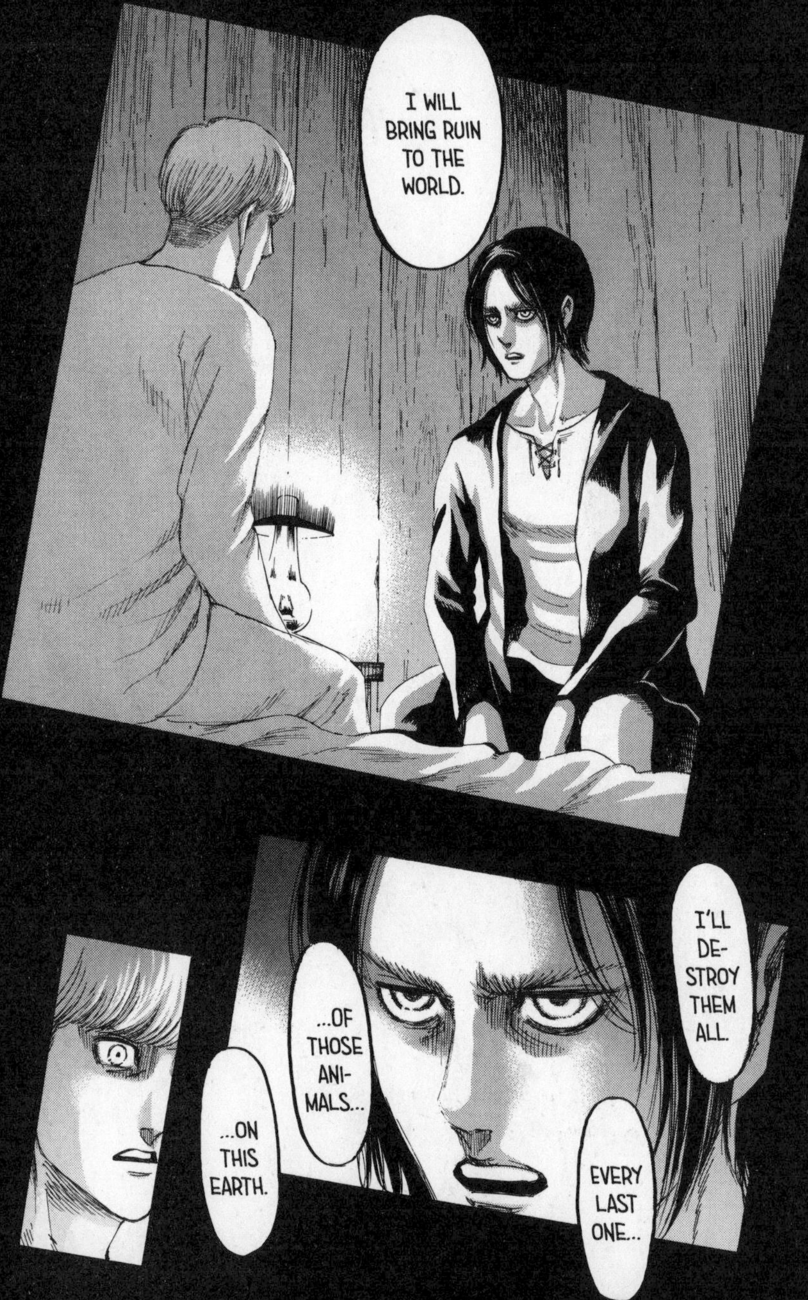
I WILL BRING RUIN TO THE WORLD.
I'LL DE-STROY THEM ALL.
EVERY LAST ONE...
...OF THOSE ANI-MALS...
...ON THIS EARTH.

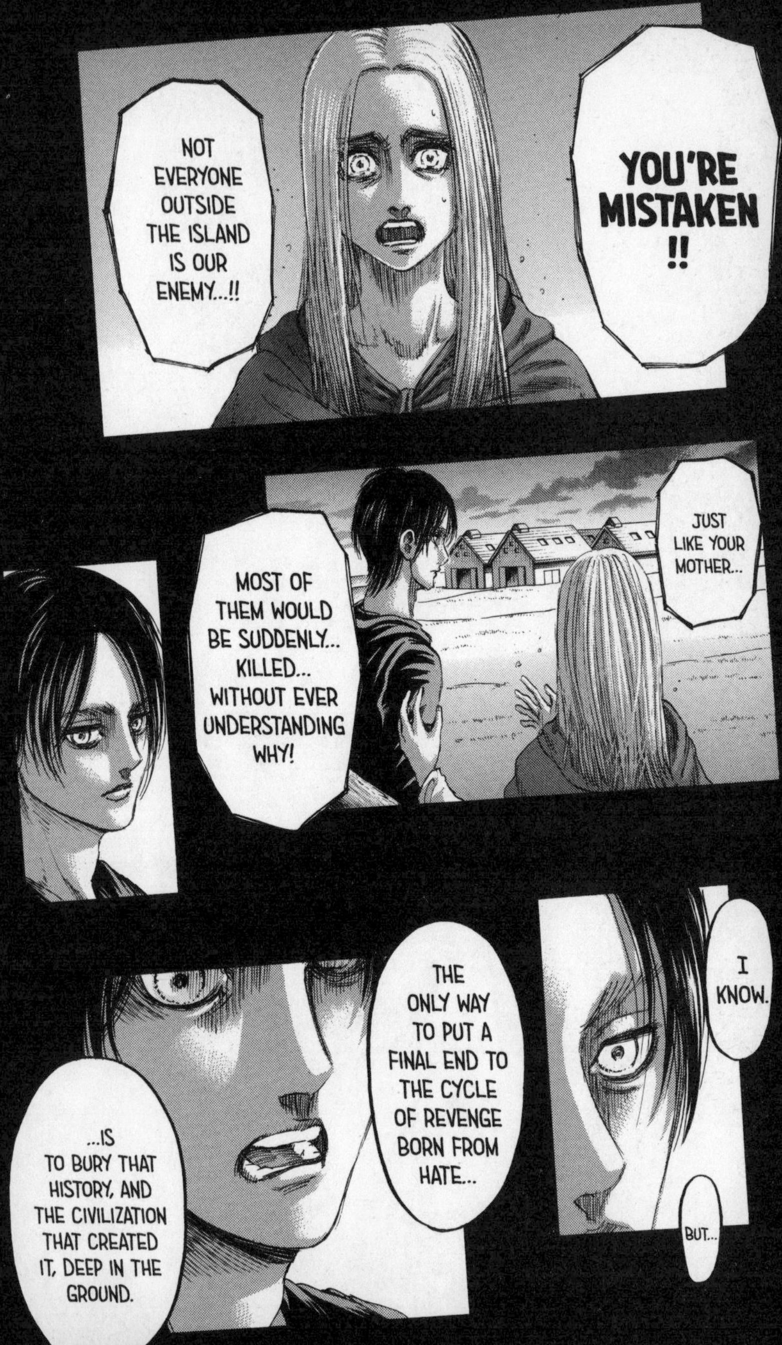
YOU'RE MISTAKEN !!
NOT EVERYONE OUTSIDE THE ISLAND IS OUR ENEMY...!!
JUST LIKE YOUR MOTHER...
MOST OF THEM WOULD BE SUDDENLY... KILLED... WITHOUT EVER UNDERSTANDING WHY!
I KNOW.
BUT...
THE ONLY WAY TO PUT A FINAL END TO THE CYCLE OF REVENGE BORN FROM HATE...
...IS TO BURY THAT HISTORY, AND THE CIVILIZATION THAT CREATED IT, DEEP IN THE GROUND.

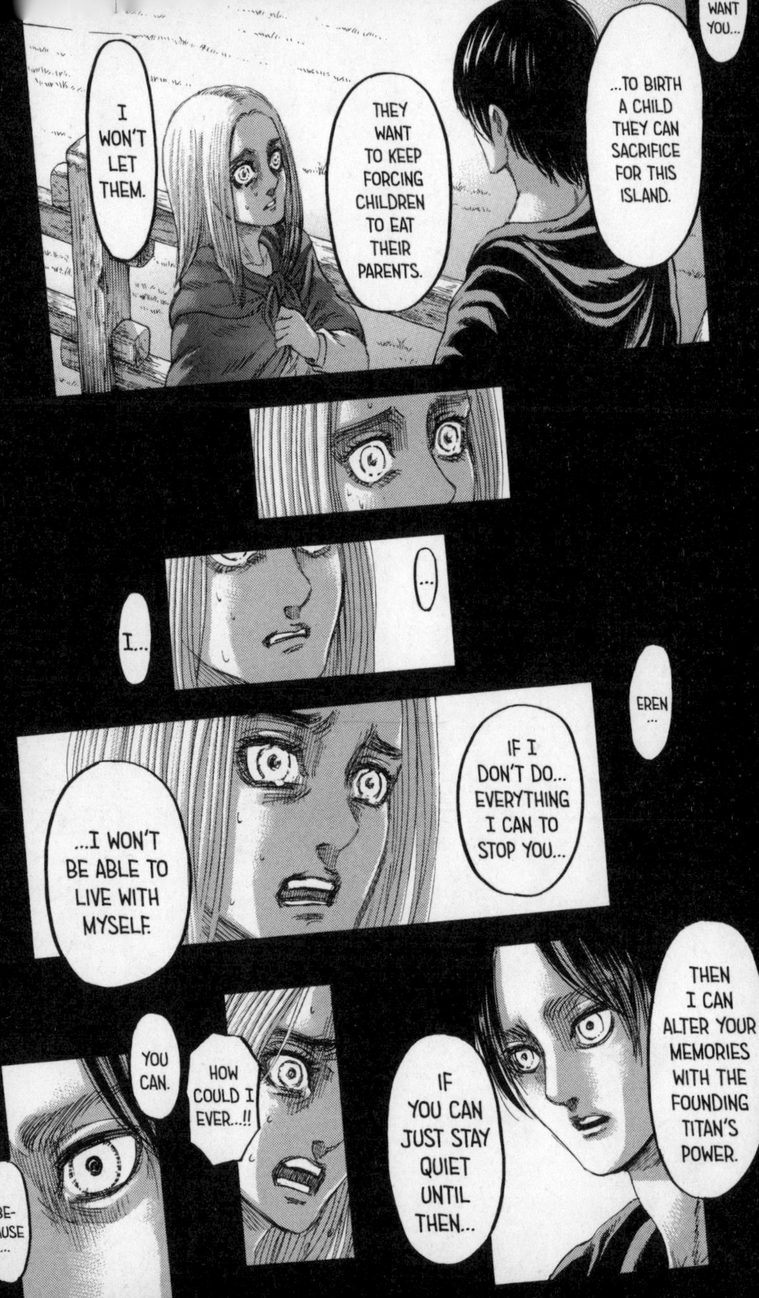
THEY WANT YOU...
...TO BIRTH A CHILD THEY CAN SACRIFICE FOR THIS ISLAND.
THEY WANT TO KEEP FORCING CHILDREN TO EAT THEIR PARENTS.
I WON'T LET THEM.
...
I...
EREN...
IF I DON'T DO... EVERYTHING I CAN TO STOP YOU...
...I WON'T BE ABLE TO LIVE WITH MYSELF.
THEN I CAN ALTER YOUR MEMORIES WITH THE FOUNDING TITAN'S POWER.
IF YOU CAN JUST STAY QUIET UNTIL THEN...
HOW COULD I EVER...!!
YOU CAN.
BE-CAUSE...

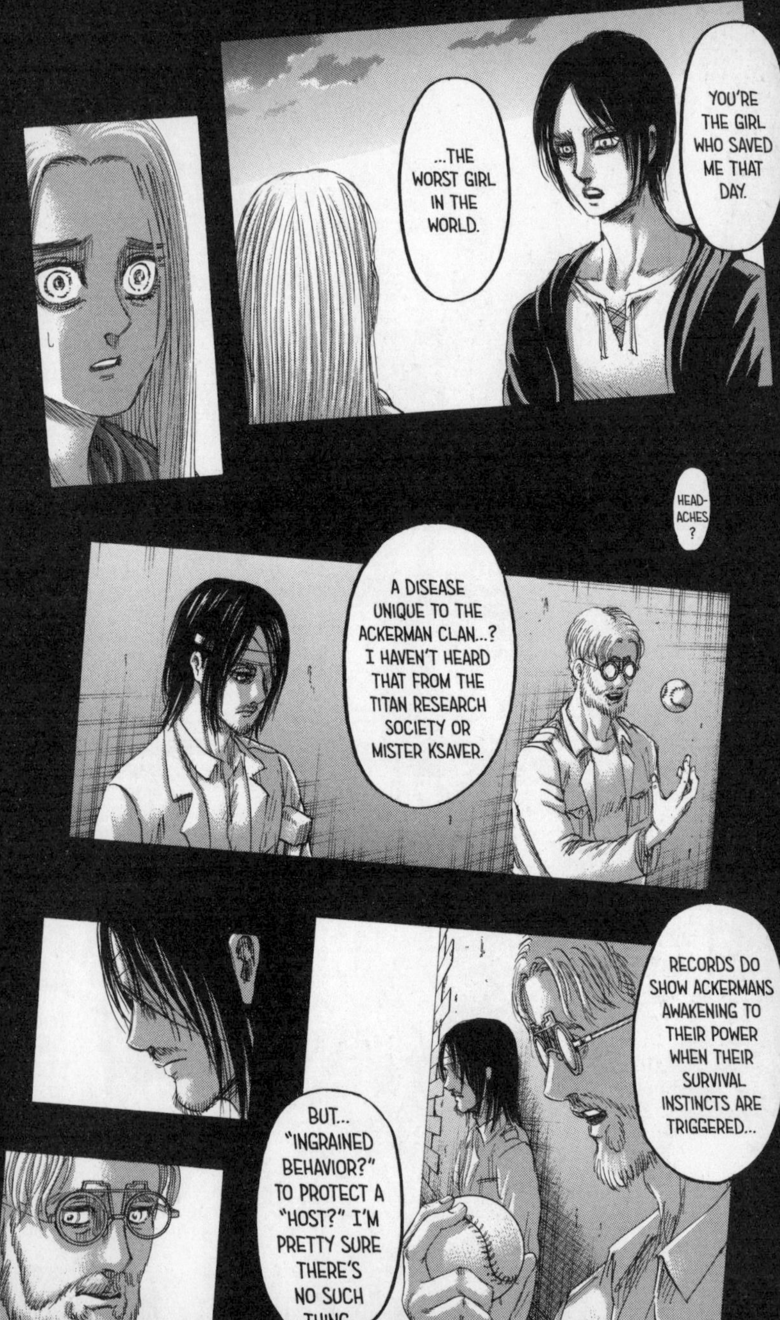
YOU'RE THE GIRL WHO SAVED ME THAT DAY.
...THE WORST GIRL IN THE WORLD.
HEAD-ACHES?
A DISEASE UNIQUE TO THE ACKERMAN CLAN...? I HAVEN'T HEARD THAT FROM THE TITAN RESEARCH SOCIETY OR MISTER KSAVER.
RECORDS DO SHOW ACKERMANS AWAKENING TO THEIR POWER WHEN THEIR SURVIVAL INSTINCTS ARE TRIGGERED...
BUT... "INGRAINED BEHAVIOR?" TO PROTECT A "HOST?" I'M PRETTY SURE THERE'S NO SUCH THING.

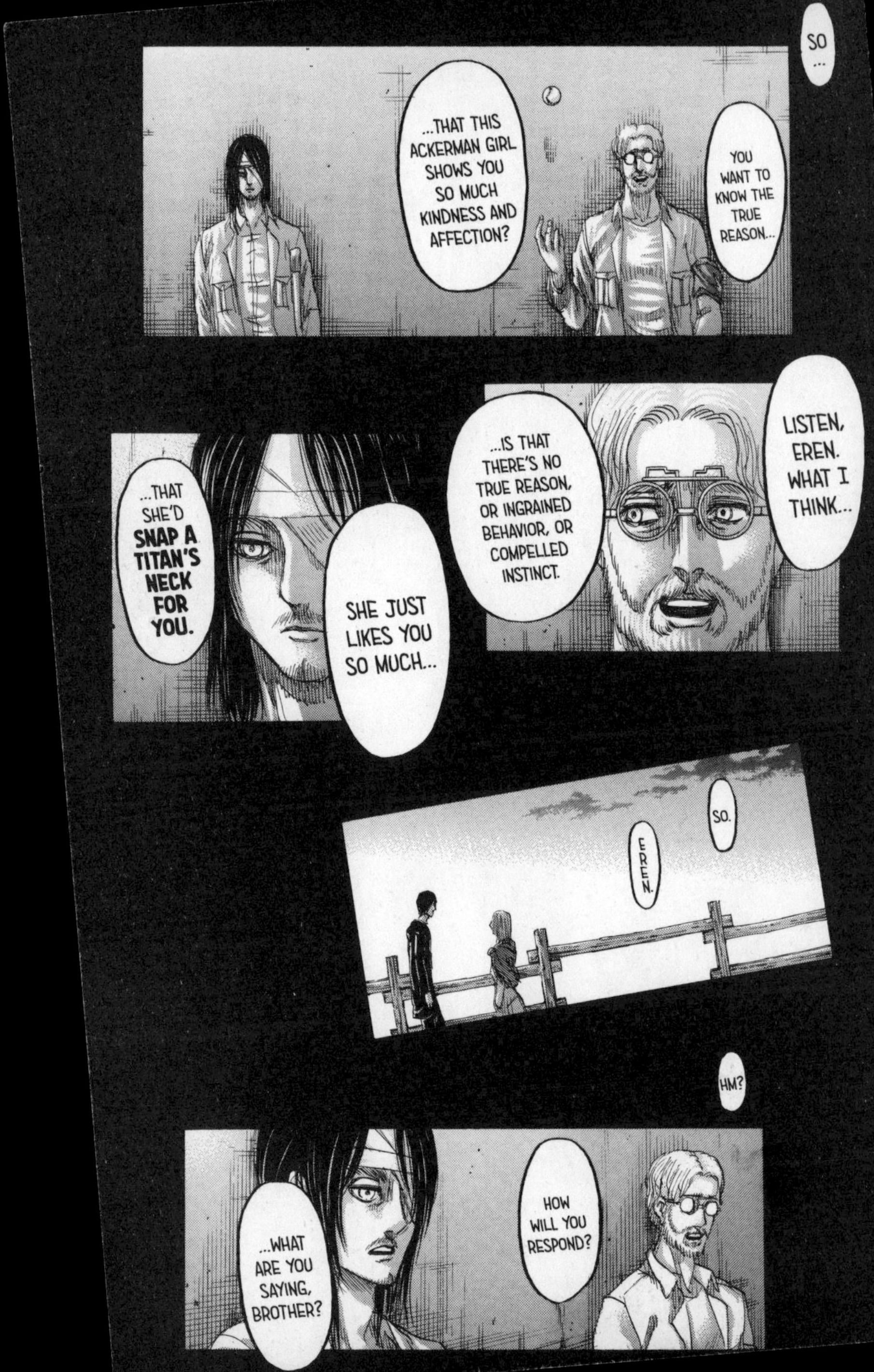
SO ...
YOU WANT TO KNOW THE TRUE REASON...
...THAT THIS ACKERMAN GIRL SHOWS YOU SO MUCH KINDNESS AND AFFECTION?
LISTEN, EREN. WHAT I THINK...
...IS THAT THERE'S NO TRUE REASON, OR INGRAINED BEHAVIOR, OR COMPELLED INSTINCT.
...THAT SHE'D **SNAP A TITAN'S NECK FOR YOU.**
SHE JUST LIKES YOU SO MUCH...
SO.
EREN.
HM?
HOW WILL YOU RESPOND?
...WHAT ARE YOU SAYING, BROTHER?

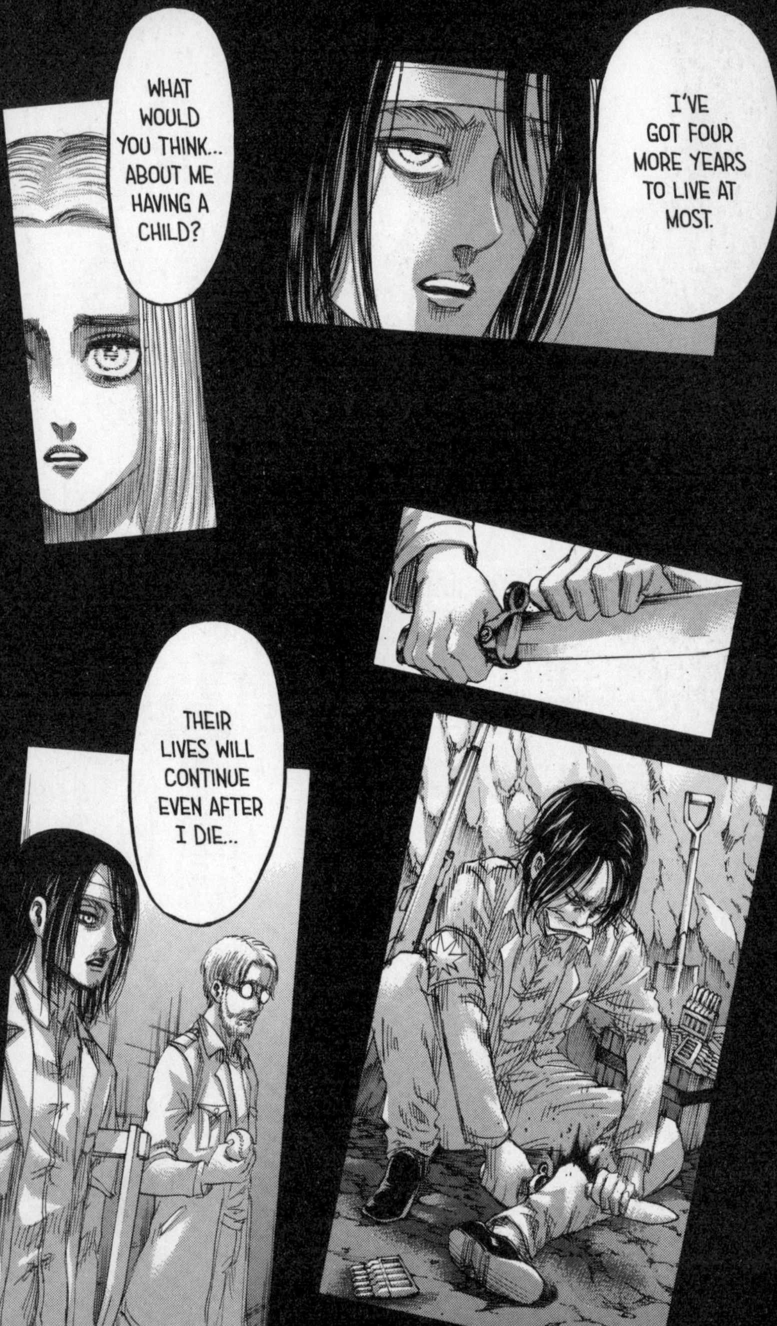
I'VE GOT FOUR MORE YEARS TO LIVE AT MOST.
WHAT WOULD YOU THINK... ABOUT ME HAVING A CHILD?
THEIR LIVES WILL CONTINUE EVEN AFTER I DIE...

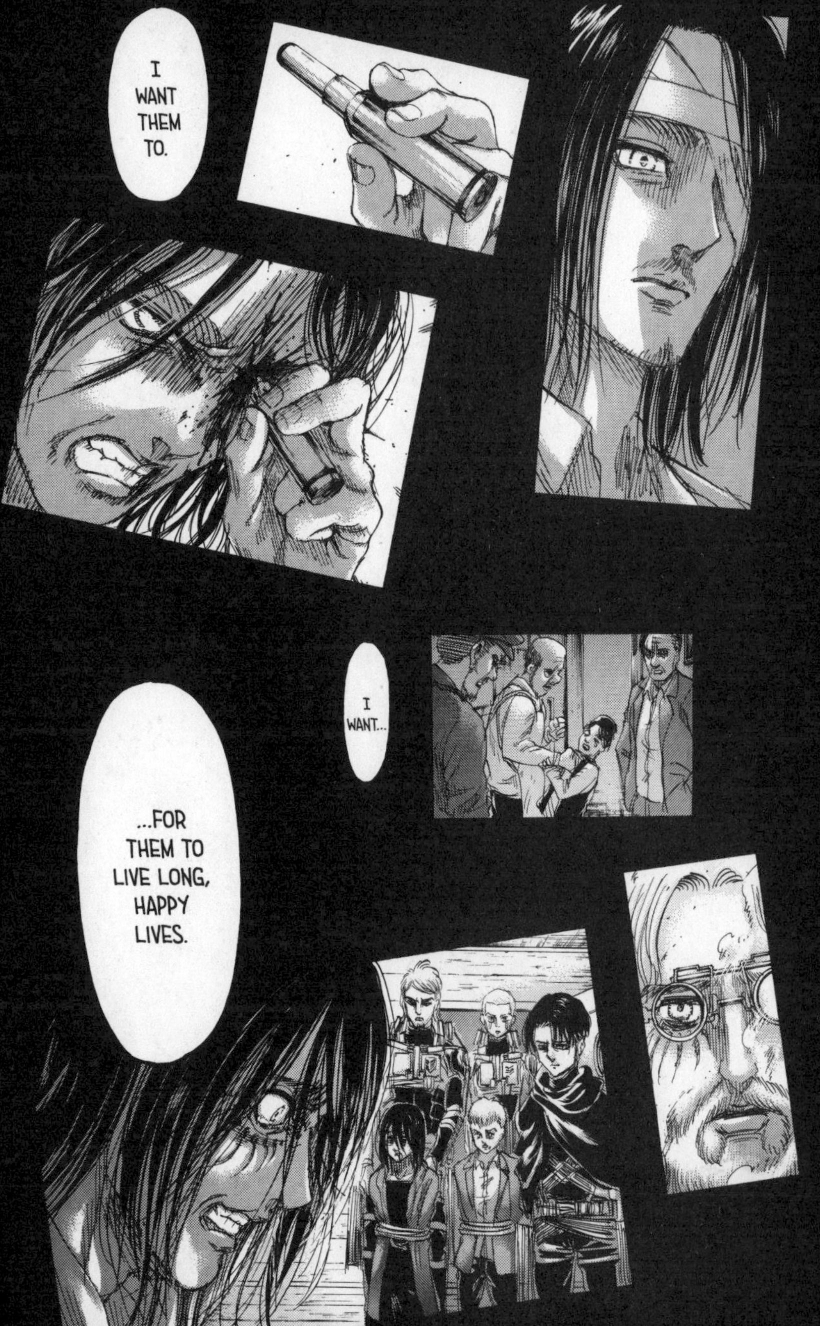
I WANT THEM TO.
I WANT...
...FOR THEM TO LIVE LONG, HAPPY LIVES.

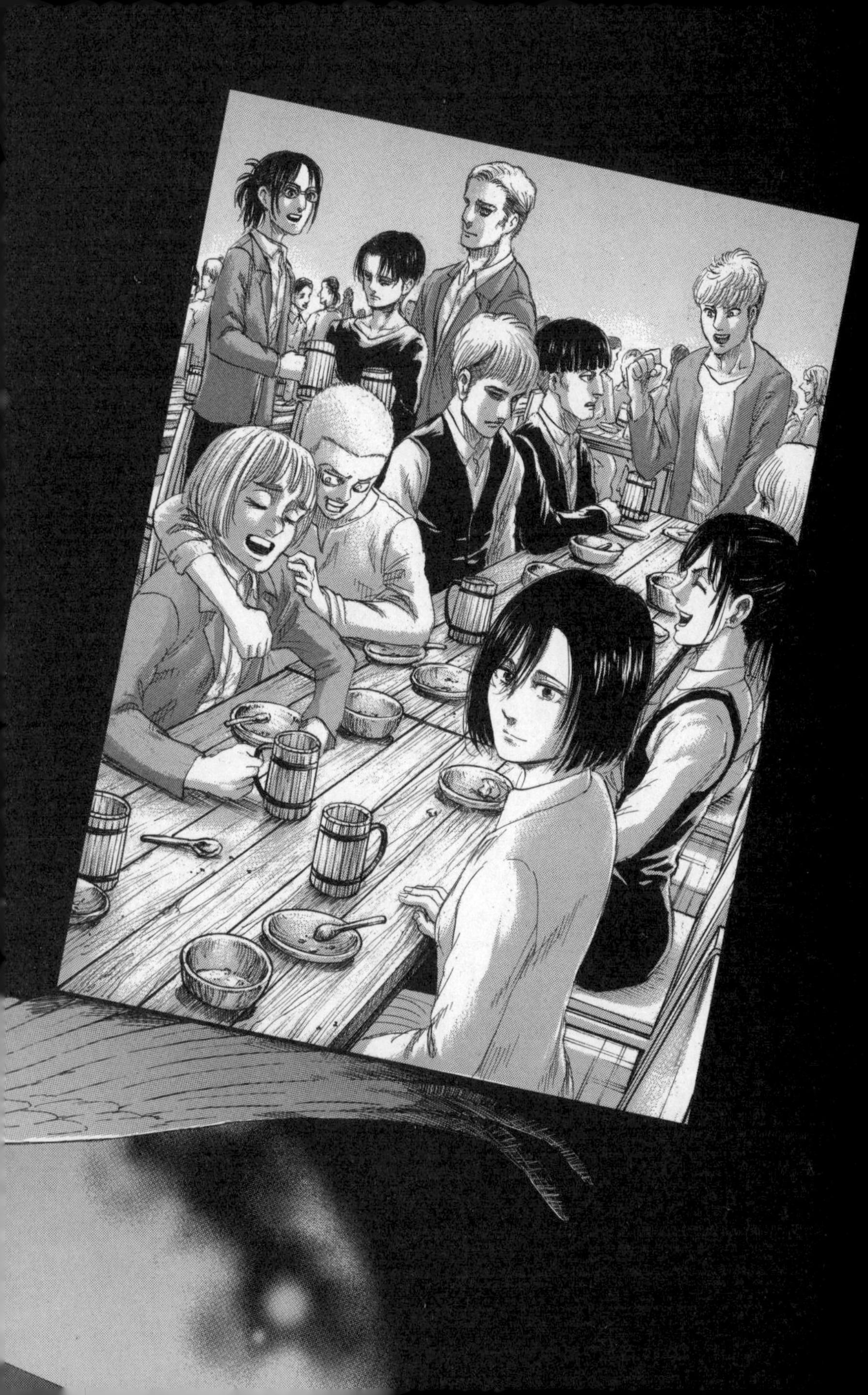

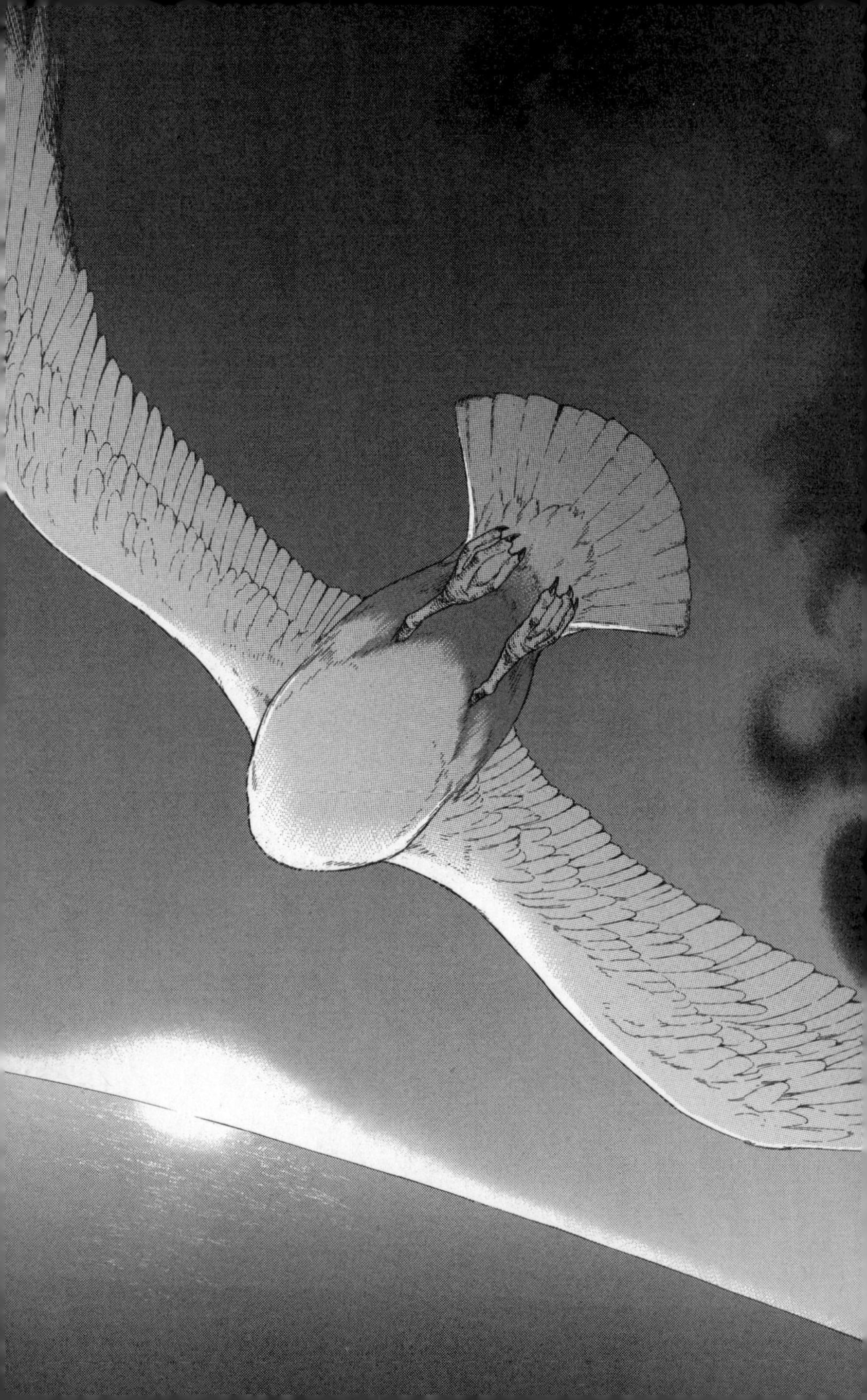

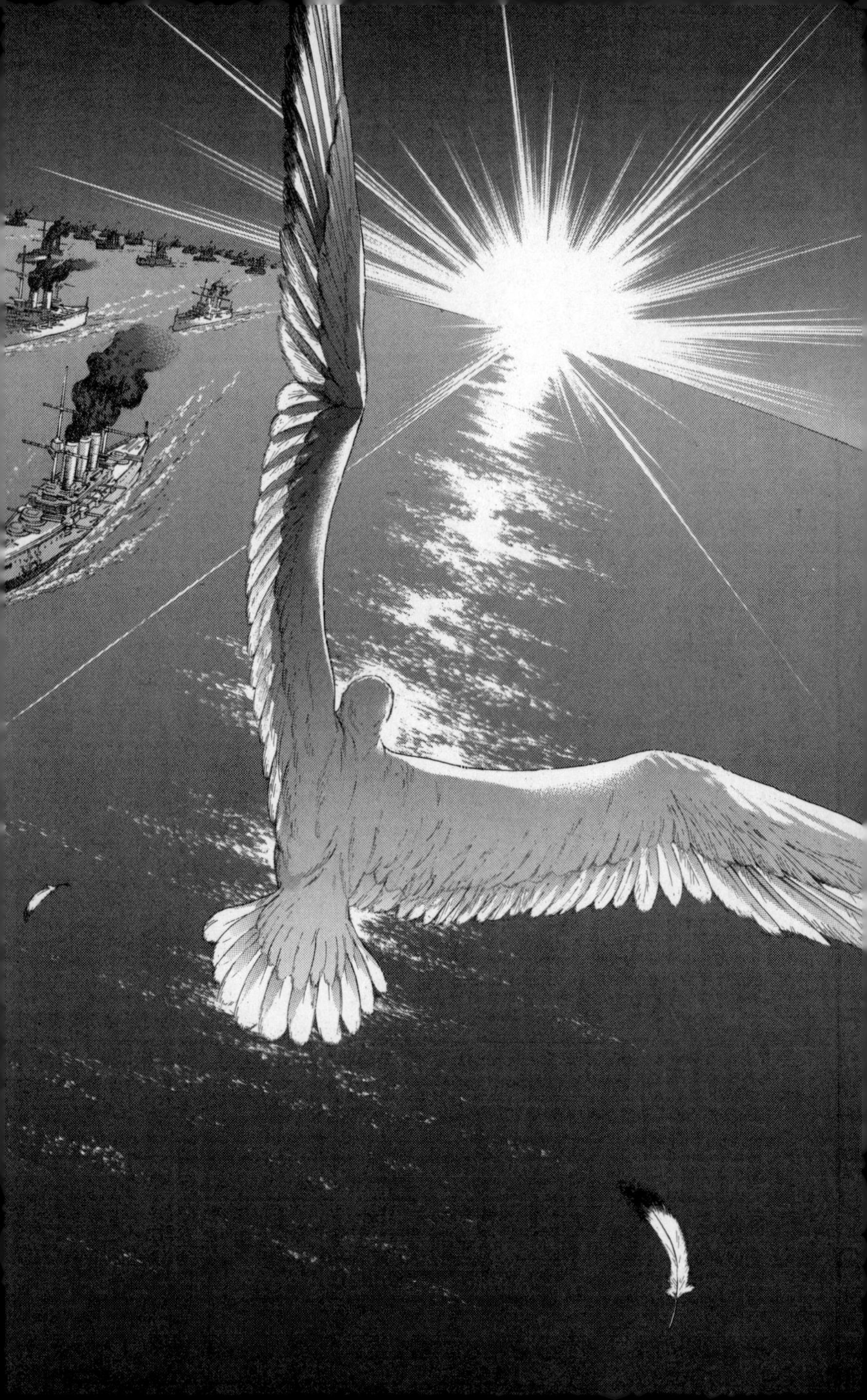

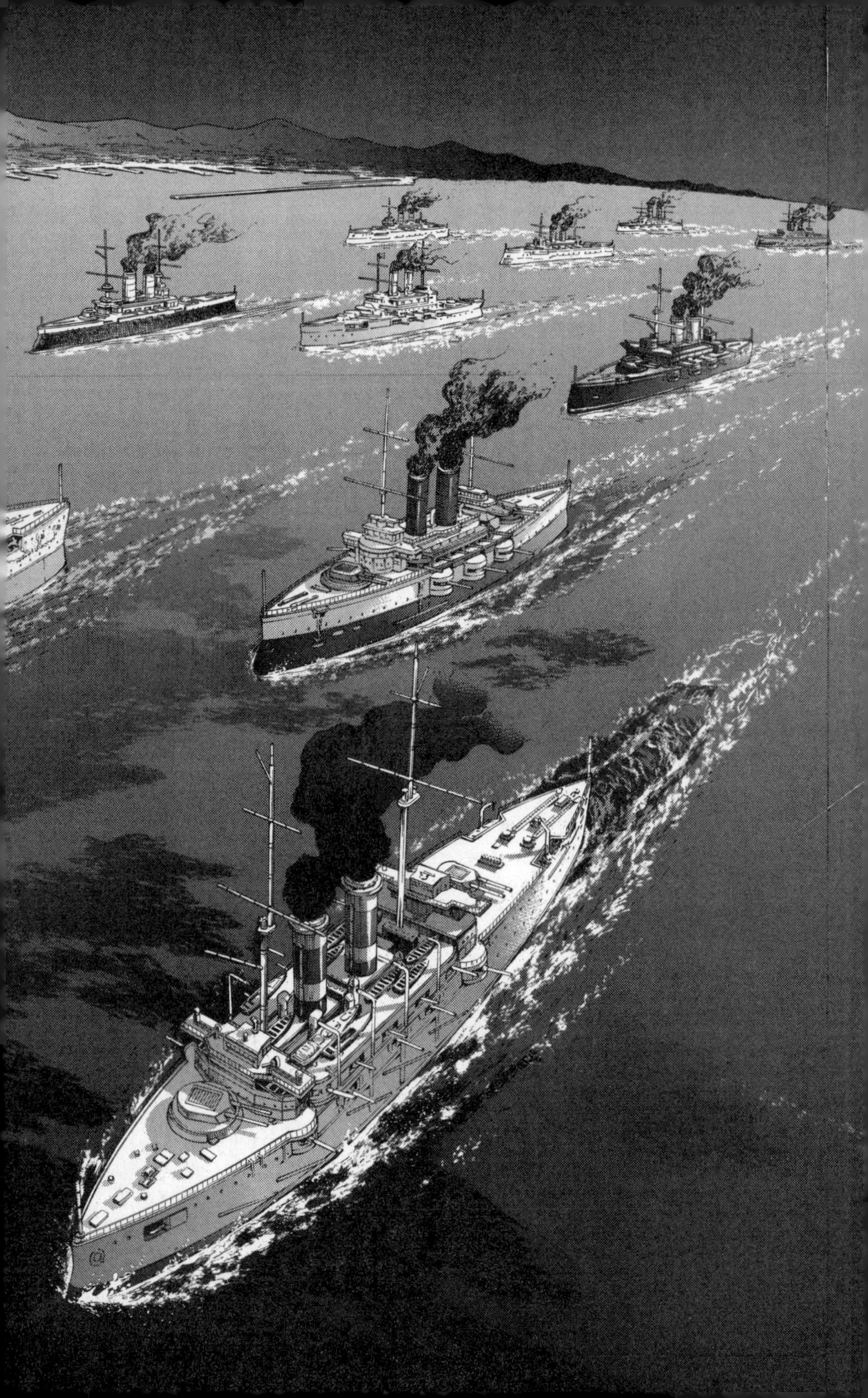

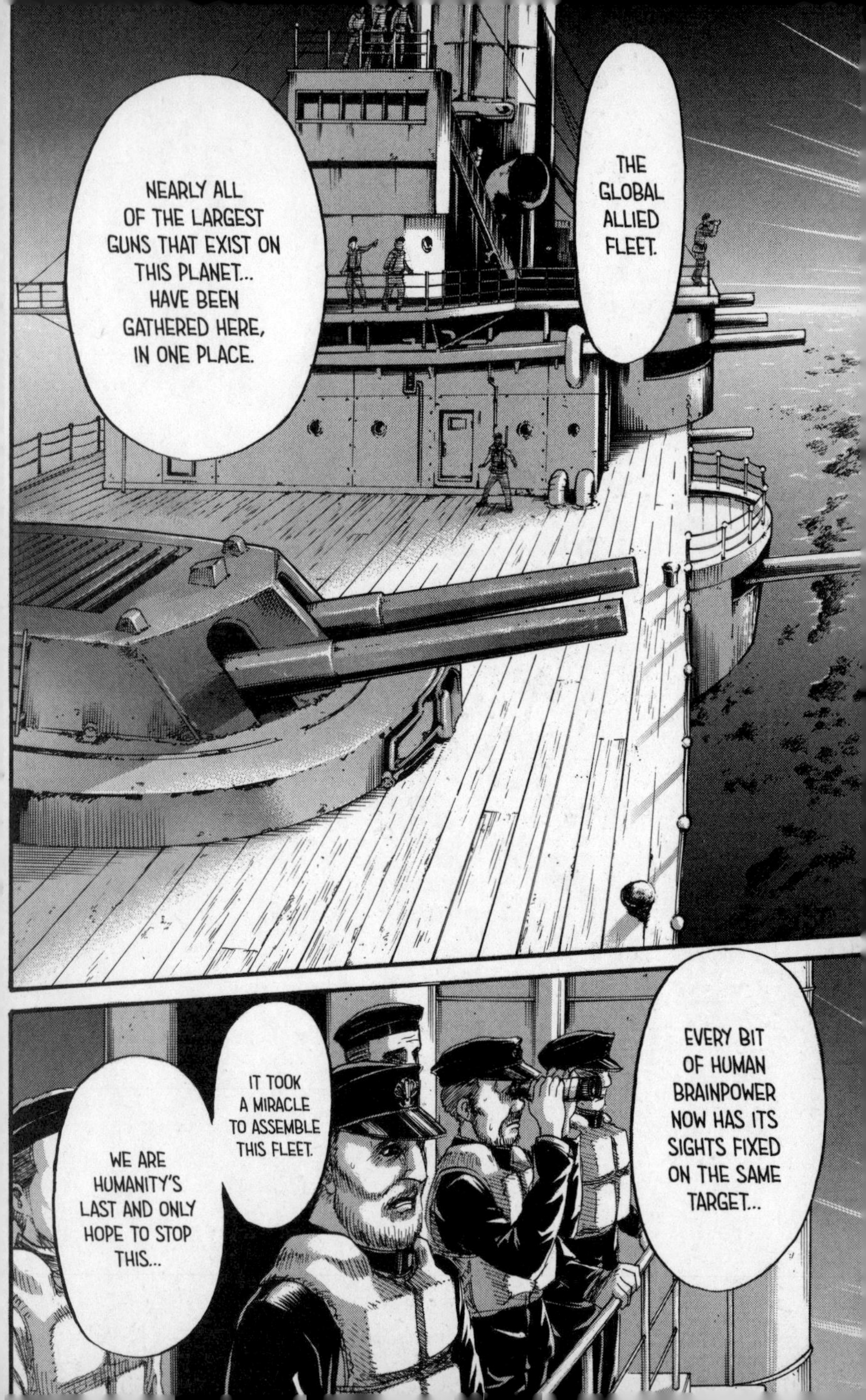
THE GLOBAL ALLIED FLEET.
NEARLY ALL OF THE LARGEST GUNS THAT EXIST ON THIS PLANET... HAVE BEEN GATHERED HERE, IN ONE PLACE.
EVERY BIT OF HUMAN BRAINPOWER NOW HAS ITS SIGHTS FIXED ON THE SAME TARGET...
IT TOOK A MIRACLE TO ASSEMBLE THIS FLEET.
WE ARE HUMANITY'S LAST AND ONLY HOPE TO STOP THIS...

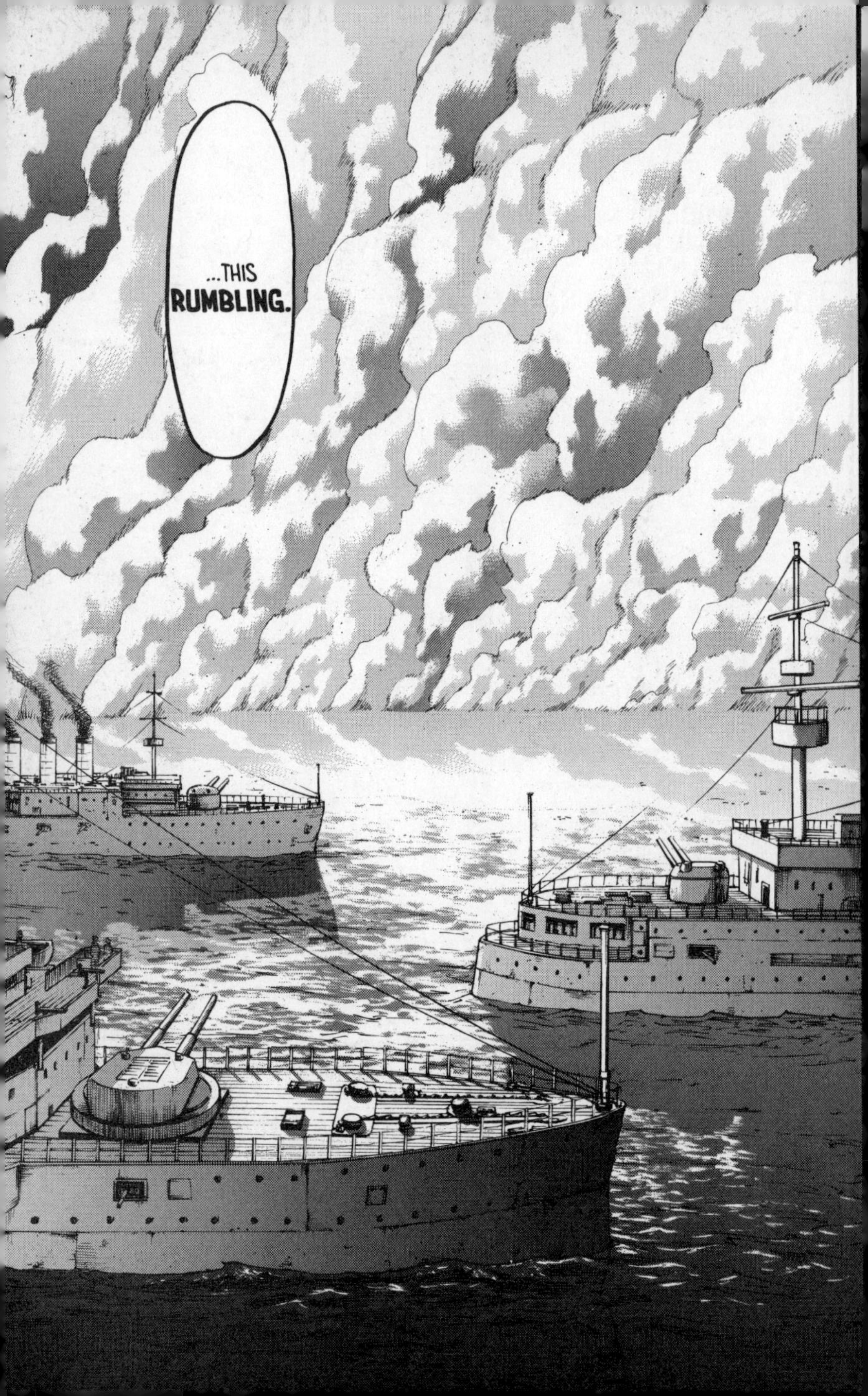
...THIS
RUMBLING.

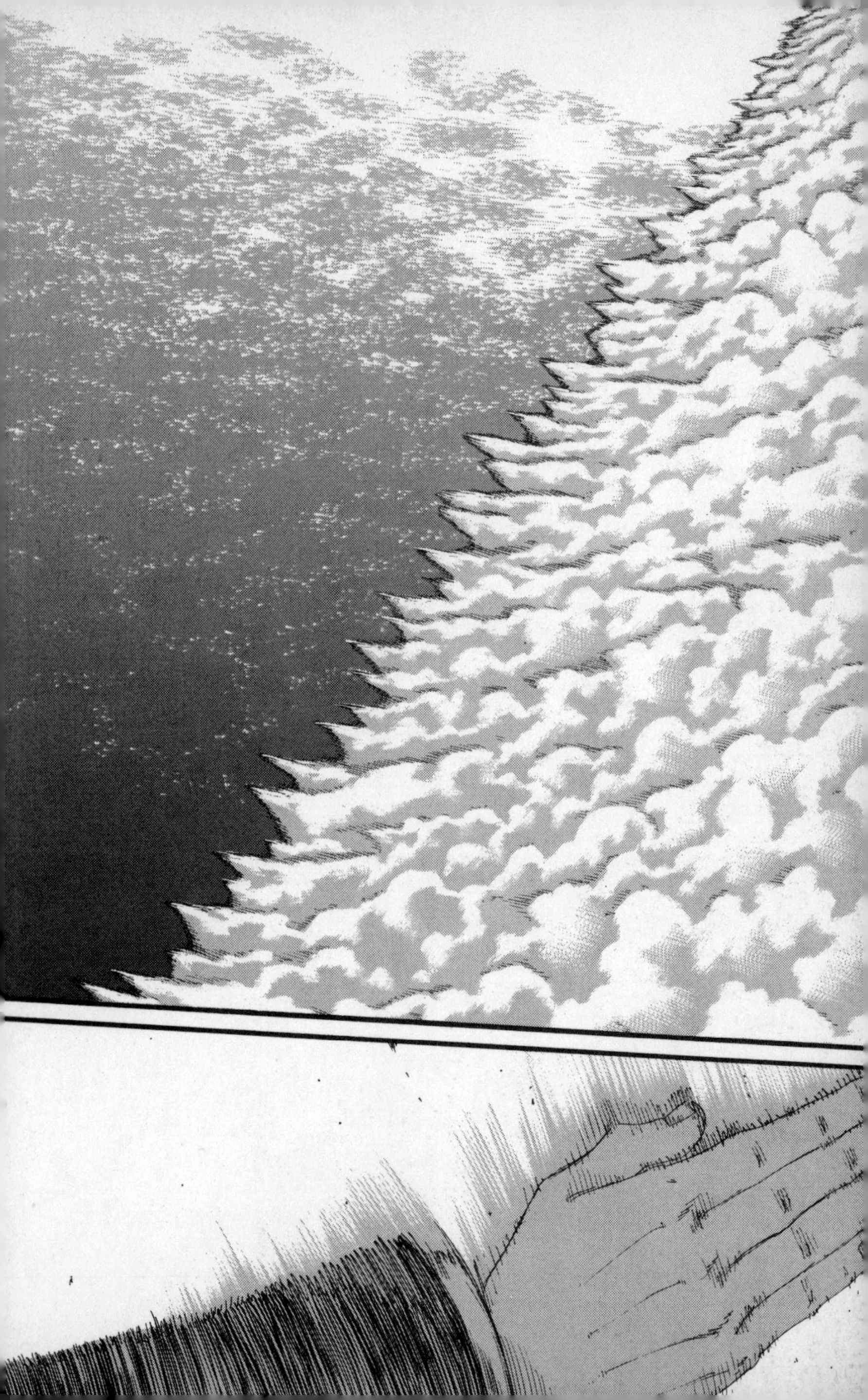

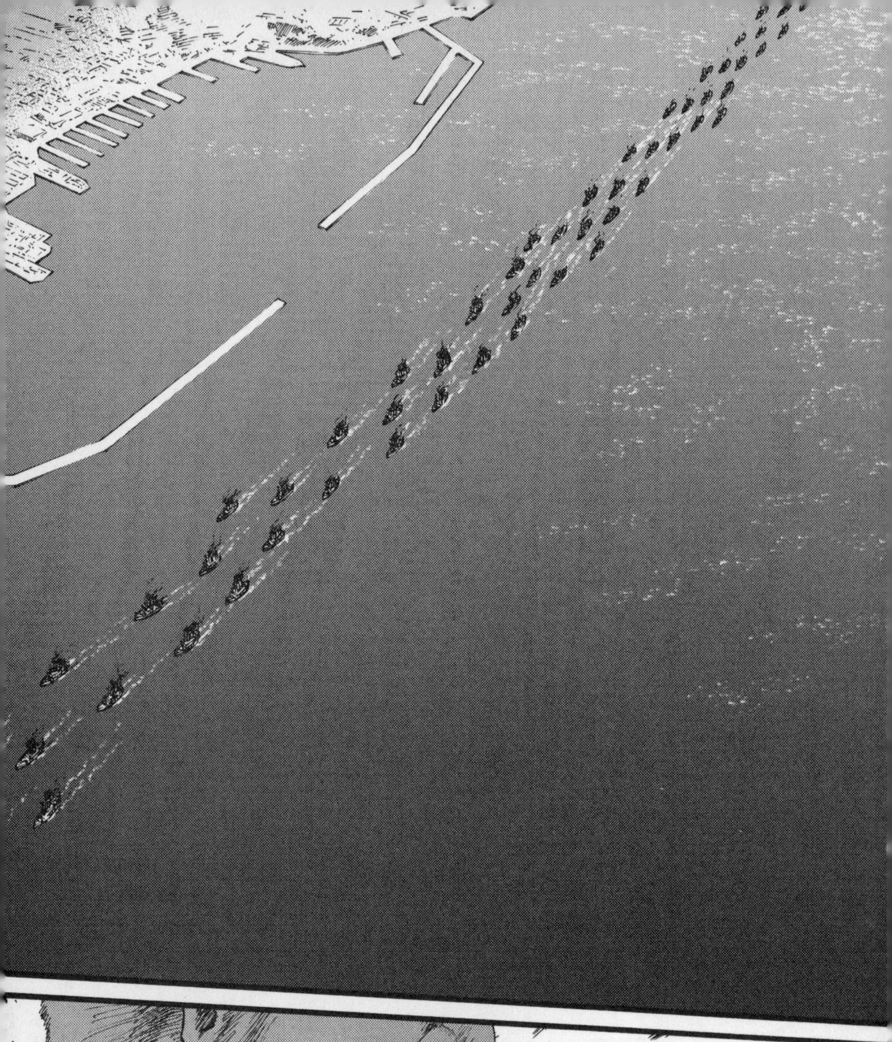
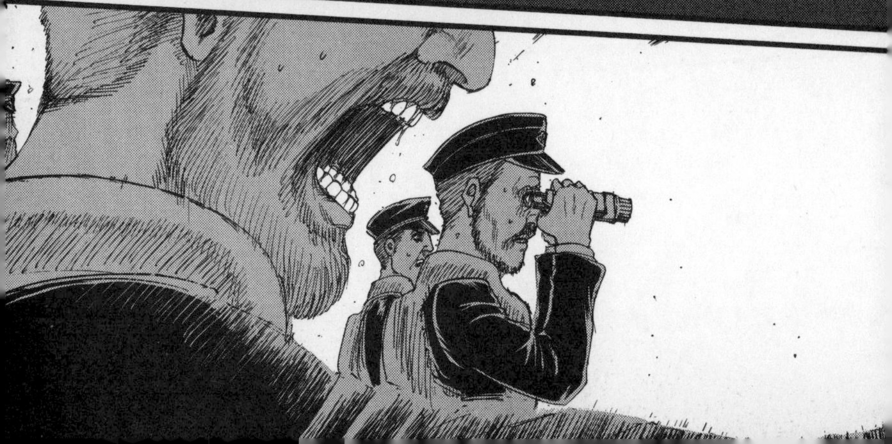

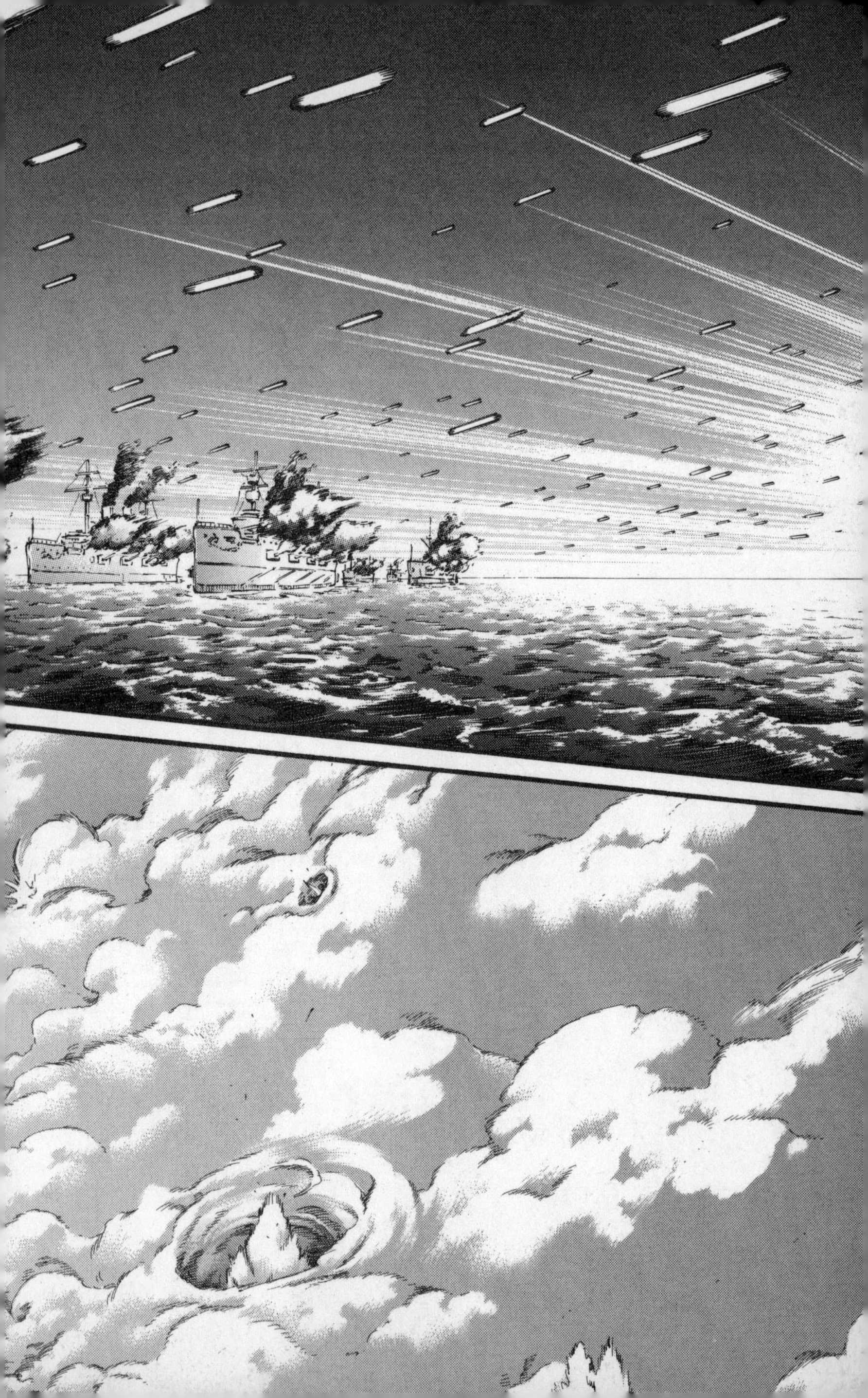

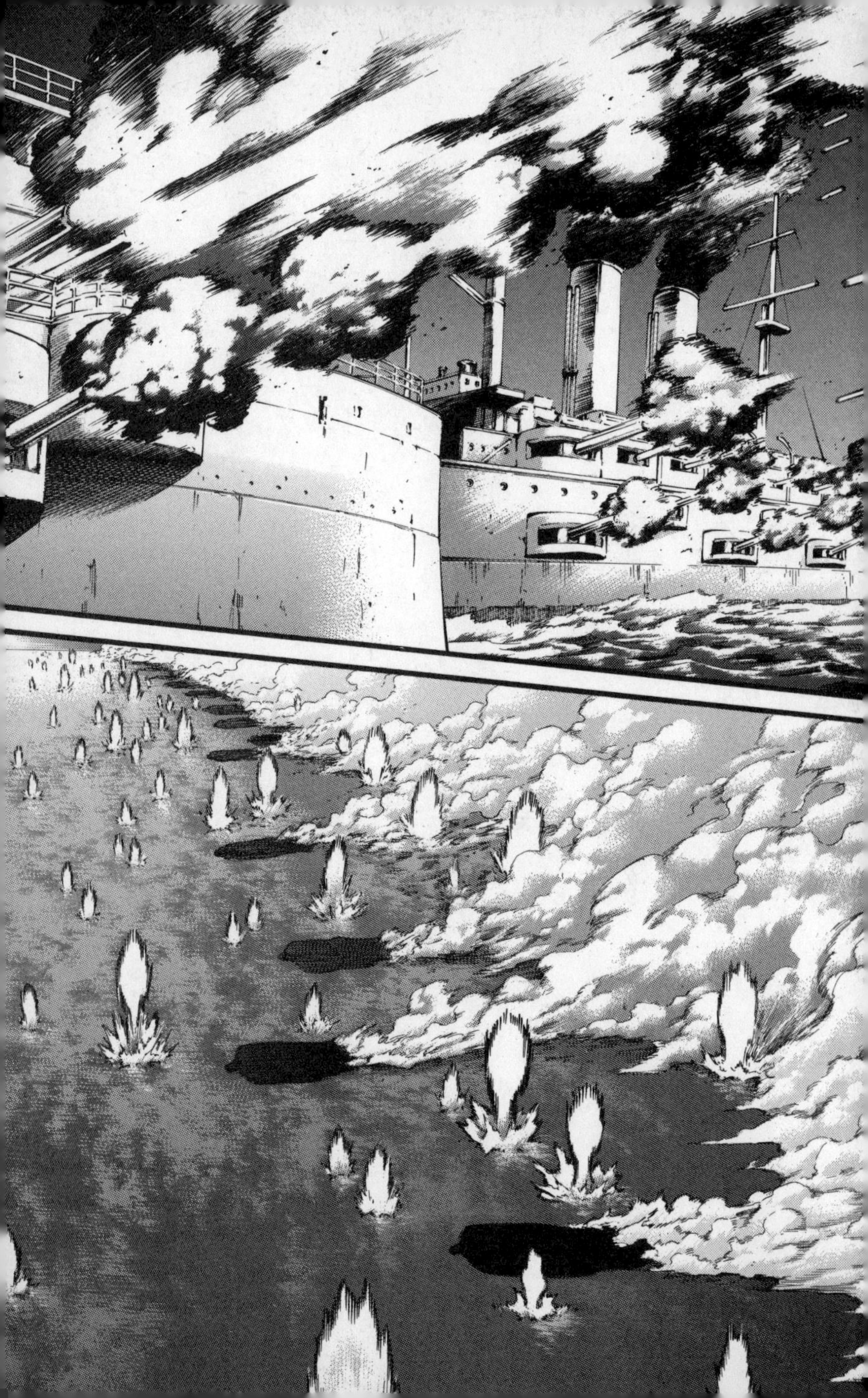

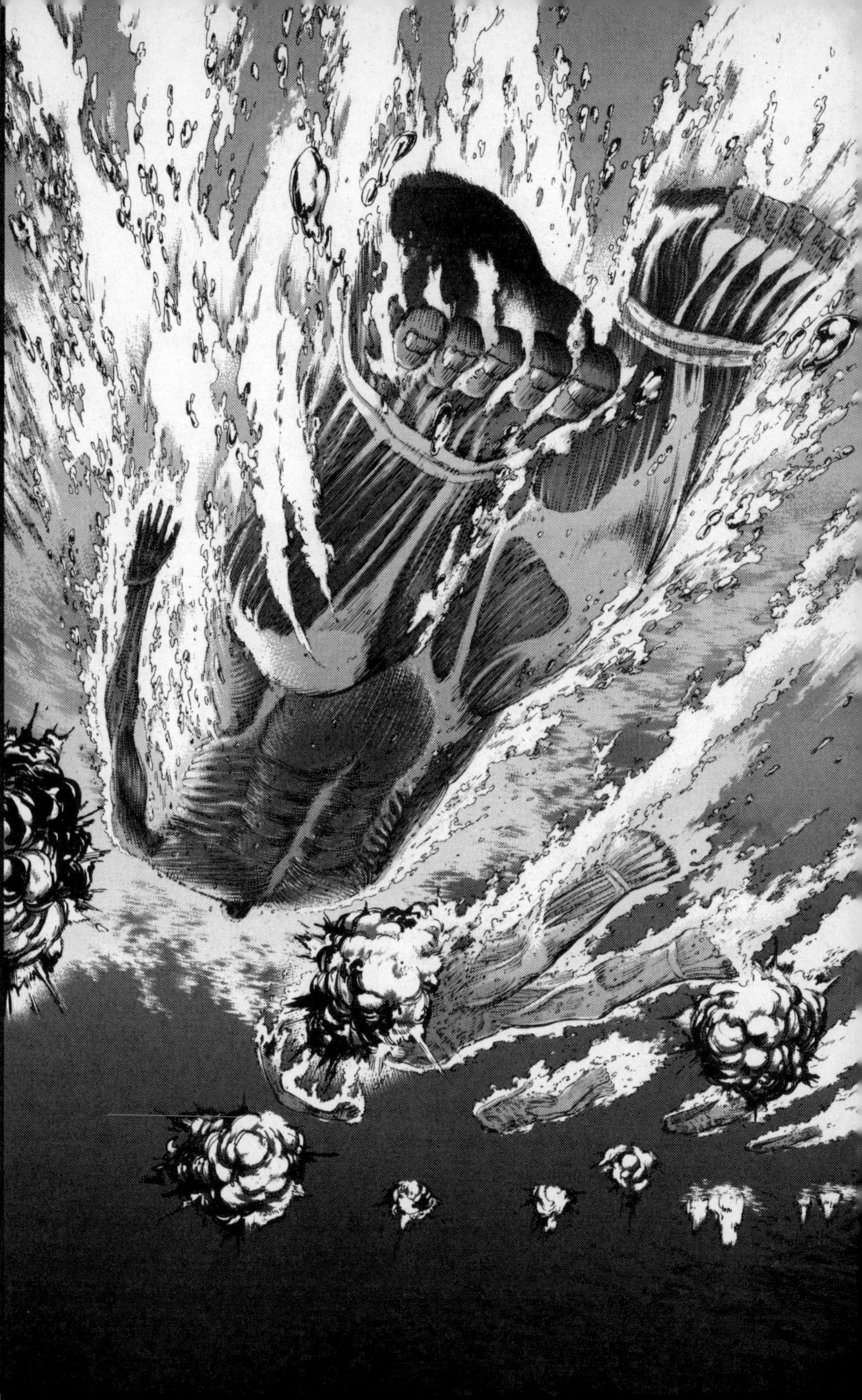

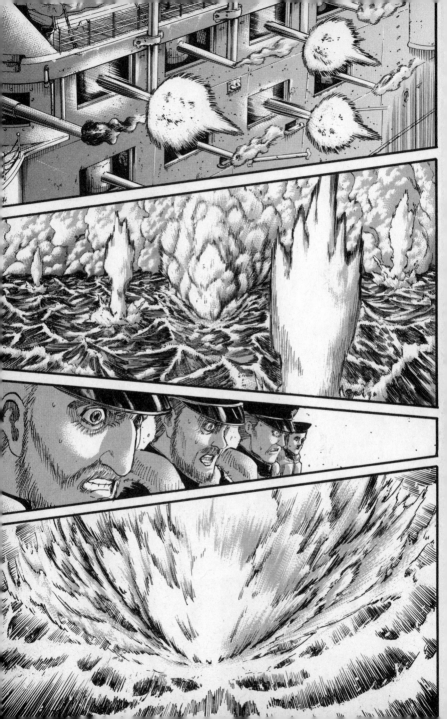

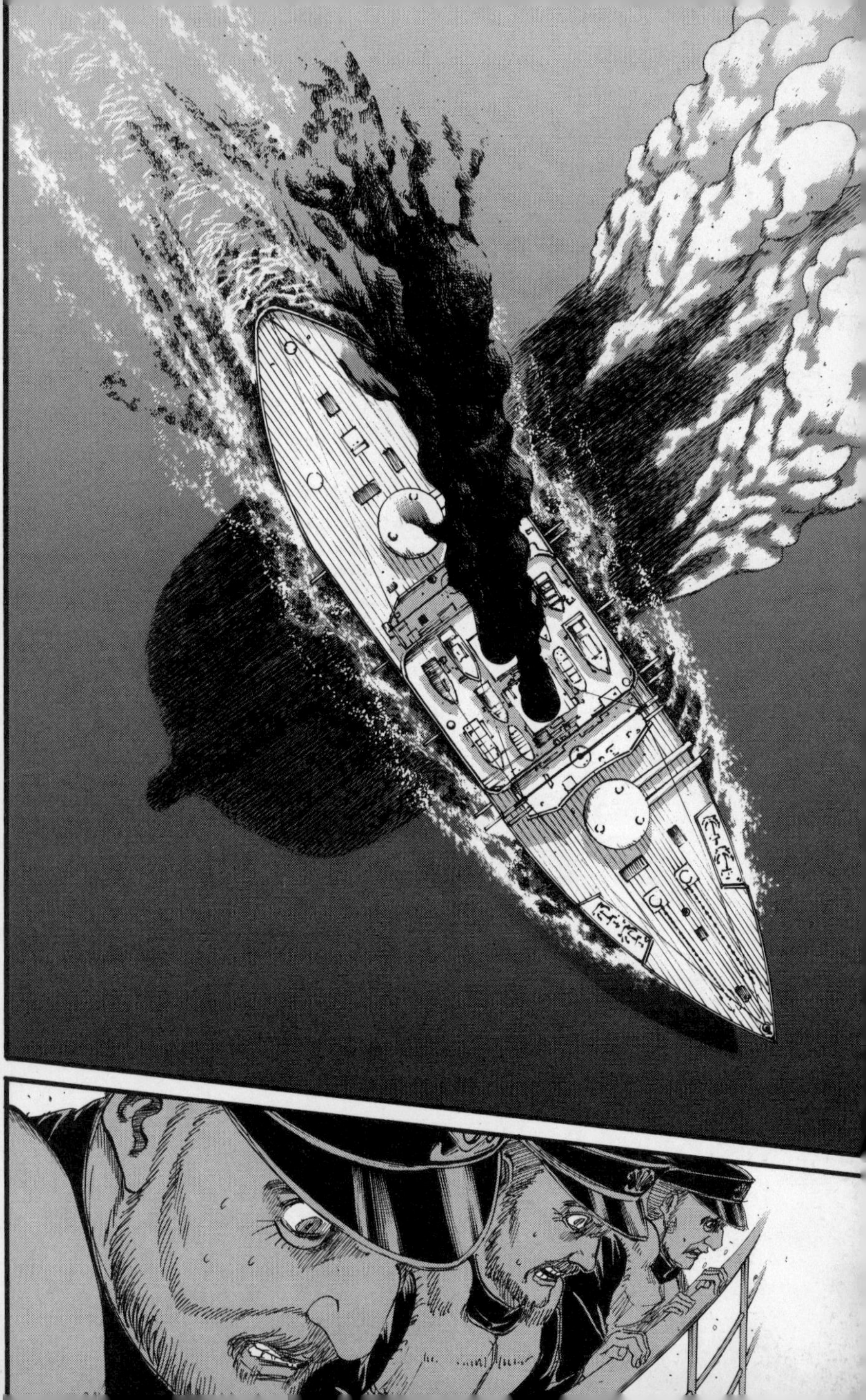

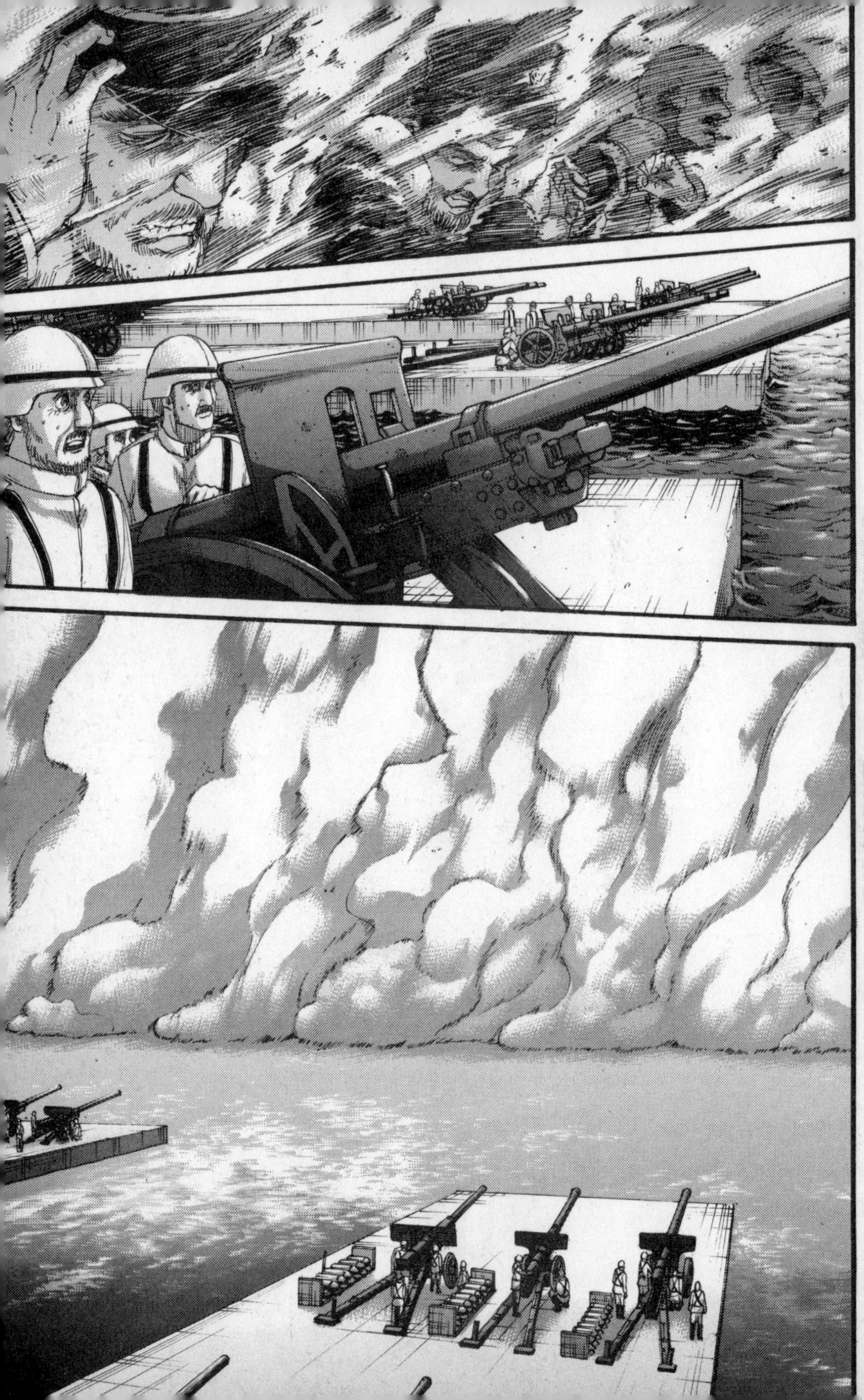

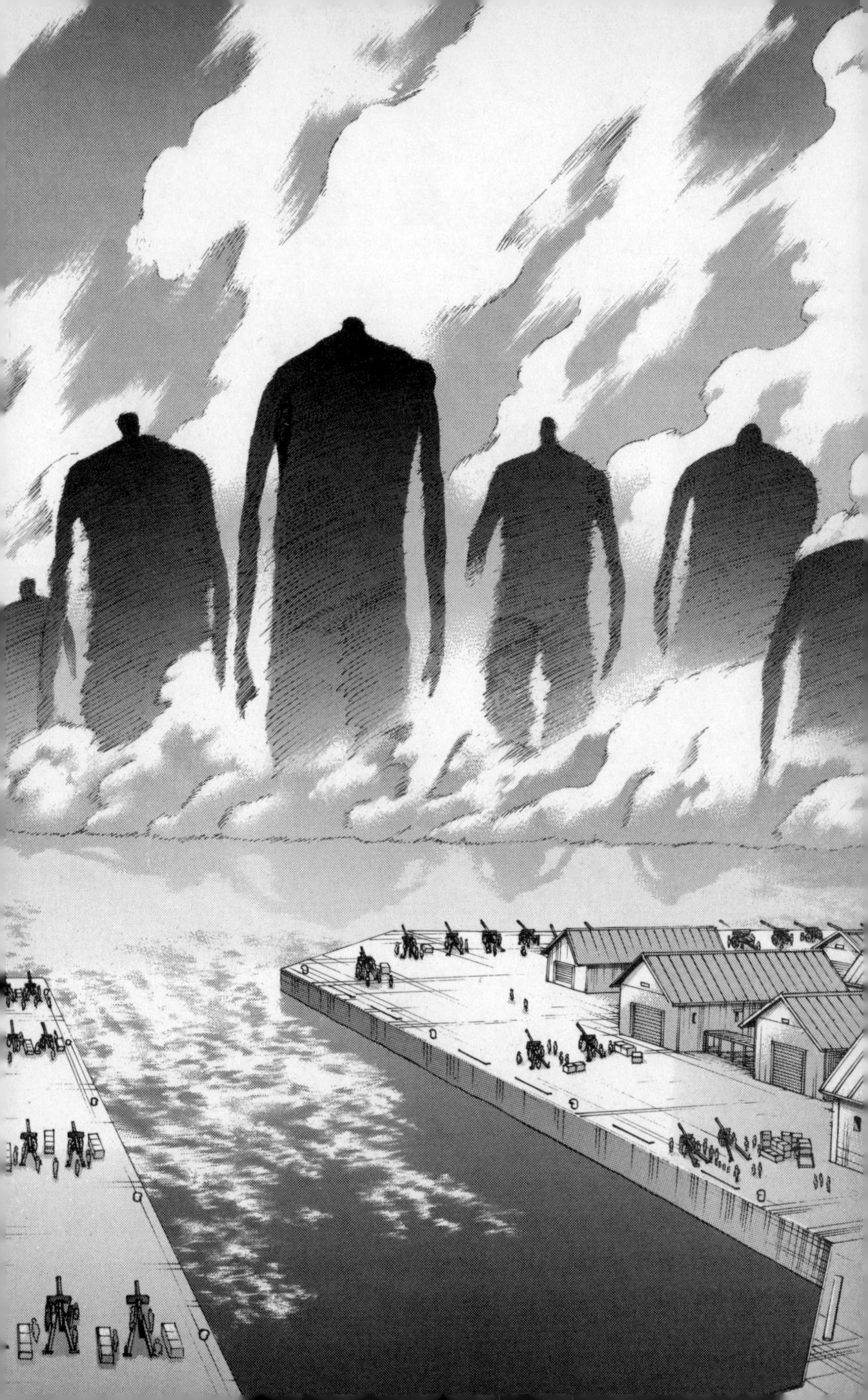

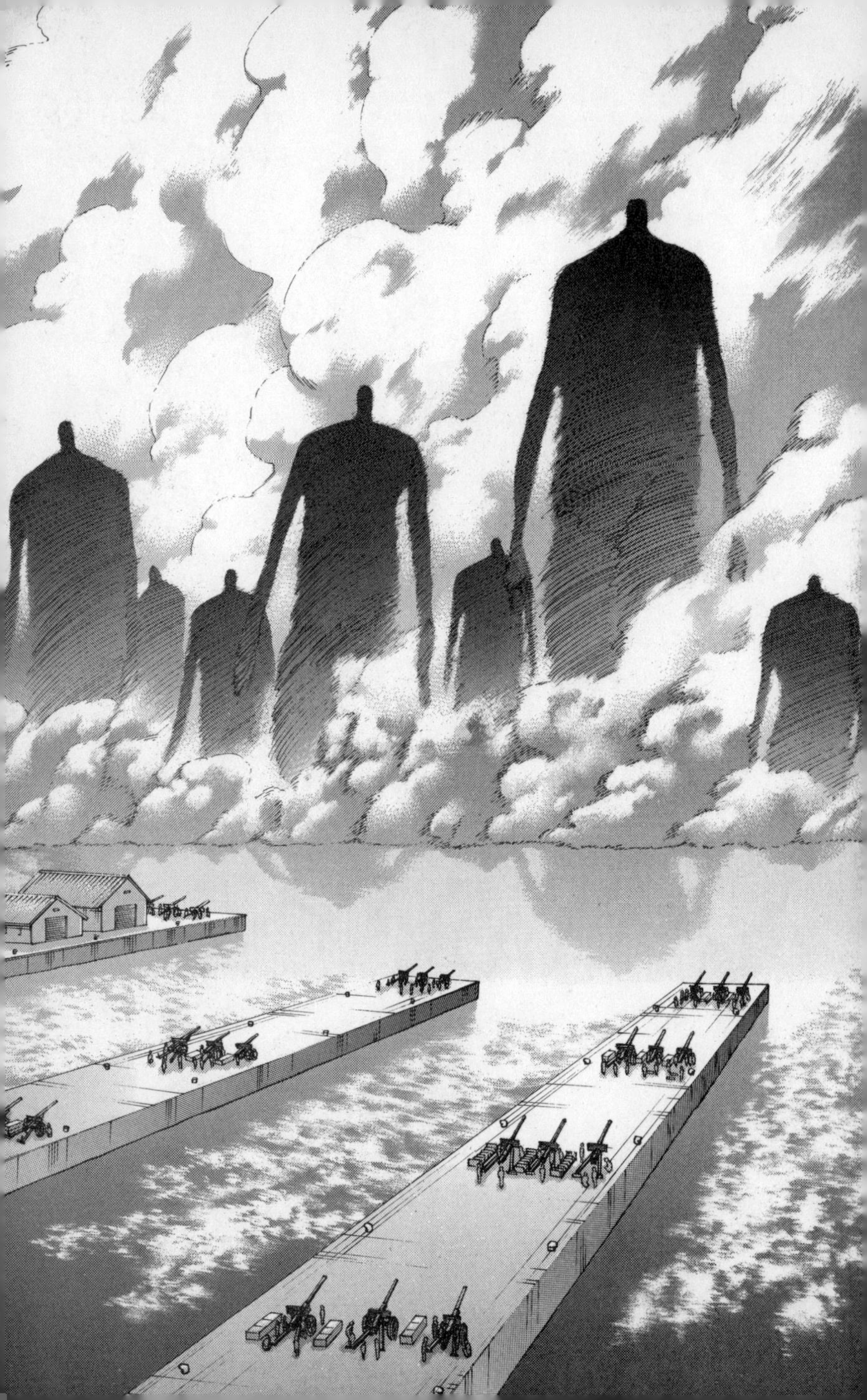

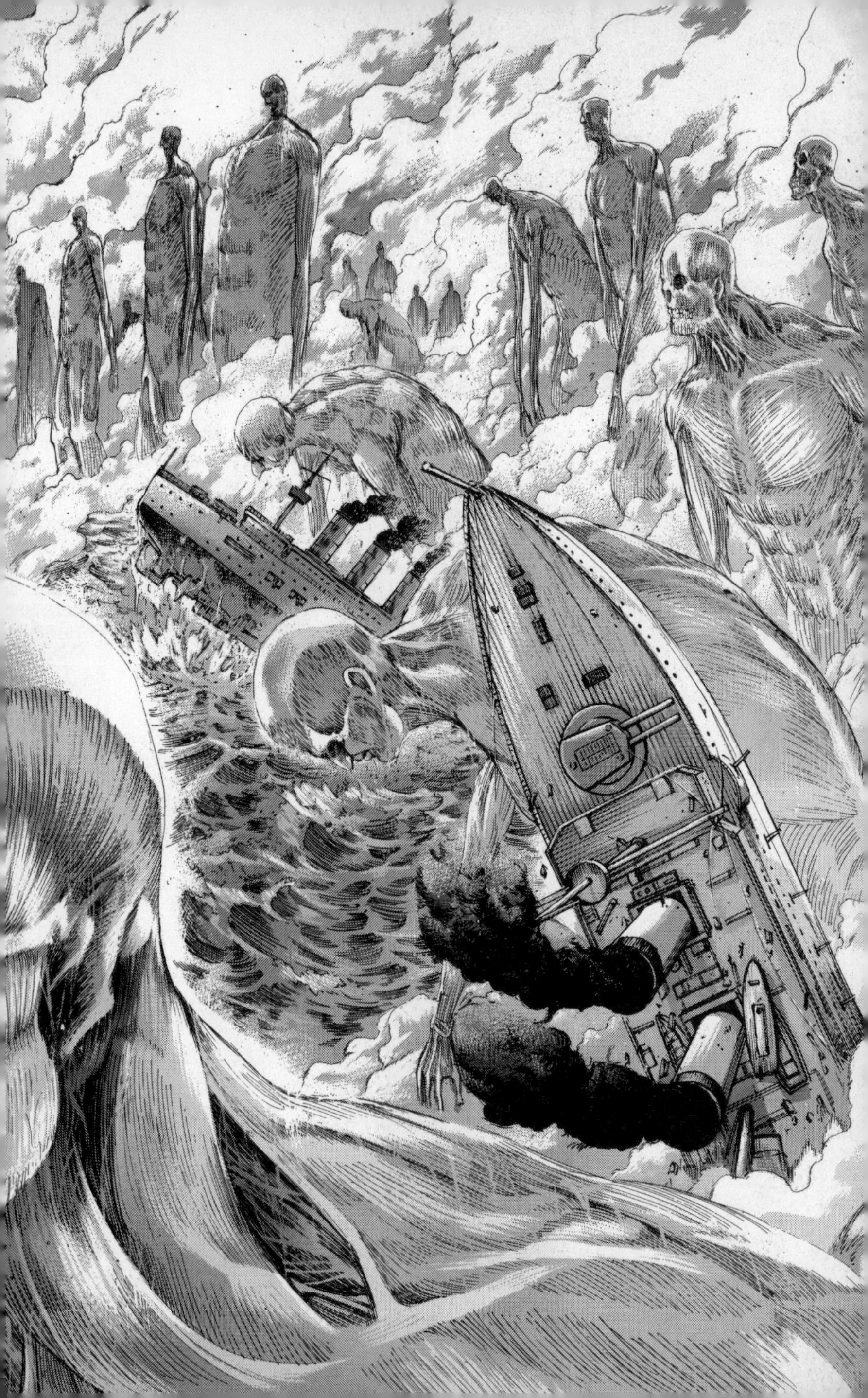

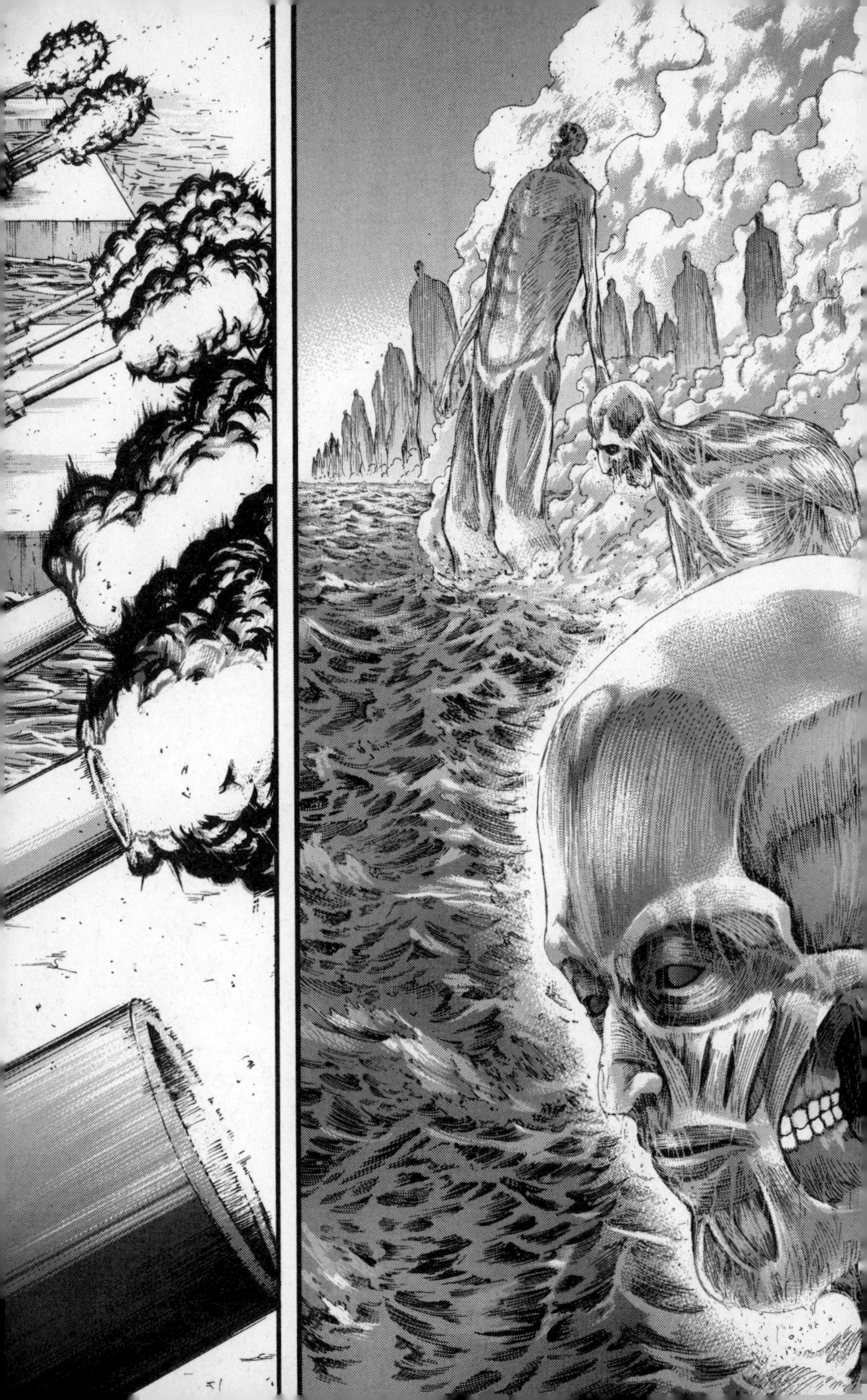

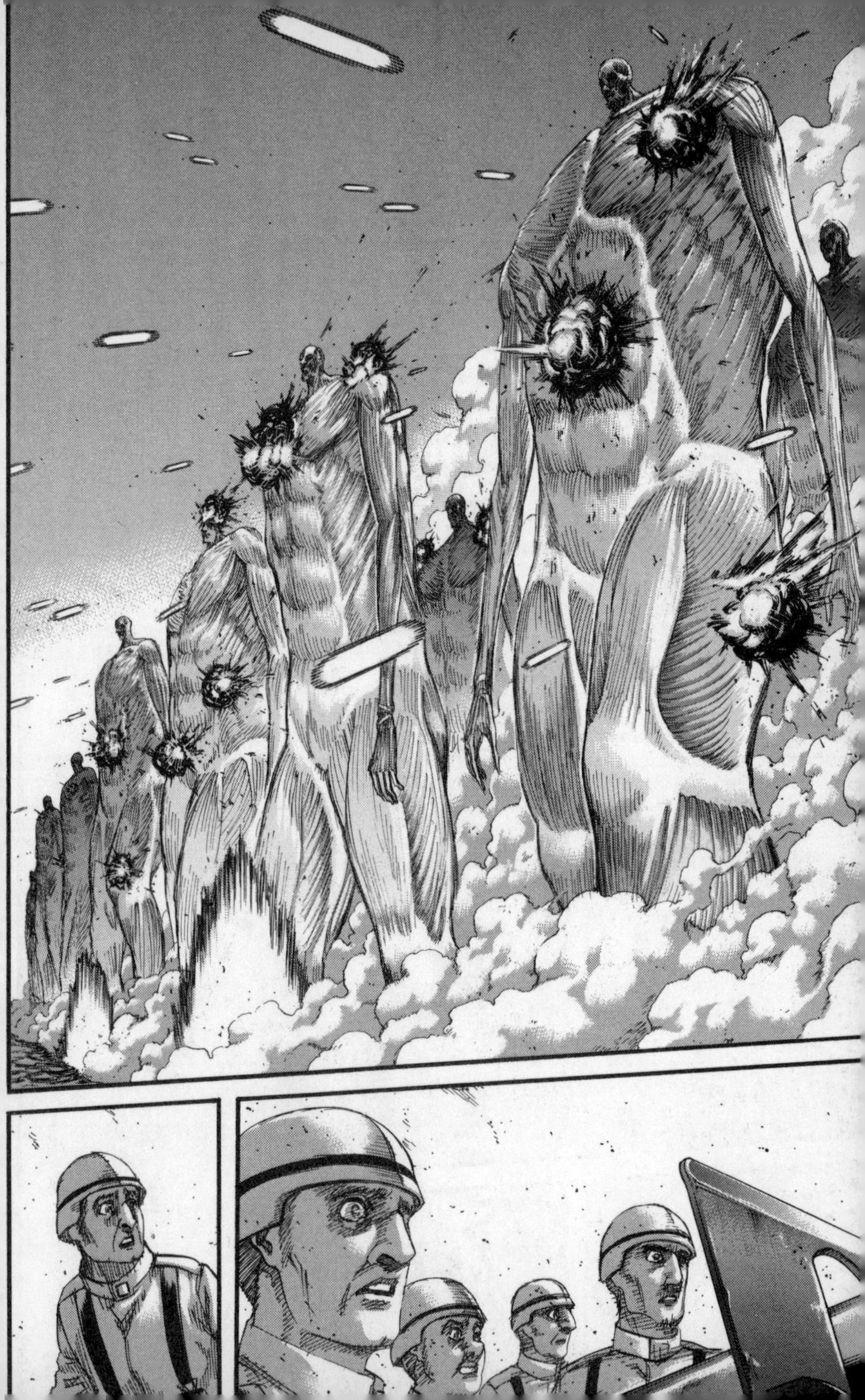

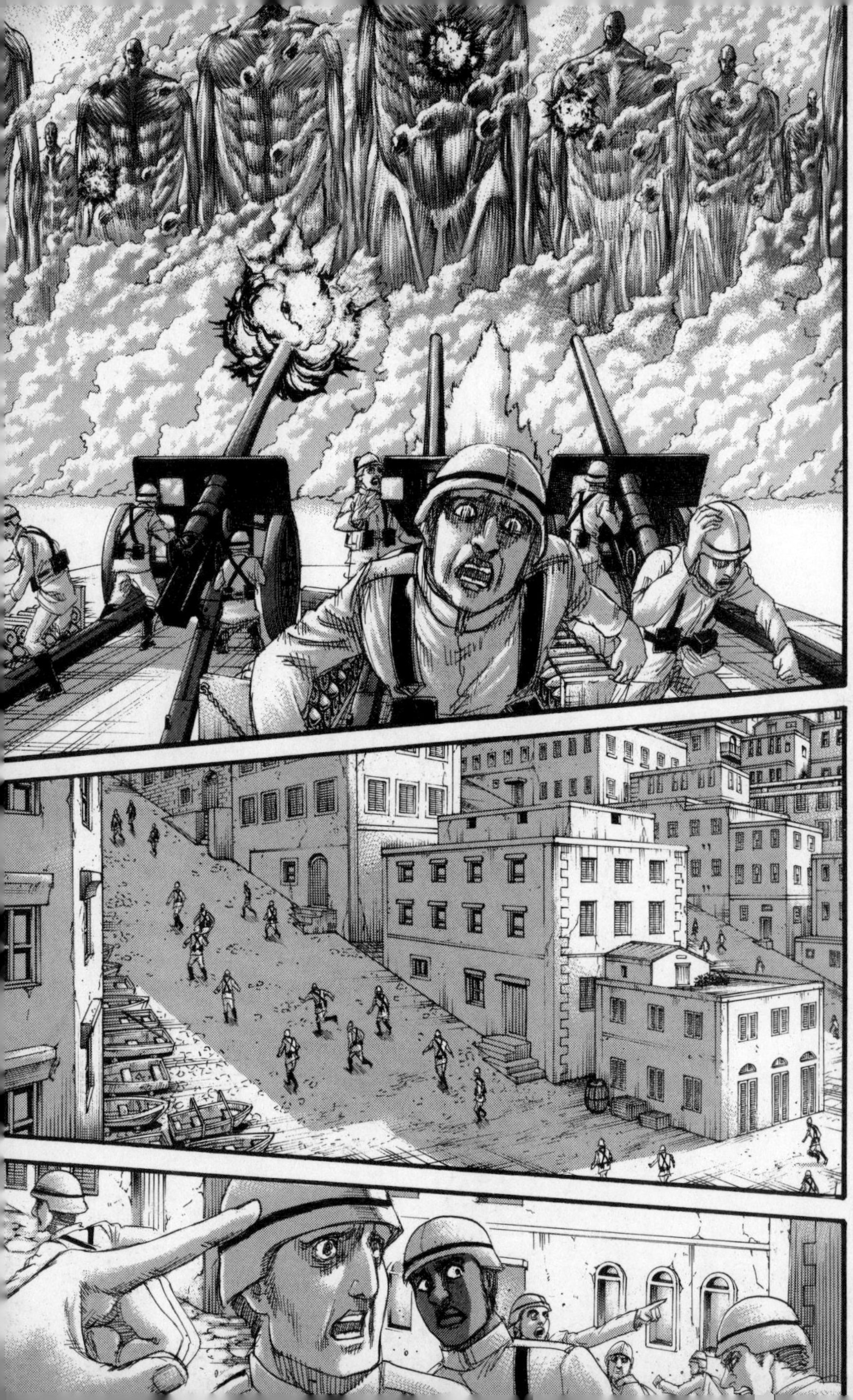

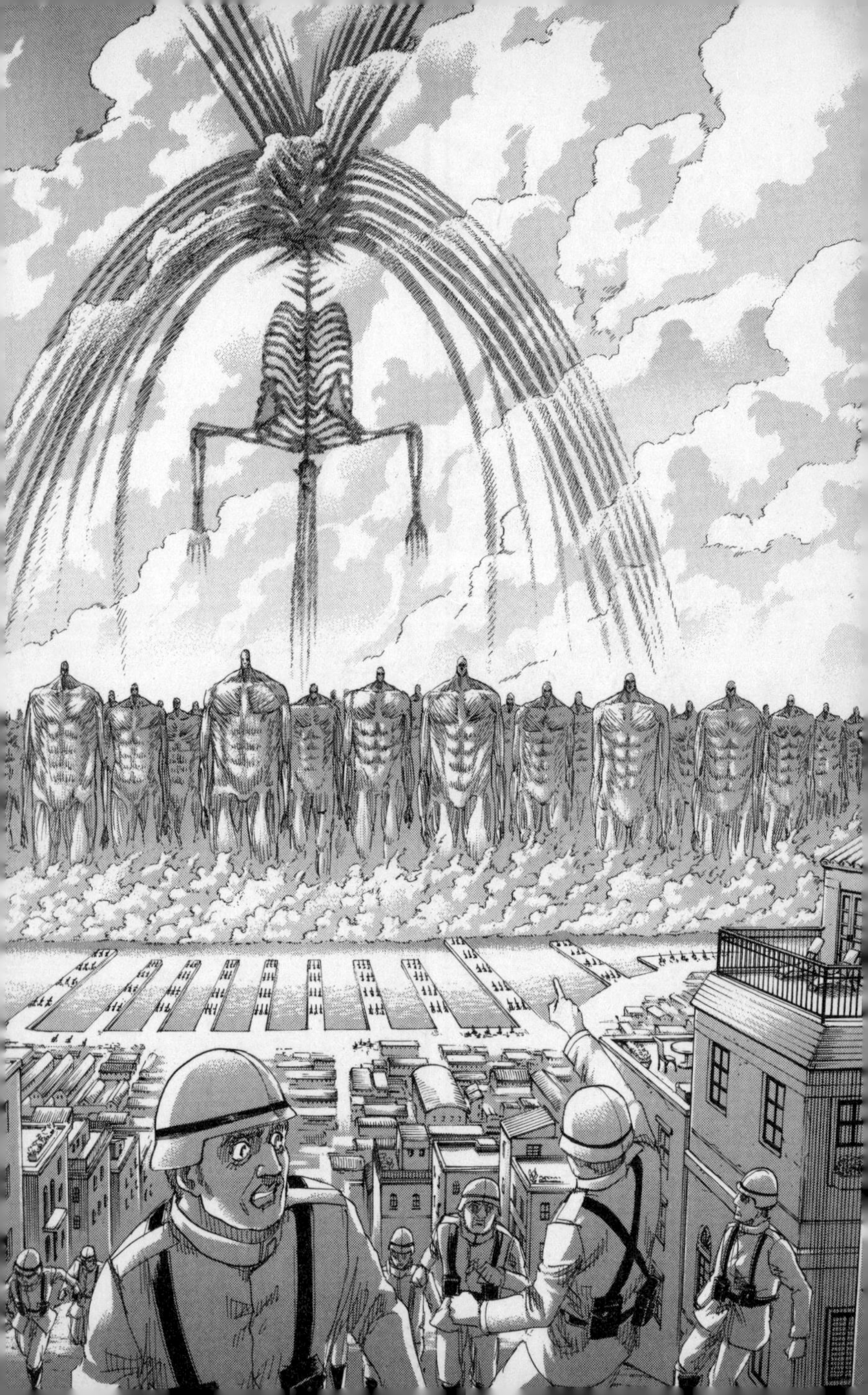

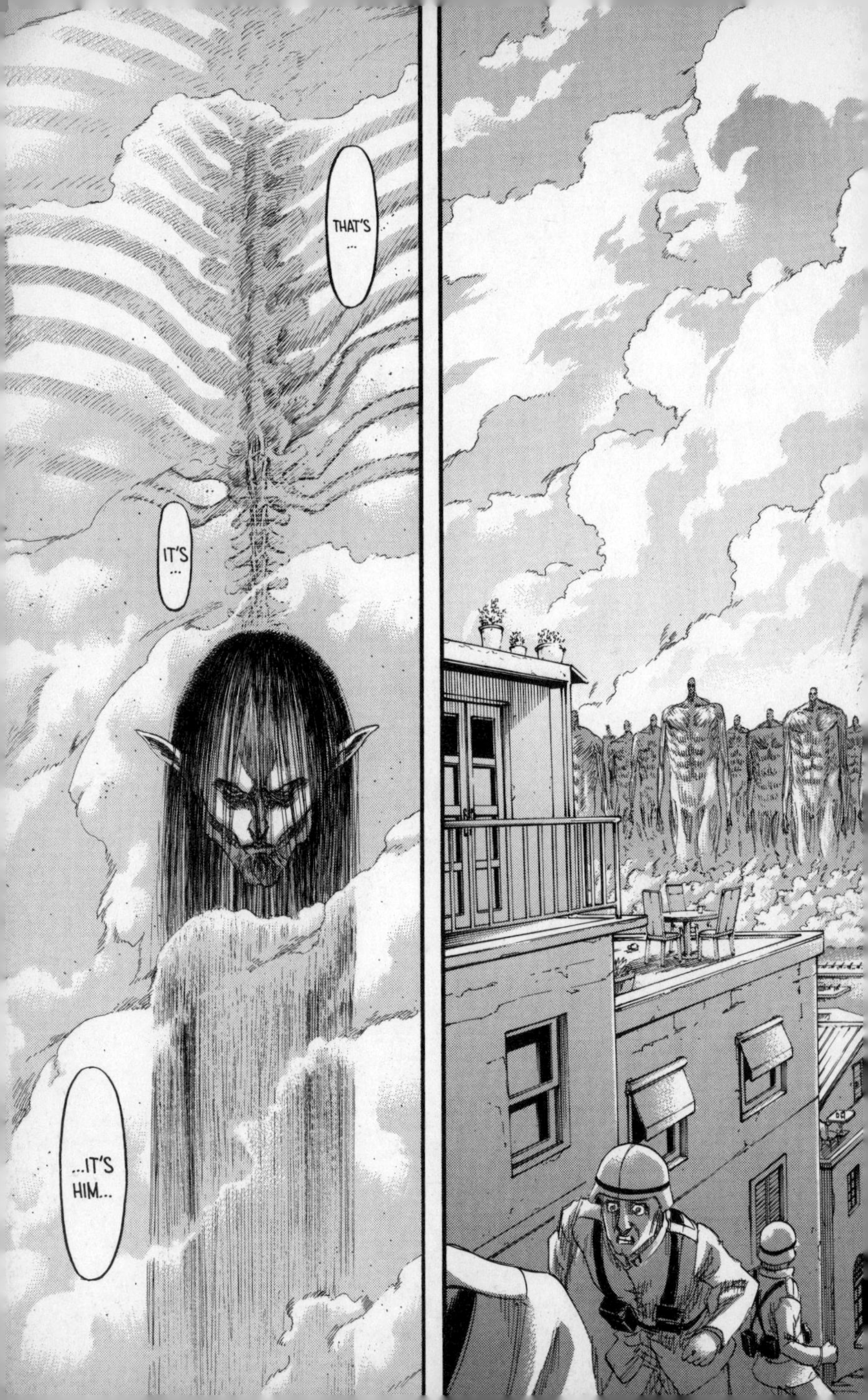
THAT'S ...
IT'S ...
...IT'S HIM...

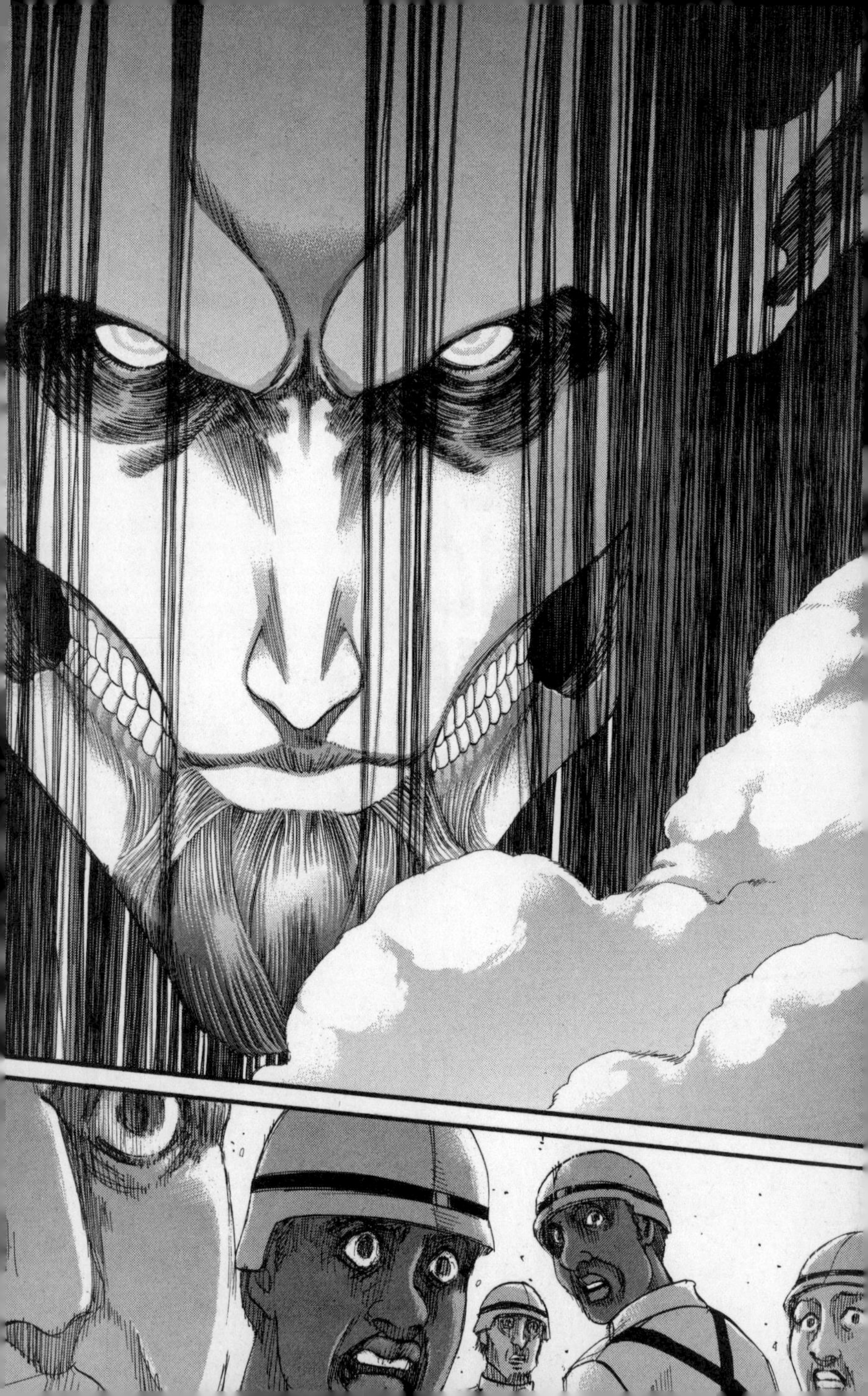

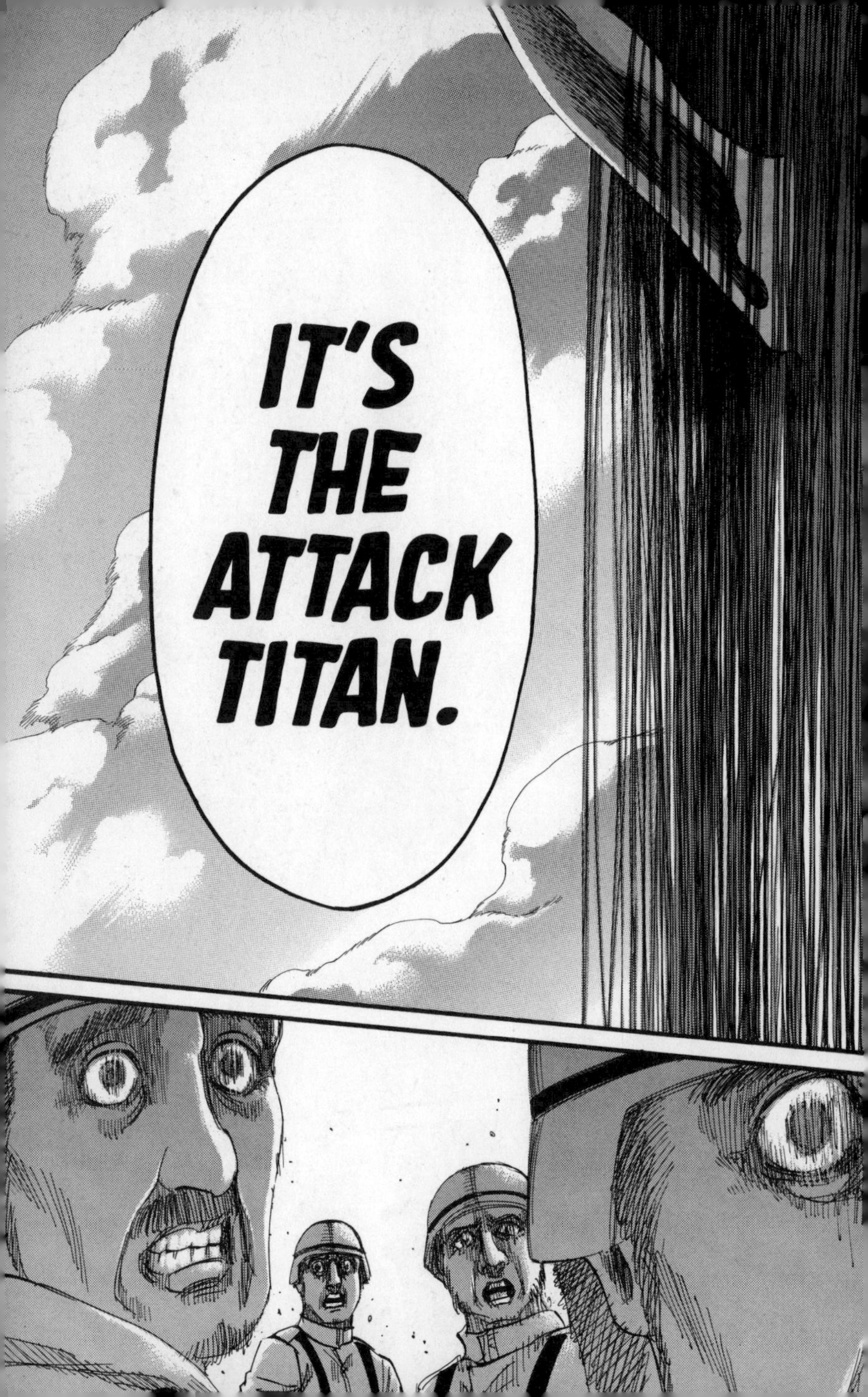
IT'S THE ATTACK TITAN.

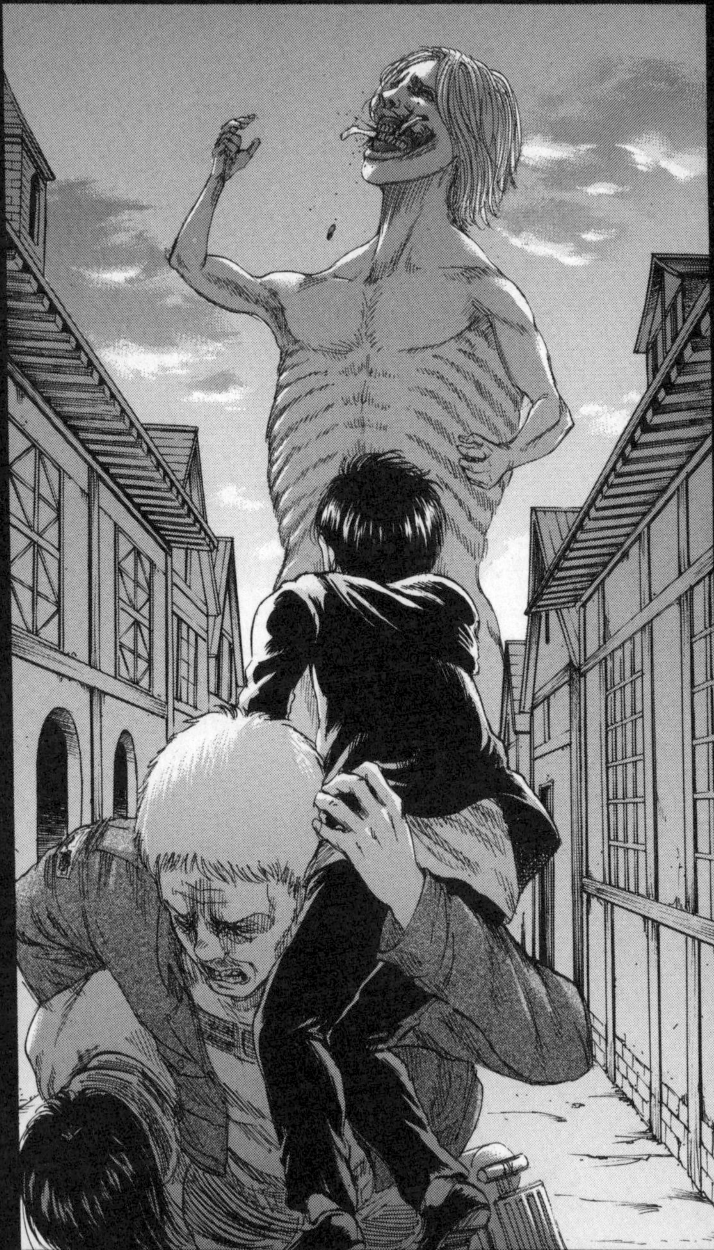

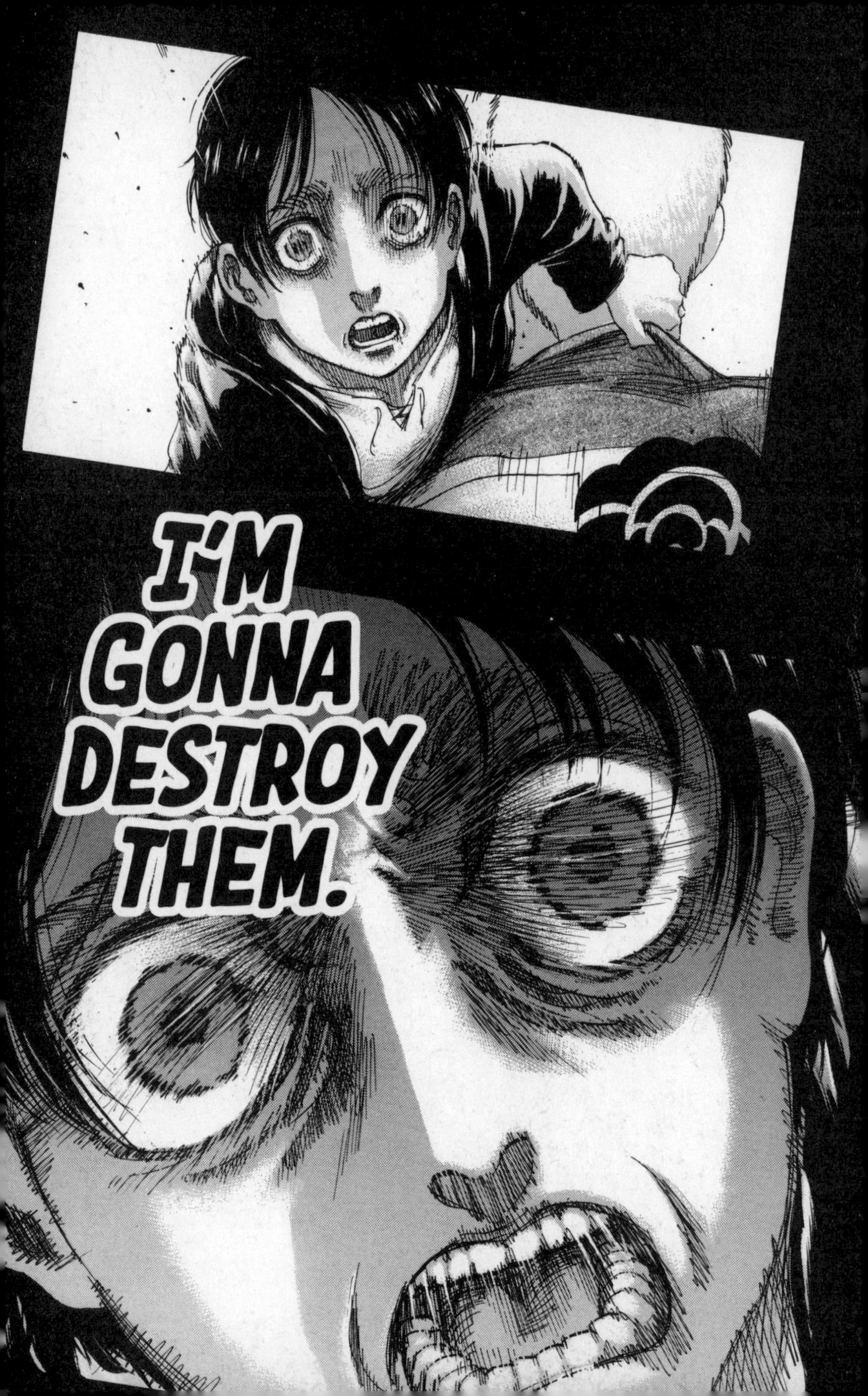
I'M GONNA DESTROY THEM.

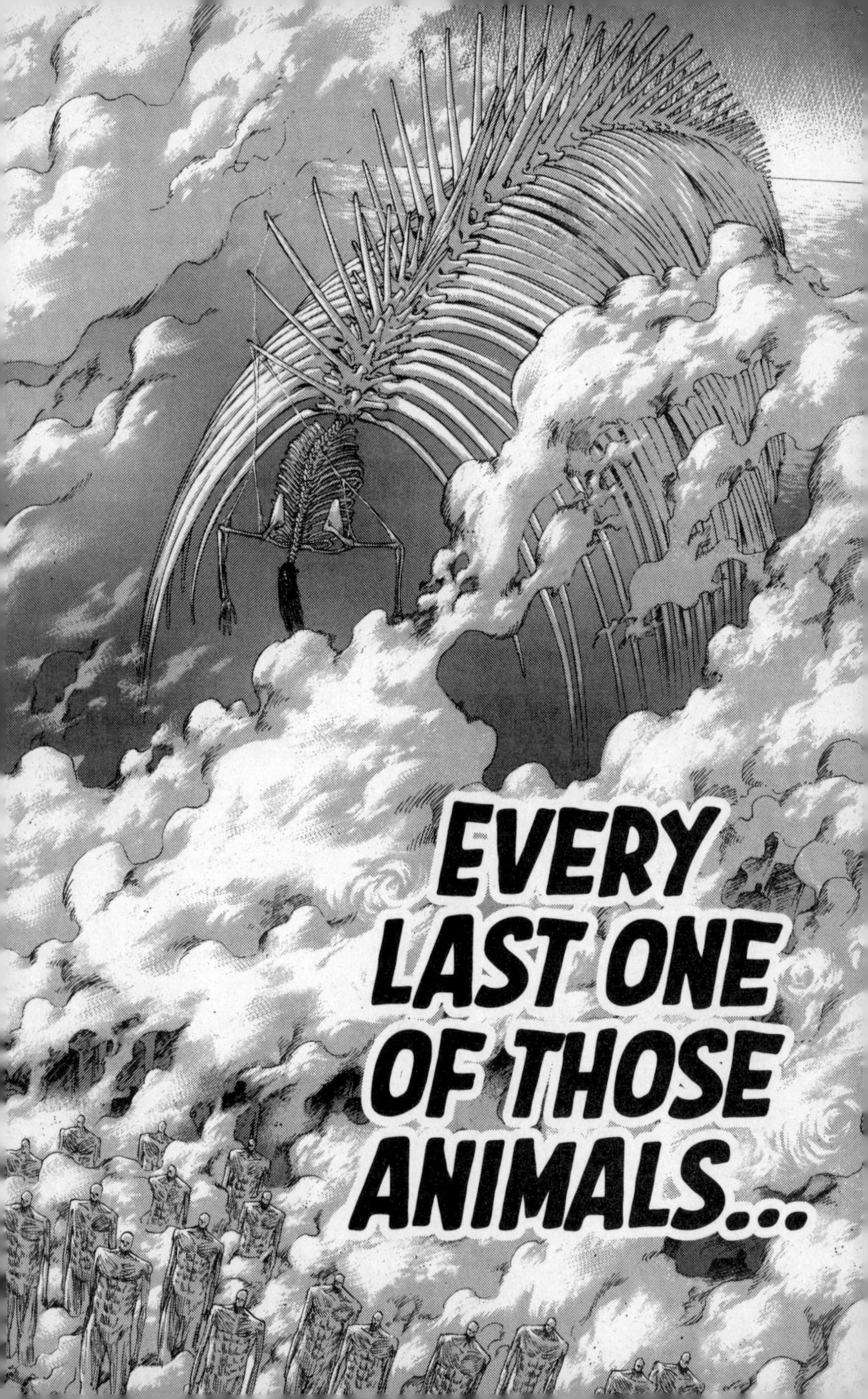
EVERY LAST ONE OF THOSE ANIMALS...

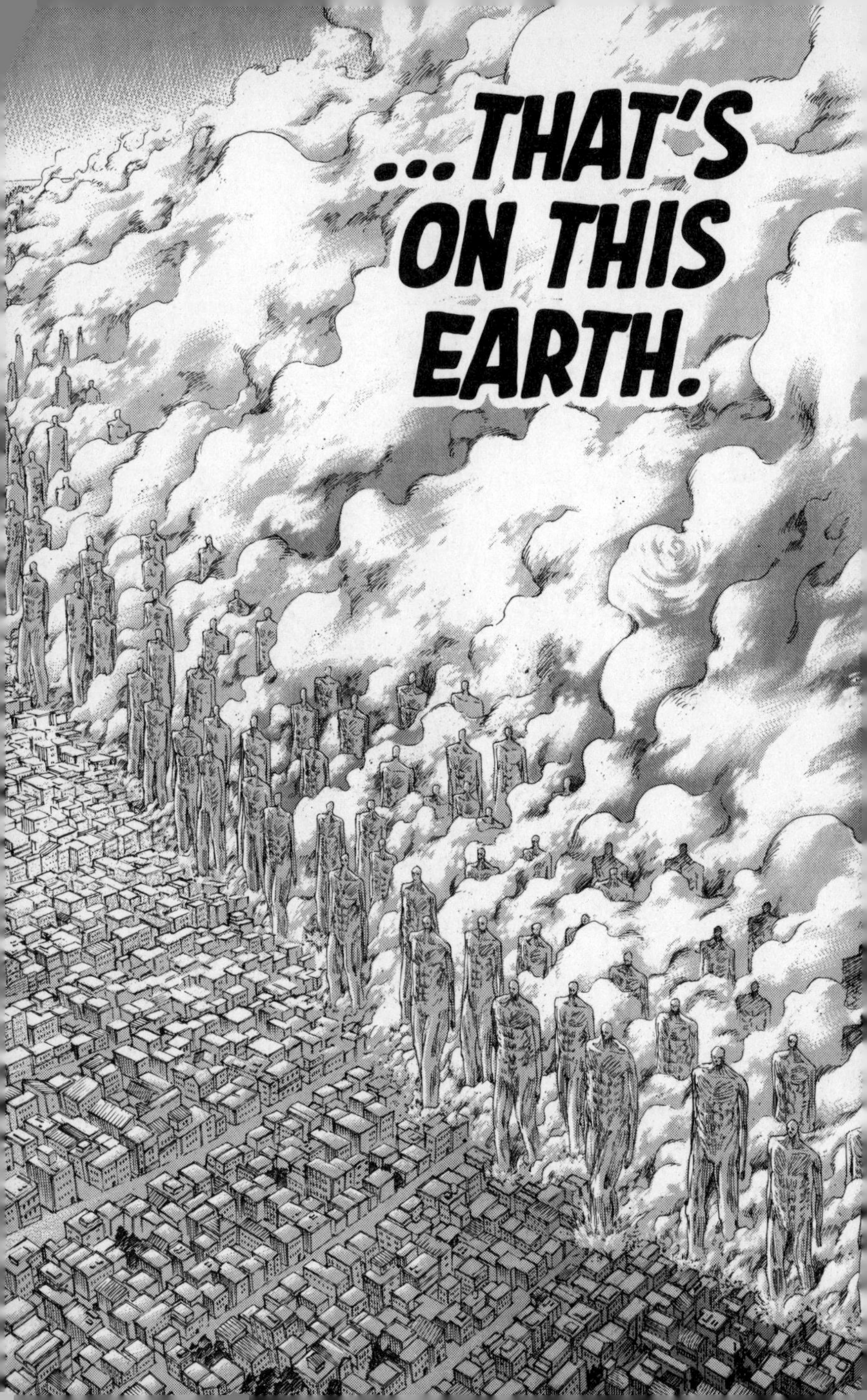
...THAT'S ON THIS EARTH.

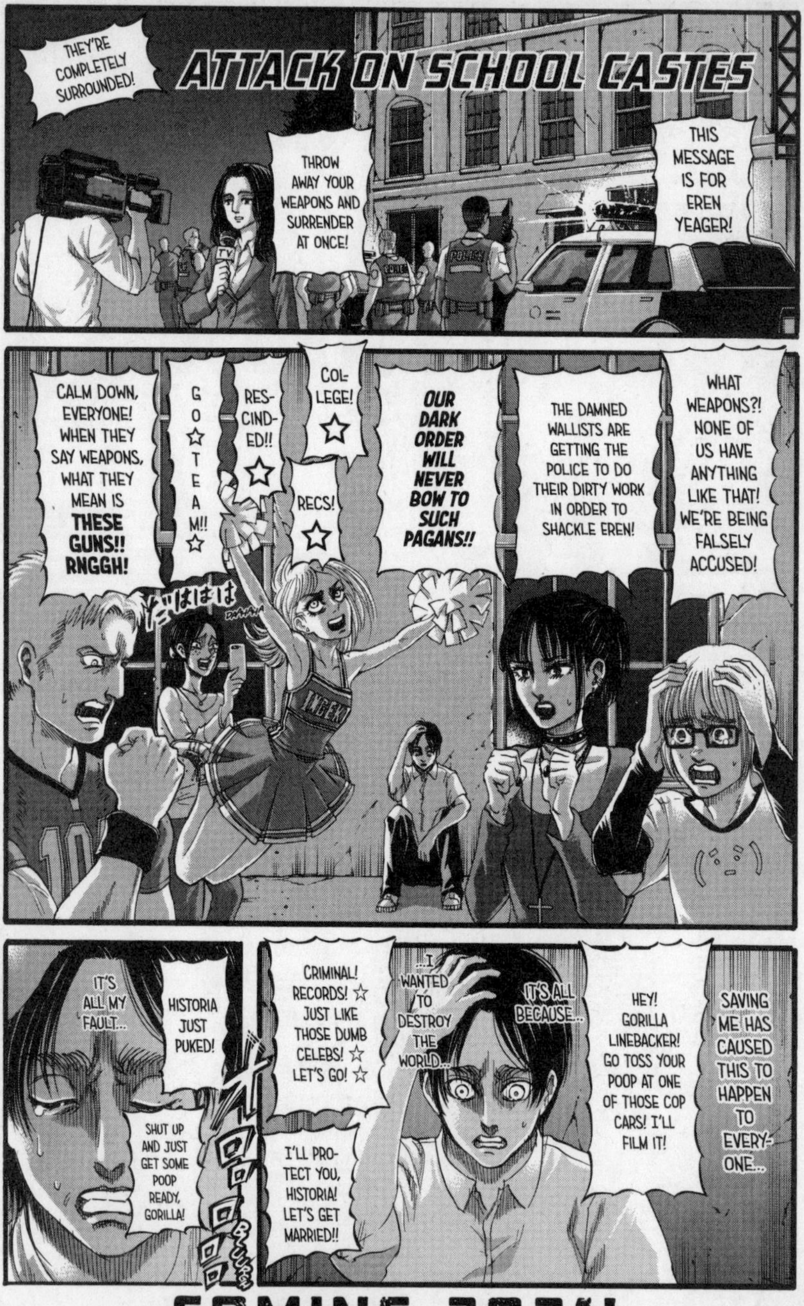
ATTACK ON SCHOOL CASTES
THIS MESSAGE IS FOR EREN YEAGER!
THROW AWAY YOUR WEAPONS AND SURRENDER AT ONCE!
THEY'RE COMPLETELY SURROUNDED!
WHAT WEAPONS?! NONE OF US HAVE ANYTHING LIKE THAT! WE'RE BEING FALSELY ACCUSED!
THE DAMNED WALLISTS ARE GETTING THE POLICE TO DO THEIR DIRTY WORK IN ORDER TO SHACKLE EREN!
OUR DARK ORDER WILL NEVER BOW TO SUCH PAGANS!!
COL-LEGE! ☆
RECS! ☆
RES-CIND-ED!! ☆
GO☆TEAM!!☆
CALM DOWN, EVERYONE! WHEN THEY SAY WEAPONS, WHAT THEY MEAN IS **THESE GUNS!! RNGGH!**
SAVING ME HAS CAUSED THIS TO HAPPEN TO EVERY-ONE...
HEY! GORILLA LINEBACKER! GO TOSS YOUR POOP AT ONE OF THOSE COP CARS! I'LL FILM IT!
IT'S ALL BECAUSE...
...I WANTED TO DESTROY THE WORLD...
CRIMINAL! RECORDS! ☆ JUST LIKE THOSE DUMB CELEBS! ☆ LET'S GO! ☆
I'LL PRO-TECT YOU, HISTORIA! LET'S GET MARRIED!!
HISTORIA JUST PUKED!
IT'S ALL MY FAULT...
SHUT UP AND JUST GET SOME POOP READY, GORILLA!

COMING 2021!

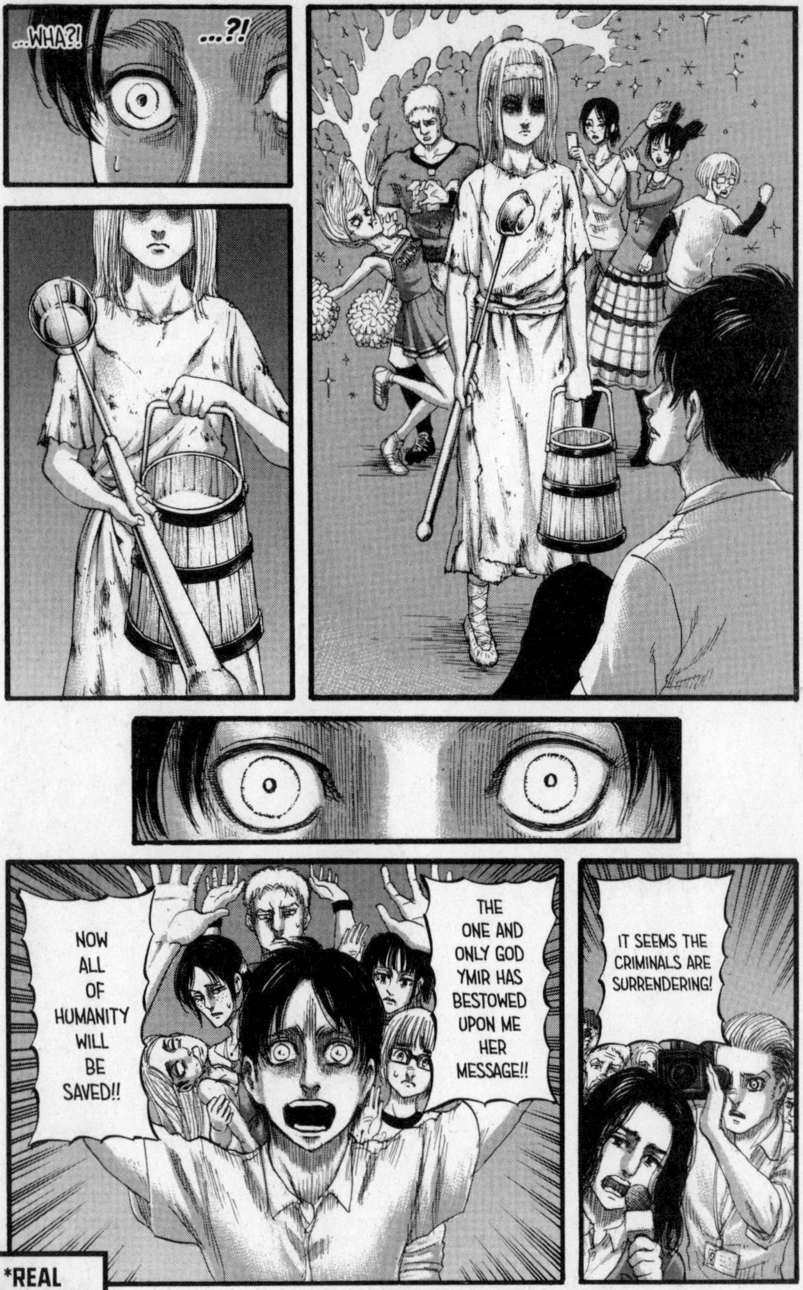
...?!
...WHA?!
IT SEEMS THE CRIMINALS ARE SURRENDERING!
THE ONE AND ONLY GOD YMIR HAS BESTOWED UPON ME HER MESSAGE!!
NOW ALL OF HUMANITY WILL BE SAVED!!

*REAL PREVIEW IS ON THE FOLLOWING PAGE!

VOLUME 33

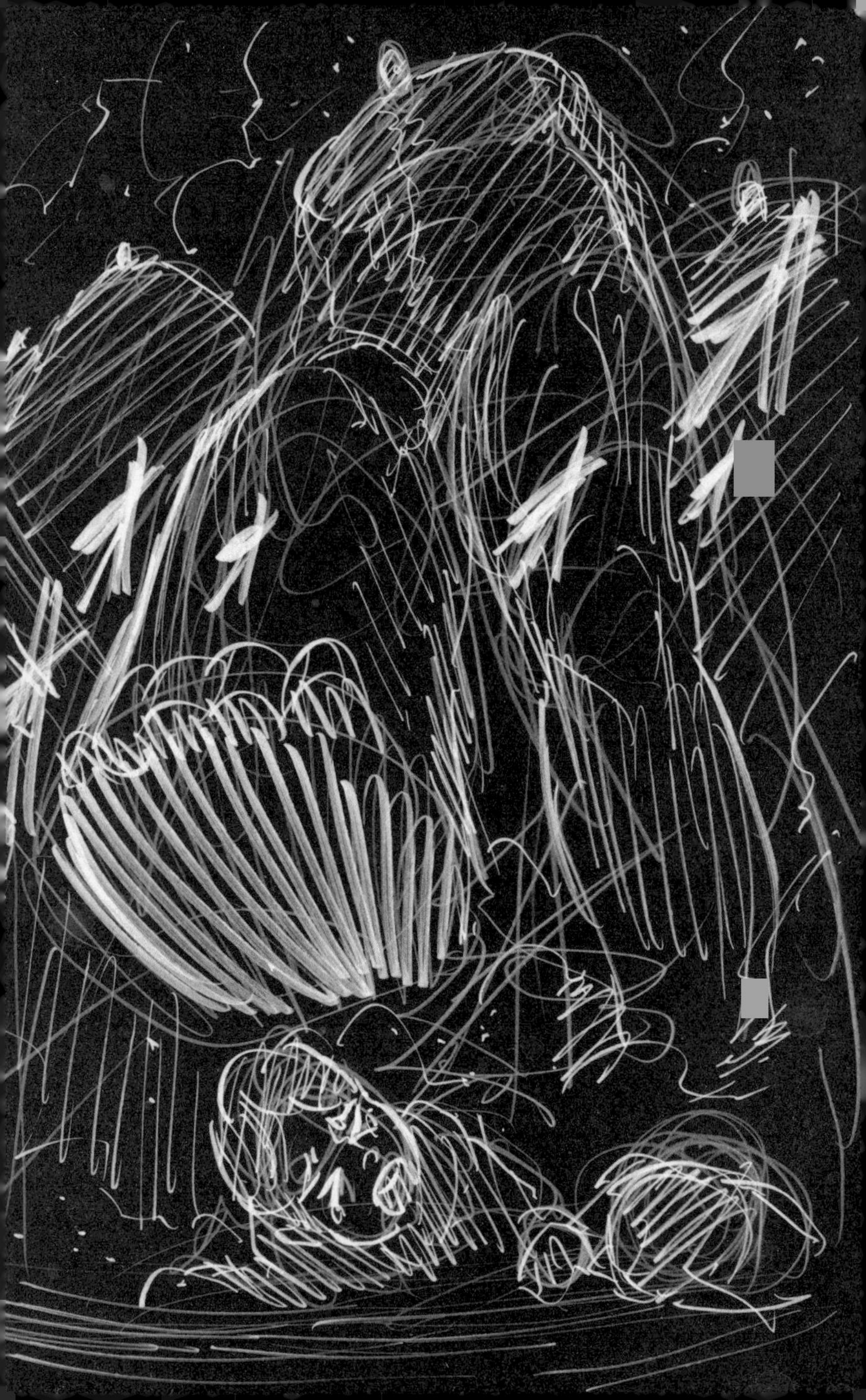

A Kodansha Comics Trade Paperback Original
Attack on Titan 32 copyright © 2020 Hajime Isayama
English translation copyright © 2020 Hajime Isayama

Published in the United States by Kodansha Comics, an imprint of Kodansha USA Publishing, LLC, New York.

Publication rights for this English edition arranged through Kodansha Ltd., Tokyo.

First published in Japan in 2020 by Kodansha Ltd., Tokyo as Shingeki no kyojin, volume 32.

ISBN 978-1-64651-031-3

Original cover design by Takashi Shimoyama/Manami Fukunaga (Red Rooster)

Printed in the United States of America.

www.kodanshacomics.com

9 8 7 6 5 4 3 2 1

Translation: Ko Ransom
Lettering: Dezi Sienty
Editing: Ben Applegate
Kodansha Comics edition cover design by Phil Balsman

Publisher: Kiichiro Sugawara
Director of publishing services: Ben Applegate
Associate director of operations: Stephen Pakula
Publishing services managing editor: Noelle Webster
Assistant production manager: Emi Lotto, Angela Zurlo

VOLUME 33 COMING 2021!

FOR YOUR
FRIENDS.

FOR YOUR
DREAMS.

TRAMPLE THE
OUTSIDE WORLD,
NO MATTER
WHAT MAY BE
UNDERFOOT.